*Praise for Karen Armstrong's*

# The Case for God

"The time is ripe for a book like *The Case for God,* which wraps a rebuke to the more militant sort of atheism in an engaging survey of Western religious thought."
—Ross Douthat, *The New York Times Book Review*

"A thoughtful explanation, well-sourced and impressively rooted in the writings of theologians, philosophers, scholars and religious figures through the ages.... If Armstrong is out to bring respect to both reason and faith in the search of that transcendent meaning, she has done well."       —Repps Hudson, *St. Louis Post-Dispatch*

"*The Case for God* is Armstrong's most concise and practical-minded book yet: a historical survey of how rather than what we believe, where we lost the 'knack' of religion and what we need to do to get it back."       —Michael Brunton, *Ode*

"*The Case for God* should be read slowly, and savored."
—Karen R. Long, *The Plain Dealer*

"Armstrong's thesis is provocative, and her book illuminates a side of Christianity that has recently been overshadowed."
—Margaret Quamme, *The Columbus Dispatch*

"Armstrong is ambitious. *The Case for God* is an entire semester at college packed into a single book—a voluminous, dizzying intellectual history.... Reading *The Case for God,* I felt smarter.... A stimulating, hopeful work. After I finished it, I felt inspired, I stopped, and I looked up at the stars again. And I wondered what could be."       —Susan Jane Gilman, NPR's *All Things Considered*

KAREN ARMSTRONG

## The Case for God

Karen Armstrong is the author of numerous other books on
religious affairs—including *A History of God*, *The Battle for
God*, *Holy War*, *Islam*, *Buddha*, and *The Great Transforma-
tion*—and two memoirs, *Through the Narrow Gate* and *The
Spiral Staircase*. Her work has been translated into forty-five
languages. She has addressed members of the U.S. Congress
on three occasions; lectured to policy makers at the U.S.
State Department; participated in the World Economic
Forum in New York, Jordan, and Davos; addressed the
Council on Foreign Relations in Washington and New
York; is increasingly invited to speak in Muslim countries;
and is now an ambassador for the UN Alliance of Civilizations. In February 2008 she was awarded the TED Prize
and recently launched with TED a Charter for Compassion, created online by the general public and crafted by
leading thinkers in Judaism, Christianity, Islam, Hinduism,
and Buddhism to restore compassion to the center of morality and religion. She lives in London.

charterforcompassion.org

ALSO BY KAREN ARMSTRONG

*Through the Narrow Gate: A Memoir of
Life In and Out of the Convent*

*Beginning the World*

*The First Christian: St. Paul's Impact on
Christianity*

*Tongues of Fire: An Anthology of Religious
and Poetic Experience*

*The Gospel According to Woman: Christianity's
Creation of the Sex War in the West*

*Holy War: The Crusades and Their
Impact on Today's World*

*The English Mystics of the Fourteenth Century*

*Muhammad: A Biography of the Prophet*

*A History of God: The 4,000-Year Quest of Judaism,
Christianity, and Islam*

*Jerusalem: One City, Three Faiths*

*In the Beginning:
A New Interpretation of Genesis*

*The Battle for God*

*Islam: A Short History*

*Buddha: A Penguin Life*

*The Spiral Staircase: My Climb Out of Darkness*

*A Short History of Myth*

*The Great Transformation: The Beginning
of Our Religious Traditions*

*The Bible: A Biography*

# The Case for God

# THE CASE

## *for*

# God

## Karen Armstrong

Anchor Books
A Division of Random House, Inc.
New York

FIRST ANCHOR BOOKS EDITION, SEPTEMBER 2010

The Library of Congress has cataloged the Knopf edition as follows:
Armstrong, Karen, [date]
The case for God / Karen Armstrong. —1st ed.
p. cm.
Includes bibliographical references (p. 379) and index.
1. God—History of doctrines. 2. Religious life—History. 3. God (Christianity)—
History of doctrines. 4. Christian life—History. 5. Apologetics. I. Title.
BL473.A76 2009
211—dc22
2009014044

Anchor ISBN: 978-0-307-38980-0

*Author photograph © J. D. Sloan*
*Book design by Wesley Gott*

www.anchorbooks.com

Printed in the United States of America

*For Joan Brown Campbell*

# Contents

# Introduction

We are talking far too much about God these days, and what we say is often facile. In our democratic society, we think that the concept of God *should* be easy and that religion ought to be readily accessible to anybody. "That book was really hard!" readers have told me reproachfully, shaking their heads in faint reproof. "Of course it was!" I want to reply. "It was about God." But many find this puzzling. Surely everybody knows what God is: the Supreme Being, a divine Personality, who created the world and everything in it. They look perplexed if you point out that it is inaccurate to call God the Supreme Being because God is not *a* being at all, and that we really don't understand what we mean when we say that he is "good," "wise," or "intelligent." People of faith admit in theory that God is utterly transcendent, but they seem sometimes to assume that *they* know exactly who "he" is and what he thinks, loves, and expects. We tend to tame and domesticate God's "otherness." We regularly ask God to bless our nation, save our queen, cure our sickness, or give us a fine day for the picnic. We remind God that he has created the world and that we are miserable sinners, as though this may have slipped his mind. Politicians quote God to justify their policies, teachers use him to keep order in the classroom, and terrorists commit atrocities in his name. We beg God to support "our" side in an election or a war, even though our opponents are, presumably, also God's children and the object of his love and care.

There is also a tendency to assume that, even though we now live in a totally transformed world and have an entirely different worldview, people have always thought about God in exactly the same way as we do today. But despite our scientific and technological brilliance, our religious thinking is sometimes remarkably undeveloped, even primitive. In some ways the modern God resembles the High God of remote antiquity, a theology that was unanimously either jettisoned or radically reinterpreted because it was found to be inept. Many people in the premodern world went out of their way to show that it was very difficult indeed to speak about God.

Theology is, of course, a very wordy discipline. People have written reams and talked unstoppably about God. But some of the greatest Jewish, Christian, and Muslim theologians made it clear that while it was important to put our ideas about the divine into words, these doctrines were man-made, and therefore were bound to be inadequate. They devised spiritual exercises that deliberately subverted normal patterns of thought and speech to help the faithful understand that the words we use to describe mundane things were simply not suitable for God. "He" was not good, divine, powerful, or intelligent in any way that we could understand. We could not even say that God "existed," because our concept of existence was too limited. Some of the sages preferred to say that God was "Nothing" because God was not another being. You certainly could not read your scriptures literally, as if they referred to divine facts. To these theologians some of our modern ideas about God would have seemed idolatrous.

It was not just a few radical theologians who took this line. Symbolism came more naturally to people in the premodern world than it does to us today. In medieval Europe, for example, Christians were taught to see the Mass as a symbolic reenactment of Jesus's life, death, and resurrection. The fact that they could not follow the Latin added to its mystique. Much of the Mass was recited by the priest in an undertone, and the solemn silence and liturgical drama, with its music and stylized gestures, put the congregation into a mental "space" that was separate from ordinary life. Today many are able to own a copy of the Bible or the Qur'an and have the literacy to read them, but in the past most people had an entirely different relationship with their scriptures. They listened to them, recited piecemeal, often in a foreign language and always in a heightened liturgical context. Preachers instructed them not to understand these texts in a purely literal way and suggested figurative interpretations. In the "mystery plays" performed annually on the feast of Corpus Christi, medievals felt free to change the biblical stories, add new characters, and transpose them into a modern setting. These stories were not historical in our sense, because they were *more* than history.

In most premodern cultures, there were two recognized ways of thinking, speaking, and acquiring knowledge. The Greeks called them *mythos* and *logos*.[1] Both were essential and neither was considered superior to the other; they were not in conflict but complementary. Each had its own sphere of competence, and it was considered unwise to mix the two. *Logos* ("reason") was the pragmatic mode of thought that enabled people to function effectively in the world. It had, therefore, to correspond accurately to external reality. People have always needed *logos* to make an efficient weapon, organize their societies, or plan an expedition. *Logos* was forward-looking, continually on the lookout for new ways of controlling the environment, improving old insights, or inventing something fresh. *Logos* was essential to the survival of our species. But it had its limitations: it could not assuage human grief or find ultimate meaning in life's struggles. For that people turned to *mythos* or "myth."

Today we live in a society of scientific *logos*, and myth has fallen into disrepute. In popular parlance, a "myth" is something that is not true. But in the past, myth was not self-indulgent fantasy; rather, like *logos*, it helped people to live effectively in our confusing world, though in a different way.[2] Myths may have told stories about the gods, but they were really focused on the more elusive, puzzling, and tragic aspects of the human predicament that lay outside the remit of *logos*. Myth has been called a primitive form of psychology. When a myth described heroes threading their way through labyrinths, descending into the underworld, or fighting monsters, these were not understood as primarily factual stories. They were designed to help people negotiate the obscure regions of the psyche, which are difficult to access but which profoundly influence our thought and behavior.[3] People had to enter the warren of their own minds and fight their personal demons. When Freud and Jung began to chart their scientific search for the soul, they instinctively turned to these ancient myths. A myth was never intended as an accurate account of a historical event; it was *something that had in some sense happened once but that also happens all the time.*

But a myth would not be effective if people simply "believed" in it. It was essentially a program of action. It could put you in the correct spiritual or psychological posture, but it was up to you to take the next step and make the "truth" of the myth a reality in your own life. The only way to assess the value and truth of any myth was to act upon it. The myth of the hero, for example, which takes the same form in nearly all cultural traditions, taught people how to unlock their own heroic potential.[4] Later the stories of historical figures such as the Buddha, Jesus, or Muhammad were made to conform to this paradigm so that their followers could imitate them in the same way. Put into practice, a myth could tell us something profoundly true about our humanity. It showed us how to live more richly and intensely, how to cope with our mortality, and how creatively to endure the suffering that flesh is heir to. But if we failed to apply it to our situation, a myth would remain abstract and incredible. From a very early date, people reenacted their myths in stylized ceremonies that worked aesthetically upon participants and, like any work of art, introduced them to a deeper dimension of existence. Myth and ritual were thus inseparable, so much so that it is often a matter of scholarly debate which came first: the mythical story or the rites attached to it.[5] Without ritual, myths made no sense and would remain as opaque as a musical score, which is impenetrable to most of us until interpreted instrumentally.

Religion, therefore, was not primarily something that people thought but something they did. Its truth was acquired by practical action. It is no use imagining that you will be able to drive a car if you simply read the manual or study the rules of the road. You cannot learn to dance, paint, or cook by perusing texts or recipes. The rules of a board game sound obscure, unnecessarily complicated, and dull until you start to play, when everything falls into place. There are some things that can be learned only by constant, dedicated practice, but if you persevere, you find that you achieve something that seemed initially impossible. Instead of sinking to the bottom of the pool, you can float. You may learn to jump higher and with more grace than seems humanly possible or sing with unearthly beauty. You do not always understand how you achieve these feats, because your mind directs your body in a way that bypasses conscious, logical deliberation. But somehow you learn to transcend your original capabilities. Some of these activities bring indescribable joy. A musician can lose herself in her music, a dancer becomes inseparable from the dance, and a skier feels entirely at one with himself and the external world as he speeds down the slope. It is a satisfaction that goes deeper than merely "feeling good." It is what the Greeks called *ekstasis,* a "stepping outside" the norm.

Religion is a practical discipline that teaches us to discover new capacities of mind and heart. This will be one of the major themes of this book. It is no use magisterially weighing up the teachings of religion to judge their truth or falsehood before embarking on a religious way of life. You will discover their truth—or lack of it—only if you translate these doctrines into ritual or ethical action. Like any skill, religion requires perseverance, hard work, and discipline. Some people will be better at it than others, some appallingly inept, and some will miss the point entirely. But those who do not apply themselves will get nowhere at all. Religious people find it hard to explain how their rituals and practices work, just as a skater may not be fully conscious of the physical laws that enable her to glide over the ice on a thin blade.

The early Daoists saw religion as a "knack" acquired by constant practice. Zhuangzi (c. 370–311 BCE), one of the most important figures in the spiritual history of China, explained that it was no good trying to analyze religious teachings logically. He cites the carpenter Bian: "When I work on a wheel, if I hit too softly, pleasant as this is, it doesn't make for a good wheel. If I hit it furiously, I get tired and the thing doesn't work! So not too soft, not too vigorous. I grasp it in my hand and hold it in my heart. I cannot express this by word of mouth, I just know it."[6] A hunchback who trapped cicadas in the forest with a sticky pole never missed a single one. He had so perfected his powers of concentration that he lost himself in the task, and his hands seemed to move by themselves. He had no idea how he did it, but knew only that he had acquired the knack after months of practice. This self-forgetfulness, Zhuangzi explained, was an *ekstasis* that enabled you to "step outside" the prism of ego and experience the sacred.[7]

People who acquired this knack discovered a transcendent dimension of life that was not simply an external reality "out there" but was identical with the deepest level of their being. This reality, which they have called God, Dao, Brahman, or Nirvana, has been a fact of human life. But it was impossible to explain what it was in terms of *logos*. This imprecision was not frustrating, as a modern Western person might imagine, but brought with it an *ekstasis* that lifted practitioners beyond the constricting confines of self. Our scientifically oriented knowledge seeks to master reality, explain it, and bring it under the control of reason, but a delight in unknowing has also been part of the human experience. Even today, poets, philosophers, mathematicians, and scientists find that the contemplation of the insoluble is a source of joy, astonishment, and contentment.

One of the peculiar characteristics of the human mind is its ability to have ideas and experiences that exceed our conceptual grasp. We constantly push our thoughts to an extreme, so that our minds seem to elide naturally into an apprehension of transcendence. Music has always been inseparable from religious expression, since, like religion at its best, music marks the "limits of reason."[8] Because a territory is defined by its extremities, it follows that music must be "definitively" rational. It is the most corporeal of the arts: it is produced by breath, voice, horsehair, shells, guts, and skins and reaches "resonances in our bodies at levels deeper than will or consciousness."[9] But it is also highly cerebral, requiring the balance of intricately complex energies and form-relations, and is intimately connected with mathematics. Yet this intensely rational activity segues into transcendence. Music goes beyond the reach of words: it is not *about* anything. A late Beethoven quartet does not represent sorrow but elicits it in hearer and player alike, and yet it is emphatically not a sad experience. Like tragedy, it brings intense pleasure and insight. We seem to experience sadness directly in a way that transcends ego, because this is not *my* sadness but sorrow itself. In music, therefore, subjective and objective become one. Language has borders that we cannot cross. When we listen critically to our stuttering attempts to express ourselves, we become aware of an inexpressible otherness. "It is decisively the fact that language does have frontiers," explains the British critic George Steiner, "that gives proof of a transcendent presence in the fabric of the world. It is just because we can go no further, because speech so marvellously fails us, that we experience the certitude of a divine meaning surpassing and enfolding ours."[10] Every day, music confronts us with a mode of knowledge that defies logical analysis and empirical proof. It is "brimful of meanings which will not translate into logical structures or verbal expression."[11] Hence all art constantly aspires to the condition of music; so too, at its best, does theology.

A modern skeptic will find it impossible to accept Steiner's conclusion that "what lies beyond man's word is eloquent of God."[12] But perhaps that is because we have too limited an idea of God. We have not been doing our practice and have lost the "knack" of religion. During the sixteenth and seventeenth centuries, a time that historians call the early modern period, Western people began to develop an entirely new kind of civilization, governed by scientific rationality and based economically on technology and capital investment. *Logos* achieved such spectacular results that myth was discredited and the scientific method was thought to be the only reliable means of attaining truth. This would make religion difficult, if not impossible. As theologians began to adopt the criteria of science, the *mythoi* of Christianity were interpreted as empirically, rationally, and historically verifiable and forced into a style of thinking that was alien to them. Philosophers and scientists could no longer see the point of ritual, and religious knowledge became theoretical rather than practical. We lost the art of interpreting the old tales of gods walking the earth, dead men striding out of tombs, or seas parting miraculously. We began to understand concepts such as faith, revelation, myth, mystery, and dogma in a way that would have been very surprising to our ancestors. In particular, the meaning of the word "belief" changed, so that a credulous acceptance of creedal doctrines became the prerequisite of faith, so much so that today we often speak of religious people as "believers," as though accepting orthodox dogma "on faith" were their most important activity.

This rationalized interpretation of religion has resulted in two distinctively modern phenomena: fundamentalism and atheism. The two are related. The defensive piety popularly known as fundamentalism erupted in almost every major faith during the twentieth century.[13] In their desire to produce a wholly rational, scientific faith that abolished *mythos* in favor of *logos,* Christian fundamentalists have interpreted scripture with a literalism that is unparalleled in the history of religion. In the United States, Protestant fundamentalists have evolved an ideology known as "creation science" that regards the *mythoi* of the Bible as scientifically accurate. They have, therefore, campaigned against the teaching of evolution in the public schools, because it contradicts the creation story in the first chapter of Genesis.

Historically, atheism has rarely been a blanket denial of the sacred per se but has nearly always rejected a particular conception of the divine. At an early stage of their history, Christians and Muslims were both called "atheists" by their pagan contemporaries, not because they denied the reality of God but because their conception of divinity was so different that it seemed blasphemous. Atheism is therefore parasitically dependent on the form of theism it seeks to eliminate and becomes its reverse mirror image. Classical Western atheism was developed during the nineteenth and early twentieth centuries by Feuerbach, Marx, Nietzsche, and Freud, whose ideology was essentially a response to and dictated by the theological perception of God that had developed in Europe and the United States during the modern period. The more recent atheism of Richard Dawkins, Christopher Hitchens, and Sam Harris is rather different, because it has focused exclusively on the God developed by the fundamentalisms, and all three insist that fundamentalism constitutes the essence and core of all religion. This has weakened their critique, because fundamentalism is in fact a defiantly unorthodox form of faith that frequently misrepresents the tradition it is trying to defend. But the "new atheists" command a wide readership, not only in secular Europe but even in the more conventionally religious United States. The popularity of their books suggests that many people are bewildered and even angered by the God concept they have inherited.

It is a pity that Dawkins, Hitchens, and Harris express themselves so intemperately, because some of their criticisms are valid. Religious people have indeed committed atrocities and crimes, and the fundamentalist theology the new atheists attack is indeed "unskillful," as the Buddhists would say. But they refuse, on principle, to dialogue with theologians who are more representative of mainstream tradition. As a result, their analysis is disappointingly shallow, because it is based on such poor theology. In fact, the new atheists are not radical enough. Jewish, Christian, and Muslim theologians have insisted for centuries that God does not exist and that there is "nothing" out there; in making these assertions, their aim was not to deny the reality of God but to safeguard God's transcendence. In our talkative and highly opinionated society, however, we seem to have lost sight of this important tradition that could solve many of our current religious problems.

I have no intention of attacking anybody's sincerely held beliefs.

Many thousands of people find that the symbolism of the modern God works well for them: backed up by inspiring rituals and the discipline of living in a vibrant community, it has given them a sense of transcendent meaning. All the world faiths insist that true spirituality must be expressed consistently in practical compassion, the ability to *feel with* the other. If a conventional idea of God inspires empathy and respect for all others, it is doing its job. But the modern God is only one of the many theologies that developed during the three-thousand-year history of monotheism. Because "God" is infinite, nobody can have the last word. I am concerned that many people are confused about the nature of religious truth, a perplexity exacerbated by the contentious nature of so much religious discussion at the moment. My aim in this book is simply to bring something fresh to the table.

I can sympathize with the irritation of the new atheists, because, as I have explained in my memoir *The Spiral Staircase,* for many years I myself wanted nothing whatsoever to do with religion and some of my first books definitely tended to the Dawkinsesque. But my study of world religion during the last twenty years has compelled me to revise my earlier opinions. Not only has it opened my mind to aspects of religion as practiced in other traditions that qualified the parochial and dogmatic faith of my childhood, but a careful assessment of the evidence has made me see Christianity differently. One of the things I have learned is that quarreling about religion is counterproductive and not conducive to enlightenment. It not only makes authentic religious experience impossible but also violates the Socratic rationalist tradition.

In the first part of this book, I have tried to show how people thought about God in the premodern world in a way that, I hope, throws light on some of the issues that people now find problematic—scripture, inspiration, creation, miracles, revelation, faith, belief, and mystery—as well as showing how religion goes wrong. In the second part, I trace the rise of the "modern God," which overturned so many traditional religious presuppositions. This cannot, of course, be an exhaustive account. I have focused on Christianity, because it was the tradition most immediately affected by the rise of scientific modernity and has also borne the brunt of the new atheistic assault. Further, within the Christian tradition I have concentrated on themes and traditions that speak directly to our present religious difficulties. Religion is complex; in every age, there are numerous strands of piety. No single tendency ever prevails in its entirety. People practice their faith in myriad contrasting and contradictory ways. But a deliberate and principled reticence about God and/or the sacred was a constant theme not only in Christianity but in the other major faith traditions until the rise of modernity in the West. People believed that God exceeded our thoughts and concepts and could be known only by dedicated practice. We have lost sight of this important insight, and this, I believe, is one of the reasons why so many Western people find the concept of God so troublesome today. Hence I have given special attention to this neglected discipline in the hope that it may throw light on our contemporary predicament. But I do not, of course, claim that this was a universal attitude; simply that it was a major element in the practice not only of Christianity but of other monotheistic and nontheistic faiths and that it needs to be drawn to our attention.

Even though so many people are antagonistic to faith, the world is currently experiencing a religious revival. Contrary to the confident secularist predictions of the mid-twentieth century, religion is not going to disappear. But if it succumbs to the violent and intolerant strain that has always been inherent not only in the monotheisms but also in the modern scientific ethos, the new religiosity will be "unskillful." We are seeing a great deal of strident dogmatism today, religious and secular, but there is also a growing appreciation of the value of unknowing. We can never re-create the past, but we can learn from its mistakes and insights. There is a long religious tradition that stressed the importance of recognizing the limits of our knowledge, of silence, reticence, and awe. That is what I hope to explore in this book. One of the conditions of enlightenment has always been a willingness to let go of what we thought we knew in order to appreciate truths we had never dreamed of. We may have to unlearn a great deal about religion before we can move on to new insight. It is not easy to talk about what we call "God," and the religious quest often begins with the deliberate dissolution of ordinary thought patterns. This may be what some of our earliest ancestors were trying to create in their extraordinary underground temples.

# PART I

---

# The Unknown God

(30,000 BCE TO 1500 CE)

# ONE

# Homo religiosus

When the guide switches off his flashlight in the underground caverns of Lascaux in the Dordogne, the effect is overwhelming. "The senses suddenly are wiped out," one visitor recalled, "the millennia drop away. . . . You were never in darker darkness in your life. It was—I don't know, just a complete knockout. You don't know whether you are looking north, south, east, or west. All orientation is gone, and you are in a darkness that never saw the sun." Normal daylight consciousness extinguished, you feel a "timeless dissociation from every concern and requirement of the upper world that you have left behind."[1] Before reaching the first of the caves decorated by our Palaeolithic ancestors in the Stone Age, seventeen thousand years ago, visitors have to stumble for some eighty feet down a sloping tunnel, sixty-five feet below ground level, penetrating ever more deeply into the bowels of the earth. Then the guide suddenly turns the beam of his flashlight onto the ceiling; and the painted animals seem to emerge from the depths of the rock. A strange beast with gravid belly and long pointed horns walks behind a line of wild cattle, horses, deer, and bulls that seem simultaneously in motion and at rest.

In all there are about six hundred frescoes and fifteen hundred engravings in the Lascaux labyrinth. There is a powerful bellowing black stag, a leaping cow, and a procession of horses moving in the opposite direction. At the entrance to another long passage known as the Nave, a frieze of elegant deer has been painted above a rocky ledge so that they appear to be swimming. We see these images far more clearly than the Palaeolithic artists did, since they had to work by the light of small flickering lamps, perched precariously on scaffolding that has left holes in the surface of the wall. They often painted new pictures over old images, even though there was ample space nearby. It seems that location was crucial and that, for reasons we cannot fathom, some places were deemed more suitable than others. The subject matter was also governed by rules that we can never hope to understand. The artists selected only a few of the species known to them, and there are no pictures of the reindeer on which they relied for food.[2] Animals are consistently paired—oxen and bison with horses, bison with mammoths—in combinations that would not occur in real life.[3] Lascaux is not unique. There are about three hundred decorated caves in this region of southern France and northern Spain. In some the artwork is more elementary, but in all these caverns the imagery and layout are basically the same. The earliest site, at Grosse Chauvet, dates from about 30,000 BCE, a time when *Homo sapiens* seems to have undergone an abrupt evolutionary change in this locality. There was a dramatic rise in population, which may have resulted in social tension. Some historians believe that the cave art records a "corpus of socially-constructed rituals . . . for conflict control . . . pictorially encoded for storage and transmission through generations."[4] But the paintings also express an intensely aesthetic appreciation of the natural world. Here we have the earliest known evidence of an ideological system, which remained in place for some twenty thousand years, after which the caves fell into disuse in about 9000 BCE.[5]

It is now generally agreed that these labyrinths were sacred places for the performance of some kind of ritual. Some historians have argued that their purpose was purely pragmatic, but their upkeep alone would have required an immense amount of unproductive labor. Some of these sites were so deep that it took hours to reach their innermost core. Visiting the caves was dangerous, exhausting, uneconomical, and time-consuming. The general consensus is that the caves were sanctuaries and that, as in any temple, their iconography reflected a vision that was radically different from that of the outside world.[6] We do not build temples like this in the modern West. Our worldview is predominantly rational, and we think more easily in concepts than images. We find it hard enough to decode the symbolism of a medieval cathedral such as the one in Chartres, so these Palaeolithic shrines offer an almost insurmountable challenge.

But there are a few clues to aid our understanding. A remarkable picture, dated to about 12,000 BCE, in a cave at Lascaux known as the Crypt because it is even deeper than the other caverns, depicts a large bison that has been eviscerated by a spear thrust through its hind-quarters. Lying in front of the wounded beast is a man, drawn in a far more rudimentary style than the animals, with arms outstretched, phallus erect, and wearing what seems to be a bird mask; his staff, which lies on the ground nearby, is also topped by a bird's head. This seems to be an illustration of a well-known legend and could have been the founding myth of the sanctuary. The same scene appears on an engraved reindeer horn at nearby Villars and on a sculpted block in a cliff shelter at Roc de Sers near Limoges, which is five thousand years older than the Lascaux painting.[7] Fifty-five similar images in the other caves and three more Palaeolithic rock drawings in Africa have been found, all showing men confronting animals in a state of trance with upraised arms.[8] They are probably shamans.

We know that shamanism developed in Africa and Europe during the Palaeolithic period and that it spread to Siberia and thence to America and Australia, where the shaman is still the chief religious practitioner among the indigenous hunting peoples. Even though they have inevitably been influenced by neighboring civilizations, many of the original structures of these societies, which were arrested at a stage similar to that of the Palaeolithic, remained intact until the late nineteenth century.[9] Today there is a remarkable continuity in the descriptions of the shaman's ecstatic flight all the way from Siberia, through the Americas to Tierra del Fuego:[10] he swoons during a public séance and believes that he flies through the air to consult the gods about the location of game. In these traditional societies, hunters do not feel that the species are distinct or permanent categories: men can become animals and animals human. Shamans have bird and animal guardians and can converse with the beasts that are revered as messengers of higher powers.[11] The shaman's vision gives meaning to the hunting and killing of animals on which these societies depend.

The hunters feel profoundly uneasy about slaughtering the beasts, who are their friends and patrons, and to assuage this anxiety, they surround the hunt with taboos and prohibitions. They say that long ago the animals made a covenant with humankind and now a god known as the Animal Master regularly sends flocks from the lower world to be killed on the hunting plains, because the hunters promised to perform the rites that will give them posthumous life. Hunters often abstain from sex before an expedition, hunt in a state of ritual purity, and feel a deep empathy with their prey. In the Kalahari Desert, where wood is scarce, the Bushmen have to rely on light weapons that can only graze the skin, so they anoint their arrows with a lethal poison that kills the animal very slowly. A tribesman has to remain with his victim, crying when it cries and participating symbolically in its death throes. Other tribes identify with their prey by donning animal costumes. After stripping the meat from the bones, some reconstruct their kill by laying out its skeleton and pelt; others bury these inedible remains, symbolically restoring the beast to the netherworld from which it came.[12]

The hunters of the Palaeolithic age may have had a similar worldview. Some of the myths and rites they devised appear to have survived in the traditions of later, literate cultures. Animal sacrifice, for example, the central rite of nearly every religious system in antiquity, preserved prehistoric hunting ceremonies and continued to honor a beast that gave its life for the sake of humankind.[13] One of the functions of ritual is to evoke an anxiety in such a way that the community is forced to confront and control it. From the very beginning, it seems, religious life was rooted in acknowledgment of the tragic fact that life depends upon the destruction of other creatures.

The Palaeolithic caves may have been the scene of similar rites. Some of the paintings include dancing men dressed as animals. The Bushmen say that their own rock paintings depict "the world behind this one that we see with our eyes," which the shamans visit during their mystical flights.[14] They smear the walls of the caves with the blood, excrement, and fat of their kill in order to restore it, symbolically, to the earth; animal blood and fat were ingredients of the Palaeolithic paints, and the act of painting itself could have been a ritual of restoration.[15] The images may depict the eternal, archetypal animals that take temporary physical form in the upper world.[16] All ancient religion was based on what has been called the perennial philosophy, because it was present in some form in so many premodern cultures. It sees every single person, object, or experience as a replica of a reality in a sacred world that is more effective and enduring than our own.[17] When an Australian Aborigine hunts his prey, he feels wholly at one with the First Hunter, caught up in a richer and more potent reality that makes him feel fully alive and complete.[18] Maybe the hunters of Lascaux reenacted the archetypal hunt in the caves amid these paintings of the eternal hunting ground before they left their tribe to embark on the perilous quest for food.[19]

We can, of course, only speculate. Some scholars believe that these caverns were likely to have been used for the initiation ceremonies that marked the adolescent boy's rite of passage from childhood to maturity. This type of initiation was crucial in ancient religion and is still practiced in traditional societies today.[20] When they reach puberty, boys are taken from their mothers and put through frightening ordeals that transform them into men. The tribe cannot afford the luxury of allowing an adolescent to "find himself" Western-style; he has to relinquish the dependency of infancy and assume the burdens of adulthood overnight. To this end, boys are incarcerated in tombs, buried in the earth, informed that they are about to be eaten by a monster, flogged, circumcised, and tattooed. If the initiation is properly conducted, a youth will be forced to reach for inner resources that he did not know he possessed. Psychologists tell us that the terror of such an experience causes a regressive disorganization of the personality that, if skillfully handled, can lead to a constructive reorganization of the young man's powers. He has faced death, come out the other side, and is now psychologically prepared to risk his life for his people.

But the purpose of the ritual is not simply to turn him into an efficient killing machine; rather, it is to train him to kill in the sacred manner. A boy is usually introduced to the more esoteric mythology of his tribe during his initiation. He first hears about the Animal Master, the covenant, the magnanimity of the beasts, and the rituals that will restore his life while he is undergoing these traumatic rites. In these extraordinary circumstances, separated from everything familiar, he is pushed into a new state of consciousness that enables him to appreciate the profound bond that links hunter and prey in their common struggle for survival. This is not the kind of knowledge we acquire by purely logical deliberations, but is akin to the understanding derived from art. A poem, a play, or, indeed, a great painting has the power to change our perception in ways that we may not be able to explain logically but that seem incontestably true. We find that things that appear distinct to the rational eye are in some way profoundly connected or that a perfectly commonplace object—a chair, a sunflower, or a pair of boots—has numinous significance. Art involves our emotions, but if it is to be more than a superficial epiphany, this new insight must go deeper than feelings that are, by their very nature, ephemeral.

If the historians are right about the function of the Lascaux caves, religion and art were inseparable from the very beginning. Like art, religion is an attempt to construct meaning in the face of the relentless pain and injustice of life. As meaning-seeking creatures, men and women fall very easily into despair. They have created religions and works of art to help them find value in their lives, despite all the dispiriting evidence to the contrary. The initiation experience also shows that a myth, like that of the Animal Master, derives much of its meaning from the ritualized context in which it is imparted.[21] It may not be empirically true, it may defy the laws of logic, but a good myth will tell us something valuable about the human predicament. Like any work of art, a myth will make no sense unless we open ourselves to it wholeheartedly and allow it to change us. If we hold ourselves aloof, it will remain opaque, incomprehensible, and even ridiculous.

Religion is hard work. Its insights are not self-evident and have to be cultivated in the same way as an appreciation of art, music, or poetry must be developed. The intense effort required is especially evident in the underground labyrinth of Trois Frères at Ariège in the Pyrenees. Doctor Herbert Kuhn, who visited the site in 1926, twelve years after its discovery, described the frightening experience of crawling through the tunnel—scarcely a foot high in some places—that leads to the heart of this magnificent Palaeolithic sanctuary. "I felt as though I were creeping through a coffin," he recalled. "My heart is pounding and it is difficult to breathe. It is terrible to have the roof so close to one's head." He could hear the other members of his party groaning as they struggled through the darkness, and when they finally arrived in the vast underground hall, it felt "like a redemption."[22] They found themselves gazing at a wall covered in spectacular engravings: mammoths, bison, wild horses, wolverines, and musk oxen; darts flying everywhere; blood spurting from the mouths of the bears; and a human figure clad in animal skin playing a flute. Dominating the scene was a large painted figure, half man, half beast, who fixed his huge, penetrating eyes on the visitors. Was this the Animal Master? Or did this hybrid creature symbolize the underlying unity of animal and human, natural and divine?

A boy would not be expected to "believe" in the Animal Master before he entered the caves. But at the culmination of his ordeal, this image would have made a powerful impression; for hours he had, perhaps, fought his way through nearly a mile of convoluted passages to the accompaniment of "songs, cries, noises or mysterious objects thrown from no one knows where," special effects that would have been "easy to arrange in such a place."[23] In archaic thinking, there is no concept of the supernatural, no huge gulf separating human and divine. If a priest donned the sacred regalia of an animal pelt to impersonate the Animal Master, he became a temporary manifestation of that divine power.[24] These rituals were not the expression of a "belief" that had to be accepted in blind faith. As the German scholar Walter Burkert explains, it is pointless to look for an idea or doctrine *behind* a rite. In the premodern world, ritual was not the product of religious ideas; on the contrary, these ideas were the product of ritual.[25] *Homo religiosus* is pragmatic in this sense only: if a ritual no longer evokes a profound conviction of life's ultimate value, he simply abandons it. But for twenty thousand years, the hunters of the region continued to thread their way through the dangerous pathways of Trois Frères in order to bring their mythology—whatever it was—to life. They must have found the effort worthwhile or they would, without a backward glance, have given it up.

Religion was not something tacked on to the human condition, an optional extra imposed on people by unscrupulous priests. The desire to cultivate a sense of the transcendent may be *the* defining human characteristic. In about 9000 BCE, when human beings developed agriculture and were no longer dependent on animal meat, the old hunting rites lost some of their appeal and people ceased to visit the caves. But they did not discard religion altogether. Instead they developed a new set of myths and rituals based on the fecundity of the soil that filled the men and women of the Neolithic age with religious awe.[26] Tilling the fields became a ritual that replaced the hunt, and the nurturing Earth took the place of the Animal Master. Before the modern period, most men and women were naturally inclined to religion and they were prepared to work at it. Today many of us are no longer willing to make this effort, so the old myths seem arbitrary, remote, and incredible.

Like art, the truths of religion require the disciplined cultivation of a different mode of consciousness. The cave experience always began with the disorientation of utter darkness, which annihilated normal habits of mind. Human beings are so constituted that periodically they seek out *ekstasis,* a "stepping outside" the norm. Today people who no longer find it in a religious setting resort to other outlets: music, dance, art, sex, drugs, or sport. We make a point of seeking out these experiences that touch us deeply within and lift us momentarily beyond ourselves. At such times, we feel that we inhabit our humanity more fully than usual and experience an enhancement of being.

Lascaux may seem impossibly distant from modern religious practice, but we cannot understand either the nature of the religious quest or our current religious predicament unless we appreciate the spirituality that emerged quite early in the history of *Homo religiosus* and continued to animate the major confessional traditions until the early modern period, when an entirely different kind of religiosity emerged in the West during the seventeenth century. To do that we must examine a number of core principles that will be of fundamental importance to our story.

The first concerns the nature of the ultimate reality—later called God, Nirvana, Brahman, or Dao. In a rocky overhang at Laussel near Lascaux, there is a small stone relief that is seventeen thousand years old and was created at about the same time as the earliest of the nearby cave paintings. It depicts a woman holding a curved bison's horn above her head so that it immediately suggests the rising, crescent moon; her right hand lies on her pregnancy. By this time, people had begun to observe the phases of the moon for practical purposes, but their religion had little or nothing to do with this protoscientific observation of the physical cosmos.[27] Instead, material reality was symbolic of an unseen dimension of existence. The little Venus of Laussel already suggests an association between the moon, the female cycle, and human reproduction. In many parts of the world, the moon was linked symbolically with a number of apparently unrelated phenomena: women, water, vegetation, serpents, and fertility. What they all have in common is the regenerative power of life that is continually able to renew itself. Everything could so easily lapse into nothingness, yet each year after the death of winter, trees sprout new leaves, the moon wanes but always waxes brilliantly once more, and the serpent, a universal symbol of initiation, sloughs off its old withered skin and comes forth gleaming and fresh.[28] The female also manifested this inexhaustible power. Ancient hunters revered a goddess known as the Great Mother. In large stone reliefs at Çatalhüyük in Turkey, she is shown giving birth, flanked by boars' skulls and bulls' horns—relics of a successful hunt. While hunters and animals died in the grim struggle for survival, the female was endlessly productive of new life.[29]

Perhaps these ancient societies were trying to express their sense of what the German philosopher Martin Heidegger (1899–1976) called "Being," a fundamental energy that supports and animates everything that exists. Being is transcendent. You could not see, touch, or hear it but could only watch it at work in the people, objects, and natural forces around you. From the documents of later Neolithic and pastoral societies, we know that Being rather than *a* being was revered as the ultimate sacred power. It was impossible to define or describe, because Being is all-encompassing and our minds are only equipped to deal with particular beings, which can merely participate in it in a restricted manner. But certain objects became eloquent symbols of the power of Being, which sustained and shone through them with particular clarity. A stone or a rock (frequent symbols of the sacred) expressed the stability and durability of Being; the moon, its power of endless renewal; the sky, its towering transcendence, ubiquity, and universality.[30] None of these symbols was worshipped for and in itself. People did not bow down and worship a rock *tout court;* the rock was simply a focus that directed their attention to the mysterious essence of life. Being bound all things together; humans, animals, plants, insects, stars, and birds all shared the divine life that sustained the entire cosmos. We know, for example, that the ancient Aryan tribes, who had lived on the Caucasian steppes since about 4500 BCE, revered an invisible, impersonal force within themselves and all other natural phenomena. Everything was a manifestation of this all-pervading "Spirit" (Sanskrit: *manya*).[31]

There was, therefore, no belief in a single supreme being in the ancient world. Any such creature could only be *a* being—bigger and better than anything else, perhaps, but still a finite, incomplete reality. People felt it natural to imagine a race of spiritual beings of a higher nature than themselves that they called "gods." There were, after all, many unseen forces at work in the world—wind, heat, emotion, and air—that were often identified with the various deities. The Aryan god Agni, for example, *was* the fire that had transformed human life, and as a personalized god symbolized the deep affinity people felt with these sacred forces. The Aryans called their gods "the shining ones" (*devas*) because Spirit shone through them more brightly than through mortal creatures, but these gods had no control over the world: they were not omniscient and were obliged, like everything else, to submit to the transcendent order that kept everything in existence, set the stars on their courses, made the seasons follow each other, and compelled the seas to remain within bounds.[32]

By the tenth century BCE, when some of the Aryans had settled in the Indian subcontinent, they gave a new name to the ultimate reality. Brahman was the unseen principle that enabled all things to grow and flourish. It was a power that was higher, deeper, and more fundamental than the gods. Because it transcended the limitations of personality, it would be entirely inappropriate to pray to Brahman or expect it to answer your prayers. Brahman was the sacred energy that held all the disparate elements of the world together and prevented it from falling apart. Brahman had an infinitely greater degree of reality than mortal creatures, whose lives were limited by ignorance, sickness, pain, and death.[33] You could never define Brahman, because language refers only to individual beings and Brahman was "the All"; it was everything that existed, as well as the inner meaning of all existence.

Even though human beings could not think about the Brahman, they had intimations of it in the hymns of the Rig Veda, the most important of the Aryan scriptures. Unlike the hunters of Lascaux, the Aryans do not seem to have thought readily in images. One of their chief symbols of the divine was sound, whose power and intangible quality seemed a particularly apt embodiment of the all-pervasive

Brahman. When the priest chanted the Vedic hymns, the music filled the air and entered the consciousness of the congregation, so that they felt surrounded by and infused with divinity. These hymns, revealed to ancient "seers" (*rishis*), did not speak of doctrines that the faithful were obliged to believe, but referred to the old myths in an allusive, riddling fashion because the truth they were trying to convey could not be contained in a neatly logical presentation. Their beauty shocked the audience into a state of awe, wonder, fear, and delight. They had to puzzle out the underlying significance of these paradoxical poems that yoked together apparently unrelated things, just as the hidden Brahman pulled the disparate elements of the universe into a coherent whole.[34]

During the tenth century, the Brahmin priests developed the Brahmodya competition, which would become a model of authentic religious discourse.[35] The contestants began by going on a retreat in the forest, where they performed spiritual exercises, such as fasting and breath control, that concentrated their minds and induced a different type of consciousness. Then the contest could begin. Its goal was to find a verbal formula to define the Brahman, in the process pushing language as far as it could go, until it finally broke down and people became vividly aware of the ineffable, the other. The challenger asked an enigmatic question, and his opponent had to reply in a way that was apt but equally inscrutable. The winner was the contestant who reduced his opponents to silence—and in that moment of silence, when language revealed its inadequacy, the Brahman was present; it became manifest only in the stunning realization of the impotence of speech.

The ultimate reality was not a personalized god, therefore, but a transcendent mystery that could never be plumbed. The Chinese called it the Dao, the fundamental "Way" of the cosmos. Because it comprised the whole of reality, the Dao had no qualities, no form; it could be experienced but never seen; it was not a god; it predated heaven and earth, and was beyond divinity. You could not say anything about the Dao, because it transcended ordinary categories: it was more ancient than antiquity and yet it was not old; because it went far beyond any form of "existence" known to humans, it was neither being nor nonbeing.[36] It contained all the myriad patterns, forms, and potential that made the world the way it was and guided the endless flux of change and becoming that we see all around us. It existed at a point where all the distinctions that characterize our normal modes of thought became irrelevant.

In the Middle East, the region in which the Western monotheisms would develop, there was a similar notion of the ultimate. In Mesopotamia, the Akkadian word for "divinity" was *ilam,* a radiant power that transcended any particular deity. The gods were not the source of *ilam* but, like everything else, could only reflect it. The chief characteristic of this "divinity" was *ellu* ("holiness"), a word that had connotations of "brightness," "purity," and "luminosity." The gods were called the "holy ones" because their symbolic stories, effigies, and cults evoked the radiance of *ellu* within their worshippers. The people of Israel called their patronal deity, the "holy one" of Israel, Elohim, a Hebrew variant on *ellu* that summed up everything that the divine could mean for human beings. But holiness was not confined to the gods. Anything that came into contact with divinity could become holy too: a priest, a king, or a temple—even the sacred utensils of the cult. In the Middle East, people would have found it far too constricting to limit *ilam* to a single god; instead, they imagined a Divine Assembly, a council of gods of many different ranks, who worked together to sustain the cosmos and expressed the multifaceted complexity of the sacred.[37]

People felt a yearning for the absolute, intuited its presence all around them, and went to great lengths to cultivate their sense of this transcendence in creative rituals. But they also felt estranged from it. Almost every culture has developed a myth of a lost paradise from which men and women were ejected at the beginning of time. It expressed an inchoate conviction that life was not *meant* to be so fragmented, hard, and full of pain. There *must* have been a time when people had enjoyed a greater share in the fullness of being and had not been subject to sorrow, disease, bereavement, loneliness, old age, and death. This nostalgia informed the cult of "sacred geography," one of the oldest and most universal religious ideas. Certain places that stood out in some way from the norm—like the labyrinthine caverns of the Dordogne—seemed to speak of "something else."[38] The sacred place was one of the earliest and most ubiquitous symbols of the divine. It was a sacred "center" that brought heaven and earth together and where the divine potency seemed particularly effective.

A popular image, found in many cultures, imagined this fructifying, sacred energy welling up like a spring from these focal places and flowing, in four sacred rivers, to the four quarters of the earth. People would settle only in sites where the sacred had once become manifest because they wanted to live as closely as possible to the wellsprings of being and become as whole and complete as they had been before they were ejected from paradise.

This brings us to the second principle of premodern religion. Religious discourse was not intended to be understood literally because it was only possible to speak about a reality that transcended language in symbolic terms. The story of the lost paradise was a myth, not a factual account of a historical event. People were not expected to "believe" it in the abstract; like any *mythos,* it depended upon the rituals associated with the cult of a particular holy place to make what it signified a reality in the lives of participants.

The same applies to the creation myth that was central to ancient religion and has now become controversial in the Western world because the Genesis story seems to clash with modern science. But until the early modern period, nobody read a cosmology as a literal account of the origins of life. In the ancient world, it was inspired by an acute sense of the contingency and frailty of existence. Why had anything come into being at all, when there could so easily have been nothing? There has never been a simple or even a possible answer to this question, but people continue to ask it, pushing their minds to the limit of what we can know. One of the earliest and most universal of the ancient cosmologies is particularly instructive to us today. It was thought that one of the gods, known as the "High God" or "Sky God" because he dwelt in the farthest reaches of the heavens, had single-handedly created heaven and earth.[39] The Aryans called him Dyaeus Pitr, the Chinese Tian ("Heaven"), the Arabians Allah (*"the* God"), and the Syrians El Elyon ("Most High God"). But the High God proved to be an unviable deity, and his myth was jettisoned.

It suffered from an internal contradiction. How could a mere being—even such a lofty one—be responsible for being itself? As if in response to this objection, people tried to elevate the High God to a special plane. He was considered too exalted for an ordinary cult: no sacrifices were performed in his honor; he had no priests, no temples, and virtually no mythology of his own. People called on him in an emergency, but otherwise he scarcely ever impinged on their daily lives. Reduced to a mere explanation—to what would later be called First Cause or Prime Mover—he became *Deus otiosus,* a "useless" or "superfluous" deity, and gradually faded from the consciousness of his people. In most mythologies, the High God is often depicted as a passive, helpless figure; unable to control events, he retreats to the periphery of the pantheon and finally fades away. Today some of the indigenous peoples—Pygmies, Aboriginal Australians, and Fuegians—also speak of a High God who created heaven and earth, but, they tell anthropologists, he has died or disappeared; he "no longer cares" and "has gone far away from us."[40]

No god can survive unless he or she is actualized by the practical activity of ritual, and people often turn against gods who fail to deliver. The High God is often mythologically deposed, sometimes violently, by a younger generation of more dynamic deities—gods of storm, grain, or war—who symbolized relevant, important realities. In Greek *mythos,* the High God Uranus ("Heaven") was brutally castrated by his son Kronos. Later Kronos himself was overthrown by his own son Zeus, head of the younger gods who lived more accessibly on Mount Olympus. In our own day, the God of the monotheistic tradition has often degenerated into a High God. The rites and practices that once made him a persuasive symbol of the sacred are no longer effective, and people have stopped participating in them. He has therefore become *otiosus,* an etiolated reality who for all intents and purposes has indeed died or "gone away."

In the ancient world, the High God myth was replaced by more relevant creation stories that were never regarded as factual. As one of the later hymns of the Rig Veda insists, nobody—not even the highest *deva*—could explain how something had issued from nothing.[41] A good creation myth did not describe an event in the distant past but told people something essential about the present. It reminded them that things often had to get worse before they got better, that creativity demanded self-sacrifice and heroic struggle, and that everybody had to work hard to preserve the energies of the cosmos and establish society on a sound foundation. A creation story was primarily therapeutic. People wanted to tap into the massive implosion of energy that had—somehow—brought the world we know into being, so they would recite a creation myth when they were in need of an infusion of sacred potency: during a political crisis, at a sickbed, or when they were building a new house. The creation myth was often reenacted during the New Year ceremonies, when the old year was ebbing away. Nobody felt obliged to "believe" in a particular cosmology; indeed, each culture usually had several creation stories, each of which had its own lesson to impart, and people thought nothing of making up a new one if their circumstances changed.

Once people had abandoned the myth of the High God, there was no concept of creation "out of nothing" (*ex nihilo*) in the ancient world. A god could only assist a creative process that was already well under way. In the tenth century, another Indian *rishi* suggested that the world had been set in motion by a primordial sacrifice—something that made sense in India, where new vegetation was often seen to sprout from a rotting tree so that it was not unnatural to think of death resulting in new life. The *rishi* imagined the Purusha ("Person"), the first, archetypal human being, striding of his own free will to the place of sacrifice and allowing the gods to put him to death; thence everything—animals, horses, cattle, heaven, earth, sun, moon, and even some of the gods—emerged from his corpse.[42] This *mythos* encapsulated an important truth: we are at our most creative when we do not cling to our selfhood but are prepared to give ourselves away.

The cosmology was not influenced by current scientific speculation because it was exploring the interior rather than the external world. The priests of Mesopotamia undertook the first successful astronomical observations, noting that the seven celestial bodies they sighted—later known as Sun, Moon, Mercury, Venus, Mars, Jupiter, and Saturn—moved in an apparently circular path through the constellations. But the chief inspiration behind their creation myth was their pioneering town planning.[43] The first cities had been established in Sumer in the Fertile Crescent in about 3500 BCE; it was an enterprise that required enormous courage and perseverance, as time and time again, the mud-brick buildings were swept away by the flooding of the Tigris and the Euphrates. Constantly it seemed that the Sumerians' fragile urban civilization would sink back into the old rural barbarism, so the city needed a regular infusion of sacred energy. And yet it seemed such an extraordinary achievement that the city was extolled as a holy place. Babylon was the "Gate of the gods" (*Babilani*), where heaven and earth could meet; it re-created the lost paradise, and the ziggurat, or temple tower, of Esagila replicated the cosmic mountain or the sacred tree, which the first men and women had climbed to meet their gods.[44]

It is difficult to understand the creation story in Genesis without reference to the Mesopotamian creation hymn known from its opening words as the *Enuma Elish*. This poem begins by describing the evolution of the gods from primordial sacred matter and their subsequent creation of heaven and earth, but it is also a meditation on contemporary Mesopotamia. The raw material of the universe, from which the gods emerge, is a sloppy, undefined substance—very like the silty soil of the region. The first gods—Tiamat, the primal Ocean; Apsu, the "Abyss"; and Mummu, "Womb" of chaos—were inseparable from the elements and shared the inertia of aboriginal barbarism and the formlessness of chaos: "When sweet and bitter mingled together, no reed was plaited, no rushes muddied the water, the gods were nameless, natureless, futureless."[45] But new gods emerged, each pair more distinct than the last, culminating in the splendid Marduk, the Sun God and the most developed specimen of the divine species. But Marduk could not establish the cosmos until he had overcome the sluggish torpor of Tiamat in a tremendous battle. Finally he stood astride Tiamat's massive carcass, split her in two to make heaven and earth, and created the first man by mixing the blood of one of the defeated gods with a handful of dust. After this triumph, the gods could build the city of Babylon and establish the ritual "from which the universe receives its structure, the hidden world is made plain, and the gods assigned their places."[46]

There was no ontological gulf separating these gods from the rest of the cosmos; everything had emerged from the same sacred stuff. All beings shared the same predicament and had to participate in a ceaseless battle against the destructive lethargy of chaos. There were similar tales in neighboring Syria, where Baal, god of storm and life-giving rain, had to fight the sea dragon Lotan, symbol of chaos, Yam, the primal sea, and Mot, god of sterility, in order to establish civilized life.[47] The Israelites also told stories of their god Yahweh slaying sea monsters to order the cosmos.[48] In Babylon, the *Enuma Elish* was chanted on the fourth day of the New Year festival in Esagila, a reen-actment that symbolically continued the process Marduk had begun and that activated this sacred energy. There was a ritualized mock battle and a saturnalia that re-created the lawlessness of chaos. In archaic spirituality, a symbolic return to the formless "nothingness" of the beginning was indispensable to any new creation.[49] It was pos-sible to move forward only if you had the courage to let go of the present, unsatisfactory state of affairs, sink back into the potent con-fusion of the beginning, and begin again.

As life became more settled, people had the leisure to develop a more interior spirituality. The Indian Aryans, always in the vanguard of religious change, pioneered this trend, achieving the groundbreaking discovery that the Brahman, being itself, was also the ground of the human psyche. The transcendent was neither external nor alien to humanity, but the two were inextricably connected. This insight would become central to the religious quest in all the major tradi-tions. In the early Upanishads, composed in the seventh century BCE, the search for this sacred Self (*atman*) became central to Vedic spiritu-ality. The Upanishadic sages did not ask their disciples to "believe" this but put them through an initiation whereby they discovered it for themselves in a series of spiritual exercises that made them look at the world differently. This practically acquired knowledge brought with it a joyous liberation from fear and anxiety.

We have a precious glimpse of the way this initiation was carried out in the Chandogya Upanishad. Here the great sage Uddalaka Aruni slowly and patiently brings this saving insight to birth within his son Shvetaketu, and has him perform a series of tasks. In the most famous of these experiments, Shvetaketu had to leave a lump of salt in a beaker of water overnight and found, of course, that even though the salt had dissolved, the water still tasted salty. "You, of course, did not see it there, son," Uddalaka pointed out, "yet it was always right there." So too was the invisible Brahman, essence and inner self of the entire world. "And you are *that,* Shvetaketu."[50] Like the salt, the Brahman could not be seen but was manifest in every single living thing. It was the subtle essence in the tiny banyan seed, from which a giant tree would grow, yet when Shvetaketu dissected the seed, he could not see anything at all. The Brahman was also the sap in every part of the tree that gave it life, and yet it could never be pinned down or analyzed.[51] All things shared the same essence, but most people did not realize this. They imagined they were unique and special and clung to these particularities—often with extreme anxiety and expenditure of effort. But in reality these qualities were no more durable than rivers that flowed into the same sea. Once they had merged, they became "just the ocean," and no longer asserted their individuality by insisting "I am that river," "I am this river." "In exactly the same way, son," Uddalaka persisted, "when all these creatures reach the Existent, they are not aware that: 'We are reaching the Existent.'" Whether they were tigers, wolves, or gnats, they all merged into Brahman. To hold on to the mundane self, therefore, was a delusion that led inescapably to pain, frustration, and confusion, which one could escape only by acquiring the deep, liberating knowledge that the Brahman was their atman, the truest thing about them.[52]

The Upanishadic sages were among the first to articulate another of the universal principles of religion—one that had already been touched upon in the Purusha myth. The truths of religion are accessible only when you are prepared to get rid of the selfishness, greed, and self-preoccupation that, perhaps inevitably, are ingrained in our thoughts and behavior but are also the source of so much of our pain. The Greeks would call this process *kenosis*, "emptying." Once you gave up the nervous craving to promote yourself, denigrate others, draw attention to your unique and special qualities, and ensure that you were first in the pecking order, you experienced an immense peace. The first Upanishads were written at a time when the Aryan communities were in the early stages of urbanization; *logos* had enabled them to master their environment. But the sages reminded them that there were some things—old age, sickness, and death— that they could not control; some things—such as their essential self—that lay beyond their intellectual grasp. When, as a result of carefully crafted spiritual exercises, people learned not only to accept but to embrace this unknowing, they found that they experienced a sense of release.

The sages began to explore the complexities of the human psyche with remarkable sophistication; they had discovered the unconscious long before Freud. But the atman, the deepest core of their personality, eluded them. Precisely *because* it was identical with the Brahman, it was indefinable. The atman had nothing to do with our normal psycho-mental states and bore no resemblance to anything in our ordinary experience, so you could speak of it only in negative terms. As the seventh-century sage Yajnavalkya explained: "About this Self [*atman*] one can only say 'not . . . not' [*neti . . . neti*]."[53]

> You can't see the Seer who does the seeing. You can't hear the Hearer who does the hearing; you can't think with the Thinker who does the thinking; and you can't perceive the Perceiver who does the perceiving. This Self within the All [*Brahman*] is this *atman* of yours.[54]

Like the Brahmodya, any discussion of the atman in the Upanishads always ended in silence, the numinous acknowledgment that the ultimate reality was beyond the competence of language.

Authentic religious discourse could not lead to clear, distinct, and empirically verified truth. Like the Brahman, the atman was "ungraspable." You could define something only when you saw it as separate from yourself. But "when the Whole [*Brahman*] has become a person's very self, then who is there for him to see and by what means? Who is there for me to think of and by what means?"[55] But if you learned to "realize" the truth that your most authentic "Self" was identical with Brahman, you understood that it too was "beyond hunger and thirst, sorrow and delusion, old age and death."[56] You could not achieve this insight by rational logic. You had to acquire the knack of thinking outside the ordinary "lowercase" self, and like any craft or skill, this required long, hard, dedicated practice.

One of the principal technologies that enabled people to achieve this self-forgetfulness was yoga.[57] Unlike the yoga practiced in Western gyms today, it was not an aerobic exercise but a systematic breakdown of instinctive behavior and normal thought patterns. It was mentally demanding and, initially, physically painful. The yogin had to do the opposite of what came naturally. He sat so still that he seemed more like a plant or a statue than a human being; he controlled his respiration, one of the most automatic and essential of our physical functions, until he acquired the ability to exist for long periods without breathing at all. He learned to silence the thoughts that coursed through his mind and concentrate "on one point" for hours at a time. If he persevered, he found that he achieved a dissolution of ordinary consciousness that extracted the "I" from his thinking.

To this day, yogins find that these disciplines, which have measurable physical and neurological effects, evoke a sense of calm, harmony, and equanimity that is comparable to the effect of music. There is a feeling of expansiveness and bliss, which yogins regard as entirely natural, possible for anybody who has the talent and application. As the "I" disappears, the most humdrum objects reveal wholly unexpected qualities, since they are no longer viewed through the distorting filter of one's own egotistic needs and desires. When she meditated on the teachings of her guru, a yogin did not simply accept them notionally but experienced them so vividly that her knowledge was, as the texts say, "direct"; bypassing the logical processes like any practically acquired skill, it had become part of her inner world.[58]

But yoga also had an ethical dimension. A beginner was not allowed to perform a single yogic exercise until he had completed an intensive moral program. Top of the list of its requirements was *ahimsa,* "nonviolence." A yogin must not swat a mosquito, make an irritable gesture, or speak unkindly to others but should maintain constant affability to all, even the most annoying monk in the community. Until his guru was satisfied that this had become second nature, a yogin could not even sit in the yogic position. A great deal of the aggression, frustration, hostility, and rage that mars our peace of mind is the result of thwarted egotism, but when the aspiring yogin became proficient in this selfless equanimity, the texts tell us that he would experience "indescribable joy."[59]

Their experience of yoga led the sages to devise a new creation myth. In the beginning, there was only a single Person, who looked around him and discovered that he was alone. In this way, he became aware of himself and cried: "Here I am!" Thus the "I," the ego principle, was born. Immediately the Person became afraid, because we instinctively feel that we must protect the fragile ego from anything that threatens it, but when the Person remembered that because he was alone, there was no such threat, his fear left him. But he was lonely, so he split his body in two to create a man and a woman, who together gave birth to every single being in the cosmos "down to the very ants." And the Person realized that even though he was no longer alone, there was still nothing to fear. Was he not identical with

Brahman, the All? He was one with all the things that he had made; indeed, he was himself his own creation.[60] He had even created the gods, who were essentially a part of himself.[61]

> Even now, if a man knows "I am *brahman*" in this way, he becomes this whole world. Not even the gods are able to prevent it, for he becomes their very self [*atman*]. So when a man venerates another deity, thinking, "He is one, and I am another," he does not understand.[62]

This insight, Yajnavalkya explained, brought with it a joy comparable to that of sexual intercourse, when one loses all sense of duality and is "oblivious to everything within or without."[63] But you would not have this experience unless you had performed the yogic exercises.

Other traditions would also find that these fundamental principles were indispensable: Buddhism, Jainism, Confucianism, and Daoism, as well as the three monotheistic faiths of Judaism, Christianity, and Islam. Each had its own unique genius and distinctive vision, each its peculiar flaws. But on these central principles they would all agree. Religion was not a notional matter. The Buddha, for example, had little time for theological speculation. One of his monks was a philosopher manqué and, instead of getting on with his yoga, constantly pestered the Buddha about metaphysical questions: Was there a god? Had the world been created in time or had it always existed? The Buddha told him that he was like a man who had been shot with a poisoned arrow and refused medical treatment until he had discovered the name of his assailant and what village he came from. He would die before he got this perfectly useless information. What difference would it make to discover that a god had created the world? Pain, hatred, grief, and sorrow would still exist. These issues were fascinating, but the Buddha refused to discuss them because they were irrelevant: "My disciples, they will not help you, they are not useful in the quest for holiness; they do not lead to peace and to the direct knowledge of Nirvana."[64]

The Buddha always refused to define Nirvana, because it could not be understood notionally and would be inexplicable to anybody who did not undertake his practical regimen of meditation and compassion. But anybody who did commit him- or herself to the Buddhist way of life could attain Nirvana, which was an entirely natural state.[65] Sometimes, however, Buddhists would speak of Nirvana using the same kind of imagery as monotheists use of God: it was the "Truth," the "Other Shore," "Peace," the "Everlasting," and "the Beyond." Nirvana was a still center that gave meaning to life, an oasis of calm, and a source of strength that you discovered in the depths of your own being. In purely mundane terms, it was "nothing," because it corresponded to no reality that we could recognize in our ego-dominated existence. But those who had managed to find this sacred peace discovered that they lived an immeasurably richer life.[66] There was no question of "believing" in the existence of Nirvana or taking it "on faith." The Buddha had no time for abstract doctrinal formulations divorced from action. Indeed, to accept a dogma on somebody else's authority was what he called "unskillful" or "unhelpful" (*akusala*). It could not lead to enlightenment because it amounted to an abdication of personal responsibility. Faith meant trust that Nirvana existed and a determination to realize it by every practical means in one's power.

Nirvana was the natural result of a life lived according to the Buddha's doctrine of *anatta* ("no self"), which was not simply a metaphysical principle but, like all his teachings, a program of action. *Anatta* required Buddhists to *behave* day by day, hour by hour, as though the self did not exist. Thoughts of "self" not only led to "unhelpful" (*akusala*) preoccupation with "me" and "mine," but also to envy, hatred of rivals, conceit, pride, cruelty, and—when the self felt under threat—violence. As a monk became expert in cultivating this dispassion, he no longer interjected his ego into passing mental states but learned to regard his fears and desires as transient and remote phenomena. He was then ripe for enlightenment: "His greed fades away, and once his cravings disappear, he experiences the release of the mind."[67] The texts indicate that when the Buddha's first disciples heard about *anatta*, their hearts were filled with joy and they immediately experienced Nirvana. To live beyond the reach of hatred, greed, and anxieties about our status proved to be a profound relief.

By far the best way of achieving *anatta* was compassion, the ability to *feel with* the other, which required that one dethrone the self from the center of one's world and put another there. Compassion would become the central practice of the religious quest. One of the first people to make it crystal clear that holiness was inseparable from altru-

ism was the Chinese sage Confucius (551–479 BCE). He preferred
not to speak about the divine, because it lay beyond the competence of
language, and theological chatter was a distraction from the real business of religion.[68] He used to say: "My Way has one thread that runs
right through it." There were no abstruse metaphysics; everything
always came back to the importance of treating others with absolute
respect.[69] It was epitomized in the Golden Rule, which, he said, his
disciples should practice "all day and every day":[70] "Never do to others what you would not like them to do to you."[71] They should look
into their own hearts, discover what gave them pain, and then refuse
under any circumstance whatsoever to inflict that pain on anybody
else.

Religion was a matter of doing rather than thinking. The traditional rituals of China enabled an individual to burnish and refine
his humanity so that he became a *junzi,* a "mature person." A *junzi*
was not born but crafted; he had to work on himself as a sculptor
shaped a rough stone and made it a thing of beauty. "How can I
achieve this?" asked Yan Hui, Confucius's most talented disciple. It
was simple, Confucius replied: "Curb your ego and surrender to ritual (*li*)."[72] A *junzi* must submit every detail of his life to the ancient
rites of consideration and respect for others. This was the answer to
China's political problems: "If a ruler could curb his ego and submit
to *li* for a single day, everyone under Heaven would respond to his
goodness."[73]

The practice of the Golden Rule "all day and every day" would
bring human beings into the state that Confucius called *ren,* a word
that would later be described as "benevolence" but that Confucius
himself refused to define because it could be understood only by
somebody who had acquired it. He preferred to remain silent about
what lay at the end of the religious journey. The practice of *ren* was an
end in itself; it was itself the transcendence you sought. Yan Hui
expressed this beautifully when he spoke of the endless struggle to
achieve *ren* "with a deep sigh."

> The more I strain my gaze towards it, the higher it soars.
> The deeper I bore down into it, the harder it becomes. I
> see it in front, but suddenly it is behind. Step by step, the
> Master skilfully lures one on. He has broadened me with

culture, restrained me with ritual. Even if I wanted to
stop, I could not. Just when I feel that I have exhausted
every resource, something seems to rise up, standing over
me sharp and clear. Yet though I long to pursue it, I can
find no way of getting to it at all.[74]

Living a compassionate, empathetic life took Yan Hui beyond
himself, giving him momentary glimpses of a sacred reality that was
not unlike the "God" worshipped by monotheists. It was both immanent and transcendent: it welled up from within but was also experienced as an external presence "standing over me sharp and clear."

Religion as defined by the great sages of India, China, and the
Middle East was not a notional activity but a practical one; it did not
require belief in a set of doctrines but rather hard, disciplined work,
without which any religious teaching remained opaque and incredible. The ultimate reality was not a Supreme Being—an idea that was
quite alien to the religious sensibility of antiquity; it was an all-
encompassing, wholly transcendent reality that lay beyond neat doctrinal formulations. So religious discourse should not attempt to
impart clear information about the divine but should lead to an
appreciation of the limits of language and understanding. The ultimate was not alien to human beings but inseparable from our
humanity. It could not be accessed by rational, discursive thought but
required a carefully cultivated state of mind and the abnegation of
selflessness.

But how would this apply to the monotheistic religions of Judaism,
Christianity, and Islam, which present themselves as religions of the
word rather than religions of silence? In the eighth century BCE,
the people of Israel were about to attempt something unusual in the
ancient world. They would try to make Yahweh, the "holy one of
Israel," the only symbol of ultimate transcendence.

# TWO

# God

At the beginning of time, the first human being (Hebrew: *adam*) found himself alone in Eden, the Land of Pleasure. This garden had been planted by the god Yahweh, who had caused a spring to gush forth in the eastern desert to create a paradisal oasis. There it divided into four separate rivers—the Pishon, the Gihon, the Tigris, and the Euphrates—that flowed from this sacred center to give life to the rest of the world. Yahweh had molded Adam from the soil (*adama*), blown the breath of life into his nostrils, and put him in charge of the garden. Eden was indeed a land of delights, and Adam could have led a blissful life. Yahweh had brought forth all the birds and animals from the ground to be his companions; there were two sacred trees marking the center of the world—the Tree of Life and the Tree of the Knowledge of Good and Evil—and there was even a talking snake to initiate him into the secret lore of the garden. But Adam was lonely. So while he was asleep, Yahweh extracted one of his ribs and constructed a female. Adam was delighted: "This-time, she-is-it! Bone from my bones, flesh from my flesh! She shall be called Woman [*Isha*], for from Man [*Ish*] she was taken!"[1] Adam named her Havva (Eve), the "Life-giver."

This immediately recalls the Upanishadic story of the lonely human person who splits in two to become male and female, but it is obviously a Middle Eastern tale and full of traditional motifs: the crafting of *adam* from clay, the river irrigating the four corners of the earth, the sacred trees and the talking animal. It is a typical lost-paradise myth. Yahweh forbids Adam and Eve to eat the fruit of the

Tree of Knowledge, the snake persuades them to disobey, and they are cast out of the garden forever. Henceforth they must toil painfully to scratch a living from the hostile earth and bring forth their children in sorrow. Like any myth, its purpose is to help us to contemplate the human predicament. Why is human life filled with suffering, back-breaking agricultural labor, agonizing childbirth, and death? Why do men and women feel so estranged from the divine?

Some Western Christians read the story as a factual account of the Original Sin that condemned the human race to everlasting perdition. But this is a peculiarly Western Christian interpretation and was introduced controversially by Saint Augustine of Hippo only in the early fifth century. The Eden story has never been understood in this way in either the Jewish or the Orthodox Christian traditions. However, we all tend to see these ancient tales through the filter of subsequent history and project current beliefs onto texts that originally meant something quite different. Today, because the modern West is a society of *logos,* some people read the Bible literally, assuming that its intention is to give us the kind of accurate information that we expect from any other supposedly historical text and that this is the way these stories have always been understood. In fact, as we shall see in subsequent chapters, until well into the modern period, Jews and Christians both insisted that it was neither possible nor desirable to read the Bible in this way, that it gives us no single, orthodox message and demands constant reinterpretation.[2]

There is also a widespread assumption that the Bible is supposed to provide us with role models and give us precise moral teaching, but this was not the intention of the biblical authors. The Eden story is certainly not a morality tale; like any paradise myth, it is an imaginary account of the infancy of the human race. In Eden, Adam and Eve are still in the womb; they have to grow up, and the snake is there to guide them through the perplexing rite of passage to maturity. To know pain and to be conscious of desire and mortality are inescapable components of human experience, but they are also symptoms of that sense of estrangement from the fullness of being that inspires the nostalgia for paradise lost. We can see Adam, Eve, and the serpent as representing different facets of our humanity.[3] In the snake is the rebelliousness and incessant compulsion to question everything that is crucial to human progress; in Eve we see our hunger for knowledge, our desire to experiment, and our longing for a life free of inhibition. Adam, a rather passive figure, displays our reluctance to take responsibility for our actions. The story shows that good and evil are inextricably intertwined in human life. Our prodigious knowledge can at one and the same time be a source of benefit and the cause of immense harm. The rabbis of the Talmudic age understood this perfectly. They did not see the "fall" of Adam as a catastrophe, because the "evil inclination" (*yeytzer ha'ra*) was an essential part of human life, and the aggression, competitive edge, and ambition that it generates are bound up with some of our greatest achievements.[4]

In the *Enuma Elish,* the cosmogony was linked with the gods' construction of the Esagila ziggurat. In the ancient Middle East, creation was regularly associated with temple building, and this Genesis myth was closely related to the temple built by King Solomon (c. 970–930 BCE) in Jerusalem:[5] one of the four sacred rivers that flow from Eden is the Gihon, the spring at the foot of the Temple Mount. The theme of Yahweh's creation was important in the temple cult, not because it provided worshippers with information about the origin of the universe but because the building of a temple was a symbolic repetition of the cosmogony.[6] It enabled mortals to participate in the creative powers of the gods and ensured that Yahweh would fight Israel's enemies just as "in the beginning" he had slain the sea monsters. In Israel, the temple was a symbol of the harmonious, pristine cosmos as originally designed by Yahweh. Hence the description of life in Eden before the "fall" is an expression of *shalom,* the sense of "peace," "wholeness," and "completion" that pilgrims experienced when they took part in these rites and felt that their separation from the divine had been momentarily healed.

The Eden story is not a historical account; it is rather a description of a ritual experience. It expresses what scholars have called the *coincidentia oppositorum* in which, during a heightened encounter with the sacred, things that normally seem opposed coincide to reveal an underlying unity. In Eden, the divine and the human are not estranged but are in the same "place": we see Yahweh "walking about in the garden at the breezy-time of the day";[7] there is no opposition between "natural" and "supernatural," since Adam is animated by the breath of God himself. Adam and Eve seem unaware of gender distinction or the difference between good and evil. This is the way that life was supposed to be. Because of their lapse, however, Adam and Eve fell into the fragmentation of our current existence and the gates of Eden were barred by cherubim brandishing a "flashing, ever-turning sword."[8] But Israelites could have intimations of this primal wholeness whenever they visited their temple and took part in its rites.

Solomon's temple was apparently designed as a replica of Eden, its walls decorated with carved cherubim, palm trees, and open flowers.[9] Its massive seven-branched candlesticks, decorated with almonds and blossoms, were like stylized trees and there was even a bronze serpent.[10] As once in Eden, Yahweh dwelled in the temple among his people. The temple was, therefore, a haven of *shalom*.[11] When the pilgrim throngs climbed the slopes of Mount Zion to enter Yahweh's house, there were exultant cries of joy and praise;[12] they yearned and pined for Yahweh's courts. Arrival in the temple was like a homecoming; as they took part in its rituals, they experienced a spiritual ascent "from height to height" and life seemed richer and more intense: "A single day in your courts is worth more than a thousand elsewhere."[13]

In the eighth century BCE, the Israelites had not yet begun to interiorize their religion and still relied on external rites. By this time, they were living in two separate kingdoms: the Kingdom of Judah in the south of what is now the West Bank, with its capital in Jerusalem, and the larger and more prosperous Kingdom of Israel in the north. The Adam and Eve story was almost certainly written by an anonymous author of the southern kingdom in the eighth century, when kings had started to commission epics for their royal archives. Eighteenth-century German scholars called him "J," the "Jahwist," because he used God's proper name, "Jahweh" ("Yahweh"). At the same time, another writer known as "E" (because he preferred to use the more formal divine title, "Elohim") was composing a similar saga for the Kingdom of Israel. After the northern kingdom was destroyed by the Assyrian army in 722, the two documents were combined in the JE narrative, which comprises the earliest stratum of the Bible.[14]

From the very beginning, therefore, there was no single, orthodox message in the Bible: J and E interpreted the history of Israel quite differently, and these differences were preserved by the editors.

There was nothing sacrosanct about these documents, and later generations would feel free to rewrite the JE epic and even make substantial changes in the story. The JE chronicle is almost certainly a collection of tales recited at the old tribal festivals. Since about 1200 BCE, the confederation of tribes collectively known as "Israel" had congregated at a number of shrines in the Canaanite highlands—in Jerusalem, Hebron, Bethel, Shechem, Gilgal, and Shiloh—where they renewed the covenant treaty that bound them together. Bards would recite poems about the exploits of local heroes: the patriarchs Abraham, Isaac, and Jacob; Moses, who led the people out of Egyptian captivity; and their great military commander Joshua. At first there was probably no master narrative, but when J and E brought all this local lore together, they wove it into the sustained epic that has become one of the founding stories of Western culture.[15]

In its final form, it relates how in about 1850 BCE, Yahweh had called Abraham to leave his home in Mesopotamia and settle in Canaan, promising that he would become the father of a mighty nation that would one day take possession of the land. Abraham, his son Isaac, and his grandson Jacob (also known as Israel) lived in the Promised Land as resident aliens, but during a famine, Jacob's twelve sons, founders of the twelve tribes of Israel, were forced to migrate to Egypt. At first they prospered there, but eventually, threatened by their great numbers, the Egyptians oppressed and enslaved the Israelites until Yahweh commanded Moses to lead his people back to Canaan. With Yahweh's miraculous help, they managed to escape Egypt and lived a nomadic life for forty years in the wilderness of the Sinai Peninsula. On Mount Sinai, Yahweh delivered his teaching (*torah*) to Moses and adopted the Israelites as his own people. Moses died on Mount Nebo on the threshold of the Promised Land, but finally, in about 1200 BCE, Joshua conquered Canaan and drove out the native inhabitants.

The excavations of Israeli archaeologists since 1967, however, do not corroborate this story. They have found no trace of the mass destruction described in the book of Joshua and no indication of a major change of population. They note that the biblical narratives reflect the conditions of the eighth, seventh, and sixth centuries, when these stories were committed to writing, rather than the period in which they are set.[16] J and E were not writing rigorously factual accounts, and this new understanding will affect the way we read the biblical stories. During the eighteenth-century philosophical Enlightenment, Western people developed a historical method that is concerned above all with giving an accurate account of the events described. But when people wrote about the past in the ancient world, they were less interested in what actually happened than in the meaning of an event. When the final editors of the Pentateuch (the first five books of the Bible) combined the J and E chronicles, they made no attempt to iron out discrepancies that would worry a modern redactor. A close examination of the text shows, for example, that J saw Abraham, a man of the south, as the prime hero of Israel and had little time for Moses, who was far more popular in the north and one of the leading protagonists of E's narrative.[17] Neither J nor E seems to have made any effort to research the history of Canaan, but were content to adapt the old stories to the conditions of their own time.

It is a mistake, therefore, to expect this saga to be historically accurate in our sense. But it is, however, true that the biblical authors were more interested in human history than most of their contemporaries. J and E paid little attention to the cosmological myths that fascinated their Syrian and Mesopotamian neighbors and were not responsible for the creation story in the first chapter of Genesis, which was not written until the sixth century. J's account of Yahweh's creation of Eden is very perfunctory, and E did not contribute at all to the "prehistory" of Israel in the first eleven chapters of Genesis but begins his chronicle with the Patriarchs, when Israel's history really begins. There were certainly tales in Israel about Yahweh creating the cosmos by fighting sea dragons, like other Middle Eastern deities, but J and E pass them by. At the very beginning of the monotheistic tradition, therefore, the doctrine of divine creation, which would later become so important, seems somewhat peripheral. If they did refer to the old cosmological myths, the biblical authors used them to supplement the meaning of historical events. One of the most famous miracle stories in the Hebrew Bible is the tale of the Israelites' crossing of the sea during their escape from Egypt, with Pharaoh's army in hot pursuit. When they reached the shore, Moses had stretched his hand over the water and Yahweh sent a fierce east wind that "made the sea into firm ground; thus the waters split." The Israelites were able to walk dry-shod across the seabed, "the waters a wall for them on their right and on their left."[18] Once they reached the opposite side, the waters closed over the heads of the Egyptians, not one of whom escaped. There have been several well-intentioned attempts to prove that this story can be explained by a tsunami or the flash flooding that was common in the region. But this entirely misses the point, because the story has been deliberately written as a myth. As we know, there were many tales in the ancient Middle East about a god splitting a sea in two to create the world, but this time what is brought to birth was not a cosmos but a people.

Immediately after the story of the crossing, the editors introduced into the narrative a much older text known as the Song of the Sea, a tenth-century poem, and put it on the lips of Moses.[19]

> *I will sing to YHWH,*
> *For he has triumphed, yes, triumphed,*
> *The horse and chariot he flung into the sea!*[20]

But a closer reading shows that originally the song celebrated an entirely different event, a victory at the River Jordan on the borders of Canaan. It describes Yahweh leading his people through the Promised Land and striking dismay *not* into the hearts of the Egyptians but into the inhabitants of Canaan and the kingdoms on the Jordan's east bank:

> *Writhing seized Philistia's settlers,*
> *and then terrified Edom's chieftains,*
> *Moav's "rams" — trembling did seize them;*
> *then melted away all Canaan's settlers.*[21]

Scholars think that the song was originally sung during the spring festival at Gilgal, where, it was said, the waters of the Jordan had miraculously parted before the Israelites to enable them to enter the Promised Land[22]—an event that utterly confounded "the kings of the Amorites on the west bank of the Jordan and all the kings of the Canaanites in the coastal region."[23] Every year, when the Jordan flooded its banks, this crossing (*pesah*) was ritually reenacted at Gilgal. Priests and laypeople would process past the floodwaters and enter the temple, where they ate unleavened bread (*mazzoth*) and roasted corn in memory of their ancestors, who had "tasted the produce of the land there for the first time."[24] It seems, therefore, that not only did the old cosmological myths shape the Israelites' understanding of their history but that the rituals of Gilgal helped to form the myth of the exodus from Egypt.

Apart from a lack of interest in cosmogony, the religion of ancient Israel did not at this date differ markedly from that of its neighbors. J and E present Abraham worshipping El, the local High God, and it seems that originally Yahweh was simply one of the "holy ones" in El's retinue.[25] But the Israelites also worshipped other gods until the sixth century, despite the campaign of a small group of prophets and priests who wanted them to worship Yahweh alone.[26] Israel would later condemn the pagan religion of the native Canaanites in the strongest terms, but at the time of J and E there seems to have been no such tension. Both, for example, record the founding myth of the temple of Bethel, which is one of the most famous of the Genesis stories.[27] Because of a family feud, Jacob was forced to flee Canaan and take refuge with relatives in Mesopotamia. On the first leg of his journey, he spent the night at Luz on the border of the Promised Land in what seemed an unremarkable spot but was in fact a Canaanite shrine, a *maqom*.[28] That night, perhaps because he used one of its sacred stones as a pillow, Jacob had a numinous dream: "A ladder was set up on the earth, its top reaching the heavens, and here: messengers of God were going up and down on it. And here: Yahweh was standing over against him."[29] Jacob awoke in astonishment: "Why, Yahweh is in this place and I did not know it!" he exclaimed. "How awe-inspiring is this *maqom*! It is none other than a house of God (*beth-El*) and that is the gate of Heaven!"[30] Before continuing his journey, Jacob upended the stone to make it a "standing pillar" (*matzebah*) and consecrated it with a libation of oil. Later generations of Israelites would try to eradicate such cult places as idolatrous and tear down the local *matzeboth,* but in this early story, these pagan symbols nourished Jacob's vision of Yahweh, and Bethel became one of their own sacred "centers."

The story shows how impossible it is to seek a single, consistent message in the Bible, since a directive in one book is likely to be countermanded in another. The editors did not eradicate potentially embarrassing early teachings that clashed with later doctrines. Later Jews would be shocked to imagine God becoming manifest in a human being, but J described Yahweh appearing to Abraham in the guise of a traveler at Mamre, near Hebron.[31] Standing in the entrance of his tent during the hottest part of the afternoon, Abraham had seen three men approaching. Strangers were dangerous people, because they were not bound by the local vendetta, but Abraham ran out to meet them, bowed before them as if they were kings or gods, brought them into his camp, and gave them an elaborate meal. Without any great fanfare, it transpires in the course of the ensuing conversation that one of these visitors was Abraham's god. The act of compassion had led to a divine encounter. Abraham's previous encounters with Yahweh had been somewhat disturbing and peremptory, but at Mamre Yahweh ate with Abraham as a friend—the first intimacy with the divine that humans had enjoyed since the expulsion from Eden.

J and E were not writing edifying morality tales, however. The characters of Genesis have moments of vision and insight, but they are also presented as flawed human beings who have to contend with a perplexing God. This is particularly evident when Yahweh commands Abraham to take his only remaining son, Isaac, to a mountain in the land of Moriyya and sacrifice him there.[32] Hitherto Abraham had not hesitated to question Yahweh's arrangements, but this time he obeyed without voicing a single objection. Perhaps he was too shocked to speak. The God he had served so long had turned out to be a heartless slayer of children, who was also cynically breaking his promise to make him the father of a great nation. At the last moment, of course, Isaac is reprieved, God renews his promise, and Abraham sacrifices a ram in Isaac's stead. This disturbing story has traditionally been related to the Jerusalem temple, which was said to have been built on Mount Moriyya. Yahweh was, therefore, making it clear that his cult must not include human sacrifice. But E's painful story goes further. Moriyya means "Seeing," and the Hebrew verb *ra'o* ("to see") sounds insistently through the Abraham stories.[33] Although Abraham is presented to us as a man of vision, the Genesis narratives show how difficult it is to see or understand the divine as we struggle with life's cruel dilemmas.

There is no clear, consistent image of God in Genesis. In the famous first chapter, the Creator God appears center stage, with no rival, supremely powerful and benign, blessing all the things that he has made. But the rest of Genesis seems to deconstruct this tidy theology. The God who was supremely powerful in chapter 1 has lost control of his creation within two chapters; the utterly fair and equitable

God who blessed everything impartially is later guilty of blatant favoritism, and his somewhat arbitrary choices (the chosen ones are rarely paragons) set human beings murderously against each other. At the time of the Flood, the benign creator becomes the cruel destroyer. And finally the God who was such a powerful presence in chapter 1 fades away and makes no further appearances, so that at the end of the book, Joseph and his brothers have to rely on their own dreams and insights—just as we do. Genesis shows that our glimpses of what we call "God" can be as partial, terrible, ambiguous, and paradoxical as the world we live in. As Abraham's plight on Mount Moriyya shows, it is not easy to "see" what God is, and there are no simple answers to life's perplexities.

The Bible traces the long process whereby this confusing deity became Israel's only icon of the sacred.[34] Traditionally in the Middle East, it was impossible to confine the holiness of *ilam* ("divinity") to a single symbol. Any image of the divine is bound to be inadequate, because it cannot possibly express the all-encompassing reality of being itself. If it is not balanced by other symbols, there is a danger that people will think of the sacred too simplistically. If that symbol is a personalized deity, they could easily start to imagine "him" functioning as if he were a human being like themselves writ large, with likes and dislikes similar to their own. Idolatry, the worship of a human image of the divine, would become one of the besetting problems of monotheism. In the Bible, we see that the Israelites were deeply vexed by the idolatry of the "foreign nations" (*goyim*), whose gods were merely "gold and silver, products of human skill."[35] But Israel's sensitivity to idolatry may have sprung from a buried anxiety. Once people forget that a particular image of the sacred can only be proximate and incomplete, there is a danger that it will cease to point to the transcendent and become an end in itself.

This became clear during the seventh century, when a group of priests, prophets, and scribes in the court of King Josiah of Judah tried to reform the religion of Israel. They are known as the Deuteronomists, because in their scriptures they presented Moses delivering a "second law" (Greek: *deuteronomion*) to the assembled people shortly before his death on Mount Nebo. For over two hundred years the region had been terrorized by the Assyrian empire, which had brought down the northern Kingdom of Israel and deported large numbers of the population. But when young Josiah became king in 649, Assyria was in decline and the Egyptians were forcing their troops to leave the Levant. At this point, the pharaoh was too fully occupied to pay much attention to Judah, where there was a surge of nationalism and eagerness for independence. Josiah's predecessors had found it perfectly acceptable to pacify the Assyrians by incorporating their gods into the temple cult, but the Deuteronomists insisted on the exclusive worship of Yahweh. They "discovered" a scroll purporting to be the lost Book of the Law (*sefer torah*) written by Moses, which had never yet been implemented. It was probably an early version of the book of Deuteronomy.[36] When they read it to Josiah, he rent his garments in distress. No wonder Israel had suffered such disasters! For centuries its kings had condoned practices that Yahweh had explicitly forbidden. The *sefer torah* revealed that he had commanded Israelites to have no dealings with the natives of Canaan, to make no treaties with them, and to wipe out their religion: "Their standing pillars (*matzeboth*) you are to smash, their sacred trees you are to cut-to-shreds and their carved images you are to burn with fire!"[37]

Josiah carried out these instructions to the letter, wiping out all traces of rival religion in Jerusalem, and also abolishing Yahweh's old rural shrines lest idolatrous practices lurk there undetected. Then, in what amounted to a *reconquista,* he invaded the territories of the former Kingdom of Israel recently vacated by Assyria, and not only destroyed every single Canaanite *maqom* as well as Yahweh's temples in Bethel and Samaria but also massacred the rural priests and contaminated their altars. Henceforth, Solomon's temple in Jerusalem would be the only legitimate national shrine.[38] Not content with this orgy of destruction, the Deuteronomists (D) also rewrote the history of Israel, making major additions to the JE narrative that gave even greater prominence to Moses, who had liberated the people from Egypt at a time when Josiah was trying to become independent of the pharaoh, and extending the saga to include the story of Joshua's conquest of the northern highlands, to which Josiah (the new Joshua) had just laid claim.

In some respects, Deuteronomy reads like a modern document.

Had it been implemented, the reformers' program would have included the establishment of a secular sphere and an independent judiciary separate from the cult;[39] a constitutional monarchy, which made the king subject to the Torah like any other citizen;[40] and a centralized state with a single, national shrine.[41] The reformers also rationalized Israelite theology to rid it of superstitious mythology.[42] You could not manipulate God by sacrifice, and God certainly did not live in his temple, which instead of being a sacred "center," as of old, was merely a house of prayer.[43]

But a rational, secular ideology is not necessarily any more tolerant than a mythical one. The Deuteronomists' reform revealed the greatest danger of idolatry. In making their national God, now the *only* symbol of the divine, endorse the national will, they had crafted a god in their own image. In the past, Marduk's power had always been challenged by Tiamat's, Baal's by Mot's. For J and E, the divine was so ambiguous that it was impossible to imagine that Yahweh was infallibly on your side or to predict what he would do next. But the Deuteronomists had no doubt that they knew exactly what Yahweh desired and felt it a sacred duty to destroy anything that seemed to oppose his/their interests. When something inherently finite—an image, an ideology, or a polity—is invested with ultimate value, its devotees feel obliged to eliminate any rival claimant, because there can be only one absolute. The type of destruction described by the Deuteronomists is an infallible indication that a sacred symbol has become idolatrous.

The vision of the Deuteronomists had been affected by the violence of their time. At about the same time as the sages of India had started to make *ahimsa,* "nonviolence," essential to the religious quest, the Deuteronomists depicted Joshua slaughtering the inhabitants of Canaan like the Assyrian generals who had terrorized the region for over two hundred years. In the event, the Deuteronomists' divinely articulated nationalism ended in tears. Their belligerent theology had blinded them to practical realities on the ground. It was only a matter of time before the great powers turned their attention to Judah. In 611 Pharaoh Necho II marched through Canaan in a bid to counter the rising power of Babylon. In a futile show of defiance, Josiah intercepted the Egyptian army at Megiddo and was killed in the very first encounter.[44]

Henceforth the tiny Kingdom of Judah would become the pawn of the great powers of Egypt and Babylon, and their foreign policy veered erratically in favor of one or the other. Some of the Israelites insisted that because Yahweh was their God, Judah could not be defeated and urged their rulers to assert their independence. But the prophet Jeremiah and others tried to force them to face facts—to no avail. Twelve years after Josiah's untimely death, a tragedy of far greater magnitude occurred. Judah rebelled against Babylonian supremacy, and in 597 Jerusalem was brought to its knees by King Nebuchadnezzar, who deported the elite—the king, the nobility, scribes, priests, the military, and artisans—to Babylonia and installed a puppet king in the Holy City. Eleven years later, in 586, after another senseless revolt, Jerusalem was destroyed and Yahweh's temple, his objective correlative on earth, was burned to the ground.

The Deuteronomists had made violence an option in the Judeo-Christian religion. It would always be possible to make these scriptures endorse intolerant policies. But the Deuteronomists did not have the last word because other biblical writers worked hard to counter this idolatrous tendency. When the redactors had put the JE document together, they used E's more transcendent image of Elohim to modify J's unabashedly anthropomorphic vision of Yahweh. In E's account of the first meeting between Moses and the God who speaks to him from the burning bush, Yahweh reveals his name: "*Ehyeh asher ehyeh*": "I am what I am."[45] Later Jews and Christians would interpret this to mean that God was being itself, He Who Is. But E did not yet think in these metaphysical terms. In his narrative, God may have been saying something far simpler. *Ehyeh asher eyeh* is a Hebrew idiom that expresses deliberate vagueness. The remark "they went where they went," for example, means "I have no idea where they went." So when Moses asked God who he was, Yahweh in effect replied: "Never mind who I am!" There must be no discussion of God's nature, and no attempt to manipulate God, as the pagans did when they called on their deities by name. Eventually Jews would refuse to pronounce the name Yahweh, as a tacit admission that any attempt to express the divine reality would be so limiting as to be almost blasphemous.

Where the very earliest accounts suggest that Moses had actually *seen* God on Mount Sinai,[46] later authors would declare this to be impossible. When Moses begged to see Yahweh's "glory" (*kavod*), Yahweh told him that no mere mortal could look upon the holiness of God and live.[47] In a scene that would become emblematic, when Moses climbed Mount Sinai to meet with God, a thick cloud and a blanket of impenetrable smoke hung over the summit. There was thunder and lightning and what sounded like deafening trumpet blasts. Moses may have stood in the place where God was, but he had no lucid vision of the divine.[48] The biblical writers made it clear that the *kavod* of Yahweh was not God himself; it was, as it were, a mere afterglow of God's presence on earth, essentially and crucially separate from the divine reality itself, which would always be beyond human ken.

The Israelites who had been deported to Babylon in 597 were not badly treated. They lived together in communities in the capital or in new settlements beside the canal and were allowed a degree of autonomy. But they were shocked, bewildered, and angry. Some wanted to pay the Babylonians back in kind and dreamed of dashing their children's heads against a rock.[49] Others felt that Yahweh had suffered a humiliating defeat at the hands of Marduk and was no longer worthy of their loyalty. How could they possibly worship a god who had no cult and no temple?[50] But five years after his deportation, a young priest called Ezekiel had a terrifying vision of Yahweh's "glory" beside the Chebar Canal.[51] It was a bewildering theophany, since it was impossible to make out anything clearly in the stormy obscurity of thunder, lightning, smoke, and wind. The trauma of exile had smashed the neat, rationalistic God of the Deuteronomists. Ezekiel's vision left him stunned for a whole week. But one thing seemed clear. God had chosen to leave Jerusalem and take up residence with the exiles. Henceforth they must live as though the "glory" previously enshrined in the temple was indeed in their midst.

But how could they do this? A small circle of exiled priests began to construct an answer, reinterpreting old symbols and stories to build an entirely new spirituality. Scholars call this priestly layer of the Bible "P": its most important sources were the Holiness Code (a miscellaneous collection of seventh-century laws)[52] and the Tabernacle Document, the centerpiece of P's narrative, which described the tent that the Israelites had built in the wilderness to house the divine presence.[53] With these and other ancient oral traditions, P compiled the two legal books of Leviticus and Numbers, which reversed the aggressive theology of the Deuteronomists by creating a series of rituals based on the experience of exile and estrangement. P also added material to the JED narrative, so that it became a story of one tragic migration after another: the expulsion from Eden, the wanderings of Cain, the dispersal of humanity after the rebellion at Babel, the departure of Abraham from Mesopotamia, the tribes' flight to Egypt, and the forty years in the wilderness. In P's revised chronicle, the climax of the Exodus was no longer the bestowal of the Torah but the gift of the divine presence in the "Tent of Meeting." God had brought his people into the Sinai desert precisely in order "to dwell (shakan), myself, in their midst."[54] The verb shakan had originally meant "to lead the life of a nomadic tent-dweller"; God would now "tent" with his wandering people wherever in the world they happened to be.[55] Instead of ending the story with Joshua's brutal conquest, P left the Israelites on the border of the Promised Land.[56] Israel was not a people because the Israelites lived in a particular country, but because they lived in the presence of a God who accompanied them wherever they happened to be. Their present exile was simply the latest instance of the tragic uprooting that had given Israel special insight into the nature of the divine.

P made a startling legal innovation. The exiles would create a sense of the divine presence by living *as if* they were priests serving in the Jerusalem temple. Hitherto the laity had never been expected to observe the ceremonial laws, purity regulations, and dietary rules of the temple personnel.[57] But now the exiles had become a nation of priests and must live as if God were dwelling in their midst, thus ritually creating an invisible, symbolic temple. There was a profound link between exile and holiness. God had told the Israelites that he was *kaddosh* ("holy"), a word that literally meant "separate," "other"; God was radically different from ordinary, mundane reality. Now the exiles must become *kaddosh* too.[58] The legislation crafted by P was based on the principle of sacred segregation. In Leviticus, Yahweh issued detailed directions about sacrifice, diet, and social, sexual, and cultic life to differentiate the exiles from their Babylonian captors. By replicating the condition of otherness, the exiles would symbolically relocate to the realm of holiness where God was. God would "walk about" in their midst, as he had once walked with Adam in the cool of the evening.[59] Babylon would become the new Eden because the rituals of separation would heal the long estrangement from the divine.

But holiness also had a strong ethical component, because it involved absolute respect for the sacred "otherness" of every single creature. Even though they kept themselves apart, Israelites must not despise the foreigner: "If a stranger lives with you in your land, do not molest him. You must treat him like one of your own people and love him as yourselves, for you were strangers in Egypt."[60] It was a law based on empathy and compassion, the ability to *feel with* the other. The experience of one's own pain must lead to an appreciation of other people's suffering. When P spoke of "love" he did not mean emotional tenderness. This was a law code, its language as technical and reticent as any legal ruling. In Middle Eastern treaties, to "love" meant to be helpful and loyal and to give practical support. Earlier biblical authors had commanded the Israelites to confine tribal loyalty (*hesed*) to their fellow Jews, but this was not true of P, whose purity regulations are remarkable in that other people are never regarded as contaminating.[61] The foreigner was not to be shunned but loved. Impurity came only from yourself, not from your enemies.

P insisted that Israelites must honor all life. Death was the great contaminator. It was an insult to come into the presence of the living God without undergoing a simple ritual of purification after coming into contact with the death of one of his creatures. In the dietary laws forbidding the eating of "unclean" animals, P developed a modified version of the Indian ideal of *ahimsa*. Like other ancient peoples, the Israelites did not regard the ritual slaughter of animals as killing; sacrifice was universally held to give the beast posthumous existence, and it was usually forbidden to eat an animal that had not been ritually consecrated in this way. P permitted the Israelites to sacrifice and consume only domestic animals from their own flocks. These were the "pure" or "clean" animals, which were members of the community; during their lifetime they must be allowed to rest on the Sabbath, and nobody could harm them in any way.[62]

But the "unclean" animals—dogs, deer, and other wild creatures—must not be killed at all; it was forbidden to trap, exploit, or eat them under any circumstances.[63] This was not because they were "dirty." It was perfectly all right to touch them while they were alive. They became unclean only after death.[64] The law that forbade contact with a dead animal's corpse protected it: because the carcass could not be skinned or dismembered, it was not worthwhile to hunt or trap it. For the same reasons, those animals classed as "abominations" (*sheqqets*) must be avoided only when they were dead. These tiny "swarming creatures" were vulnerable and should inspire compassion; because they were prolific and "teemed," they enjoyed God's blessing, so it was an "abomination" to harm them.[65] God had blessed the unclean animals on the day of creation, and had saved pure and impure animals during the Flood. To damage any one of them was an affront to his holiness.

This is the context in which we should read P's most famous work, the creation hymn in the first chapter of Genesis. Like all ancient cosmogonies, its purpose was primarily therapeutic. In Babylon, the Israelites would have been painfully aware of the magnificent New Year rituals in Esagila that celebrated Marduk's victory over Tiamat. P's cosmogony is, first, a gentle polemic against Babylonian religion that would have been balm to the exiles' bruised spirits. Marduk may have appeared to defeat Yahweh, but in reality Yahweh was far more powerful. Like all ancient cosmogonies, this was no creation ex nihilo. Elohim simply brings order to preexistent chaos, "when earth was wild and waste (*tohu va bohu*), darkness over the face of Ocean, rushing-spirit hovering over the face of the waters."[66] The Ocean would immediately have recalled Tiamat, but instead of being a frightening goddess, it was merely the raw material of the universe. The sun, moon, and stars were not deities but functionaries, timekeepers that brought light to the earth.[67] The "great sea-serpents" were no longer threatening adversaries like Yam or Lotan but simply God's creatures. He did not have to slaughter or split them in two, and at the end of the day, he blessed them.[68] Marduk's victory had to be reactivated every year in order to make the cosmos viable, but Yahweh finished his creative work in a mere six days and was able to rest on the seventh.

This was a nonviolent cosmogony. When P's first audience heard the opening words "At the beginning of God's creating of the heavens and the earth," they would have expected a story of fearsome battles. But P surprised them: there was no fighting, no killing. Unlike Marduk, Elohim did not have to fight to the death to create an ordered cosmos; instead he simply issued a series of commands: "Let there be light!" "Let the earth sprout forth with sprouting growth!" "Let there be lights in the dome of the heavens, to separate the day from the night" and each time, without any struggle at all, "it was so."[69] Yahweh had no competition and was the sole power in the universe.[70] But there was no stridency in P's polemic. On the last day of his creation, Elohim "saw everything that he had made and here: it was exceedingly good."[71] P knew that some of the exiles routinely cursed the Babylonians, but, he implied, this was not the way to go because God had blessed everything that he had made. Everybody should be like Elohim, resting calmly on the Sabbath and blessing all his creatures without exception—even, perhaps, the Babylonians.

This was emphatically not intended as a literal account of the physical origins of life. P was saying something much more relevant to the exiles. If J's creation story had been a myth of Solomon's temple, P's was the myth of the virtual temple he was encouraging the exiles to build by means of the new rituals of separation. Yahweh's creation of the cosmos had been an important theme in the cult of Solomon's temple, and in the Near East a temple was widely regarded as a symbolic replica of the cosmos. Temple building thus enabled human beings to participate in the gods' ordering of the universe. With this in mind, P's creation hymn was deliberately linked to his elaborate description of the construction of the tent shrine.[72] After God has issued his very detailed instructions for the tabernacle, we have a laborious and repetitive description of Moses carrying them out, point by point. At each stage, Moses "saw all the work" and "blessed" the people, just as Yahweh had "seen" all he had made and "blessed" it at the end of each day of creation. The sanctuary was built on the first day of the first month of the year; Bezalel, its architect, was blessed by the "rushing-spirit" of God that had brooded over the primal waters, and both the creation hymn and the Tabernacle Document emphasized the importance of the Sabbath rest.[73] The temple, the Israelites' replica of the divinely ordered cosmos, was in ruins; their world had been annihilated, but they could build a symbolic temple in the wilderness of exile that brought order to their dislocated lives. This would restore them to the intimacy of Eden, because an Israelite temple symbolized the original harmony before *adam* had ruined the world.

But P's creation myth was not the last word on the subject and nobody was required to "believe" it to the exclusion of all others. Alternative cosmogonies continued to flourish in Israel. Toward the end of their seventy-year exile in Babylonia, an anonymous prophet, usually known as Second Isaiah, revised the old tales of Yahweh fighting a sea monster in order to bring "comfort" to his people.[74] And again, he told his creation story therapeutically, not as a factual cosmogony but to throw light on the hidden meaning of history. At the beginning of time, Yahweh had slaughtered his enemies, splitting the cosmic Sea in two and drying up the waters of the great Abyss, just as he had parted the Egyptian sea "to make the seabed a road for the redeemed to cross."[75] Now he would end the exile and bring the deportees home.[76] It is in Second Isaiah that we find the first unequivocal statement of monotheism in the Bible. "I am Yahweh unrivalled," God announces proudly. "There is no other god besides me."[77] But this was a far cry from P's *ahimsa*. Second Isaiah imagined Yahweh marching aggressively through the world like the divine warrior of early Israelite tradition.[78] The strident insistence on a single symbol of the divine was linked once again with a blatant projection of the national will and the destruction of its enemies. Yahweh has nothing but contempt for other deities: "You are nothing," he tells the gods of the *goyim*, "and your works are nothingness."[79] All the gentiles would be "destroyed and brought to nothing," scattered like chaff on the wind. Even those foreign rulers who helped Israel would fall prostrate before the Israelites, licking the dust at their feet.[80]

Yet these fierce oracles are interspersed in the extant text with four songs that are redolent of compassion, nonviolence, and universal concern, sung by an individual who called himself Yahweh's servant.[81] We do not know who he was, but these songs clearly represented an ideal active in the exiled community that was very different from Second Isaiah's aggressive monotheism. The servant's task was to establish justice throughout the world, not by force but by a nonviolent, compassionate campaign:

> He does not cry out or shout aloud
> Or make his voice heard in the street.
> He does not break the crushed reed
> Nor quench the wavering flame.[82]

When attacked, the servant turns the other cheek and refuses to retaliate.[83] Despised and rejected, he will eventually be "lifted up, exalted, rise to great height," and the people will realize that his serene resignation has healed them.[84] He will become, Yahweh promises, "the light to the nations, so that my salvation will reach to the ends of the earth."[85]

Second Isaiah's predictions were fulfilled. When Cyrus, king of Persia, conquered the Babylonian empire, he gave all deportees the option of returning to their homelands. Most of the Jewish exiles had acclimatized to life in the Diaspora and decided to stay in Babylonia, but in 530 a party of Jews made the decision to return home, and ten years later, after many trials and tribulations, they rebuilt the temple. The return was difficult: the Second Temple failed to live up to the fabled glories of Solomon's, and the returning exiles had to contend with opposition from their pagan neighbors as well as from those Israelites who had not been deported and found the new religious ideas of the Golah, the community of exiles, alien and exclusive.

The Hebrew Bible was almost complete: preaching tolerance and respect for difference on the one hand and a strident chauvinism on the other, it was a difficult document to decipher, and it is not clear that at this stage it had any official religious significance or that it was used in the cult. A transitional figure was Ezra, a scribe in the Persian court who had "set his heart to investigate the Torah of Yahweh and to do and teach the law and ordinance in Israel."[86] In about 398, the Persian king sent him to Jerusalem with a mandate to enforce the Torah of Moses as the law of the land.[87] The Persians were reviewing the legal systems of the subject peoples to make sure that they were compatible with imperial security, and Ezra had probably worked out a satisfactory modus vivendi between Mosaic and Persian jurisprudence.

When he arrived in Jerusalem, Ezra was horrified to find that instead of maintaining the separation that P had prescribed, some of the people had actually taken foreign wives. On New Year's Day, Ezra brought the Torah to the square in front of the Water Gate and read it aloud, "translating and giving the sense, so that the people understood what was read," while Levites, lower-ranking priests, circulated among the crowds, supplementing his commentary.[88] We cannot be sure of his text, but whatever it was, it reduced the people to tears. They had clearly never heard it before and were dismayed by these unfamiliar demands. Read "neat," as it were, scripture could be daunting and alarming. "Do not weep!" Ezra insisted. It was the month of Sukkoth, and the law commanded Israelites to spend these weeks in special "booths" (*sukkoth*) in memory of their ancestors' forty years in the Sinai wilderness. Again, this was a novel instruction: the First Temple rituals had celebrated Sukkoth very differently. At once, the people rushed into the hills to pick branches of olive, myrtle, pine, and palm, and leafy shelters mushroomed all over the city. There was a festive atmosphere as the people assembled each evening to hear Ezra's exposition.

But later Ezra held a more somber assembly in the square in front of the new temple, during which the people stood shivering as the torrential winter rains deluged the city and they heard Ezra commanding them to send away their foreign wives.[89] Membership in Israel was now confined to the Golah and to those who submitted to the Torah, the official law of the land. Ezra had interpreted the scriptures in an exclusive manner, emphasizing the duty of separation but neglecting P's equally stringent demand that Israelites treat the stranger with "love" and respect. The Bible consists of many contradictory texts, so our reading is always selective. Tragically, however, a selective reading of scripture to enforce a particular point of view or marginalize others would be a constant temptation for monotheists.

Ezra's reading, accompanied as it was by his own running commentary, also made it clear that the Torah required interpretation. This is the first time we hear of these miscellaneous texts being treated as scripture with binding force. Ezra's presentation at the Water Gate marked the beginning of classical Judaism, a religion that focuses not merely on the reception and preservation of revelation but on its constant reinterpretation.[90] When he had expounded the text, Ezra did not merely recite the Torah given to Moses in the distant past but created something new and unexpected. The biblical writers had worked in the same way, making radical revisions to the texts and traditions they had inherited. In classical Judaism, revelation would never be something that had happened once and for all time, but an ongoing process that could never end, because there was always something fresh to be discovered. If it was simply read like any other text, the Torah could be disturbing. It must be heard in the context of rituals, like those of Sukkoth, which separated it from ordinary life and put the audience in a different frame of mind. And in any reading of the Torah, the commentary was as important as the text itself. The Jews had discovered that religious discourse was essentially interpretive. Ezra had not swallowed the text gullibly but had "set his heart to investigate (*li-drosh*)" it. Jewish exegesis would be called *midrash,* which derives from the verb *darash,* "to search," "investigate," "to go in pursuit of something" as yet undiscovered. Midrash would become a new ritual evoking the divine and would always retain connotations of dedication, emotional involvement, and expectant inquiry.[91]

# THREE

# Reason

At about the same time as P was writing his creation story, a handful of philosophers in the thriving Greek colony of Miletus on the Ionian coast of Asia Minor had begun to think about the cosmos in an entirely different way.[1] What they were attempting was so new that they had no name for it, but they became known as the *phusikoi,* the "naturalists," because their thinking was based entirely on the material world. The Milesians were merchants; their interests—sailing, land surveying, astronomy, mathematical calculation, and geography—were pragmatic and geared to their trade, but their wealth had given them leisure for speculation. They came to a startling conclusion. Despite the flux and change that were apparent everywhere in the universe, they were convinced that there was an underlying order and that the universe was governed by intelligible laws. They believed that there was an explanation for everything and that stringent rational inquiry would enable them to find it. These Ionian naturalists had launched the Western scientific tradition.

They did not have a large following, since very few people could understand their ideas and only fragments of their writings have survived. But it seems that from the first the *phusikoi* pushed their minds to the limits of human knowledge, looking more deeply into the natural world than was deemed possible at the time. Why was the world the way it was? They believed that they could find an answer by examining the *arche,* the "beginning" of the cosmos. If they could discover the raw material that had existed before the universe as we know it had emerged, they would understand the substance of the cosmos, and everything else would follow.

They were not hostile to religion; indeed, there was nothing in Greek religion that was incompatible with this type of investigation. As an Aryan people, the Greeks accepted the idea of an overarching cosmic order to which all beings were subject. There were no orthodox doctrines of creation, and the gods of Mount Olympus were neither omnipotent nor cosmic powers. They differed only in being more anthropomorphically conceived than the gods of most other pantheons. In his eighth-century epics, Homer had fixed the gods' personalities for all time, and their endless feuds symbolized the agonistic relationship of the sacred forces that the Greeks sensed all around them. When they contemplated the complex Olympian family, Greeks were able to glimpse a unity that drew its warring contradictions together.[2] The gods might meddle irresponsibly in human affairs, but their similarity to mortal men and women emphasized their compatibility with the human race. The Greeks sensed the presence of a deity in any exceptional human achievement.[3] When a warrior was possessed by the fury of battle, he knew that Ares was present; when his world was transfigured by the overwhelming reality of erotic love, he called this emotion Aphrodite. Hephaestus was revealed in the work of an artist and Athena in each and every cultural attainment.

But the Milesians, who had encountered Eastern culture during their trade missions, may have regarded traditional Greek *mythos* more dispassionately than was possible on the mainland. They wanted to show that thunderbolts and lightning were not arbitrary whims of Zeus but expressions of fundamental physical laws. The *phusikoi* were beginning to think differently from other people. Their talent for working things out independently and logically may have been encouraged by the political organization of the *polis*, the city-state, in which every citizen had to participate in the deliberations of the Assembly. Because the polis was ruled by impersonal, uniform laws, the Greeks were learning to ferret out abstract, general principles instead of reaching for immediate, short-term solutions. Their democracy may also have inspired the naturalists to develop a more egalitarian cosmology, so that they saw the physical elements of the universe evolving according to inherent natural principles, independently of a monarchical creator. But we must not exaggerate their egalitarianism. Greek aristocrats led extremely privileged lives. The

Western pursuit of disinterested, scientific truth was rooted in a way of life that depended upon the institution of slavery and the subjugation of women. From the beginning, science, like religion, had its ambiguities and shadows.[4]

At the same time as it sought to emancipate itself from the older worldview, the new naturalism was also affected by traditional ideas. Thales (fl. c. 580), the earliest of the *phusikoi,* may have been influenced by the *mythos* of the primal Sea when he argued that water was the original ingredient of the universe. The only sentence of his work to have survived is "Everything is water and the world is full of gods." But unlike the poets and mythmakers, Thales felt compelled to find the reason why water had been the primordial stuff. Water was indispensable to life; it could change its form, becoming ice or steam, and so had the capacity to evolve into something different. But Thales's scientific naturalism did not lead him to jettison religion; he still saw the world as "full of gods." In a similar vein, Anaximenes (c. 560–496) believed that the *arche* was air, which was even more fundamental to life than water and had transmuted itself from a purely ethereal substance into matter by coagulating progressively into wind, clouds, water, earth, and rock.

Anaximander (610–556) took another approach. He believed that the naturalist must go beyond sense data and look for an *arche* that was entirely different from any of the beings we know. The cosmos must have emerged from a larger entity that contained all subsequent beings in embryo. He called it the *apeiron,* the "indefinite," because it had no qualities of its own and was, therefore, indefinable. It was infinite, divine (but not a mere god), and the source of all life. By means of a process that Anaximander was unable to explain satisfactorily, individual beings had "separated out" from the *apeiron.* A seed had broken away and grown into a cold, damp mass that became the earth. Then, like a tree shedding its bark, the *apeiron* had sloughed off rings of fire, each surrounded by thick mist, which had encircled the earth. Without empirical proof, this was little more than fantasy, but Anaximander understood that the scientist could throw light on the unknown only if he laid aside conventional modes of thought.

When Miletus was conquered by the Persians at the end of the sixth century, the scientific capital moved to Elea, a Greek colony in southern Italy. Here Parmenides developed a radical skepticism. How could we know that the way we analyzed the cosmos bore any relation to the reality itself?[5] Were the laws and phenomena that we thought we observed real and objective, or did they merely explain the few aspects of the world that we were able to see? Parmenides became convinced that to attain the truth, human reason must rise above common sense and unverified opinion. The idea of change, for example, was pure convention. The Milesians had been wrong to imagine that the world had developed gradually. Reality consisted of a unified, single, complete, and eternal being. It might *appear* that creatures came into being and passed away, but true reality was unaffected by time. A rational person should not speak of things that did not exist, so we should never say that something had been born, because that implied that there had been a time when it did not exist; for the same reason, we must not say that something had died or moved or changed. But how could one function in such a world? What were we to make of the physical changes we noted in our bodies? How could you say anything without mentioning past or future? One of Parmenides' disciples was a commander in the navy: How could he guide a ship that was not supposed to move?

Parmenides' contemporaries complained that he had left them nothing to think about. Leucippus (fl. c. 400) and his pupil Democritus (466–370) tried to soften this austere rationalism.[6] They agreed that the world consisted of a unitary, changeless substance but argued that it was not a single being, as Parmenides thought. Instead it took the form of an infinite number of tiny, invisible, and "indivisible" (*atomos*) particles that were ceaselessly in motion in the boundless void of empty space. There was no overseeing creator God: each atom moved at random, propelled mechanically, its direction dictated by pure chance. Periodically, atoms collided, stuck together, and formed the physical phenomena—men, women, plants, animals, rocks, and trees—that we see around us. But these were only temporary conglomerations; eventually these objects would disintegrate, and the atoms of which they were made would mill around in the void until they formed another object.

Even though the naturalists could not prove their theories, some of their insights were remarkable. In attempting to find a simple, first principle as an explanation for the cosmos, Thales and Anaximenes had already started to think like scientists. Parmenides realized that the moon reflects the light of the sun; Democritus's atomism would be revived to great effect during the seventeenth-century scientific revolution. But some of their contemporaries were doubtful about the new philosophy, fearing that in seeking to know the mysteries of the cosmos, the *phusikoi* were dangerously guilty of hubris. They were like the Titan Prometheus, who had stolen fire from the gods and given it to men so that they could develop technology. But Zeus had retaliated by having the divine craftsman Hephaestus fashion the first woman, Pandora, who was beautiful but evil, the source of the world's sorrow.

The mathematician Pythagoras (570–500), however, took science in a different direction.[7] He had been born and educated on the island of Samos, off the Ionian coast, where he became famous for his asceticism and mystical insight, and had studied in Mesopotamia and Egypt before settling in southern Italy. There he established a religious community, dedicated to the cult of Apollo and the Muses, where the study of mathematics, astronomy, geometry, and music were not merely tools for the exploration of the physical world but also spiritual exercises. Apart from his famous theorem of the right-angled triangle, we know very little about Pythagoras himself—later Pythagoreans tended to attribute their own discoveries to the Master—but it may have been he who coined the term *philosophia,* the "love of wisdom." Philosophy was not a coldly rational discipline but an ardent spiritual quest that would transform the seeker. This was the kind of philosophy that would develop in Athens during the fourth century; the rationalism of classical Greece would not consist of abstract speculation for its own sake. It was rather rooted in a search for transcendence and a dedicated practical lifestyle.

Pythagoras's vision was in part shaped by religious changes in Greece during the sixth century. The Greeks had a uniquely tragic vision of the world. Their rituals were designed to teach participants to come to terms with the sorrow of life by making them face up squarely to the unspeakable. Every year at the festival of Thesmophoria, for example, they reenacted the story of Demeter, goddess of the grain that provided the economic basis of civilization.[8] She had borne Zeus a beautiful daughter called Persephone. Even though he knew that Demeter would never agree to the match, Zeus had betrothed the girl to his brother Hades, lord of the underworld, and helped him to abduct her. Distraught with rage, Demeter left Olympus and withdrew all her gifts from humanity. Without corn, the people began to starve, so the Olympians arranged for Persephone's return on condition that she spend four months each year with her husband. When Persephone was reunited with her mother, the earth burst into flower, but when she returned to Hades during the winter, it seemed to die in sympathy. Thesmophoria compelled the Greeks to imagine what might have happened if Demeter's favors had been permanently withdrawn. Married women left their husbands and, like the goddess, disappeared from the polis. Together they fasted, slept on the ground as people had done in primitive times, and ritually cursed the male sex. The festival forced the Greeks to contemplate the destruction of civilization, which depended upon the institution of marriage, and to appreciate the real antagonism that existed between the sexes. They also meditated on the catastrophe that would ensue if the crops ceased to grow. At the end of the festival, the women went home and life returned to normal, but everybody knew that the alternative was a lurking, fearful possibility.

As the concept of the individual developed in the polis, however, Greeks wanted a more personal spirituality alongside the public cult and developed the Mystery Cult. The word "mystery" needs clarification. The *musterion* was neither a hazy abandonment of rationality nor a self-indulgent wallowing in mumbo jumbo. In fact, the Mysteries would have a profound effect on the new philosophical rationalism. *Musterion* was closely related to *myesis*, "initiation"; it was not something that you thought (or failed to think!) but something that you did.[9] The Mysteries that developed during the sixth century were carefully constructed psychodramas in which *mystai* ("initiates") had a direct and overwhelming experience of the sacred that, in many cases, entirely transformed their perception of life and death.

The most famous of the Mysteries was celebrated annually at Eleusis, some twenty miles west of Athens. When Demeter had stormed off Mount Olympus after Persephone's abduction, she wandered all over the earth, disguised as an old woman, searching for her daughter. Metaneira, queen of Eleusis, had taken her into the royal household as a nurse for her son Demophon, and to repay her kindness, Demeter decided to make the child divine by burning away his mortal parts each night in the fire. One night, however, she was interrupted by Metaneira, who was understandably horrified to see her little boy in the flames. Revealing herself in all her glory, Demeter left the palace in a rage but later returned to teach the Eleusinians how to cultivate grain and instruct them in her secret rites. There had probably been some kind of festival at Eleusis since the Neolithic era. But in the sixth century, an enormous new cult hall was built, and for over a millennium the Eleusinian Mysteries would remain an integral part of the religious life of Athens.[10]

Each autumn, a new set of *mystai* voluntarily applied for initiation. What happened inside the cult hall was kept secret because a mere recital of events would sound trivial to an outsider, but the secrecy means we have only partial glimpses of what went on. It seems, however, that the *mystai* reenacted Demeter's sojourn in Eleusis. Like any ancient initiation, these rituals were frightening. The *mystai* understood that the rites and the myth of Eleusis were symbolic: if you had asked them if there was sufficient historical evidence for Demeter's visit, they would have found the query somewhat inept. *Mythos* was *theologia* ("speaking about a god"), and like any religious discourse, it made sense only in the context of the disciplined exercises that brought it to life.[11] The fact that the myth could not be understood literally made it more effective. "What is surmised (but not overtly expressed) is more frightening," explained the Hellenistic writer Demetrius. "What is clear and manifest is easily despised, like naked men. Therefore the mysteries too are expressed in the form of allegory, in order to arouse consternation and dread, just as they are performed in darkness at night."[12] The rites enabled the *mystai* to share Demeter's suffering. Her cult showed that there was no life without death. Seeds had to be buried in the depths of the earth before they could bring forth life-giving food, so Demeter, goddess of grain, was also a mistress of the underworld. The Mystery would force initiates to face up to their own mortality, experience the terror of death, and learn to accept it as an integral part of life.

But it was a hard, exhausting process. It began in Athens, where the *mystai* fasted for two whole days, sacrificed a piglet in honor of Persephone, and set off in a huge throng on the long, hot march to Eleusis. By this time, they were weak and apprehensive. The *epoptai*, who had been initiated the previous year, walked with them, abusing and threatening the *mystai* while they called hypnotically on Diony-sus, god of transformation, driving the crowd into a frenzy of excite-ment. By the time the *mystai* arrived in Eleusis, confused, elated, exhausted, and scared, it was evening, and they were herded to and fro through the streets by flickering torchlight until, thoroughly dis-oriented, they finally plunged into the pitch darkness of the initiation hall. From this point, we have only brief, disconnected glimpses of the rites. Animals were sacrificed; there was a shocking event—a child may have been pushed, like little Demophon, into the fire, only to be reprieved at the eleventh hour—and a "revelation." Some-thing—a sheaf of corn, perhaps—was lifted out of a covered basket. But the Mystery ended joyfully, with tableaux depicting Perseph-one's return from the world of the dead and her reunion with her mother.

No secret doctrine was imparted in which the *mystai* had to "believe." The "revelation" was significant only as the culmination of the intense ritual experience. In a superb summary of the religious process, Aristotle would later make it clear that the *mystai* did not go to Eleusis to learn (*mathein*) anything but to have an experience (*pathein*) and a radical change of mind (*diatethenai*).[13] The rites seem to have left a powerful impression. No *mystes* could fail to be stunned by a ceremony so "overwhelming in its beauty and size," wrote the Greek rhetorician Dio of Prusa (50–117 CE); he would behold "many mystic views and hear many sounds of the kind, with darkness and light appearing in sudden changes and other innumerable things happening"; it was impossible that he would "experience just nothing in his soul, and that he should not come to surmise that there is some wiser insight or plan in all that is going on."[14] The historian Plutarch (c. 46–120 CE) thought that the initiation was a foretaste of death. It began with the dissolution of one's mental processes, disorientation, frightening paths that seemed to lead nowhere, and, just before the end, "panic, shivering, sweat and amazement." But finally a "won-derful light . . . pure regions and meadows are there to greet you, with sounds and dances and solemn sacred words and holy views."[15]

The carefully crafted drama introduced *mystai* to a wholly new dimension of life and put them in touch with a deeper, unconscious level of the psyche so that afterward many felt entirely different. "I came out of the mystery hall," one recalled, "feeling a stranger to myself."[16] They found that they were no longer afraid of death: they had achieved an *ekstasis,* a "stepping out" of their workaday selves, and, for a short time, had felt something akin to the beatitude of the gods. But not everybody was skilled at these ritual games. The Athenian philosopher Proclus (c. 412–85 CE) explained that some *mystai* were "stricken with panic" during the darker part of the rite and remained trapped in their fear; they were not sufficiently adept in this ritual of make-believe. But others achieved a *sympatheia,* an affinity that made them one with the ritual, so that they lost themselves in it "in a way that is unintelligible to us and divine." Their *ekstasis* was a *kenosis,* a self-forgetfulness that enabled them to "assimilate themselves to the holy symbols, leave their own identity, become at home with the gods, and experience divine possession."[17]

Some Greeks, however, were beginning to be critical of the old mythology. How could anybody imagine that the gods "are born, and have clothes and speech and shape like our own," asked the Ionian poet Xenophanes (560–480), or that they were guilty of theft, adultery, and deception?[18] To be truly divine, a god should transcend such human qualities and be beyond time and change.[19] The naturalist Anaxagoras of Smyrna (508–435) insisted that the moon and stars were just massive rocks; it was not the gods but Mind (*nous*), composed of sacred matter, that controlled the universe. Protagoras of Abdera caused a sensation when he arrived in Athens in 430 and delivered a lecture in the home of the playwright Euripides (480–406). No god could impose his will on human beings, and as for the Olympians, who could tell whether they existed or not? "There are many obstacles to such knowledge, including the obscurity of the subject and the shortness of human life."[20] There was simply not the evidence to pronounce definitively on the existence of the divine, one way or the other.

Athens was still a very religious city and Protagoras and Anaxagoras were both expelled from the polis. But people were looking for a deeper form of theism. For the tragedian Aeschylus (525–456) the ineluctable pain of human life was the path to wisdom. Zeus—"whoever Zeus may be"—had "taught men to think" and reflect on the sorrow of human experience. It was therefore ordained

> *that we must suffer, suffer into truth.*
> *We cannot sleep, and drop by drop at the heart*
> *the pain of pain remembered comes again,*
> *and we resist, but ripeness comes as well.*
> *From the gods enthroned on the awesome rowing-bench*
> *there comes a violent love.*[21]

Euripides wanted a more transcendent god: "O you who give the earth support and me by it supported," prays Queen Hecuba in his *Trojan Women,* "whoever you are, power beyond our knowledge, Zeus, be you stern law of nature or intelligence in man, to you I make my prayers; for you direct in the way of justice all mortal affairs, moving with noiseless tread."[22] Euripides seems to have concluded that "the *nous* of each one of us is a god."[23] The philosophers of Athens were about to arrive at the same conclusion.

In the 420s, during the darkest phase of the Peloponnesian War, a new philosopher started to attract a devoted circle of disciples in Athens. The son of a stonecutter and a midwife, an unprepossessing man with protruding lips, a flat, snubbed nose, and a paunch, Socrates (c. 469–399) cast a spell over a group of young men from some of the noblest families in the city. But he would talk to anybody at all, rich or poor. Indeed, he needed conversation to achieve his mission. Socrates was intent above all on dismantling received ideas and exploring the true meaning of virtue. But he was asking the right questions at the wrong time. During this crisis, people wanted certainty rather than stringent criticism, and in 399 Socrates was condemned to death for corrupting the young, refusing to honor the gods of the polis, and introducing new gods. He denied the charges, insisting that he was no atheist like Anaxagoras. How could teaching about goodness be corrupting? He could have escaped and was probably expected to do so. But even though the sentence was unjust, he preferred to obey the laws of his beloved Athens to the end: he would die a witness (*martys*) to the untruth currently in the ascendant.

Socrates did not commit any of his teachings to writing, so we have to rely on the dialogues composed by his pupil Plato (c. 427–347) that claim to record these conversations. Socrates himself had a poor opinion of written discourse. People who read a lot imagined that they knew a great deal, but because they had not inscribed what they had read indelibly on their minds, they knew nothing at all.[24] Written words were like figures in a painting. They seemed alive, but if you questioned them they remained "solemnly silent." Without the spirited interchange of a human encounter, the knowledge imparted by a written text tended to become static: it "continues to signify just that very same thing forever."[25] Socrates did not approve of fixed, dogmatically held opinions. When *philosophia* was written down, it was easily misunderstood, because the author had not been able to tailor his discourse to the needs of a particular group. But a living dialogue could transform a person who took part in it, making him "as happy as any human being can be."[26]

It is difficult for us today to appreciate the power attributed to the spoken word in the premodern world. In his conversations Socrates sought not merely to inform but to form the minds of his interlocutors, producing within them a profound psychological change. Wisdom was about insight—not amassing information. To his dying day, Socrates insisted that he had no interest in teaching anybody anything, because he knew nothing at all. At the end of his life, he recalled an occasion when he was attacked by one of the leading politicians of Athens and said to himself, "I am wiser than this man; it is likely that neither of us knows anything worthwhile, but he thinks he knows something when he does not, whereas when I do not know, neither do I think I know; so I am likely to be wiser than he to this small extent, that I do not think I know what I do not know."[27] Instead of being aggressively dogmatic about his ideas, Socrates was profoundly and determinedly agnostic and sought to show those who came to him how little they really knew.

This was one of the reasons why he had become impatient with the *phusikoi*. In a dialogue that Plato set in the prison where Socrates had spent his last days, he makes Socrates explain that as a young man he had been "wonderfully keen" on natural science. He thought it would be splendid to know the causes of everything: "why it comes to be, why it perishes, and why it exists."[28] He discovered, however, that the naturalists were not interested in these matters but concentrated solely on the material explanation of phenomena. He had been delighted to hear about Anaxagoras's theories of the cosmic Mind but, to his disappointment, found that "the man made no use of Mind, nor gave it any responsibility for the management of things, but mentioned as causes air and ether and water and many other strange things." This concentration on the purely physical left too much out. It would be like saying that the reason he was sitting in jail was because "my body consists of bones and sinews," and that the "relaxation of the sinews enables me to bend my limbs, and that is the cause of my sitting here with my limbs bent."[29] But why were his bones and sinews not safely in Megara or Boeotia, "taken there by my belief as to the best course, if I had not thought it more right and honourable to endure whatever penalty the city ordered rather than escape or run away?"[30] Science should, of course, continue, but Socrates felt that the *phusikoi* were not asking the really important questions. If you were interested in morality or meaning, you would have to look elsewhere.

Like the *mystai* at Eleusis, the people who came to converse with Socrates did not come to learn anything but to have an experience and a radical change of mind. The Socratic dialogue was a spiritual exercise. The French historian and philosopher Pierre Hadot has shown that unlike modern philosophy, which tends to be purely notional, Athenian rationalism derived its insights from practical exercises and a disciplined lifestyle.[31] The conceptual writings of philosophers like Plato or Aristotle were either teaching aids or merely served as a preliminary guide for those looking for a new way of living. Unlike the *phusikoi,* Socrates was primarily interested in goodness, which, like Confucius, he refused to define. Instead of analyzing the concept of virtue, he wanted to live a virtuous life. When asked for a definition of justice, for example, Socrates replied: "Instead of speaking it, I make it understood in my acts."[32] It was only when a person chose to behave justly that he could form any idea of a wholly just existence.

For Socrates and those who came after him, a philosopher was essentially a "lover of wisdom." He yearned for wisdom precisely because he realized that he lacked it. As Paul Friedländer has explained, there was "a tension between *ignorance* — that is, the impossibility ultimately to put into words 'what justice is' — and the direct experience of the unknown, the existence of the just man, whom justice raises to the level of the divine."[33] As far as we can tell from Plato's dialogues, Socrates seems to have been reaching toward a transcendent notion of absolute virtue that could never be adequately conceived or expressed but could be intuited by such spiritual disciplines as meditation. Socrates was famous for his formidable powers of concentration. "Every now and then he just goes off," a friend remarked, "and stands motionless, wherever he happens to be."[34] Alcibiades, the famous Athenian politician, recalled that during a military campaign, Socrates had started thinking about a problem, could not resolve it, and to the astonishment of his fellow soldiers "stood there, glued to the spot," all day and all night, leaving his station only at dawn, "when the sun came out and he made his prayers to the new day."[35] Plato's dialogues were a model for the type of meditation that Socrates and his followers practiced; it was nothing like yoga but took the form of a conversation with oneself—conducted either in solitude or together with others—that pushed thought to the very limit.

But this type of internal dialogue was possible only if the self that you were conversing with was authentic. Socrates' mission was to awaken genuine self-knowledge in the people who came to talk to him. He had invented what is known as dialectic, a rigorous discipline designed to expose false beliefs and elicit truth. Consequently a conversation with Socrates could be disturbing. Even if somebody started to talk to him about something quite different, his friend Niceas explained, he would finally be forced to "submit to answering questions about himself concerning both his present manner of life and the life he has lived hitherto. And . . . Socrates will not let him go before he has well and truly tested every last detail."[36] He would discuss only those subjects that his conversation partners felt comfortable with. Laches, for example, as a general in the army, thought he understood the nature of courage and was convinced that it was a noble quality. And yet, Socrates pointed out, relentlessly piling up one example after another, a courageous act could seem stupid and foolhardy. When Niceas pointed out that, on the contrary, courage required the intelligence to appreciate terror, Socrates replied that in fact all the terrible things we feared lay in the future and were unknown to us, so we could not separate the knowledge of future evil from our present and past experience. How could we separate courage from the other virtues when a truly valiant person must also be temperate, just, and wise and good? A single virtue like courage must in reality be identical with all the rest. By the end of the conversation, these veterans of the Peloponnesian War, who had all endured the trauma of battle and should have been experts on the subject, found that they did not have the first idea what courage was. They felt deeply perplexed and rather stupid, as though they were ignorant children who needed to go back to school.

Socrates' dialectic was a rational version of the Indian Brahmodya, which had led participants to a direct appreciation of the transcendent otherness that lay beyond the reach of words. However closely he and his partners reasoned, something always eluded them, so the Socratic dialogue led people to the shocking realization of the profundity of their ignorance. Instead of achieving intellectual certainty, his rigorous *logos* had uncovered a transcendence that seemed an inescapable part of human experience. But Socrates did not see this unknowing as a handicap. People *must* interrogate their most fundamental prejudices or they would live superficial, expedient lives. As he explained to the court that condemned him to death: "It is the greatest good for a man to discuss virtue every day and those other things about which you hear me conversing and testing myself and others, for the unexamined life is not worth living."[37]

Socrates was a living summons to the paramount duty of stringent self-examination. He described himself as a gadfly, perpetually stinging people into awareness, forcing them to wake up to themselves, question their every opinion, and attend to their spiritual progress.[38] The important thing was not the solution to a problem but the path that people traveled in search of it. To philosophize was not to bludgeon your opponent into accepting your point of view but to do battle with yourself. At the end of his unsettling conversation with Socrates, Laches had a "conversion" (*metanoia*), literally a "turning around."[39] This did not mean that he had accepted a new doctrinal truth; on the contrary, he had discovered that, like Socrates himself, he knew nothing at all. Socrates had made him realize that the value system by which he had lived was without foundation; as a result, in order to go forward authentically, his new self must be based on doubt (*aporia*) rather than certainty. The type of wisdom that Socrates offered was not gained by acquiring items of knowledge but by learning to *be* in a different way.

In our society, rational discussion is often aggressive, since participants are not usually battling with themselves but are doing their best to demonstrate the invalidity of their opponent's viewpoint. This was the kind of debate that was going on in the Athenian assemblies, and Socrates did not like it.[40] He told the ambitious young aristocrat Meno that if he was one of the "clever and disputatious debaters" currently in vogue, he would simply state his case and challenge Meno to refute it. But this was not appropriate in a discussion between people who "are friends, as you and I are, and *want* to discuss with each other." In true dialogue the interlocutors "must answer in a manner more gentle and more proper to discussion."[41] In a Socratic dialogue, therefore, the "winner" did not try force an unwilling opponent to accept his point of view. It was a joint effort. You expressed yourself clearly as a gift to your partner, whose beautifully expressed argument would, in turn, touch *you* at a profound level. In the dialogues recorded by Plato, the conversation halts, digresses to another subject, and returns to the original idea in a way that prevents it from becoming dogmatic. It was essential that at each stage of the debate, Socrates and his interlocutors maintain a disciplined, openhearted accord.

Because the Socratic dialogue was experienced as an initiation (*myesis*), Plato used the language of the Mysteries to describe its effect on people. Socrates once said that, like his mother, he was a midwife whose task was to help his interlocutor engender a new self.[42] Like any good initiation, a successful dialogue should lead to *ekstasis:* by learning to inhabit each other's point of view, the conversationalists were taken beyond themselves. Anybody who entered into dialogue with Socrates had to be willing to change; he had to have faith (*pistis*) that Socrates would guide him through the initial vertigo of *aporia* in such a way that he found pleasure in it. At the end of this intellectual ritual, if he had responded honestly and generously, the initiate would have become a philosopher, somebody who realized that he lacked wisdom, longed for it, but knew that he was not what he ought to be. Like a *mystes,* he had become "a stranger to himself." This relentless search for wisdom made a philosopher *atopos,* "unclassifiable." That was why Socrates was not like other people; he did not care about money or advancement and was not even concerned about his own security.

In the *Symposium,* Plato made Socrates describe his quest for wisdom as a love affair that grasped the seeker's entire being until he achieved an *ekstasis* that was an ascent, stage by stage, to a higher state of being. If the philosopher surrendered himself to an "unstinting love of wisdom," he would acquire joyous knowledge of a beauty that went beyond finite beings because it was being itself: "It always *is* and neither comes to be nor passes away, neither waxes nor wanes."[43] It was not confined to

> one idea or one kind of knowledge. It is not anywhere in another thing, as in an animal, or in earth, or in heaven, or in anything else, but itself by itself with itself, it is always one in form; and all the other beautiful things share in that in such a way that when these others come to be or pass away, this does not become the least bit smaller or greater nor suffer any change.[44]

It was "absolute, pure, unmixed, unique, eternal"[45]—like Brahman, Nirvana, or God. Wisdom transformed the philosopher so that he himself enjoyed a measure of divinity. "The love of the gods belongs to anyone who has given birth to true virtue and nourished it, and if any human being could become immortal, it would be he."[46]

As Socrates finished this moving explanation, Alcibiades burst in upon the company and, his tongue loosened by drink, described the extraordinary effect Socrates had upon him. He might be as ugly as a satyr, but he was like the popular effigies of the satyr Silenus that had a tiny statue of a god inside. He was like the satyr Marsyas, whose music propelled an audience into a tranced yearning for union with the gods, except that Socrates did not need a musical instrument because his words alone stirred people to the depths. He had made Alcibiades aware of how deficient he was in wisdom and how lacking in self-knowledge: "He always traps me, you see, and he makes me admit that my political career is a waste of time, while all that matters is just what I most neglect: my personal shortcomings, which cry out for the closest attention."[47] He tried to stop his ears against Socrates' imperative summons to virtue but simply could not keep away from him. "I swear to you, the moment he starts to speak, I am beside myself: my heart starts leaping in my chest, the tears come streaming down my face." The *logoi* of Socrates filled him with the same kind of "frenzy" as the Mysteries of Dionysus; the listener felt "unhinged" (*explexis*) and on the brink of illumination: "I don't know if any of you have seen him when he's really serious. But I once caught him when he was open like Silenus' statues, and I had a glimpse of the figures he keeps hidden within: they were so godlike—so bright and beautiful, so utterly amazing—that I no longer had a choice—I just had to do whatever he told me."[48]

For his followers, Socrates had become an incarnation of divine beatitude, a symbol of the wisdom to which his whole life was directed. Henceforth each school of Greek philosophy would revere its founding sage as an avatar of a transcendent idea that was natural to humanity but almost impossibly difficult to achieve.[49] The Greeks had always seen the gods as immanent in human excellence; now the sage would express in human form the rational idea of God that had left the old Olympian theology far behind. Despite his humanity— and Alcibiades makes it clear that he was all too human—Socrates' unique qualities pointed beyond himself to the transcendence that informed his moral quest. This became especially evident in the manner of his death. Socrates admitted that his conflict with the polis was inevitable. He had approached each of the magistrates of the city personally, trying to persuade him "not to care for any of his belongings before caring that he himself should be as good and as wise as possible; not to care for the city's possessions more than for the city itself, and to care for other things in the same way."[50] This advice would not have appealed to many politicians. Before he drank the hemlock, he washed his body to spare the women, thanked his jailer courteously for his kindness, and made mild jokes about his predicament. Instead of destructive, consuming rage, there was a quiet, receptive peace as he looked death calmly in the face, forbade his friends to mourn, and lovingly accepted their companionship.

The execution of Socrates made a lasting impression on Plato, who became so disillusioned that he abandoned his dream of a political career and traveled in the eastern Mediterranean, where he became acquainted with Pythagorean spirituality. When he returned to Athens, he founded a school of philosophy and mathematics in a grove dedicated to the hero Academius on the outskirts of the city. The Academy was nothing like a department of philosophy in a modern Western university. It was a religious association; everybody attended the daily sacrifice to the gods performed by one of the students, who came not only to hear Plato's ideas but to learn how to conduct their lives.[51]

Plato regarded philosophy as an apprenticeship for death,[52] and claimed that this had also been the goal of Socrates: "Those who practise philosophy in the right way are in training for dying and they fear death least of all men."[53] At the moment of death the soul would become free of the body, so Plato's disciples had to live out this separation on a daily, hourly basis, paying careful attention to their behavior, as if each moment were their last. They must constantly be on their guard against pettiness and triviality, thus transcending the individualized personality that they would one day leave behind, and strive instead for a panoptic perspective that grasped "both divine and human as a whole."[54] A philosopher must not be a money lover, a coward, or a braggart; he should be reliable and just in his dealings with others.[55] A man who consistently behaved as if he were already dead should not take earthly affairs too seriously, but should be calm in misfortune. He must eat and drink in moderation, feeding his rational powers instead with "fine arguments and speculations." If he applied himself faithfully to this regimen, the philosopher would no longer resent his mortality; it would be quite absurd for a man who had lived in this way to be upset when death finally arrived. If he had already set his soul free of the toils of the body, he could "leave it alone, pure and by itself, to get on with its investigations, to yearn after and perceive something, it knows not what."[56]

Like the Pythagoreans, Plato regarded mathematics as a spiritual exercise that helped the philosopher to wean himself from sense perceptions and achieve a level of abstraction that enabled him to view the world in a different way. Geometry was the hidden principle of the cosmos. Even though a perfect circle or triangle was never seen in the physical world, all material objects were structured on these ideal forms. Indeed, every single earthly reality was modeled on a heavenly archetype in a world of perfect ideas. Plato departed from Socrates in one important respect. He believed that we did not arrive at a conception of virtue by accumulating examples of virtuous behavior in daily life. Like everything else, virtue was an objective phenomenon that existed independently and on a higher plane than the material world.

Plato's "doctrine of the forms" is an extraordinary notion to us moderns. We regard thinking as something that *we* do, so we naturally assume that our ideas are our own creation. But in the ancient world, people experienced an idea as something that happened to them. It was not a question of the "I" knowing something; instead, the "Known" drew one to itself. People said, in effect, "I think—therefore there is that which I think."[57] So everything that was thought about had an objective existence in an ideal world. The doctrine of the forms was really a rationalized expression of the ancient perennial philosophy, in which every earthly object or experience here below had its counterpart in the divine sphere.[58] For Plato, the forms were in a realm apart. Numinous and timeless, they became manifest in the imperfect realities of our world but were not themselves involved in the endless process of change. The philosopher's task was to become vividly aware of this superior level of being by cultivating his powers of reason.

Plato's vision of the transcendent forms seems to have been influenced by his experience of the Mysteries, which, like his philosophy, helped people to live creatively with their mortality. In the *Phaedrus,* he has left us one of the fullest—albeit discreetly veiled—accounts of the Eleusinian experience. Most people, he explained, were unable to see the forms shining through their earthly counterparts because "the senses are so murky." But during their initiation, the *mystai* had all glimpsed their radiant beauty when,

> along with the glorious chorus . . . [we] saw that blessed and spectacular vision and were ushered into the mystery that we may rightly call the most blessed of all: And we who celebrated it were wholly perfect and free of all the troubles that awaited us in time to come, and we gazed in rapture at sacred revealed objects that were perfect, and simple, and unshakeable and blissful. That was the ultimate vision, and we saw it in pure light because we were pure ourselves, not buried in this thing we are carrying around now, which we call a body, locked in it like an oyster in its shell.[59]

Plato's pupils were not required to "believe" in the existence of the forms but received a philosophical initiation that gave them a direct experience of this vision.

Plato did not impose his ideas on his pupils or expound them systematically, like a modern academic, but introduced them playfully and allusively in the course of a conversation in which other viewpoints were also expressed. In his writings we find no definitive account of the "doctrine of the forms," for example, because each dialogue was addressed to a different audience with its own needs and problems. His written work, a mere teaching aid, was no substitute for the intensity of an oral dialogue that had an emotional aspect that was essential to the philosophical experience. Like any ritual, it was extremely hard work, requiring "a great expense of time and trouble." Like Socrates, Plato insisted that it must be conducted in a gentle, compassionate manner so that participants "felt with" their partners.

> It is only when all these things, names and definitions, visual and other sensations, are rubbed together and subjected to tests in which questions and answers are exchanged in good faith and without malice that finally, when human capacity is stretched to its limit, a spark of understanding and intelligence flashes out and illuminates the subject at issue.[60]

If the argument was spiteful and competitive, the initiation would not work. The transcendent insight achieved was as much the product of a dedicated lifestyle as of intellectual striving. It was "not something that can be put into words like other branches of learning; only after long partnership in a common life devoted to this very thing does truth flash upon the soul, like a flame kindled by a leaping spark, and once it is born there it nourishes itself thereafter."[61]

In *The Republic,* Plato's description of an ideal polis, he described the process of philosophical initiation in his famous allegory of the cave.[62] He imagined a group of men who had been chained up all their lives in a cave; turned away from the sunlight, they could see only shadows of objects in the outside world cast on the rocky wall. This was an image of the unenlightened human condition. We are so inured to our deprived vision that, like the prisoners, we assume that the ephemeral shadows we see are the true reality. If the prisoners were taken into the upper world, they would be bewildered and dazzled by its light, brilliance, and vibrancy; they would find it too much and would want to go back to their twilight existence. So they must be initiated gradually into this new mode of being. The sunlight was a symbol of the Good, the highest of the forms, source of knowledge and existence. The Good lay beyond anything we could experience in ordinary life. But at the end of a long apprenticeship, enlightened souls would be able to bask in its light. They would want to linger in the upper world, but had a duty to go back to the cave and enlighten their companions. They would be able to assess the problems of their shadowy world far more clearly now, but they would get no credit for it. Their former companions would probably laugh at them. They might even turn on their liberators and kill them—just, Plato implied, as the Athenians had executed Socrates.

Toward the end of Plato's life, as the political situation in Athens deteriorated, his vision became more elitist and hard-line. In *The Laws,* his last work, which described another utopian republic, he even introduced an inquisitorial mechanism to enforce a theological orthodoxy that took precedence over ethical behavior. The first duty of the state was to inculcate "the right thoughts about the gods, and *then* to live accordingly, well or not well."[63] This was an entirely new development, alien to both ancient religion and philosophy.[64] A "nocturnal council" must supervise the thinking of the citizens, who were required to submit to three articles of faith: that the gods existed, that they cared for human beings, and that they could not be influenced by sacrifice and worship. A convicted atheist was allowed five years to recant, but if he persisted in his heresy, he would be executed.[65] It is sobering to note that the inquisitorial methods that the Enlightenment philosophes castigated in the revealed religions made an early appearance in the Greek rational tradition they so much admired.

In his later work, Plato's theology also became more concrete and prepared the ground for the religious preoccupation with the physical cosmos that would characterize a great deal of Western religion. In the *Timaeus,* he devised a creation myth—not, of course, intended to be taken literally—that presented the world as shaped by a divine craftsman (*demiourgos*), who was eternal, good but not omnipotent. He was not the supreme God. There was a higher deity who was virtually unknowable, so removed from us that he was basically irrelevant. "To find the maker and father of this universe is hard enough,"

Plato remarked, "and even if I succeeded, to declare him to everyone is impossible."[66] This was no creation ex nihilo: the craftsman merely worked on preexistent matter and had to model his creation on the eternal forms. The point of the story was to show that the universe, based as it was on the forms, was intelligible. The cosmos was a living organism, with a rational mind and soul that could be discerned in its mathematical proportions and the regular revolutions of the heavenly bodies. Participating in the divinity of the archetypal forms, the stars were "visible and generated gods" and Earth, the mythical Gaia, was the principal deity. So too the *nous* of each human person was a divine spark that, if nourished correctly, could "raise us up away from the earth and toward what is akin to us in heaven."[67] Plato had helped to lay the foundations of the important Western belief that human beings lived in a perfectly rational world and that the scientific exploration of the cosmos was a spiritual discipline.

Aristotle (c. 384–322), Plato's most brilliant pupil, brought philosophical rationalism down to earth. A biologist rather than a mathematician, he was intrigued by the process of decay and development that so disturbed Plato, because he saw it as the key to the understanding of life. Aristotle spent years in Asia Minor dissecting animals and plants and writing detailed descriptions of his investigations. He had no interest in leaving Plato's cave but found beauty and absorbing interest in the fascinating design that he saw everywhere in the physical world. For Aristotle, a "form" was not an eternal archetype but the immanent structure that determined the development of every single substance. Aristotelian science was dominated by the idea of *telos:* like any human artifact, everything in the cosmos was directed toward a particular "end" and had a specific purpose, a "final cause." Like the acorn that was programmed to become an oak tree, its entire being was devoted to achieving this potential. So change should be celebrated, because it represented a dynamic and universal striving for fulfillment.

Aristotle's writings are often inconsistent and contradictory, but his aim was not to devise a coherent philosophical system, rather to establish a scientific method of inquiry. His writings were simply lecture notes, and a treatise was not meant to be definitive but was always adapted to the needs of a particular group of students, some of whom would be more advanced than others and would need different material. In the Greek world, *dogma* ("teaching") was not cast in stone once it was committed to writing but usually varied according to the understanding and expertise of the people to whom it was addressed. Like Plato, Aristotle was chiefly concerned not with imparting information but with promoting the philosophical way of life.[68] His scientific research was not an end in itself, therefore, but a method of conducting the *bios theoretikos,* the "contemplative life" that introduced human beings to the supreme happiness. What distinguished men—Aristotle had little time for the female—from other animals was their ability to think rationally. This was their "form," the end for which they were designed, so in order to achieve *eudaimonia* ("well-being") they must strive to think clearly, calculate, study, and work things out. This would also affect a man's moral health, since qualities such as courage or generosity had to be regulated by reason. "The life according to reason is best and pleasantest," he wrote in one of his later treatises, "since reason, more than anything else, *is* man."[69]

Like Plato, Aristotle believed that human intelligence was divine and immortal. It linked human beings to the gods and gave them the ability to grasp ultimate truth. Unlike sensual pleasure or purely practical activity, the pleasures of *theoria* (the "contemplation" of truth for its own sake) did not wax and wane but were a continuous joy, giving the thinker that self-sufficiency that characterized the highest life of all. "We must, therefore, in so far as we can, strain every nerve to live in accordance with the best thing in us," Aristotle insisted. *Theoria* was a divine activity, so a man could practice it only "in so far as something divine is present in him."[70] His biological research was a spiritual exercise: people who were "inclined to philosophy" and could "trace the links of causation" would find that it brought them "immense pleasure"[71] because, by exercising his reason, a scientist was participating in the hidden life of God.

Aristotle thought that the universe was eternal. So his God was not the Creator, the First Cause of being, but the Unmoved Mover that set the cosmos in motion. Aristotle's cosmology would determine Western ideas about the universe until the sixteenth century: the earth was at the center of the cosmos, and the other heavenly bodies, each in its own celestial sphere, revolved around it. What had set the stars and planets in their unchanging revolutions? He had noticed that the motion of an earthly object was always activated by something outside itself. But the force responsible for celestial motion must itself be immobile, since reason demanded that the chain of cause and effect have a starting point. In the animal kingdom, movement could be sparked by desire. A hungry lion would stalk a lamb because he wanted to eat. So perhaps longing had set the stars in motion. They were themselves so perfect that they could only yearn toward a still greater perfection, impelled by an intellectual love of the entirely self-sufficient God that was absorbed in the supreme activity of *noesis noeseos* ("thinking about thinking"), the ceaseless contemplation of itself.

For Aristotle, *theologia,* "discourse about God," was the "first philosophy" because it was concerned with the highest mode of being, but Aristotle's God was utterly impersonal and bore no resemblance to either Yahweh or the Olympians. It had no appeal for ordinary folk.[72] Aristotle was convinced, however, that a philosopher who exercised his reasoning powers to the full would be able to experience this remote deity. Like any Greek, Aristotle believed that when he thought about something, his intellect was activated by the object of his thought, so it followed that when he was engaged in the contemplation of God, he participated to a degree in the divine life. "Thought thinks on itself because it shares the nature of the object of thought," he explained,

> for . . . thought and object of thought are the same: The act of contemplation [*theoria*] is what is most pleasant and best. If, then, God is always in that good state in which we sometimes are, this compels our wonder; and if in a better this compels it yet more. And God *is* in a better state. And life also belongs to God; for the actuality of thought is life, and God is that actuality; and God's self-dependent actuality is life most good and eternal. We say therefore that God is living being, eternal, most good, so that life and duration continuous and eternal belong to God; for this *is* God.[73]

Even for the down-to-earth Aristotle, philosophy was not merely a body of knowledge but an activity that involved spiritual transformation.

By the beginning of the third century BCE, six main philosophical schools had emerged: Platonism, Aristotelianism, Skepticism, Cynicism, Epicureanism, and Stoicism. They all saw theory as secondary to and dependent upon practice, and all regarded philosophy as a transformative way of life rather than a purely theoretical system. Each school developed its own scholasticism, building huge doctrinal edifices of written reflection on the teaching of the sages, but these writings were secondary to the oral transmission of the tradition.[74] When a philosopher expounded an authority, such as Plato or Aristotle, his chief purpose was to shape the spirituality of his pupils. He would, therefore, feel free to give the old texts an entirely new interpretation if this met the needs of a particular group. What mattered was the prestige and antiquity of the old texts, not the author's original intention. Until the early modern period, most Western thought developed in a way that was reminiscent of the modern design technique of bricolage, where something new is constructed from an assemblage of whatever materials happen to lie at hand.

The Hellenistic era that followed the establishment of the empire of Alexander the Great (c. 356–323) and its subsequent disintegration was a period of political and social turbulence.[75] Consequently, Hellenistic philosophy was chiefly concerned with the cultivation of interior peace.[76] Epicurus (341–270), for example, established a community outside Athens near the Academy, where his disciples could lead a frugal, secluded life and avoid mental disturbance. At the same time, Zeno (342–270), who lectured in the Painted Stoa in the Athenian agora, preached a philosophy of *ataraxia*, "freedom from pain": Stoics hoped to achieve total serenity by means of meditation and a disciplined, sober lifestyle.

Like Plato and Aristotle, Stoics and Epicureans both regarded science primarily as a spiritual discipline. "We must not suppose that any other end is served by knowledge of celestial phenomena," Epicurus wrote to a friend, "than *ataraxia* and firm confidence, just as in other fields of study."[77] Epicureans discovered that when they meditated on the cosmos described by the "atomists" Leucippus and Democritus, they were released from needless anxiety. Because the gods themselves were produced by chance combinations of atoms, they could not affect our destiny, so it was pointless to be afraid of them.[78] When they contemplated the vastness of empty space with its swirling particles, Epicureans felt they had achieved a godlike perspective. Your own life span may be short, Metrodorus, a disciple of Epicurus, told his pupils, "yet you have risen, through contemplation of nature, to the infinity of space and time, and you have seen all the past and the future."[79] Stoics also discovered that meditating on the immensity of the cosmos revealed the utter insignificance of human affairs, and that this gave them a saner perspective. They saw the whole of reality as animated by a fiery vaporous breath that Zeno called Logos ("Reason"), Pneuma ("Spirit"), and God. Instead of railing against his fate, the philosopher must align his life to this Spirit and surrender his entire being to the inexorable world process. Thus he himself would become an embodiment of Logos.

The philosophers may have been critical of popular religion, but their way of life required an act of faith (*pistis*) that had to be renewed every day. This did not, of course, mean that they had to "believe" blindly in the doctrines of their school, whose truth became evident only in the context of its spiritual and moral disciplines. *Pistis* meant "trust," "loyalty," "engagement," and "commitment." Against all the depressing evidence to the contrary, the philosopher trusted that the cosmos was indeed rational, engaged himself in the exacting regimen prescribed by the sages, and committed daily to the heroic endeavor of living a truly philosophical life in the hope that he would one day achieve the peace of *ataraxia* and intellectual enlightenment.

The rationalism of ancient Greece was not opposed to religion; indeed, it was itself a faith tradition that evolved its own distinctive version of the principles that guided most of the religious systems. *Philosophia* was a yearning for transcendent wisdom; it had a healthy respect for the limitations of *logos* and held that the highest wisdom was rooted in unknowing. Its insights were the result of practical meditative exercises and a disciplined lifestyle. In their dealings with others, the Greeks had developed their own form of *kenosis* and compassion, seeing the achievement of enlightenment as a joint, communal activity that must be conducted with kindness, gentleness, and consideration.

The God of Aristotle could not be more different from Yahweh, but even though many Jews were hostile to the Hellenistic culture that was beginning to infiltrate the Near East, some were inspired by these Greek ideas, which they used to help them refine their understanding of God. In the third century BCE, a Jewish writer personified the Wisdom of God that had brought the world into being. He imagined her at God's side, like Plato's *demiourgos*, "a master craftsman . . . delighting to be with the sons of men."[80] She was identical with the Word that God had spoken at creation and the Spirit that had brooded over the primal Ocean.[81] Word, Wisdom, and Spirit were not separate gods but aspects of the ineffable God that our frail minds were able to recognize in the marvels of the physical world and in human life—not unlike the "glory" (*kavod*) described by the Prophets. Later, in rather the same way, a Jewish writer living in the Hellenistic polis of Alexandria in Egypt in the first century BCE would see wisdom (*sophia*) as the human perception of God, an idea in our minds that was only a pale shadow of the utterly transcendent reality that would always elude our understanding: "the breath of the power of God . . . a reflection of the eternal light, untarnished mirror of God's active power, image of his goodness."[82]

In Alexandria, Jews exercised in the gymnasium with the Greeks, taking part in the spiritual and intellectual exercises that always accompanied athletic training. Philo (c. 30 BCE–45 CE), a Jewish Platonist, made the immensely important and influential distinction between God's *ousia,* his essential nature, and his *dunamis* ("powers") or *energeiai* ("energies").[83] We could never know God's *ousia,* but in order to adapt his indescribable nature to our limited intellect, God communicated with us through his activities in the world. They were not God itself but the highest realities that the human mind could grasp, and they enabled us to catch a glimpse of a transcendent reality beyond anything we could conceive. Philo also allegorized the stories of the Hebrew Bible in the same way as the Greeks were allegorizing the epics of Homer in order to make them conform to the philosophic ideal. He suggested that God's master plan (*logos*) of creation corresponded to the world of the forms that had been incarnated in the physical universe.

Philo was far from typical, however. Mainstream Judaism was still a temple religion, dominated by the sacrificial rituals, elaborate liturgy, and huge temple festivals that seemed to introduce Jewish participants into the presence of the divine. But in the year 70 CE, a political catastrophe forced Jews to seek a different religious focus. Two new Jewish movements emerged, both influenced, in different ways, by the Greek ethos; both were widely regarded as "schools of philosophy," and both would develop their teachings in a manner similar to the intellectual "bricolage" of the Greek academies.

# FOUR

# Faith

Early in the year 70, the Roman armies laid siege to Jerusalem. Judaea had long been restive under Roman occupation, and in 66 the rumbling discontent had exploded in outright revolt. The leaders of the Jewish war did not command universal support: many Jews believed it utterly foolhardy to take on the might of Rome. But a radical party of Zealots had overpowered the moderates, convinced that Rome was in decline and that the Jews had a good chance of success. For three years, however, the brilliant Roman general Vespasian had systematically defeated the pockets of resistance in Galilee in northern Palestine until in 70 he was made emperor and returned to Rome, leaving his son Titus in charge of the Jewish war. By May Titus had broken through the northern wall of Jerusalem, but still the Jews would not give up. When Titus's army finally fought their way into the inner courts of the magnificent temple built by Herod the Great (c. 73–4 BCE), they found six thousand Zealots ready to fight to the death, deeming it an honor to die in defense of their temple. They fought with extraordinary courage, but when the building caught fire, a terrible cry of horror arose. Some flung themselves on the swords of the Romans; others hurled themselves into the flames. Once the temple had gone, the Jews gave up; they did not even bother to defend the rest of the city or try to recover it from other nearby fortresses. Most of the survivors simply stood numbly, helplessly watching Titus's officers efficiently demolish what was left of the buildings. The Jews had lost their temple once before, but this time it would not be rebuilt.

In the years leading up to the war, there had been an extraordinarily diverse eruption of Jewish religiosity, which had blossomed into multifarious sects, each convinced that it alone was the authentic voice of Judaism.[1] New scriptures were written. Despite the efforts of Ezra and other reformers, there was still no Jewish orthodoxy. Some of the sects even spoke of abolishing the Sinai revelation and starting again. But everybody agreed that the temple was of prime importance. Some were critical of the temple establishment, which they felt had been corrupted by the Roman occupation; the Qumran ascetics and the related sect of the Essenes held aloof from the cult but looked forward to a new temple that God would build when he had vanquished the wicked. In the meantime, their own communities would become a symbolic shrine and their members would observe the laws of priestly purity. The Pharisees attended regular temple worship, but they also observed the purity laws and temple rituals in their own homes; their spirituality revolved around an imaginary, virtual temple, and they tried to conduct their entire lives as though they were literally standing before the Shekhinah, the divine presence in the temple's inner sanctum, the Holy of Holies. The Christians, who believed that their teacher Jesus of Nazareth had been the Messiah, had reservations about the temple but still participated in its liturgy. Even though Jesus had been crucified by the Romans in about 30 CE, his disciples believed that he had risen from the tomb and would soon return in glory to inaugurate the Kingdom of God. In the meantime, the Christian leaders lived in Jerusalem in expectation of his coming, and worshipped as a body in the temple every day.

The destruction of the temple sent shock waves throughout the entire Jewish world. Only two of the sects that had developed during the Late Second Temple period would survive the catastrophe. Toward the end of the siege, Rabbi Yohanan ben Zakkai, leader of the Pharisees, had himself smuggled out of the city in a coffin to get past the Zealot guards at the gates. Once outside, he made his way to the Roman camp and asked the emperor's permission to settle with a group of scholars in the coastal town of Yavneh to the south of Jerusalem. After the fall of the city, a community of scribes, priests, and Pharisees gathered there and, under the leadership of Yohanan and his pupils Eliezer and Joshua, began the heroic task of transforming Judaism from a temple faith to a religion of the book. The Torah would replace the Holy of Holies, and the study of scripture would substitute for animal sacrifice. But in the first years after the disaster, the Pharisees simply could not believe that the temple was gone forever; they began to collect and preserve all its ancient traditions so that they would be ready for the new temple and the resumption of the cult.[2]

Rabbi Yohanan and his colleagues belonged to the more flexible strand of the Pharisee movement. His teachers had been disciples of the great Hillel (c. 80 BCE–30 CE), who had emphasized the importance of the spirit rather than the letter of Mosaic law. In a famous Talmudic story, it was said that Hillel had formulated a Jewish version of Confucius's Golden Rule. One day, a pagan had approached Hillel and promised to convert to Judaism if Hillel could teach him the entire Torah standing on one leg. Hillel replied: "What is hateful to yourself, do not to your fellow man. That is the whole of the Torah and the remainder is but commentary. Go learn it."[3] It was a provocative and daring piece of exegesis. Hillel did not mention any of the doctrines that seemed central to Judaism—the unity of God, the creation of the world, the Exodus, Sinai, the 613 commandments of the Torah, or the Promised Land. The essence of Jewish teaching was the disciplined refusal to inflict pain on other human beings: everything else was only "commentary."

Rabbi Yohanan had absorbed this lesson. Shortly after the destruction of Jerusalem, when he and his companions had occasion to walk past the ruined temple buildings, Rabbi Joshua had been unable to contain his grief: "Woe is it that the place, where the sins of Israel find atonement, is laid waste." But Rabbi Yohanan replied calmly, "Grieve not, we have an atonement equal to the Temple, the doing of loving deeds, as it is said, 'I desire love and not sacrifice.' "[4] Kindness would replace the temple ritual; compassion, one of the pillars on which the world depended, was the new priestly task. Compassion was also the key to the interpretation of scripture. As Hillel had pointed out, everything in the Torah was simply a "commentary"—a mere gloss—on the Golden Rule. Scholars had a mandate to reveal the core of compassion that lay at the heart of all the legislation and narratives of the Bible—even if this meant twisting the original meaning of the text. In this spirit, Rabbi Akiva, Yohanan's successor, insisted that the chief principle of the Torah was "Thou shalt love thy neighbour as thyself."[5] Only one of the rabbis disagreed, preferring the simple sentence "This is the roll of Adam's descendants," because it revealed the unity of the entire human race.[6]

In Rabbinic Judaism, the religion of Israel came of age, developing the same kind of compassionate ethos as the Eastern traditions. The rabbis regarded hatred of any human being made in God's image as tantamount to atheism, so murder was not just a crime against humanity but a sacrilege: "Scripture instructs us that whatsoever sheds human blood is regarded as if he had diminished the divine image."[7] God had created only one man at the beginning of time to teach us that the destruction of a single life was equivalent to annihilating the entire world; conversely, to save a life redeemed the whole of humanity.[8] To humiliate anybody, even a slave or a goy, was a sacrilegious defacing of God's image[9] and a malicious libel denied God's existence.[10] Any interpretation of scripture that bred hatred or disdain for others was illegitimate, while a good piece of exegesis sowed affection and dispelled discord. Anybody who studied scripture properly was full of love, explained Rabbi Meir; he "loves the Divine Presence *(Shekhinah)* and all creatures, makes the Divine Presence glad and makes glad all creatures."[11]

The rabbis continued to use terms such as the Glory *(kavod)*, Shekhinah, and Spirit *(ruach)* to distinguish their inherently limited, earthly experience of God from the ineffable reality itself. Their new spiritual exercises made the divine a vibrant and immanent presence. Exegesis would do for them what yoga did for Buddhists and Hindus. The truth they sought was not abstract or theoretical but derived from the practice of spiritual exercises. To put themselves into a different state of consciousness, they would fast before they approached the sacred text, lay their heads between their knees, and whisper God's praises like a mantra. They found that when two or three of them studied the Torah together, they became aware of the Shekhinah in their midst.[12] One day, when Rabbi Yohanan was studying the Torah with his pupils, the Holy Spirit seemed to descend upon them in the form of fire and a rushing wind.[13] On another occasion, Rabbi Akiva heard that his student Ben Azzai was expounding the Torah surrounded by a nimbus of flashing fire. He hurried off to investigate. Was Ben Azzai attempting a dangerous mystical flight to the throne of God? "No," Ben Azzai replied. "I was only linking up the words of the Torah with one another, and then with the words of the prophets and the prophets with the Writings, and the words rejoiced, as when they were delivered from Sinai, and they were sweet as at their original utterance."[14] As Ezra had indicated so long ago, scripture was not a closed book and revelation was not a distant historical event. It was renewed every time a Jew confronted the text, opened himself to it, and applied it to his own situation. The rabbis called scripture *miqra:* it was a "summons to action." No exegesis was complete until the interpreter had found a practical new ruling that would answer the immediate needs of his community. This dynamic vision could set the world aflame.

Anybody who imagines that revealed religion requires a craven clinging to a fixed, unalterable, and self-evident truth should read the rabbis. Midrash required them to "investigate" and "go in search" of fresh insight. The rabbis used the old scriptures not to retreat into the past but to propel them into the uncertainties of the post-temple world. Like the Hellenistic philosophers, Jews had started to build an intellectual "bricolage," creatively reinterpreting the available authoritative texts to carry the tradition forward. But already they had moved instinctively toward some of the great principles that had inspired the other major traditions to find a transcendent meaning amid life's tragedy. They too now stressed the centrality of compassion and were developing a more interior spirituality.

But during the Second Temple period, midrash had been a minority pursuit. It would take the rabbis about twenty years to make any serious impact on the wider Jewish community. It was not easy to make textual study attractive to the masses. How could it possibly compete with the dramatic temple rituals? By the late 80s and 90s, as we shall see later in this chapter, the hard work of the rabbis and their colleagues at Yavneh finally paid off, but in the first years after the disaster, another Jewish sect seemed to be making more headway.

The Christians got organized more quickly. The first of the four canonical gospels was written either shortly before or immediately after the destruction. We know very little about the historical Jesus, since all our information comes from the texts of the New Testament, which were not primarily concerned with factual accuracy. He seems to have been a charismatic healer and a man of *ahimsa* who told his followers to love their enemies.[15] Like other prophets at this time, he preached the imminent arrival of the Kingdom of God, a new world order in which the mighty would be cast down and the lowly exalted, the righteous dead would rise from their tombs, and the whole world would worship the God of Israel.

Jesus does not seem to have attracted a large following during his lifetime. But that changed in about 30 CE when—for reasons that are not entirely clear—he was crucified by the Romans. His disciples had visions that convinced them that he had been raised by God from the dead in advance of the Last Days; he was the *messhiach* (Greek: *christos*), the "anointed one" who would soon return in glory to establish the Kingdom.[16] The first Christians prepared for this great event by living a dedicated Jewish life, holding all property in common, and giving generously to the poor.[17] They had no intention of founding a new religion but observed the Torah, worshipped in the temple, and kept the dietary laws.[18] Like the Pharisees, they regarded the Golden Rule as central to Judaism.[19] They continued to think about God in the traditional Jewish way and, like the rabbis, experienced the Holy Spirit, the immanent presence of God, as a tangible, empowering, and electrifying force.[20] Christian missionaries preached the "gospel" or "good news" in such marginal regions of Palestine as Samaria and Gaza, and established congregations in the Diaspora to ensure that all Jews, even "sinners," were prepared for the Kingdom.[21] They also took the highly unusual step of admitting non-Jews into their community. Some of the prophets had predicted that in the Last Days the foreign nations would share Israel's triumph and would voluntarily throw away their idols.[22] When the Christians discovered that they were attracting gentile converts, many of them already sympathetic to Judaism, this confirmed them in their belief that the old order was indeed passing away.[23]

One of the most forceful champions of this view was Paul, a Greek-speaking Jew from Tarsus in Cilicia, who joined the Christian movement some three years after Jesus's death. Paul's letters to his converts, written during the 50s and 60s, are the earliest extant Christian writings and show that the Christians had already started to engage in a radically inventive exegesis of the Torah and the Prophets to demonstrate that Jesus was the culmination of Jewish history. Paul was convinced that his mixed congregations of Jews and gentiles were the first fruits of the new Israel. These were astonishing claims. There was nothing in the scriptures to suggest that a future redeemer would be crucified and rise from the dead, and many found the idea utterly scandalous.[24] After the disaster of 70, Christians saw the destruction of the temple as an *apokalypsis,* a "revelation" of a terrifying truth. The old Israel was dead. The catastrophe had been predicted by Daniel,[25] and the prophets Jeremiah and Isaiah had criticized the cult and insisted that God wanted the temple to be a house of prayer for all peoples.[26] Now in the new Israel Jews must encounter the Shekhinah, the divine presence formerly enshrined in the Holy of Holies, in the person of Jesus, the *christos.*[27]

The twenty-seven books of the New Testament, completed by the middle of the second century, represented a heroic effort to rebuild a shattered tradition. Like the rabbis, the Christians used midrashic techniques to enable Jews to move forward.[28] The authors of the four gospels later attributed to Matthew, Mark, Luke, and John were Jewish Christians who wrote in Greek, read the Bible in its Greek translation, and lived in the Hellenistic cities of the Near East.[29] Mark was written in about 70; Matthew and Luke in the 80s; and John in the late 90s. The gospels were not biographies in our sense but should, rather, be seen as commentaries on the Hebrew Bible. Like Paul, the evangelists searched the scriptures to find any mention of a *christos* — be it a king, prophet, or priest—who had been "anointed" in the past by God for a special mission and was now seen to be a coded prediction of Jesus. They believed that Jesus's life and death had been foretold in the four servant songs, and some even thought that he was the Word and Wisdom of God, who had descended to earth in human form.

This was not simply a clever exercise in public relations. Jews had long realized that all religious discourse was basically interpretive. They had always looked for new meaning in the ancient texts during a crisis, and the basic methodology of Christian *pesher* ("deciphering") exegesis, which had also been practiced by the Qumran sectarians, was not unlike Greek "bricolage" or rabbinical midrash. Above all, it was a spiritual exercise. Luke has shown the way it may have worked in his story of a numinous encounter on the road to Emmaus.[30] Three days after Jesus's crucifixion, two of his disciples had been walking sadly from Jerusalem to the nearby village of Emmaus and had fallen in with a stranger who asked them why they were so despondent. They explained what had happened to Jesus, the man they thought had been the messiah. The stranger gently rebuked them: Did they not realize that the scriptures had foretold that the *christos* would suffer before attaining his glory? Starting with Moses, he began to expound "the full message" of the prophets, and later the disciples recalled how their hearts had "burned" within them when he had "opened" the scriptures to them in this way. When they arrived at their destination, they begged the stranger to dine with them, and it was only when he blessed the bread that they realized it was Jesus himself, but that their "eyes had been held" from recognizing him.

Like the rabbis, the Christians gathered "in twos and threes" to decipher the old texts. As they conversed together, the scriptures would "open" and bring them fresh insight. This illumination might last only a moment—just as Jesus had vanished as soon as the disciples had recognized him—but the act of bringing hitherto unconnected texts together to form an unexpected harmony gave them intimations of the *coincidentia oppositorum* that had characterized the temple experience. Apparent contradictions locked together in the luminous "wholeness" of *shalom.* The stranger had a crucial role. In Luke's congregation Jews and gentiles were discovering that, like Abraham at Mamre, when they reached out to the "other," they experienced the divine. The story also shows how the early Christians understood Jesus's resurrection. They did not have a simplistic notion of his corpse walking out of the tomb. Henceforth, as Paul had made clear, they would no longer know Jesus "in the flesh" but would find him in one another, in scripture, and in the ritual meals they ate together.

Jesus was acquiring mythical and symbolic status, but like any *mythos,* this would make no sense unless it was put into practice. In his letter to his converts in Philippi in Asia Minor, Paul quoted a hymn already well-known to the Christian communities, which shows that from this very early date (c. 54–57) Christians saw Jesus's life as a *kenosis,* a humble "self-emptying."[31] Although, like all human beings, Jesus was the image of God, he did not cling to this high dignity,

> *But emptied himself* [heauton ekenosen]
> *To assume the condition of a slave. . . .*
> *And was humbler yet, even to accepting death, death on a cross.*

Because of this humiliating descent, God had raised him high and given him the supreme title *kyrios* ("lord"), "to the glory of God the Father." This text is often quoted to show that Christians saw Jesus as the incarnate son of God from the very beginning, but Paul was not giving the Philippians a lesson in Christian doctrine. He had introduced the hymn to them with a moral instruction: "In your minds, you must be the same as Christ Jesus."

> There must be no competition among you, no conceit;
> but everybody is to be self-effacing. Always consider the
> other person to be better than yourself, so that nobody
> thinks of his own interests first, but everybody thinks of
> other people's interests instead.[32]

Unless they imitated Jesus's *kenosis* in the smallest details of their own lives, they would not understand the *mythos* of the lord Jesus. Like all great religious teaching, Christian doctrine would always be a *miqra* that would make sense only when translated into a ritual, meditative, or ethical program.

When he gave Jesus the title "lord," Paul did not mean that he was God. The careful wording of the hymn made it clear that there was a distinction between the *kyrios* and God. Even though Paul and the evangelists all called Jesus the "son of God," they were not making divine claims for him. They would have been quite shocked by this idea. For Jews, a "son of God" was a perfectly normal human being who had been raised to special intimacy with God and had been given a divine mandate. Prophets, kings, and priests had all been called "sons of God"; indeed, the scriptures saw all Israelites as the "sons of God" in this sense.[33] In the gospels, Jesus called God his "father," but he made it clear that God was the father of his disciples too.[34]

Today it is often assumed that when they told the story of Jesus's virgin birth, the evangelists alleged that he was somehow impregnated by God in the womb of his mother and was a "son of God" in the same way as Dionysus, who was the son of Zeus by an earthly woman. But no Jewish reader would have understood the story in this way. There are a number of unusual conceptions in the Hebrew Bible: Isaac, for example, was born when his mother was ninety years old. A tale of this kind is regularly attached to an exceptional human being to show that the child had been marked out for greatness from the first instant of his life. The virgin birth is found only in Matthew and Luke—the other New Testament writers do not appear to have heard of it—but both trace Jesus's lineage through Joseph, his natural father, in the normal way; Mark takes it for granted that Joseph was Jesus's father and that he had brothers and sisters who were well known to the earliest Christian communities;[35] like the other evangelists, he sees Jesus primarily as a prophet.[36] Skeptics point derisively to the obvious discrepancies in the infancy narratives, but these were not supposed to be factual, and the final redactors felt no qualms about including such contradictory accounts. These stories are exercises in creative midrash, their object being to show that Jesus's coming was foretold in the Hebrew scriptures. Placed at the beginning of these two gospels, they give the reader a foretaste of how each evangelist understood Jesus's mission. Like the Hebrew Bible, the New Testament records a wide range of views rather than a single orthodox teaching. Matthew was anxious to show that Jesus was the *christos* of the gentiles as well as the Jews, so he has the Magi come from the Far East to worship at the crib. Luke, on the other hand, always stressed Jesus's mission to the poor and marginalized, so in his gospel a group of shepherds are the first to hear the "good news" of his birth.

Jesus's unusual conception and birth were by no means the chief ways in which the first Christians expressed their sense of his divine sonship. Paul believed that he was "designated" the "son of God" at his resurrection.[37] Mark thought he received his commission at his baptism, like the ancient kings of Israel, who had been "adopted" by Yahweh at their coronation. He even quotes the ancient coronation psalm.[38] On another occasion, when Jesus took three of his disciples up a high mountain, the gospels show him being "anointed" as a prophet. He was "transfigured" before them, his face and garments shining like the sun; the disciples saw him speaking with Moses and Elijah while a heavenly voice, quoting the same hymn, declared, "This is my Son, the Beloved; he enjoys my favor."[39]

Yet did not Jesus constantly insist that his followers acknowledge his divine status—almost as a condition of discipleship?[40] In the gospels we continually hear him berating his disciples for their lack of "faith" and praising the "faith" of gentiles, who seem to understand him better than his fellow Jews. Those who beg him for healing are required to have "faith" before he can work a miracle, and some pray:

"Lord, I believe, help thou my unbelief."[41] We do not find this preoccupation with "belief" in the other major traditions. Why did Jesus set such store by it? The simple answer is that he did not. The word translated as "faith" in the New Testament is the Greek *pistis* (verbal form: *pisteuo*), which means "trust; loyalty; engagement; commitment."[42] Jesus was not asking people to "believe" in his divinity, because he was making no such claim. He was asking for commitment. He wanted disciples who would engage with his mission, give all they had to the poor, feed the hungry, refuse to be hampered by family ties, abandon their pride, lay aside their self-importance and sense of entitlement, live like the birds of the air and the lilies of the field, and trust in the God who was their father. They must spread the good news of the Kingdom to everyone in Israel—even the prostitutes and tax collectors—and live compassionate lives, not confining their benevolence to the respectable and conventionally virtuous. Such *pistis* could move mountains and unleash unsuspected human potential.[43]

When the New Testament was translated from Greek into Latin by Saint Jerome (c. 342–420), *pistis* became *fides* ("loyalty"). *Fides* had no verbal form, so for *pisteuo* Jerome used the Latin verb *credo,* a word that derived from *cor do,* "I give my heart." He did not think of using *opinor* ("I hold an opinion"). When the Bible was translated into English, *credo* and *pisteuo* became "I believe" in the King James version (1611). But the word "belief" has since changed its meaning. In Middle English, *bileven* meant "to prize; to value; to hold dear." It was related to the German *belieben* ("to love"), *liebe* ("beloved"), and the Latin *libido.* So "belief" originally meant "loyalty to a person to whom one is bound in promise or duty."[44] When Chaucer's knight begged his patron to "accepte my bileve," he meant "accept my fealty, my loyalty."[45] In Shakespeare's *All's Well That Ends Well,* which was probably written around 1603, shortly before the publication of the King James Bible, the young nobleman Bertram is urged to "believe not thy disdain": he must not entertain his contempt for lowborn Helena and allow it to take deep root in his heart.[46] During the late seventeenth century, however, as our concept of knowledge became more theoretical, the word "belief" started to be used to describe an intellectual assent to a hypothetical—and often dubious—proposition. Scientists and philosophers were the first to use it in this sense, but in religious contexts the Latin *credere* and the English "belief" both retained their original connotations well into the nineteenth century.

It is in this context, perhaps, that we should discuss the vexed question of Jesus's miracles. Since the Enlightenment, when empirical verification became important in the substantiation of any "belief," many people—Christians and atheists alike—have assumed that Jesus performed these miracles to prove his divinity. But in the ancient world, "miracles" were quite commonplace and, however remarkable and significant, were not thought to indicate that the miracle worker was in any way superhuman.[47] There were so many unseen forces for which the science of the day could not account that it seemed quite reasonable to assume that spirits affected human life, and Greeks routinely consulted a god rather than a doctor. Indeed, given the state of medicine before the modern period, this was probably a safer and more prudent option. Some people had a special ability to manipulate the malign powers that were thought to cause disease, and Jews in particular were known to be skilled healers. In the ninth century BCE, the prophets Elijah and Elisha had both performed miracles similar to Jesus's, but nobody ever suggested that they were gods.

Jesus came from Galilee in northern Palestine, where there was a tradition of devout men (*hasidim*) who were miracle workers.[48] In the middle of the first century BCE, the prayers of Honi the Circle Drawer had brought a severe drought to an end, and shortly before the destruction of the temple, Hanina ben Dosa was able, like Jesus, to cure a patient without even visiting his bedside. But nobody, least of all the *hasidim* themselves, thought that they were anything other than ordinary human beings. Jesus probably presented himself as a *hasid* in this tradition, and he seems to have been a particularly skilled exorcist. People suffering from epilepsy or mental illnesses for which there was no other cure naturally consulted exorcists, some of whom may have been able to effect an improvement in diseases that had a strong psychosomatic component. But like Honi, Jesus made it clear that he owed his miracles to the "powers" (*dunamis*) of God that worked through him and insisted that anybody who trusted God sufficiently would be able to do still greater things.[49]

Far from these miracles being central to the gospel, the evangelists seem rather ambivalent about them. Mark tells us that even though the fame of these marvels spread far and wide, Jesus regularly asked people to keep quiet about their cure;[50] Matthew tends to play down the miracles, using them simply to show how Jesus fulfilled ancient prophecy,[51] while for Luke, the miracles merely showed that Jesus was "a great prophet" like Elijah.[52] The evangelists knew that, despite these signs and wonders, Jesus had not won many followers during his lifetime. The miracles had *not* inspired "faith"; people who witnessed them agreed that Jesus was a "son of God" but were not prepared to disrupt their lives and commit themselves wholeheartedly to his mission—any more than they had been willing to sell all they had and follow Honi the Circle Drawer.

Even the inner circle of apostles lacked *pistis*. They made no comment at all when Jesus fed a crowd of five thousand people with a few loaves and fishes; and when they saw him walking on water, Mark tells us, they were "utterly and completely dumbfounded . . . their minds were closed."[53] Matthew relates that the disciples did indeed bow down before him after this miracle, crying: "Truly, you are the Son of God,"[54] but in no time at all Jesus had to rebuke them for their lack of faith.[55] The miracle stories probably reflect the disciples' understanding of these events *after* the resurrection apparitions. With hindsight, they could see that God had already been working through Jesus to usher in the Kingdom, when God would vanquish the demons that caused suffering, sickness, and death and trample the destructive powers of chaos underfoot.[56] They did not think that Jesus was God, so did not argue that these miracles proved his divinity. But after the resurrection they were convinced that like any person of *pistis,* Jesus had been able to call upon God's *dunamis* when he stilled the storm at sea and walked on the windswept waters.

The rabbis knew that miracles proved nothing. One day, during the early years at Yavneh, Rabbi Eliezer was engaged in a fierce argument about a legal ruling (*halakah*) arising from the Torah. When his colleagues refused to accept his opinion, he asked God to prove his point with a series of miracles. A carob tree moved four hundred cubits of its own accord, water in a nearby canal flowed backward, and the walls of the house of studies caved in, as if on the point of collapse. But the rabbis remained unconvinced and seemed somewhat disapproving of this divine extravaganza. In desperation, Rabbi Eliezer asked for a *bat qol,* a heavenly voice, to support his case, and obligingly a celestial voice cried, "What have you against Rabbi Eliezer? The *halakah* is always as he says." Unimpressed, Rabbi Joshua simply quoted God's own Torah back to him: "It is not in heaven."[57] The Torah was no longer the property of heaven; it had descended to earth on Mount Sinai and was now enshrined in the heart of every Jew. So "we pay no attention to a *bat qol,*" he concluded firmly. It was said that when God heard this, he laughed and said, "My children have conquered me." They had grown up. Instead of meekly accepting opinions foisted on them from above, they were thinking for themselves.[58]

Revelation did not mean that every word of scripture had to be accepted verbatim,[59] and midrash was unconcerned about the original intention of the biblical author. Because the word of God was infinite, a text proved its divine origin by being productive of fresh meaning. Every time a Jew exposed himself to the ancient text, the words could mean something different. By the 80s and 90s, the rabbis were beginning to persuade their fellow Jews that this—rather than Christianity—was the authentic way for Israel to go forward. It was Rabbi Akiva who perfected this innovative style of midrash. It was said that his fame had reached heaven and that, intrigued, Moses decided to come down to earth and attend one of his classes. He sat in the eighth row behind the other students and discovered, to his embarrassment, that he could not understand a word of Akiva's exposition of the Torah that had been revealed to *him,* Moses, on Mount Sinai. "My sons have surpassed me," Moses reflected ruefully, like any proud parent, as he made his way back to heaven.[60] Another rabbi put it more succinctly: "Matters that had not been revealed to Moses were disclosed to Rabbi Akiva and his generation."[61] Some people thought that Rabbi Akiva went too far, but his method carried the day because it kept scripture open. A modern scholar may feel that midrash violates the integrity of the original, but this kind of textual "bricolage" was a creative method of moving a tradition forward at a time when new material was harder to get hold of and people had to work with what they had.

The rabbis believed that the Sinai revelation had not been God's last word to humanity but just the beginning. Scripture was not a finished product; its potential had to be brought out by human ingenuity, in the same way as people had learned to extract flour from wheat and linen from flax.[62] Revelation was an ongoing process that continued from one generation to another.[63] A text that could not speak to the present was dead, and the exegete had a duty to revive it. The rabbis used to link together verses that originally had no connection with one another in a "chain" (horoz) that, in this new combination, meant something entirely different.[64] They would sometimes alter a word in the text, creating a pun by substituting a single letter that entirely changed the original meaning, telling their pupils, "Don't read this . . . but that."[65] They did not intend the emendation to be permanent; like any teacher in antiquity, they were mainly concerned with speaking directly to the needs of a particular group of students. They were happy to interpret a text in a way that bore no relation to the original, so that the Song of Songs, a profane love song sung in taverns that did not even mention God, became an allegory of Yahweh's love for his people.

Midrash was not a solitary exercise; rather, like the Socratic dialogue, it was a joint enterprise. The rabbis had retained the ancient reverence for oral communication and in the early days at Yavneh did not commit their traditions to writing but learned them by heart. Graduates of the academy were called tannaim, "repeaters," because they recited the Torah aloud and developed their midrash together in conversation. The House of Studies was not like a hushed modern library but was noisy with clamorous debate. As the political situation deteriorated in Palestine, however, the rabbis decided that they needed a written record of these discussions, and between 135 and 160 they compiled an entirely new scripture, which they called the Mishnah, an anthology of the oral teachings collected at Yavneh. The Mishnah was deliberately constructed as a replica of the lost temple, its six sections (sederim) supporting the literary edifice like pillars.[66] By studying the laws and ordinances now tragically rendered obsolete, students could still honor the divine Presence in the post-temple world.

It had been one thing for the early Pharisees to base their lives on an imaginary temple when Herod's temple was still a fully functioning reality, but quite another when it had been reduced to a pile of charred rubble. In the Mishnah, the rabbis amassed thousands of new rulings that regulated the lives of Jews down to the smallest detail to help them become aware of the Shekhinah's continued presence in their midst. They had no interest in "beliefs" but focused on practical behavior. If all Jews were to live as if they were priests serving the Holy of Holies, how should they deal with gentiles? How could each household observe the purity laws? What was the role of women in the home that was now a temple? The rabbis would never have been able to persuade the people to accept this formidable body of law had it not yielded a satisfying spirituality.

The Mishnah did not cling nervously to the Hebrew Bible, but held proudly aloof and rarely quoted the old scriptures. It felt no need to discuss its relation to the Sinai tradition, but loftily assumed that its competence was beyond question. The rabbis continued to love and revere the older scriptures, but knew that the world they represented had gone forever; like the Christians, they took from them what they needed and respectfully laid the rest to one side. Religion must be allowed to move forward freely and could not be constrained by misplaced loyalty to the past. Divine revelation, they decided, had come in two forms: a written Torah and an ongoing Oral Torah that evolved from one generation to another. Both were sacred, both came from God, but the rabbis valued the Oral Torah more than any written scripture because this living tradition reflected the fluctuations of human thought and kept the Word responsive to change. Undue reliance on a written text could encourage inflexibility and backward-looking timidity.[67] The insights of all Jews—past, present, and to come—had been anticipated symbolically in the Sinai revelation, so when they developed the Oral Torah together in their discussions in the House of Studies, the rabbis felt as though they were standing beside Moses on the mountaintop, and were participating in a never-ending conversation with the great sages of the past and with their God. They were the recipients of God's word just as surely as were the ancient prophets and patriarchs.[68]

The two Talmuds moved even more firmly away from the Bible. The Jerusalem Talmud, compiled during the fifth century, and the more authoritative Babylonian Talmud (known as the Bavli) a century later, were commentaries on the Mishnah, not the Bible. Like the New Testament, the Bavli was regarded as the completion of the Hebrew Bible, a new revelation for a changed world.[69] As Christians would always read the Hebrew Bible from the perspective of the New Testament, Jews would study it only in conjunction with the Bavli, which completely transformed it. The author-editors felt free to reverse the Mishnah's legislation, play one rabbi off against another, and point out serious gaps in their arguments. They did exactly the same with the Bible, even suggesting what the biblical authors should have said and substituting their own rulings for biblical law. The Bavli gave no definitive answers to the many questions it raised. We hear many different voices: Abraham, Moses, the Prophets, the early Pharisees, and the rabbis of Yavneh were all brought together on the same page, so that they seem to be on the same level and taking part in a communal debate across the centuries.

The study of Talmud is democratic and open-ended. If a student finds that none of these august authorities resolve a problem to his satisfaction, he must sort it out for himself. The Bavli has thus been described as the first interactive text.[70] Because students are taught to follow the rabbinic method of study, they engage in the same discussions and must make their own contribution to this never-ending conversation. In some versions of the Talmud, there was a space on each page for a student to add his own commentary. He learned that nobody had the last word, that truth was constantly changing, and that while tradition was of immense importance, it must not compromise his own judgment. If he did not add his own remarks to the sacred page, the line of tradition would come to an end. Religious discourse should not be cast in stone; the ancient teachings required constant revision. "What is Torah?" asked the Bavli. "It is the interpretation of Torah."[71]

As Christianity spread in the Hellenistic world, the more educated converts brought with them the insights and expectations of their own Greek education. From an early date, they regarded Christianity as a *philosophia* that had much in common with the Greek schools. It took courage to become a Christian, as the churches were subjected to sporadic but intense bouts of persecution by the Roman authorities. When Jesus had failed to return, Jewish Christianity petered out, and by the beginning of the second century, Christianity and Rabbinic Judaism had parted company. Once Christians made it clear that they were no longer members of the synagogue, they were regarded by the

Romans as impious fanatics who had committed the cardinal sin of breaking with the parent faith. Christians were accused of atheism because they refused to honor the patronal gods of the empire, so some tried to prove that Christianity was no *superstitio* but a new school of philosophy.

One of the earliest of these apologists was Justin (100–160), a pagan convert from Samaria in the Holy Land. He had dabbled in Stoicism and Pythagorean spirituality but found what he was looking for in Christianity, which he regarded as the culmination of both Judaism and Greek philosophy. Philosophers also saw their great sages— Socrates, Plato, Zeno, Epicurus—as "sons of God," and Christians used the same kind of terminology—Logos, Spirit, and God—as the Stoics. In the prologue to his gospel, Saint John had said that Jesus was the incarnate "Word" or "Logos" of God[72]—the very same Logos, Justin argued, that had inspired Plato and Socrates. There was no Greek equivalent to the Hebrew *Shekhinah,* so increasingly Christians used the term *Logos* to describe the divine Presence that they could experience but that was essentially separate from God's inmost nature. Justin was not an intellectual of the first caliber, but his conception of Christ as the eternal Logos was crucial to the theologians who developed the seminal ideas of Christianity and are therefore known as the "fathers" of the Church.

The Greek-educated fathers sought references to the Logos in every sentence of the Hebrew Bible. Finding the Hebrew texts difficult to understand and the ancient biblical ethos somewhat alien, they transformed them into an allegory, in which all the events and characters of what they called the Old Testament became precursors of Christ in the New. The Christians of Antioch preferred to concentrate on the literal sense of scripture and discover what the biblical authors themselves had intended to teach, but they were not as popular as the exegetes of Alexandria, who followed in the footsteps of Philo and the Greek allegorists.

One of the most brilliant and influential of these early exegetes was Origen (185–254), who had studied *allegoria* with Greek and Jewish scholars in Alexandria and midrash with rabbis in Palestine. In his search for the deeper significance of scripture, Origen did not cavalierly cast the original aside but took the plain sense of scripture very seriously. He learned Hebrew, consulted rabbis about Jewish lore, studied the flora and fauna of the Holy Land, and, in a mammoth effort to establish the best possible text, set the Hebrew alongside five different Greek translations. But he believed that it was impossible for a modern, Greek-educated Christian to read the Bible in a wholly literal manner. How could anybody imagine that God had really "walked" in the Garden of Eden? What possible relevance to Christians were the lengthy instructions for the construction of a tabernacle in the Sinai wilderness? Was a Christian obliged to take literally Christ's instruction that his disciples should never wear shoes? What could we make of the highly dubious story of Abraham selling his wife to Pharaoh? The answer was to treat these difficult texts as *allegoria,* the literary form that describes one thing under the guise of another.

Indeed, Origen argued, the glaring anomalies and inconsistencies in scripture forced us to look beyond the literal sense. God had planted these "stumbling blocks and interruptions of the historical sense" to make us look deeper. These "impossibilities and incongruities . . . present a barrier to the reader and lead him to refuse to proceed along the pathway of the ordinary meaning."[73] Origen never tired of telling his readers that exegesis was hard work and that, like any philosophical exercise, it required discipline and dedication. Like any philosopher, the exegete must live a life of prayer, purity, sobriety, and virtue; he must be prepared to study all night long.[74] But if he persevered, he would find that "in the very act of reading and diligently studying" these outwardly unpromising texts, he would feel "touched by the divine spirit (*pneuma*)."[75] For the Christians as for the rabbis, scripture was a symbol, its words and stories merely the outward "images of divine things."[76] For Origen, exegesis was a *musterion,* an initiation that required hard labor but finally brought the *mystes* into the divine presence.[77]

Like a human person, scripture consisted of a body, a psyche, and a spirit that transcended mortal nature; these corresponded to the three senses in which scripture could be understood. The *mystes* had to master the "body" of the sacred text (its *literal* sense) before he could progress to anything higher. Then he was ready for the *moral* sense, an interpretation that represented the "psyche," the natural powers of mind and heart: it provided us with ethical guidance but was largely a matter of common sense. The *mystes* that pressed on to the end of his initiation was introduced to the *spiritual,* allegorical sense, when he encountered the Word that lay hidden in the earthly body of the sacred page.

But this would not be possible without the spiritual exercises that put the *mystes* into a different frame of mind. At first Origen's exegesis seems strained and far-fetched to a modern reader, because he reads into the text things that are simply not there. But Origen was not asking the reader to "believe" his conclusions. Like any philosophical theory, his insights made no sense unless the disciple undertook the same spiritual exercises as his master. His commentaries were a *miqra.* Readers had to take the next step for themselves, meditating on the text with the same intensity as Origen, until they too were "capable of receiving the principles of truth."[78] Without long hours of *theoria* ("contemplation"), Origen's exegesis was both incomprehensible and incredible.

Origen's method of reading scripture according to the literal, moral, and spiritual senses became standard throughout the Christian world. The monastic reformer John Cassian (360–435) introduced this type of exegesis to western Europe and added a fourth sense: the *anagogical,* which described the eschatological dimension of any given text. This fourfold method remained in place in the West until the Reformation. It was imparted to the laity by preachers in the pulpit and used by monks when they meditated on the biblical text. You began always with the literal reading but then progressed up the ladder of the moral, allegorical, and anagogical senses in a symbolic "ascent" from the physical to the spiritual levels of existence. Until the modern period, nobody thought of confining their attention to a literal reading of the plain sense of scripture. When Christians started to insist on the literal truth of every word of the Bible in the late nineteenth century, many would find that it was as alien, incredible, and paradoxical as Origen had described.

For the fathers of the Church, scripture was a "mystery" not because it taught a lot of incomprehensible doctrines, but because it directed the attention of Christians toward a hidden level of reality. Scripture was also a "mystery," because exegesis was a spiritual process that, like any initiation, proceeded stage by stage until the final moment of illumination. You could not hope to understand it without undergoing this disciplined ascesis of heart and mind. Scrip-

ture was not just a text but an "activity"; you did not merely read it—
you had to *do it*.[79] Scholars and lay folk alike usually read it in a liturgical setting, which separated it from secular modes of thought. As
we know from Paul's letters, the early Christians had developed their
own rituals. Baptism and the Eucharist (a reenactment of Jesus's last
supper with his disciples) were also "mysteries," not because they
could not be understood by natural reason but because they were initiations, during which the congregation were taught to look beneath
the symbolic gestures to find the sacred kernel within and thus experience a "change of mind."

In the lectures of Cyril, bishop of Jerusalem (c. 315–86), we have
one of the earliest accounts of the way candidates were introduced to
the rituals and doctrines of the church.[80] In Cyril's church, the ceremony of baptism took place in the small hours of Easter Sunday
morning in the Basilica of the Resurrection. During the six weeks of
Lent, converts had undergone an intensive period of preparation.
They had to fast, attend vigils, pray, and receive instruction about the
*kerygma,* the basic factual message of the gospel. They were not
required to believe anything in advance. They would be instructed in
the deeper truths of Christianity only after the initiation of baptism,
because these dogmas would make sense only after the transformative experience of the ritual. As in any philosophical school, theory
was secondary to the rites and spiritual exercises that had produced
it. Like any *mythoi,* the doctrines of Christianity were only ever
imparted in a ritualized setting to people who were properly prepared and were eager to be transformed by it.[81] Like the insights of
any initiation, the doctrines that were revealed at the end of the ritualized process would seem trivial or even absurd to outsiders. It was
only *after* they had been through the transformative process that new
Christians were asked to recite the "creed," a proclamation not of
"belief" but of commitment to the God that had become a reality in
their lives as a result of this rite of passage.

Cyril's lectures, therefore, were not metaphysical doctrinal explanations demanding credulous "belief" but *mystagogy;* this had been
the technical term for the instruction that enabled *mystai* in the
Greek Mysteries "to assimilate themselves with the holy symbols,
leave their own identity, become at home with the gods, and experience divine possession." When the ceremony began, baptismal candi-

dates were lined up outside the church facing westward, in the direction of Egypt, the realm of sunset and death. As a first step in their reenactment of the Israelites' liberation from slavery, they renounced Satan. They were then "turned around" in a "conversion" toward the east—to the dawn, new life, and the pristine innocence of Eden. Processing into the church, they discarded their clothes, symbolically shedding their old selves, so that they stood naked, like Adam and Eve before the fall. Each *mystes* was then plunged three times into the waters of the baptismal pool. This was their crossing of the Sea and their symbolic immersion in the death of Christ, whose tomb stood only a few yards away. Each time they were pulled underwater, the bishop asked them: Do you have *pistis* in the Father—in the Son—and in the Holy Spirit? And each time, the *mystes* cried, *"Pisteuo!"*: "I give him my heart, my loyalty and my commitment!" When they emerged from the pool, they had themselves become *christoi* ("anointed ones").[82] They were clothed in white garments, symbolizing their new identity, received the Eucharist for the first time, and, like Christ at his own baptism, were ritually adopted as "sons of God." In the Latin-speaking West, neophytes would cry *"Credo!"* when they were immersed in the water. This was not an intellectual assent to obligatory doctrines; much of the *dogma* would not be imparted to them until the following week. The *mystai* were not simply stating their "belief" in a set of empirically unproven propositions. The cry *"Pisteuo!"* or *"Credo!"* was more like "I will!" in the marriage service.

The carefully devised rituals had evoked an *ekstasis,* a "stepping out" of their accustomed modes of thought. As Theodore, bishop of Mopsuestia in Cilicia from 392 to 428, explained to his catechumens:

> When you say *"pisteuo"* ["I engage myself"] before God,
> you show that you will remain steadfastly with him, that
> you will never separate yourself from him and that you
> will think it higher than anything else to be and to live
> with him and to conduct yourself in a way that is in har-
> mony with his commandments.[83]

"Belief" in our modern sense did not come into it. Even though Theodore was a leading proponent of the literal exegesis practiced in Antioch, he did not require his candidates to "believe" any "mysterious" doctrines. Faith was purely a matter of commitment and practical living.

This would also be true of the third of the monotheisms, which would not emerge until the early years of the seventh century. In 610, Muhammad ibn Abdullah (c. 560–632), a merchant of the thriving commercial city of Mecca in the Arabian Hijaz, began to have revelations that he believed came from the God of the Jews and Christians. These divine messages were eventually brought together in the scripture known as the *Qur'an*, the "Recitation," and its text was finalized a mere twenty years after the Prophet's death. The religion of the Qur'an would eventually be known as *islam,* a word that means "surrender" to God, and was based on the same basic principles as the two other monotheistic traditions.

The Qur'an has no interest in "belief"; indeed, this concept is quite alien to Islam.[84] Theological speculation that results in the formulation of abstruse doctrines is dismissed as *zannah,* self-indulgent guesswork about matters that nobody can prove one way or the other but that makes people quarrelsome and stupidly sectarian.[85] Like any religion or *philosophia,* Islam was a way of life (*din*). The fundamental message of the Qur'an was not a doctrine but an ethical summons to practically expressed compassion: it is wrong to build a private fortune and good to share your wealth fairly and create a just society where poor and vulnerable people are treated with respect.[86] The five "pillars" of Islam are a *miqra,* a summons to dedicated activity: prayer, fasting, almsgiving, and pilgrimage. This is also true of the first "pillar," the declaration of faith: "I bear witness that there is no God but Allah and that Muhammad is his prophet." This is not a "creed" in the modern Western sense; the Muslim who makes this *shahadah* "bears witness" in his life and in every single one of his actions that his chief priority is Allah and that no other "gods"—which include political, material, economic, and personal ambitions—can take precedence over his commitment to God alone. In the Qur'an, faith (*iman*) is something that people do: they share their wealth, perform the "works of justice" (*salihat*), and prostrate their bodies to the ground in the kenotic, ego-deflating act of prayer (*salat*).[87]

In the Qur'an, the people who opposed Islam when Muhammad

began to preach in Mecca are called the *kafirun*. The usual English translation is extremely misleading: it does not mean "unbeliever" or "infidel"; the root *KFR* means "blatant ingratitude," a discourteous and arrogant refusal of something offered with great kindness.[88] The theology of the *kafirun* was quite correct: they all took it for granted that God created the world, for example.[89] They were not condemned for their "unbelief" but for their braying, offensive manner to others, their pride, self-importance, chauvinism, and inability to accept criticism.[90] The *kafirun* never give serious consideration to an idea that is new to them, because they think they know everything already. Hence they sneer at the Qur'an, seizing every opportunity to display their own cleverness.[91] Above all, they are *jahili:* chronically "irascible," acutely sensitive about their honor and prestige, with a destructive tendency to violent retaliation.[92] Muslims are commanded to respond to such abusive behavior with *hilm* ("forbearance") and quiet courtesy, leaving revenge to Allah.[93] They must "walk gently on the earth," and whenever the *jahilun* insult them, they should simply reply, "Peace."[94]

There was no question of a literal, simplistic reading of scripture. Every single image, statement, and verse in the Qur'an is called an *ayah* ("sign," "symbol," "parable"), because we can speak of God only analogically. The great *ayat* of the creation and the last judgment are not introduced to enforce "belief," but they are a summons to action. Muslims must translate these doctrines into practical behavior. The *ayah* of the last day, when people will find that their wealth cannot save them, should make Muslims examine their conduct here and now: Are they behaving kindly and fairly to the needy? They must imitate the generosity of Allah, who created the wonders of this world so munificently and sustains it so benevolently. At first, the religion was known as *tazakka* ("refinement"). By looking after the poor compassionately, freeing their slaves, and performing small acts of kindness on a daily, hourly basis, Muslims would acquire a responsible, caring spirit, purging themselves of pride and selfishness. By modeling their behavior on that of the Creator, they would achieve spiritual refinement.[95]

In these early days, Muslims did not see Islam as a new, exclusive religion but as a continuation of the primordial faith of the "People of the Book," the Jews and Christians. In one remarkable passage, God insists that Muslims must accept indiscriminately the revelations of every single one of God's messengers: Abraham, Isaac, Ishmael, Jacob, Moses, Jesus, and all the other prophets.[96] The Qur'an is simply a "confirmation" of the previous scriptures.[97] Nobody must be forced to accept Islam, because each of the revealed traditions had its own *din;* it was not God's will that all human beings should belong to the same faith community.[98] God was not the exclusive property of any one tradition; the divine light could not be confined to a single lamp, belonged neither to the East nor to the West, but enlightened all human beings.[99] Muslims must speak courteously to the People of the Book, debate with them only in "the most kindly manner," remember that they worshipped the same God, and not engage in pointless, aggressive disputes.[100]

All this would require a ceaseless *jihad* (which did not mean "holy war" but "effort," "struggle"), because it was extremely difficult to implement the will of God in a tragically flawed world. Muslims must make a determined endeavor on all fronts—intellectual, social, economic, moral, spiritual, and political. Sometimes they might have to fight, as Muhammad did when the Meccan *kafirun* vowed to exterminate the Muslim community. But aggressive warfare was outlawed, and the only justification for war was self-defense.[101] Warfare was far from being the prime Muslim duty. An important and oft-quoted tradition (*hadith*) has Muhammad say on his way home after a battle: "We are returning from the Lesser Jihad [the battle] and going to the Greater Jihad," the far more important and difficult struggle to reform one's own society and one's own heart. Eventually, when the war with Mecca was turning in his favor, Muhammad adopted a policy of nonviolence.[102] When Mecca finally opened its gates voluntarily, nobody was forced to enter Islam and Muhammad made no attempt to implement an exclusively Islamic state there.

Like any religious tradition, Islam would change and evolve. Muslims acquired a large empire, stretching from the Pyrenees to the Himalayas, but true to Qur'anic principles, nobody was forced to become Muslim. Indeed, for the first hundred years after the Prophet's death, conversion to Islam was actually discouraged, because Islam was a *din* for the Arabs, the descendants of Abraham's elder son, Ishmael, just as Judaism was for the sons of Isaac and Christianity for the followers of the gospel.

Faith, therefore, was a matter of practical insight and active commitment; it had little to do with abstract belief or theological conjecture.
Judaism and Islam have remained religions of practice; they promote
orthopraxy, right practice, rather than orthodoxy, right teaching. In
the early fourth century, however, Christianity had begun to move in
a slightly different direction and developed a preoccupation with
doctrinal correctness that would become its Achilles' heel. Yet even
while some Christians stridently argued about abstruse dogmatic
definitions, others—perhaps in reaction—developed a spirituality of
silence and unknowing that would be just as important, characteristic, and influential.

# FIVE

# Silence

I n 312, Constantine defeated his rival for the imperial throne at the battle of Milvian Bridge and would always believe that he owed his victory to the God of the Christians. The following year, he declared Christianity *religio licita,* one of the permitted religions of the Roman Empire. This was a dramatic and fateful reversal. From being persecuted members of an outlawed sect, Christians could now own property, build churches, worship freely, and make a distinctive contribution to public life. Even though Constantine continued to preside over the official pagan cult as *pontifex maximus* and was baptized only on his deathbed, it was clear that he favored Christianity. He had hoped that, once legalized, the church would become a cohesive force in his far-flung empire. This state support proved a mixed blessing, however. Constantine had very little understanding of Christian theology, but that did not prevent him from meddling in doctrinal affairs when he discovered that the church that was supposed to unify his subjects was itself torn apart by a dogmatic dispute.

Christians had to adapt to their changed circumstances. They had to find a way of instructing the flood of new converts presenting themselves for baptism, some, doubtless, with an eye on the main chance. They realized that their faith could be puzzling. Now that Christianity was a predominantly gentile religion, the Hebrew terminology of the first Jewish Christians needed to be translated into a Greco-Roman idiom. Christianity claimed to be a monotheistic religion, but what was the status of Jesus, the incarnate Logos? Was he a second God? What did Christians mean when they called him "Son of God"? Or was he a hybrid—half human and half divine—like Dionysus? And who was the Holy Spirit? The problem was exacerbated by a marked change in the intellectual and spiritual climate of late antiquity.

There seems to have been a profound loss of confidence in both the physical world and human nature. Hitherto Greeks, like most other peoples, had seen no impassable gulf between God and humanity. Their philosophers had agreed that as rational animals, human beings contained a spark of the divine within themselves; a sage like Socrates, who incarnated the transcendent ideal of wisdom, was a son of God and an avatar of the divine. People had no doubt that they could ascend to the Good by their own natural powers. Origen, a Platonist, believed that he could get to know God by contemplating the universe and had seen the Christian life as a Platonic ascent that would continue after death until the soul was fully assimilated to the divine. The Egyptian Neoplatonist philosopher Plotinus (c. 205–70) believed that the universe emanated from God eternally, like rays from the sun, so that the material world was a kind of overflowing of God's very being; when you meditated on the universe, you were, therefore, meditating upon God. But by the early fourth century, people felt that the cosmos was separated from God by a vast, almost unbridgeable chasm. The universe was now experienced as so fragile, moribund, and contingent that it could have nothing in common with the God that was being itself. A terrifying void lay ready to engulf all living things. The primordial question (Why does anything exist rather than nothing at all?) no longer inspired awe, wonder, and delight but had been replaced by a sickening vertigo. The possibility of nothingness lurked threateningly at both the beginning and the end of human existence.

Some Christians had already started to promote the new doctrine, entirely unknown in antiquity, of creation ex nihilo. Clement of Alexandria (c. 150–215) believed that the philosophical idea of an eternal cosmos was idolatrous, because it presented nature as a second coeternal god. Nothing could come from nothing, so the universe could only have been summoned out of the primal void by the God that was Life itself. Instead of "deifying the universe," people needed to know that "the sheer volition of God is the making of the universe."[1] The idea that God had deliberately created all things posed huge problems: Did it not imply that God was responsible for evil? Yet the belief that matter was eternal seemed to compromise God's omnipotence and sovereign freedom. Monotheism implied that there was only one omnipotent power, so God's decisions could surely not be influenced by the independent requirements of matter, which, like Plato's craftsman, he was merely permitted to arrange and finish off.[2]

Today the doctrine of creation ex nihilo is regarded as the linchpin of Christianity, the truth on which theism stands or falls. So it is interesting to note how slowly and uncertainly this idea emerged. It was entirely alien to Greek philosophy. It would have seemed absurd to Aristotle to imagine the timeless God who was wholly absorbed in ceaseless contemplation of itself suddenly deciding to create the cosmos. Creation out of nothing represented a fundamental change in the Christian understanding of both God and the world. There was no longer a chain of being emanating eternally from God to the material universe, no longer an intermediate realm of spiritual beings that transmitted the divine energy to the nether regions. Instead, God had called every single creature from an abysmal and unimaginable nothingness and could at any moment withdraw his sustaining hand. Creation ex nihilo tore the universe away from God. The physical world could not tell us anything about the divine, because it had not emanated naturally from God, as the philosophers had imagined, but was made out of nothing. It was, therefore, of an entirely different nature (*ontos*) from the substance of the living God. A "natural theology" that argued from our rational observation of the world to God was no longer possible, because the new doctrine made it clear that, left to ourselves, we could know nothing at all about God.

Yet Christians did not feel that God was entirely unknowable. The man Jesus had been an image (*eikon*) of the divine and had given them an inkling of what the utterly transcendent God was like. They were also convinced that, in spite of everything, they had entered a hitherto-unexplored dimension of their humanity that in some sense enabled them to participate in the divine life. They called this Christian experience *theosis* ("deification"): like the incarnate Logos, they too had become the sons of God, as Paul had explained. But because this chasm had opened up between the material and divine worlds, they now realized that they could not have achieved this by their own efforts. It had happened only because of a divine initiative. The God who had called all things into being had somehow bridged the immense gulf when "the Word was made flesh and lived among us."[3] But who was Jesus? On which side of the abyss was the Logos "through whom all things came to be"?[4] Some Christians argued that because, as Saint John said, the Word had been "with God" from the beginning and, indeed "was God,"[5] Jesus, the incarnate Word, belonged in the divine sphere. But others pointed out that because he had become a man and died an agonizing death, he shared the fragility and contingency of matter. Did that mean that the Word had been created from nothing like everything else?

In 320, a heated debate about these issues erupted in Alexandria. It seems to have started with an argument about the meaning of Wisdom's words in the book of Proverbs, which Christians had always applied to Christ—"Yahweh created me when his purpose first unfolded, before the oldest of his works"[6]—and went on to say that Wisdom had been God's "master craftsman," his agent of creation. Arius, a handsome and charismatic young presbyter of Alexandria, argued that this text made it clear that the Word and Wisdom of the Father was the first and most privileged of God's creatures. It followed that the Word must also have been created ex nihilo. Arius did not deny that Jesus was God, but suggested that he had merely been promoted to divine status. God had foreseen that when the Logos became a man, he would behave with perfect obedience, and as a reward had raised him to divine status in advance of his mission. The Logos thus became the prototype of the perfected human being; if Christians imitated his wholehearted *kenosis*, they too could become "sons of God"; they too could become divine.[7] Alexander, bishop of Alexandria, and his brilliant young assistant Athanasius immediately realized that Arius had put his finger on an ambiguity in the Alexandrian view of Christ that needed to be cleared up.[8]

The debate was not confined to a coterie of learned experts. Arius set his ideas to music, and it was not long before sailors and travelers were singing popular songs proclaiming that the Father was God by nature and had given life and being to the Son, who was neither coeternal with him nor uncreated. Soon the controversy had spread to the churches of Asia Minor and Syria. We hear of a bath attendant who engaged the bathers in heated discussion about whether the Son had come from nothingness; a money changer who, when asked for the exchange rate, held forth on the distinction between the Creator and his creation; and a baker who argued with his customers that the Father was greater than the Son.[9] People were discussing the question with the same enthusiasm and passion as they discuss football today, because it touched the heart of their Christian experience. In the past, the creeds and explanations of the faith had often been changed to meet pastoral needs.[10] The Arian crisis showed that they would probably have to be changed yet again.

Over the centuries, Arianism has become a byword for heresy but at the time there was no officially orthodox position and nobody knew whether Arius or Athanasius was right.[11] Arius was anxious to safeguard the transcendence of God. God was unique, "the only unbegotten, the only eternal, the only one without beginning, the only true, the only one who has immortality, the only wise, the only good."[12] His power was so overwhelming that it had to be mediated through the Logos at the creation, because frail creatures "could not endure to be made by the absolute hand of the Unoriginate."[13] The immense and all-powerful God could not possibly have been in the man Jesus: for Arius that would be like cramming a whale into a can of shrimp or a mountain into a box.

Athanasius wanted to safeguard the liturgical practice of the Church, which regularly referred—albeit imprecisely—to Jesus as divine. If, he argued, the Arians really believed Christ to be a mere creature, were they not guilty of idolatry when they worshipped him?[14] Like Arius, Athanasius had accepted the new doctrine of creation ex nihilo, but he argued that Arius did not understand its full implications. Creation ex nihilo had revealed an utter incompatibility between being itself and creatures that came from nothing.[15] The only things that we could know by our natural, unaided reason were the objects of the material world, which told us nothing about God. Our brains were equipped to recognize only finite realities created ex nihilo, so we had no idea what the substance (*ousia*) of the uncreated God was like. God was not like any immense thing in our experience, and Arius "should not think of him in [such] human terms."[16] Further, being and nonbeing had absolutely nothing in common; it was impossible to speak in these human terms about the Logos, the agent of creation, "by whom all things were made": "What sort of resemblance is there between things which are from nothing and the one who rendered the things which are nothing into being?"[17] Jesus had not been linked to a very large and powerful being, as the Arians seemed to imagine; all that could be said was that there was an incomprehensible transcendence in Jesus that was entirely distinct from anything in human experience.

The relationship between the unknowable God and the incarnate Logos, who had brought all things into existence, must, therefore, be entirely different from a relationship between two created beings. If, like the Arians, you simply thought of God as another being, albeit bigger and better than us, then it was absolutely impossible for God to become human. It was only because we had no idea what God was that we could say that God had been in the man Jesus. It was also impossible to say that God's substance was *not* in Christ, because we could not identify the *ousia* of God; it lay completely beyond our ken, so we did not know what we were denying. Christians would not have been able to experience the "deification" of *theosis* or even imagine the unknowable God unless God had—in some unfathomable way—taken the initiative and entered the realm of fragile creatures. "The Word became human that we might become divine," Athanasius wrote in his treatise *On the Incarnation;* "he revealed himself through a body that we might receive an idea of the invisible Father."[18] When we looked at the man Jesus, therefore, we had a partial glimpse of the otherwise unknowable God, and God's Spirit, an immanent presence within us, enabled us to recognize this.

Unfortunately, Constantine, who had no understanding of the issues, decided to intervene and summoned all the bishops to Nicaea in Asia Minor on May 20, 325. Athanasius managed to impose his views on the delegates, and the council issued a statement that Christ, the Word, had not been created but had been begotten "in an ineffable, indescribable manner" from the *ousia* of the Father—not from nothingness like everything else. So he was "from God" in an entirely different manner from all other creatures.[19] The paradoxical terminology of the Nicene statement revealed the new emphasis on the absolute unknowability of the "ineffable, indescribable" God.[20] But this authoritative ruling solved nothing. Because of imperial pressure, all the delegates except Arius and two of his colleagues signed the statement, but once they had returned to their dioceses, they continued to teach as they had always done—for the most part midway between Arius and Athanasius. This attempt to impose a uniform belief on the bishops and the faithful was counterproductive. Nicaea led to another fifty years of acrimony, divisions, conciliar deliberations, and even to violence, as creedal orthodoxy became politicized. The Nicene Council would eventually become a symbol of orthodoxy, but it would be centuries before Athanasius's formula was restated in a form that Christians were willing to accept—and even then there was no uniformity.

Eastern and Western Christians would understand the incarnation very differently. Anselm of Canterbury (1033–1109) defined the doctrine of atonement that became normative in the West: God became man in order to expiate the sin of Adam. Orthodox Christians have never accepted this. The Orthodox view of Jesus was defined by Maximus the Confessor (c. 580–662), who believed that the Word would have become flesh even if Adam had not sinned. Jesus was the first human being to be wholly "deified," entirely possessed and permeated by the divine, and we could all be like him, even in this life. The Word had become incarnate in order that "the whole human being would become God, deified by the grace of God become man, soul and body, by nature and becoming whole God, soul and body by grace."[21] As a result of this divine initiative, God and humanity had become inseparable. The man Jesus gave us our only hint of what God was like and had shown that human beings could participate in some indefinable way in the being of the incomprehensible God. We could no longer think "God" without thinking "human," or "human" without thinking "God."

Maximus fully accepted Athanasius's appreciation of the absolute transcendence of God. The revelation of the incarnate Logos made it clear that God must be absolutely unknowable. It was only because we did *not* regard God as an immense being (as Arius did) that we could say that God could remain the all-powerful God at the same time as assuming the frailty of human flesh, because any mere being of our experience could not be two incompatible things at once. It was only because we did not know what God was that we could say that human beings could in some way share the divine nature. Even when we contemplated Christ the man, God itself remained opaque and elusive. Revelation did not provide us with clear information about God but told us that God was incomprehensible to us. Paradoxical as it might sound, the purpose of revelation was to tell us that we knew nothing about God. And the supreme revelation of the incarnate Logos made this clearer than ever. After all, we have to be *told* about something we do not know or we would remain completely unaware of it.

> For having become man . . . [God] himself remains completely incomprehensible. . . . What could do more to demonstrate the proof of the divine transcendence of being than this? Revelation shows that it is hidden, reason that it is unspeakable, and intellect that it is transcendently unknowable.[22]

These matters could not be settled by doctrinal formulations, because human language is not adequate to express the reality that we call "God." Even words such as "life" and "light" mean something entirely different when we use them of God, so silence is the only medium in which it is possible to apprehend the divine.

But this did not mean that people had merely to "believe" these unfathomable truths; on the contrary, they had to work very hard to achieve the mental stillness that made the experience of unknowing a numinous reality in their lives. Maximus's theology was based on a spirituality that had developed shortly after Nicaea. At a time when many Christians recoiled from the specter of primordial nothingness, others moved forward to embrace it. While some were engaged in wordy disputes and technical Christological definitions, others opted for a spirituality of silence—not dissimilar to the Indian Brahmodya. The monks had become the Christian heroes par excellence; they flocked into the deserts of Egypt and Syria to live in solitude, meditating on the scriptural texts they had memorized and practicing spiritual exercises that brought them the same kind of serenity as that sought by Epicureans, Stoics, and Cynics. The Greek fathers regarded monasticism as a new school of *philosophia*. The monks practiced the Stoic virtue of *prosoche*, "attention to oneself"; they too prepared for death and adopted a way of life that made them *atopos*, an "unclassifiable" breach with the norm.[23] By the mid-fourth century, some of these desert monks had pioneered an apophatic or "wordless" spirituality that brought them inner tranquillity (*hesychia*).

Evagrius of Pontus (c. 348–99), who became one of the leading hesychasts of the Egyptian desert, taught his monks yogic techniques of concentration that stilled the mind, so that instead of seeking to limit the divine by confining it within rationalistic, human categories, they could cultivate an attentive, listening silence.[24] Prayer was not conversation with God or a busy meditation on the divine nature; it meant a "shedding of thoughts." Because God lay beyond all words and concepts, the mind must be "naked": "When you are praying, do not shape within yourself any image of the Deity," Evagrius advised, "and do not let your mind be stamped with the impress of any forms."[25] It was possible to gain an intuitive apprehension of God that was quite different from any knowledge derived from discursive reasoning. The contemplative must not expect exotic feelings, visions, or heavenly voices; these did not come from God but from his own fevered imagination and would merely distract him from his true objective: "Blessed is the intellect that has acquired complete freedom from sensations during prayer."[26] Some of the Greek fathers called prayer an activity of the heart (kardia), but this did not imply that it was an emotional experience. The "heart" represented the spiritual center of the human being, what the Upanishads called the atman, his or her true self.[27]

Today religious experience is often understood as intensely emotional, so Evagrius's prohibition of "sensations" may seem perverse. In all the great traditions, however, teachers have constantly proclaimed that far from being essential to the spiritual quest, visions, voices, and feelings of devotion could in fact be a distraction. The apprehension of God, Brahman, Nirvana, or Dao had nothing to do with the emotions. Christians had been aware of this from the very beginning; worship had often been noisy and unrestrained: under the inspiration of the Spirit, there had been speaking in strange languages, ecstatic trance, and spontaneous prophecy. But Saint Paul sternly and memorably told his Corinthian converts that these transports had to remain within due bounds and that by far the most important of the spiritual gifts was charity. In all the major traditions, the iron rule of religious experience is that it be integrated successfully with daily life. A disorderly spirituality that makes the practitioner dreamy, eccentric, or uncontrolled is a very bad sign indeed.

In warning his monks against "sensations," Evagrius was reiterating this central insight. Many of the disciplines of contemplation, such as yoga or *hesychia,* were designed precisely to wean the mind and heart away from these earthbound modes of perception and help people discover another mode of experience. To cultivate and luxuriate in ordinary feelings and sensations meant that the contemplative remained trapped in the mundane cast of mind that he or she was supposed to transcend. A contemplative must not think of undertaking this journey into the depths of the psyche without a spiritual director or guru. Plunging into the subconscious is risky, and a good director can lead disciples past dangerous swings of mood to the disciplined equanimity of *hesychia,* which was rooted in a level of the self that lies deeper than the emotions.

The life of the desert monks was extremely monotonous. It is no accident that in all the faith traditions, people who wanted to engage in this kind of meditative activity organized a monastic life to cater to their needs. Details and emphases differ from one culture to another, but the similarities are striking. The withdrawal from the world, the silence, the disciplines of community—everybody wearing the same clothes and doing the same thing day after day—have been found to support the contemplative during his frequently lonely journey, to earth him in reality and wean him away from an excitement and drama inimical to the authentic religious experience. These practices provided an element of stability to counterbalance the mental extremity to which the monk, yogin, or hesychast was continually exposed. Once religious experience is equated with fervid enthusiasm, this can indicate that people are losing touch with the psychological rhythms of the interior life.

*Hesychia* was not what we call "mysticism" today. It was not a specialized form of prayer, characterized by impressive spiritual visions and available only to an elite group of practitioners. The monks were the professionals, certainly, because they could devote themselves to it full-time, but *hesychia* was also prescribed for the laity. All the regular Christian practices—theology, liturgy, exegesis, morality, and acts of kindness—were supposed to be informed by the silent, reticent attitude of *hesychia.* It was not just for solitaries but could also be experienced in public worship and human relationships.[28] One of the most famous exponents of the new apophatic theology was a married man who had been a professional orator until he became bishop of the small Cappadocian town of Nyssa. Gregory of

Nyssa (c. 331–95) had become involved in the political turmoil of the Arian controversy with great reluctance. He was uneasy about these theological disputes, because it was impossible to adjudicate Christian teaching from a position of magisterial detachment. Theology depended on practice, and its truth could be assessed only by people who allowed its doctrines to change them. We could not speak about God rationally, as we speak about ordinary beings, but that did not mean that we should give up thinking about God at all.[29] We had to press on, pushing our minds to the limits of what we could know, descending ever deeper into the darkness of unknowing and acknowledging that there could be no final clarity. After an initial frustration, the soul would realize that "the true satisfaction of her desire consists in constantly going on with her quest and never ceasing in her ascent, seeing that every fulfillment of her desire continually generates further desire for the Transcendent."[30] You had to leave behind "all that can be grasped by sense or reason" so that "the only thing left for contemplation is the invisible and the incomprehensible."[31]

Gregory could see this process at work in the life of Moses. His first encounter with God had been the revelation of the Burning Bush, where he had learned that the God that called itself "I Am" was being itself. Everything else in the universe "that the senses perceive or intelligence contemplates" could only participate in the being that sustained it at every second.[32] After this initial revelation, Moses, like the great philosophers, had engaged in a disciplined contemplation of the natural world. But while nature could lead us to the Logos, through whom the world was made, it could not bring us to God itself. When Moses climbed Mount Sinai and entered the impenetrable darkness on its summit, however, he was in the place where God was—even though he could not see anything. He had at last left normal modes of perception behind and achieved an entirely different kind of seeing. Pushing his reason to the point where it could go no further, he had intuited the silent otherness that existed beyond the reach of words and concepts. Once the hesychast understood this, he realized that any attempt to define God clearly "becomes an idol of God and does not make him known."[33]

Gregory knew that many Christians were confused by the Nicaean statement. How could the Son have the same nature as the Father without becoming a second God? No longer familiar with traditional

Jewish terminology, they were also puzzled about the identity of the Holy Spirit. Gregory's older brother Basil, bishop of Caesarea (c. 330–79), took time out from his diocese to find a solution. Christians must stop thinking about God as *a* mere being, a larger and more powerful version of themselves. That was not what God was. The new doctrine of creation had made it clear that God was unknowable; our minds could think only about beings in the universe; we could not imagine the "nothingness" out of which our world was formed, because we could think only about things that had some kind of spatial extension or qualities. It was impossible for us to understand what had happened before our world was created, because we could think only in terms of time. This was what Saint John meant when he wrote "In the beginning was the Word."

> For thought cannot travel outside *was*, nor imagination beyond *beginning*. Let your thought travel ever so far backward you cannot get beyond the *was*, and however you may strain and strive to see what is beyond the Son, you will find it impossible to get back further than the *beginning*.[34]

What lies behind or beyond the universe is inconceivable to us. When we try to think of its "Creator" our minds simply seize up. But we could see signs and traces of God in our world. Reviving Philo's distinction between God's essential nature (*ousia*) and his "activities" (*energeiai*) in the world, Basil insisted that we could never know God's *ousia*; indeed, we should not even speak of it. Silence alone is appropriate for what lies beyond words. But we could form an idea about the divine "energies" that have, as it were, translated the ineffable God into a human idiom: the incarnate Word and the immanent divine presence within us that scripture calls the Holy Spirit.[35]

To show Christians that Father, Son, and Spirit were not three distinct "Gods," Basil formulated the doctrine of the Trinity. At first Christians thought that Jesus, the incarnate Logos, and the Holy Spirit were two separate divine beings. But Paul had explained that they were one and the same: "This Lord is the Spirit."[36] Because they were divine forces, Logos and Spirit were not finite or discrete like the beings of our ordinary experience. Over time Christians realized that because the divine energies they experienced in the rituals and practices of the church were indefinable and illimitable, "Logos" and "Spirit" must refer to the same divine power. God was not the sort of being that was defined by number or extension, so Father, Son, and Spirit were not three separate "gods." Pagans thought of their "gods" as members of the cosmos, with separate personalities and functions, but the Christian God was not that sort of being. When we spoke of Father, Son, and Spirit being One God, we were not saying "One plus one plus one equals three" but "Unknown infinity plus unknown infinity plus unknown infinity equals unknown infinity."[37] We think of the beings we know as single items or collections of different items. But God is not like that. Again, the absolute ineffability of the divine was the key to understanding the Trinity. The reason the Trinity is not a logical or numerical absurdity is because God is not a being that can be restricted to such human categories as number.

The Trinity has been very puzzling to Western Christians, but it has been central to Eastern Orthodox spirituality.[38] In the early modern period, when the West was developing a wholly rational way of thinking about God and the world, philosophers and scientists were appalled by the irrationality of the Trinity. But for the Cappadocian fathers—Basil, Gregory, and their friend Gregory of Nazianzus (329–90)—the whole point of the doctrine was to stop Christians from thinking about God in rational terms. If you did that, you could only think about God as *a* being, because that was all our minds were capable of. The Trinity was not a "mystery" that had to be believed but an image that Christians were supposed to contemplate in a particular way. It was a *mythos,* because it spoke of a truth that was not accessible to *logos,* and, like any myth, it made sense only when you translated it into practical action. When they meditated on the God that they had known as Three and One, Christians would become aware that God bore no relation at all to any being in their experience.[39] The Trinity reminded Christians *not* to think about God as a simple personality and that what we call "God" was inaccessible to rational analysis.[40] It was a meditative device to counter the idolatrous tendency of people like Arius, who had seen God as a mere being.

When they presented the Trinity to their new converts after the initiation of baptism, the three Cappadocians distinguished between the *ousia* of a thing, its inner nature, which made it what it was, and its *hypostases,* its external qualities. Each one of us has an *ousia* that we find very difficult to pin down but that we know to be the irreducible essence of our personality. It is what makes us the person we are, but it is very difficult to define. We try to express this *ousia* to the outside world in various *hypostases*—our work, offspring, possessions, clothes, facial expressions, and mannerisms, which can give outsiders only a partial knowledge of our inner, essential nature. Language is a very common *hypostasis:* my words are distinctively my own, but they are not the whole of me; they nearly always leave something unsaid. So in God there was, as it were, a single, divine self-consciousness that remained unknowable, unnameable, and unspeakable. But Christians had experienced this ineffability in *hypostases* that had translated it into something more accessible to limited, sense-bound, time-bound human beings. The Cappadocians sometimes substituted the term *prosopon* ("face," "mask") for *hypostasis;* the word also meant a facial expression or a role that an actor had chosen to play. When *prosopon* was translated into Latin, it became *persona,* the "mask" used by an actor that enabled the audience to recognize his character and contained a sound-enhancing device that made him audible.

But nobody was required to "believe" this as a divine fact. The Trinity was a "mystery" not because it was an incomprehensible conundrum that had to be taken "on faith." It was a *musterion* because it was an "initiation" that inducted Christians into a wholly different way of thinking about the divine. Basil always distinguished between the *kerygma* of the Church (its public message) and its *dogma,* the inner meaning of the *kerygma,* which could be grasped only after long immersion in liturgical prayer.[41] The Trinity was a prime example of *dogma,* a truth that brought us up against the limits of language but could be suggested by the symbolic gestures of the liturgy and the silent practice of *hesychia.* The initiation consisted of a spiritual exercise that was explained to new *mystai* after their baptism in a liturgical context. They were instructed to keep their minds in continuous motion, swinging back and forth between the One and the Three. This mental discipline would enable them gradually to experience within themselves the inner balance of the threefold mind.[42] Gregory of Nazianzus explained the kind of *ekstasis* this produced:

No sooner do I conceive of the One than I am illumined
by the splendour of the Three; no sooner do I distinguish

Three than I am carried back into the One. When I think
of any of the Three I think of him as the whole, and my
eyes are filled, and the greater part of what I am thinking
escapes me. I cannot grasp the greatness of that One so as
to attribute a greater greatness to the rest. When I see the
Three together, I see but one Torch, and cannot divine or
measure the undivided light.[43]

Trinity was not unlike a mandala, the icon of concentric circles
that Buddhists visualize in meditation to find within themselves an
ineffable "center" that pulls the scattered aspects of their being into
harmony. Trinity was an activity rather than an abstract metaphysical
doctrine. It is probably because most Western Christians have not
been instructed in this exercise that the Trinity remains pointless,
incomprehensible, and even absurd.

The *dogma* of Trinity also symbolized the *kenosis* that Christians
glimpsed at the heart of being. Each persona of the Trinity defers to
the others; none is sufficient unto itself. It is, perhaps, easier to express
this in a pictorial image. In Orthodox Christianity, the icon has a *dogmatic* function that expresses the inner truth of a doctrine, and a great
icon can have the same status as scripture.[44] One of the most famous
icons of all time is *The Old Testament Trinity* by the fifteenth-century
Russian painter Alexander Rublev, which has become an archetypal
image of the divine in the Orthodox world.[45] It is based on the story of
Abraham and the three strangers, whom Rublev depicts as angels,
messengers of the unknowable God. Each represents one of the
Trinitarian "persons"; they look interchangeable and can be identified only by their symbolically colored garments and the emblem
behind each one. Abraham's table has become an altar, and the elaborate meal he prepared has been reduced to the Eucharistic cup. The
three angels sit in a circle, emblem of perfection and infinity, and the
viewer is positioned on the empty side of the table. Immediately
Rublev suggests that Christians can experience the truth of the Trinity in the Eucharistic liturgy, in communion with God and one
another, and—recalling the Genesis story—in a life of compassion.
The central angel representing the Son immediately attracts our
attention, yet he does not return our gaze but looks toward the
Father, the angel on his right. Instead of returning his regard, the

Father directs his attention to the figure at the right of the painting, whose gaze is directed within. We are thus drawn into the perpetual circling motion described by Gregory of Nazianzus. This is not an overbearing deity, demanding exclusive loyalty and total attention to himself. We meet none of the *prosopoi* head-on; each refers us to the other in eternal personal dispossession.

There is no selfhood in the Trinity.[46] Instead there is silence and *kenosis*. The Father, the ground of being, empties itself of all that it is and transmits it to the Son, giving up everything, even the possibility of expressing itself in another Word. Once that Word has been spoken, the Father no longer has an "I" and remains forever silent and unknowable. There is nothing that we can say about the Father, since the only God we know is the Son. At the very source of being is the speechless "nothingness" of Brahman, Dao, and Nirvana, because the Father is not another being and resembles nothing in our mundane experience. The Father confounds all our notions of personality and, since the Father is presented in the New Testament as the end of the Christian quest, this becomes a journey to no place, no thing, and no one. In the same way, the Son, our only access to the divine, is merely an *eikon* of the ultimate reality, which remains, as the Upanishads insisted, "ungraspable." Like any symbol, the Son points beyond itself to the Father, while the Spirit is simply the atman of the Father and the "we" between Father and Son. We cannot pray *to* the Spirit, because the Spirit is the ultimate innerness of every being, ourselves included.

The Christians of Western Europe arrived at a similar understanding of the Trinity by a more psychological route, charted by Augustine (354–430), bishop of Hippo in North Africa.[47] Before his conversion to Christianity, Augustine had experienced a restless dissatisfaction that drove him from one *philosophia* to another. He tried materialism, hedonism, and Manichaeism (a Gnostic Christian sect) before he discovered Neoplatonism, which burst upon him, he recalled later, in a blaze of light and saved him from despair. Like his contemporaries, Augustine was appalled by the instability of the material world, which seemed to tremble on the brink of nothingness. At first he fought shy of Christianity. He found the idea of the incarnation offensive and was disappointed by the literary quality of the Bible. But his reading of Paul and the counsel of Ambrose, the saintly bishop of Milan (339–97), led to a dramatic conversion when "the light of steadfast trust poured into my heart, and all the shadows of hesitation fled away."[48] Apart from Saint Paul, no other Western theologian has been more influential than Augustine in both Protestant and Catholic Christianity. We know him more intimately than any other thinker of late antiquity because of his *Confessions,* a memoir that revealed his fascination with the working of the human mind that is also evident in his treatise *On the Trinity.*

Augustine fully understood the implications of the new creation doctrine that had rendered God unknowable. In one of the most famous passages of *The Confessions,* he made it clear that the study of the natural world could not give us information about God:

> Late have I loved you, Beauty so ancient and so new, late
> have I loved you! Behold, you were within and I was
> without [*foris*]; and there I sought you, plunging un-
> formed as I was into the fair things that you have formed
> and made. You were with me, and I was not with you. I
> was kept from you by the things that would not have
> been, were they not in you.[49]

God was "within" but Augustine could not find him because he was "outside himself" (*foris*). As long as he confined his quest to the external world, he remained trapped in the fragile mutability that so disturbed him.[50] When he questioned the physical world about God, the earth, the sea, the sky, and the heavenly bodies all replied, "I am not he, but it is he that made me."[51] But when he asked, "What, then, do I love in loving my God?"[52] Augustine knew that, like the Upanishadic sages, he could only answer, *"neti . . . neti":*

> No physical beauty, no temporal glory, no radiancy of
> light that commends itself to these eyes of mine; no sweet
> melody of songs tuned to every mode, no soft scent of
> flowers or of ointments or of perfumes, no manna, no
> honey, no limbs that can conceive corporal embrace.[53]

But God was all these things "to my inner man. There it is that a light shines on my soul that no place can contain, a sound is uttered no time can take away, a fragrance cast that no breath of wind can disperse, a savour given forth that eating cannot blunt. . . . This is what I love in loving my God."[54]

Scripture told us that we had been made in God's image and it was therefore possible to find an *eikon* within ourselves that, like any Platonic image, yearned toward its archetype. If we looked within, we would discover a triad in our minds in the faculties of memory (*memoria*), understanding (*intellectus*), and will or love (*voluntas*) that gave us an insight into the triune life of God. Augustine was fascinated by memory. It was far more than the faculty of recollection but comprised the whole mind, conscious and unconscious, and was the source of our mental life in the same way as the Father was the ground of being. When he contemplated *memoria*, Augustine was filled with awe: "It is something to be shuddered at, my God, a deep and endless multiplicity."

> What, then, am I, my God? What manner of creature am I? A life unconstant, manifold and utterly unmeasured. In the countless fields and grots and caverns of my memory, full beyond counting with countless kinds of things . . . I range, flitting this way and that. I go as deep in as I can, and nowhere is there an end; such is the force of memory. Such is the force of life in a man that lives this mortal life![55]

Memory gave us intimations of infinity, but to encounter the divine, it had to strain beyond itself to the *intellectus,* the place where the soul could encounter God in deepest intimacy.

When Augustine spoke of "intellect," he meant something different from a modern intellectual. *Intellectus* was not simply the faculty of logic, calculation, and argument.[56] In the ancient world, people saw "reason" as a hinterland, bounded on the one hand by our powers of discursive rationality (*ratio*) and on the other by *intellectus,* a kind of pure intelligence, which in India was called *buddhi.* So intellect was higher than reason, but without it we would not be able to reason at all. Left to itself, the human mind was incapable of looking dispassionately at the mutable beings of our world and making any kind of valid judgment about them, because it was itself fraught with impermanence and change. Augustine had only been able to recognize the inconstancy and impermanence of the world that had so troubled him before his conversion, because the Platonists told him that he had within him an innate standard of stability, a light within, "unchangeable and true that was above my changeable mind."[57] There was, therefore, a realm in the psyche where the mind was able to reach beyond itself. That was the intellect, the mind's *acies,* its "cutting edge,"[58] and *scintilla* ("spark").[59]

So when Augustine looked into the depths of his mind, he saw that it was modeled on the Trinity, the archetype of all being. In the human mind, memory generates the intellect, as the Father begets a Word that expresses the Father's essential nature. In the human mind, the intellect seeks out and loves the self it finds in the caverns of the memory that generated it, just as memory seeks out and loves the self-knowledge encapsulated in the intellect. This activity in our own minds is a pale reflection of the Spirit, the bond of love between Father and Son. As in God, the three different faculties—memory, understanding, and love—constitute "one life, one mind, and one essence" within ourselves.[60]

For Augustine, the Platonist, "knowing" was not an activity that he had initiated but something that happened to his mind. Knowledge was not a matter of assessing, defining, and manipulating an external object; the Known drew the thinker into an intimate relationship with itself.[61] In Augustine's Trinity, knowledge of God was inseparable from love of God. But Augustine did not expect his readers simply to take his word for all this; they too must undertake the introspection and meditation that had led to him to adopt this theology and make it a reality for themselves, otherwise, like any *mythos,* it would remain incredible.

Augustine was a complex man, and neither he nor his theology was flawless. He could be intolerant, misogynist, and depressive—this last tendency exacerbated by the fact that he witnessed the collapse of the western provinces of the Roman Empire, a calamity that was like a huge environmental disaster. A deep sadness pervades Augustine's later work. When he was ordained bishop of Hippo in 396, he became the subject of a vitriolic campaign of slander, was burdened by the administration of a viciously divided diocese, and was in poor health. That same year Alaric and his Visigoths invaded Greece, the first of the barbarian hordes that would bring the Roman Empire to its knees: in 410 Alaric sacked the city of Rome itself. The fall of Rome plunged Western Europe into a dark age that lasted some seven hundred years, its culture preserved only in isolated monasteries and libraries, bastions of civilization in a sea of barbarism. When Augustine died in 430, the Vandals had besieged Hippo and would burn the town to the ground the following year.

This is the context of Augustine's doctrine of Original Sin, one of his less positive contributions to Western theology. He produced an entirely novel exegesis of the second and third chapters of Genesis, which claimed that the sin of Adam had condemned all his descendants to eternal damnation. Despite the salvation wrought by Christ, humanity was still weakened by what Augustine called "concupiscence," the irrational desire to take pleasure in beings instead of God itself. It was experienced most acutely in the sexual act, when our reasoning powers are swamped by passion, God is forgotten, and creatures revel shamelessly in one another. The specter of reason dragged down by the chaos of lawless sensation reflected the tragedy of Rome, source of order, law, and civilization, brought low by the barbarian tribes. Jewish exegetes had never seen the sin of Adam in this catastrophic light, and the Greek Christians, who were not affected by the barbarian scourge, have never accepted the doctrine of Original Sin. Born in grief and fear, this doctrine has left Western Christians with a difficult legacy that linked sexuality indissolubly with sin and helped to alienate men and women from their humanity.

Even though the Greeks found his interpretation of the story of Adam and Eve far too literal, Augustine was no die-hard biblical literalist. He took science very seriously, and his "principle of accommodation" would dominate biblical interpretation in the West until well into the early modern period. God had, as it were, adapted revelation to the cultural norms of the people who had first received it.[62] One of the psalms, for example, clearly reflects the ancient view, long outmoded by Augustine's time, that there was a body of water above the earth that caused rainfall.[63] It would be absurd to interpret this text literally. God had simply accommodated the truths of revelation to the science of the day so that the people of Israel could understand it; today a text like this must be interpreted differently. Whenever the literal meaning of scripture clashed with reliable scientific information, Augustine insisted, the interpreter must respect the integrity of science or he would bring scripture into disrepute.[64] And there must be no unseemly quarreling about the Bible. People who engaged in acrimonious discussion of religious truth were simply in love with their own opinions and had forgotten the cardinal teaching of the Bible, which was the love of God and neighbor.[65] The exegete must not leave a text until he could make it "establish the reign of charity," and if a literal understanding of any biblical passage seemed to teach hatred, the text must be interpreted allegorically and forced to preach love.[66]

Augustine had absorbed the underlying spirit of Greek apophatic theology, but the West did not develop a fully fledged spirituality of silence until the ninth century, when the writings of an unknown Greek author were translated into Latin and achieved near-canonical status in Europe. He used the pseudonym Denys the Areopagite, Saint Paul's first Athenian convert,[67] but he was almost certainly writing toward the end of the fifth and the beginning of the sixth centuries. During the medieval period, Denys had a profound influence on nearly every major Western theologian. The fact that very few people have even heard of him today is, perhaps, a symptom of our current religious malaise.[68]

Denys saw no conflict between the Neoplatonic *philosophia* and Christianity, even though he was almost certainly writing in 529, when Emperor Justinian had closed down the Academy, driven its philosophers underground, and abolished the Eleusinian Mysteries. Plotinus had seen all beings radiating from the One, an outward movement that was balanced by the yearning of all beings to return to the primal Unity. In rather the same way, Denys imagined the creation as an *ekstatic,* almost erotic eruption of divine goodness, when God was, as it were, "carried outside of himself in the loving care he has for everything." Creation was not something that had happened once in the distant past but was a *mythos,* a continuous, timeless process in which, paradoxically, God was eternally "enticed away from his transcendent dwelling-place and comes to abide within all things," and yet had the "capacity to remain, nevertheless, within himself."[69]

But, of course, this was impossible to understand rationally, because our minds cannot think outside a universe of beings that are unable to do two irreconcilable things at once. Religious people are always talking about God, and it is important that they do so. But they also need to know when to fall silent. Denys's theological method was a deliberate attempt to bring all the Christians he taught—lay folk, monks, and clergy alike—to that point by making them conscious of the limits of language. We can do that only by talking about God and listening carefully to what we say. As Denys pointed out, in the Bible God is given fifty-two names.[70] God is called a rock and is likened to the sky, the sea, and a warrior. All that is fine, as far as it goes. Because God is always pouring itself into creatures, any one of them—even a rock—can tell us something about the divine. A rock is a very good symbol of God's permanence and stability. But because a rock is not alive, it is obviously worlds apart from the God that is life itself, so we will never be tempted to say that God *is* a rock. But the more sophisticated attributes of God—Ineffability, Unity, Goodness, and the like—are more dangerous, because they give us the false impression that we know exactly what God is like. "He" *is* Good, Wise, and Intelligent; "He" *is* One; "He" *is* Trinity.

In his treatise *The Divine Names,* Denys symbolically reproduced God's descent from his exalted solitude into the material world, so he began by discussing the more elevated and lofty divine attributes. At first, each one sounds perfectly appropriate, but closer examination reveals it to be inherently unsatisfactory. It is true that God is One—but this term properly applies only to beings defined by numerical quantities. God is Trinity but that does not mean that the three personae add up to any kind of triad that is familiar to us. God is Nameless—yet he has a multiplicity of names. God must be Intelligible—and yet God is Unknowable; God is certainly not "good" like a "good" human being or a "good" meal. Gradually, we become aware that even the most exalted things we say about God are bound to be misleading.[71]

Then, following God's descent into the depths of the material world, we consider the physical and obviously inadequate images of God in the Bible. These texts cannot, of course, be read literally, because they are full of "so many incredible or fictitious fairy tales." From the very first chapter of Genesis, the Bible calls God a creator "as if he was a mere artisan" but goes on to say even more ludicrous things. Scripture supplies God

> with horses and chariots and thrones and provides delicately prepared banquets and depicts Him drinking and drunk, and drowsy and suffering from a hangover.

> And what about God's fits of anger, His griefs, His vari-
> ous oaths, His moments of repentance, His curses, His
> wraths, the manifold and crooked reasons given for His
> failure to fulfil promises?[72]

But crass as this seems, it is valuable, because this gross *theologia* shocks us into an appreciation of the limitations of all theological language.[73] We have to remember this when we speak about God, listen critically to ourselves, realize that we are babbling incoherently, and fall into an embarrassed silence.

When we listen to the sacred text read aloud during Mass and apply this method to the readings, we start to understand that even though God has revealed these names to us, we have no idea what they can mean. So we have to deny them, one after the other, and in the process make a symbolic *ascent* from earthly modes of perception to the divine. It is easy to deny the physical names: God is plainly *not* a rock, a gentle breeze, a warrior, or a creator. But when we come to the more conceptual descriptions of God, we find that we have to deny these too. God is *not* Mind in any sense that we can understand; God is *not* Greatness, Power, Light, Life, Truth, Imagination, Conviction, Understanding, Goodness—or even Divinity.[74] We cannot even say that God "exists" because our experience of existence is based solely on individual, finite beings whose mode of being bears no relation to being itself:

> Therefore . . . God is known by knowledge and by
> unknowing; of him there *is* understanding, reason,
> knowledge, touch, perception, opinion, imagination,
> name and many other things, but he is *not* understood,
> *nothing* can be said of him, he *cannot* be named. He is *not*
> one of the things that *are,* nor is he known in any of the
> things that are; he *is* all things in everything and *nothing*
> in anything.[75]

This was not simply an arid logical conundrum that left people in a baffled, thwarted state. It was a spiritual exercise that, if properly performed, would bring participants to the same kind of stunned insight as did the Brahmodya competition.

Denys's spiritual exercise took the form of a dialectical process, consisting of three phases. First we must affirm what God is: God is a rock; God is One; God is good; God exists. But when we listen carefully to ourselves, we fall silent, felled by the weight of absurdity in such God talk. In the second phase, we deny each one of these attributes. But the "way of denial" is just as inaccurate as the "way of affirmation." Because we do not know what God is, we cannot know what God is not, so we must then deny the denials: God is therefore *not* placeless, mindless, lifeless, or nonexistent. In the course of this exercise, we learn that God transcends the capability of human speech and "is beyond every assertion" and "beyond every denial."[76] It is as inaccurate to say that God is "darkness" as to say that God is "light"; to say that God "exists" as to say that God does "not exist," because what we call God falls "neither within the predicate of existence or non-existence."[77] But what can this mean? The exercise leads us to *apophasis,* the breakdown of speech, which cracks and disintegrates before the absolute unknowability of what we call God.

As our language fails, we experience an intellectual *ekstasis.* We no longer pay mere lip service to God's ineffability; the fact that "there is no kind of thing that God is"[78] has become an insight that we have made our own, a *kenosis* that "drives us out of ourselves."[79] Like the *mystai* of Eleusis, we have become strangers to our former ways of thinking and speaking. This new understanding is not an emotional experience. If we cannot know God, we certainly can neither feel nor have any sensation of unity with God. Denys's dialectical method leads to an intellectual rapture that takes us beyond everyday perceptions and introduces us to another mode of seeing. Like Moses at the top of the mountain, we embrace the darkness and experience no clarity, but know that, once we have rinsed our minds of inadequate ideas that block our understanding, we are somehow in the place where God is.

> Renouncing all that the mind may conceive, wrapped entirely in the intangible and the invisible, [Moses] belongs completely to him who is beyond everything. Here, being neither oneself nor someone else, one is supremely united to the completely unknown by an inactivity of all knowledge, and knows beyond the mind by knowing nothing.[80]

Once we have left the idols of thought behind, we are no longer worshipping a simulacrum, a projection of our own ideas and desires. There are no longer any false ideas obstructing our access to the inexpressible truth, and, like Moses, forgetful of self, we can remain silently in the presence of the unknown God.

But this would, of course, be incomprehensible unless you had personally put yourself through this spiritual exercise again and again. Denys did not regard this *ekstasis* as an exotic "peak" experience. Everybody, priests and lay folk alike, should apply this threefold dialectical method to the scriptures as they listened to them read aloud during the liturgy. When they heard God called "Rock," "Creator," "Wise," or "Good," they must affirm, deny, and then deny the denial, becoming in the process ever more conscious of the inadequacy of all theological language—even the inspired words of scripture. At key moments they would be able to "hear" the silence of the ineffable other that lay beyond the limits of speech. In his *Mystical Theology*, Denys applied his method to the ceremonies of the liturgy, to bring to light the deeper meaning of these ritualized symbolic gestures.[81] This was a communal rather than a solitary *ekstasis*. Priests and congregants should plunge *together* "into that darkness which is beyond intellect." Eventually, Denys concluded, "*We* shall find ourselves not simply running short of words but actually speechless and unknowing."[82]

Denys's theology was based on the liturgy of Alexandria, which instead of simply regarding the Eucharist as a reenactment of Jesus's last supper also saw it as an allegory of the soul's ascent to God.[83] His method was not for an elite group of contemplatives but seems to have been part of the public instruction of all the baptized faithful, who would have found it easy to follow his imagery of descent and ascent because it was familiar to them in the liturgy. When the celebrant left the sanctuary and walked among the congregation, sprinkling them with holy water, the people should see this as a symbolic reenactment of the *ekstasis* in which God perpetually abandoned its lonely solitude and merged with creation. When the celebrant turned his back on the congregation, entered the inner sanctum, and disappeared from view to consecrate the bread and wine, Denys compared him to Moses, when he left the people and, "accompanied by certain priests," entered the "mysterious darkness of unknowing" on the summit of Mount Sinai.[84]

Like all doctrinal instruction in the Greek Orthodox world, Denys's method was practiced in the heightened atmosphere of the liturgy. The evocative music, stylized drama, clouds of fragrant incense, and numinous solemnity all ensured that the dialectical process was not a dry, cerebral exercise but was performed in a context that, like any great aesthetic performance, touched people and stirred them at a deeper level of their being. As they heard the words of scripture read aloud in a special chant that separated it from normal discourse, and attended critically, as Denys had taught them, to the words of the prayers and hymns, clergy and congregants would in effect be saying to themselves, *"Neti . . . neti":* the reality we call God was *not* this, *not* that, but immeasurably other. The liturgy had always been a *musterion,* a ritual that initiated all the participants into a different mode of seeing. When Denys spoke of his mentor Bishop Hierotheus, he used terms associated with the Eleusinian Mysteries that Emperor Justinian had just abolished. Hierotheus did not "learn" (*mathein*) these truths simply by studying the doctrines of the church, but by allowing the beauty and symbolism of the liturgy to act upon him, he "experienced" or "suffered (*pathein*) divine things." Denys implies that Hierotheus imparted the knowledge he had intuited to the people not by speaking about it but in the way he performed the liturgy, which made it obvious that he had achieved an empathetic *sympatheia* with the rites.[85]

In the East, Denys was merely regarded as a disciple of the Cappadocians and Maximus, the major luminaries of Greek Orthodoxy, but in the West he enjoyed enormous prestige and became a leading authority. His writings were translated into Latin by the Irish theologian John Scotus Erigena (810–877), who worked in the court of Charles the Bald, king of the West Franks. In his writings, like Denys, Erigena insisted that God is "Nothing" because he does not possess "being" in any sense that we could understand. But God is also "Everything," because every single creature that God informs becomes a theophany, a manifestation of God. Erigena also translated the works of Gregory of Nyssa, Maximus, and other Greek fathers, making Orthodox wisdom available to the traumatized West, which was beginning to crawl out of the long period of barbarism that had succeeded the fall of Rome and rejoin the outside world. In the West, people took Denys's pseudonym seriously, and his supposed connection with Saint Paul gave him near-apostolic status. Western theologians tended not to apply his method liturgically, since their Mass was different from the Alexandrian ritual. But the apophatic method was central to the way leading European theologians understood religious truth and to the way they instructed the laity to think about God. By the medieval period, the apophatic habit had become ingrained in Western Christian consciousness.

# SIX

# Faith and Reason

B y the end of the eleventh century, philosophers and theologians in the West had embarked on a project that, they believed, was entirely new. They had begun to apply their reasoning powers systematically to the truths of faith. By now Europe was beginning to recover from the dark age that had descended after the fall of Rome. The Benedictine monks of Cluny in Burgundy had initiated a campaign to educate the clergy and laity, many of whom were woefully ignorant of the rudiments of Christianity. Hundreds of churches were built throughout Christendom, even in quite small villages and settlements, where people could attend Mass and hear the biblical readings. This instruction was reinforced by the cult of pilgrimage. During the long, difficult trek to a holy place— Jerusalem, Rome, Santiago de Compostela, Conques, or Glastonbury—lay folk experienced a "conversion" of life, turning away from their secular affairs and toward the centers of holiness. They traveled in a community of pilgrims, dedicated for the duration to the monastic ideals of austerity, charity, celibacy, and nonviolence. The rich had to share the hardships of the poor, who, in turn, realized that their poverty had spiritual value.[1] Instead of being educated in the niceties of doctrine, Western Christians were introduced to their faith as a practical way of life. By the end of the century, there was a marked rise in commitment among the laity, and Europeans had begun to forge a new and distinctively Western Christian identity.

Meanwhile, as they became reacquainted with the intellectual heritage of their more sophisticated neighbors in the Greek Byzantine and Islamic worlds, European monks had started to think and pray in a more "rational" way. One of the leading exponents of this new spirituality was Anselm of Laon, abbot of the prestigious monastery and school at Bec in Normandy, who was appointed archbishop of Canterbury by William Rufus in 1093.[2] Excited by the new vogue for reasoning, he wanted to make traditional Christian teaching rationally coherent. There was no question of making his loyalty to God dependent upon rational proof; instead he saw his writings "advancing through faith to understanding, rather than proceeding through understanding to faith."[3] Men and women had to use all their faculties when they approached God, and Anselm wanted to make truths grasped intuitively intelligible, so that every part of his mind was involved in the contemplation of God. Augustine had taught the Christians of the West that all their mental activities reflected the divine, and this was particularly true of their reasoning powers. "I confess, Lord, with thanksgiving," Anselm prayed in his *Proslogion* ("Colloquy") with God, "that you have made me in your image, so that I can remember you, think of you and love you."[4] This was the raison d'être of every "rational creature," so people must spare no effort in "remembering, understanding and loving the Supreme Good."[5]

But it was extremely difficult to think about God or even to work up any enthusiasm for contemplation. Anselm was acutely aware of the torpor that made prayer so difficult. In the opening verses of the *Proslogion,* which takes the form of a highly wrought poem, he laments his sense of alienation from the divine. The image of God within him was so obscured by his imperfections that, try as he would, he could not perform the task for which he had been created. He must, therefore, shake off this mental sloth, using his intellect, reason, imagination, and emotion to stir up and excite his mind; his newfound rational powers in particular were a God-given tool for rousing and kindling the spirit.

But he had no illusions about human reason, which he knew was incapable of understanding the unknowable God. "Lord, I am not trying to make my way to your height," he prayed, "for my understanding is in no way equal to that."[6] He simply wanted to grasp

> a little of your truth, to which my heart is already loyal
> and which it loves [*quem credit et amat cor meum*]. For I

do not seek to understand in order that I may have faith
[*intellegere ut credam*], but I commit myself in order that I
may understand [*credo ut intellgam*]; and what is more, I
am certain that unless I so commit myself I shall not
understand.[7]

Anselm is still using the verb *credere* in its original sense: it is an affair
of the "heart," the center of the human being, rather than a purely
notional act and, as for Augustine, inseparable from love. Because the
word "belief" has changed its meaning since Anselm's day, it is misleading to translate, as is often done, *credo ut intellgam* as: "I believe in
order that I may understand." This gives the impression that before
one can have any comprehension of the loyalty and trust of faith, one
must first force one's mind to accept blindly a host of incomprehensible doctrines. Anselm is saying something quite different: religious
truth made no sense without practically expressed commitment. Perhaps a better translation is "I involve myself in order that I may
understand." Anselm was trying to shake off his lethargy in prayer by
engaging all his faculties, and was certain that "unless I so involve
myself, I shall not understand." So to spark his reader's interest, he
invites him to consider what has been called the "ontological proof"
for the existence of God.

In the second chapter of the *Proslogion,* he asks God to help him to
understand "that you exist" in the way that he has been taught.[8]
Denys would not have approved of such a project, because God could
not be said to "exist" in any way that human beings could understand.
But Anselm was trying to express a similar insight in the new fash-
ionably metaphysical terminology, in a way that would excite an
eleventh-century reader. He defined God as "that thing than which
nothing more perfect can be thought [*aliquid quo nihil maius cogitari
possit*]."[9] He was asking his readers to think of the greatest thing that
they could imagine or conceive—but then go on to reflect that God
was even greater and more perfect than that. God must transcend any
"thing" that the human mind could envisage.

As a Platonist, it was natural for Anselm to think that the very
nature (*ontos*) of God contains within it the necessity for God's existence. "Lord my God," he prays, "you so truly *are,* that it is not possible to think of you as not existing."[10] Since thought was something

that happened to the thinker, an idea in the mind was an intimate encounter with the Known, so in an intellectual world still dominated by Platonism, this was a perfectly acceptable argument. Anselm had no doubt that God existed, so he was not trying to convince a skeptic. The only "atheist" he could imagine was the "fool" quoted in the Psalms who says that "there is no God."[11] Anselm believed that the idea of God was innate: even this atheist had an idea of God in his mind or he would not have been able to deny it. Even though we live in such an imperfect world, we have a notion of absolute perfection and completeness. But a perfect thing that existed only in the mind would be a contradiction in terms, since to exist in reality (*in re*) is both greater and more complete than to exist merely as a mental concept:

> If that than which nothing greater [*maius*] can be thought exists in the understanding alone, then this thing than which nothing greater can be thought is something than which a greater can be thought. And this is clearly impossible.[12]

Therefore, Anselm concluded, "there can be no doubt at all" that this "something greater" exists "both in the understanding and in reality."[13] A modern person, who inhabits an entirely different intellectual universe, cannot assume that simply because he thinks he has a hundred dollars, the money will materialize in his pocket.[14] But Anselm was not attempting a scientific or logical "proof"; rather, he was using his reasoning powers to stir up his sluggish mind so that it could "involve" itself with the immanent divine reality. And built into this "proof" was the apophatic conviction that any idea that human beings could conceive of God would inevitably fall short of the reality.

For the monks of medieval Europe, *lectio* ("reading") was not conducted simply to acquire information but was a spiritual exercise that enabled them to enter their inner world and there confront the truths revealed in scripture to see how they measured up. Reading—in private or in the communal practice of the liturgy—was part of a process of personal transformation.[15] Every day, a monk spent time in *lectio divina,* ruminating on the sacred page until it had become an interior reality. *Lectio* was a pleasant, leisurely exercise; a monk could proceed at his own pace until the words ignited and he "heard" their inner meaning. In his *Prayers and Meditations,* Anselm was taking this practice a stage further. Instead of communicating with the divine through the words of the Bible, he addressed God directly in his own words. He was also writing for men and women who wanted to practice *lectio divina.* In the preface, he explained that these prayers were "not to be read in a turmoil, but quietly, not skimmed or hurried through, but taken a little at a time with deep and thoughtful meditation."[16] Readers must feel free to dip into the book and leave off wherever they choose. Its purpose was not to inform but to "stir up the mind of the reader to the love and fear of God or to self-examination."[17] In this way, *lectio* would lead to a moment of reflection, awe, or insight. So in order to benefit, the reader must withdraw, mentally and physically, from the pressures of daily life and approach each meditation in a receptive frame of mind:

> Come now, little man, turn aside for a while from your
> daily employment, escape for a moment from the tumult
> of thoughts. . . . Enter into the inner chamber of your
> soul, shut out everything except God and that which can
> help you in seeking him, and when you shut the door,
> seek him.[18]

You could not approach religious ideas in the same way as you conducted business or engaged in an argument in daily life. This *logos*-driven mentality had to be set to one side in order for these prayers and meditations to come to life in the mind.

Anselm did not arrive at his "proof" by means of a strictly rational, logical process. His monks had begged him for a meditation on the meaning of faith (*fides*), and for a long time he had struggled to find a single, self-evident argument for the reality of God. He was about to give up when an idea forced itself upon him with increasing urgency, until finally, "when I was tired out with resisting its importunity, that which I had despaired of finally came to me."[19] His biographer Eadmer said that the "proof" arrived in a moment of rapture involving both heart and head: "Suddenly one night during matins, the grace of God illumined his heart, the whole matter becoming clear in his mind, and a great joy and exultation filled his whole being."[20] Later writers would have dwelled in detail on this "experience," but it does not seem to have interested either Anselm or Eadmer. Anselm was simply concerned with how best he could use it to help others. "It seemed to me that this thing which had given me such joy to discover would, if it were written down, give pleasure to any who might read it," he explained. So he gave the *Proslogion* the subtitle *fides quaerens intellectum,* "Faith in Search of Understanding."[21]

Anselm was not the first to attempt a "proof" of God's existence. During the eighth and ninth centuries, the Muslims in the Abbasid Empire had enjoyed a cultural florescence, inspired by the encounter with ancient Greek, Syriac, and Sanskrit texts, which had recently been translated into Arabic. Many of these translators were local Christians. First they had tackled the more positive sciences, such as medicine and astronomy; then they had turned their attention to the metaphysical works of Plato, Aristotle, and Plotinus, so that gradually the philosophical and scientific heritage of ancient Greece became available to the Arabic-speaking world—but with a scientific bias. Muslims began to study astronomy, alchemy, medicine, and mathematics with such success that they made impressive discoveries of their own and developed their own tradition of what they called *falsafah* (philosophy). Like the European philosophes of the eighteenth century, the *faylasufs* wanted to live in accordance with the rational laws that, they believed, governed the cosmos. They were scientists and mathematicians and wanted to apply what they had learned to their religion.

Following the example of the Greek philosophers, they began to devise their own proofs for God's existence, based on Aristotle's arguments for the Prime Mover and Plotinus's doctrine of emanation.[22] Like Anselm, none of the leading *faylasufs*—Yaqub ibn Ishaq al-Kindi (d. c. 870), Muhammad ibn Zakaria ar-Razi (d. c. 930), and Abu Nasr al-Farabi (d. 980)—had any doubts of God's existence, but they wanted to integrate their scientific knowledge with Qur'anic teaching. Many practiced the spiritual exercises of the Sufis, the mystics of Islam, finding that these yogic techniques of concentration and chanting of mantras added a new dimension to their studies. The more radical found the idea of creation ex nihilo unacceptable on philosophical grounds, but they believed that *falsafah* and scripture were both valid paths to God, because they served the needs of different individuals. At the same time, they were convinced that *falsafah* was a more developed form of religiosity because it was not rooted in a particular time and place but had universal appeal. The most distinguished *faylasuf,* Abu Ali ibn Sina (c. 980–1037), known in the West as Avicenna, argued that a prophet enjoyed a direct, intuitive knowledge of God that was similar to the Sufis' and had therefore been able to bypass reason and logic, but *falsafah* could refine the idea of the divine, purge it of superstition and anthropomorphism, and prevent it from becoming idolatrous.

*Falsafah* was a valuable and instructive experiment. The Muslim philosophers were open to new ideas and had no qualms about learning from Greeks who had sacrificed to idols. "We should not be ashamed to acknowledge truth and to assimilate it from whatever source it comes to us, even if it is brought to us by former generations and foreign peoples," al-Kindi had remarked.[23] It is always dangerous to isolate religious ideas from contemporary thought. As one tenth-century *faylasuf* insisted, the seeker after truth must "shun no sciences, scorn no book, nor cling fanatically to a single creed."[24] Their stringent rationalism led some to develop a radically apophatic vision. Ibn Sina argued that God's oneness meant that God was perfectly simple: Allah had no attributes that were distinct from his essential being, so there was absolutely nothing that reason could say about him, even though we could infer God's goodness, life, and power from our own experience of these qualities. In the same vein, Abu Yaqub al-Sijistani (d. 971), who belonged to the Ismaili sect, developed a dialectical method similar to Denys's, based on the affirmation and denial of the divine names.

But the God of the philosophers seemed dangerously close to the old Sky Gods, who had become so remote that they faded from the consciousness of their worshippers. Despite its desire to accommodate the faith of the masses, *falsafah* remained a minority pursuit and put down no roots in the Muslim world. Most Muslims found it impossible to engage with this distant God, who seemed a mere abstraction, was unaware that human beings existed, and could not possibly communicate with them. The *faylasufs* themselves may have found that the Sufi rituals helped to make this austere deity a more vibrant reality for them, and at the end of his life, Ibn Sina seems to have been evolving a philosophy based on intuitive insight as well as reason.

So did Abu Hamid al-Ghazzali (1058–1111), an emblematic figure in the history of religious philosophy. A rising star in the intellectual establishment of Baghdad, he had made an intensive study of *falsafah* and could tackle the ideas of al-Farabi and Ibn Sina on their own terms. Finally, in *The Incoherence of the Philosophers*, al-Ghazzali declared that the *faylasufs* had contravened their own principles. Our rational powers could investigate only observable data, so while *falsafah* was competent in mathematics, astronomy, and medicine, it could tell us nothing about matters that lay beyond the reach of the senses. When the *faylasufs* spoke of God, therefore, they were guilty of *zannah,* fanciful guesswork. How could they prove the theory of divine emanation? What was their evidence for saying that God knew nothing of mundane affairs? In going beyond their brief, the philosophers had been unphilosophical.

Al-Ghazzali was looking for certainty, but he could not find it in any contemporary intellectual movement. His doubts became so severe that he suffered a breakdown and was forced to abandon his prestigious academic post. For ten years he lived in Jerusalem, engaged in the rituals and contemplative disciplines of the Sufis; and when he returned to his teaching duties, he insisted that only spiritual exercises of this kind could provide us with certainty (*wujud*) about the existence of God. It was a waste of time to try to prove the existence of Allah, as the *faylasufs* had done: because God was being itself, an all-encompassing reality, it could not be perceived in the same way as the mere beings that we see, hear, or touch. But that did not mean that the divine was wholly inaccessible. We could, as it were, catch a glimpse of God by cultivating a different mode of perception, as the Sufis did when they chanted the names of Allah like a mantra and performed the meditative exercises that induced an altered state of consciousness.

But those who did not have the time, talent, or inclination for this type of spirituality could make themselves conscious of God in the smallest details of daily life. Al-Ghazzali developed a spirituality that would enable every single Muslim to become aware of the interior dimension of Muslim law. They should deliberately call to mind the divine presence when they performed such ordinary actions as eating, washing, preparing for bed, praying, almsgiving, and greeting one another. They must guard their ears from slander and obscenity, their tongues from lies; they must refrain from cursing or sneering at others. Their hands must not harm another creature; their hearts must remain free of envy, anger, hypocrisy, and pride.[25] This vigilance—similar to that practiced by Stoics, Epicureans, Buddhists, and Jains—would bridge the gap between outward observance and interior commitment; it would transform the smallest action of daily life into a ritual that made God present in the lives of ordinary men and women, even if they could not prove this rationally.

It has been said that al-Ghazzali was the most important Muslim since the Prophet Muhammad. After al-Ghazzali, one great philosopher after another—Yahya Suhrawardi (d. 1191), Muid ad-Din ibn al-Arabi (1165–1240), Jalal ad-Din Rumi (1207–73), Mir Dimad (d. 1631), and his pupil Mulla Sadra (1571–1640)—insisted that theology must be fused with spirituality. The philosopher had a sacred duty to be as intellectually rigorous as Aristotle and as mystical as a Sufi; reason was indispensable for science, medicine, and mathematics, but a reality that transcended the senses could be approached only by more intuitive modes of thought. During the twelfth and thirteenth centuries, Sufism ceased to be a fringe movement and remained the dominant Islamic mode until the nineteenth century. Ordinary laypeople practiced Sufi exercises, and these disciplines helped them to get beyond simplistically anthropomorphic ideas of God and experience the divine as a transcendent presence within.

The Jews in the Islamic empire, who were so excited by *falsafah* that they developed a philosophical movement of their own, had a similar experience. Writing for the most part in Arabic, they introduced a metaphysical dimension into Judaism. From the beginning, they were concerned about the contrast between the remote God of the philosophers and the highly personalized God of the Bible. One of the first Jewish *faylasufs*, Saadia ibn Joseph (882–942), for example, found the idea of creation ex nihilo fraught with philosophical difficulties. In the main, however, Jewish philosophers tended to be less radical than the Muslims, did not concern themselves with science, confined their attention to religious matters, and concluded in the main that reason's chief use was to help the philosopher give a more systematic explanation of religious truth. Maimonides (1134–1204), the greatest of the Jewish rationalists, believed that *falsafah* was unsuitable for the laity, but it could wean Jews from their more facile ideas of God. Maimonides developed an apophatic spirituality that denied any positive attributes to God, arguing that we could not even say that God was good or existed. A person who relied on this kind of affirmation would make God incredible, he warned in his *Guide to the Perplexed,* and "unconsciously loses his belief in God."[26]

But again, for most Jews the God of the philosophers was too abstract, unable to offer any consolation in times of persecution and suffering. Increasingly they turned to the mystical spirituality of the Kabbalah, which was developed in Spain during the late thirteenth century. Some of the pioneers of this spirituality—Abraham Abulafia, Moses de Leon, Isaac de Latif, and Joseph Gikatilla—had been involved in *falsafah* but found its attenuated God empty of religious content.[27] Yet they used philosophic motifs, such as divine emanation, to describe the process whereby the utterly unknowable Godhead, which they called En Sof ("Without End"), had emerged from its lonely inaccessibility and made itself known to humanity. Like Sufism, Kabbalah was an unashamedly mythical and imaginative spirituality. Until the modern period, it would inform the piety of many Jews and, as we shall see, would even become a mass movement.

In the Muslim world, Jews, Christians, and Muslims were able to collaborate and learn from one another. But in Western Europe, during the last years of Anselm's life, the first Crusades were launched against Islam. In 1096, some of the Crusaders attacked the Jewish communities along the Rhine valley, and when they finally conquered Jerusalem in July 1099, they massacred some thirty thousand Jews and Muslims; the blood was said to have come up to the knees of their horses. Crusading was the first cooperative act of the new Europe as it struggled back onto the international stage. It appealed to the knights, who were men of war and wanted an aggressive religion, and would remain a major passion in the West until the end of the thirteenth century. This was, of course, an idolatrous catastrophe and one of the most shameful developments in Western Christian history. The Crusaders' God was an idol; they had foisted their own fear and loathing of these rival faiths onto a deity they had created in their own likeness and thus given themselves a sacred seal of absolute approval. Crusading made anti-Semitism an incurable disease in Europe and would indelibly scar relations between Islam and the West.

But it was not the whole story. At the same time as Christians were slaughtering Muslims in the Near East, others were traveling to Spain to study under Muslim scholars in Córdoba and Toledo. Here they discovered the works of Aristotle and other Greek scientists and philosophers whose work had been lost to them after the fall of Rome. They also encountered the work of the Jewish and Muslim *faylasufs*. With the help of the local Jews, European scholars translated these writings from Arabic into Latin, and by the beginning of the thirteenth century, a wide array of Greek and Arabic scientific and philosophical works had become available to Europeans. This influx of new knowledge sparked an intellectual renaissance. The discovery of Aristotle in particular showed theologians how to present their doctrines in a coherent system.

This reminds us that in any age, the religious life is always multifarious, varied, and contradictory—even within a single individual. One of the most famous Europeans of the period was Francis of Assisi (1181–1226). His life and career show us that while some Europeans were engaged in scholarly rationalism, others like Francis had no time for theology of any kind and were far more literal-minded than the apophatic Anselm. Yet Francis's literalism, like that of the pilgrims, was neither intellectual nor doctrinal but practical. He represented a strand of popular piety that saw the life of Christ as primarily a *miqra* to be imitated literally down to the last detail. Francis emulated the absolute poverty of Christ in his own life; he and the Franciscan friars who followed him begged for their food, went barefoot, owned no property, and slept rough. He even reproduced the wounds of Christ in his own body. And yet this gentle saint seems to have approved of the Crusades and accompanied the Fifth Crusade to Egypt, though he did not take part in the fighting but preached to the sultan.

As I explained at the outset, my aim is not to give an exhaustive account of religion in any given period, but to highlight a particular trend—the apophatic—that speaks strongly to our current religious perplexity. This was, of course, not the only strand of medieval piety, but it was not a minor movement; it was promoted by some of the most influential thinkers and spiritual leaders of the time. In the Eastern Church, it had been crafted by Athanasius, the Cappadocians, and Maximus, who were revered as heroes of Orthodoxy. In the West, we see it in both Augustine and Anselm, as well as in the towering figure of Thomas Aquinas (1225–74).

Nobody did more to absorb Aristotelian rationalism than Thomas. Destined for a monastic life, at the age of fourteen Thomas was attracted to the Dominican friars he encountered at the University of Naples, the only school in Christendom at that time to teach Aristotelian logic and philosophy. Like the Franciscans, the Dominicans were the men of the hour; these friars were not monks sequestered in a monastery but lived a life of evangelical poverty in the world, putting themselves at the service of the people. After a struggle with his family, Thomas threw in his lot with the Dominicans, studied in Paris under Albert the Great (1200–80), who was completing his magisterial commentary on Aristotle, and at the tender age of thirty-two, succeeded to his chair. Like the *faylasufs*, Thomas was wide open to change and new ideas. He quoted Arab and Jewish philosophers while most of his contemporaries were still committed to crusading, and his voluminous writings integrated the new sciences with traditional faith at a time when Aristotle was still a controversial figure.[28]

It is difficult for us to read Thomas today. He wrote in the technical language of the new metaphysics, and his style is dry, understated, and dense. But it is also confident. Within a hundred years, the intellectual climate would change and theologians would become warier of the intellect, but Thomas had no qualms about making affirmative, positive statements about God. He thought Maimonides was wrong to insist that it was only appropriate to use negative terms that said what God was *not*. For Thomas—as for Denys, whom he greatly revered—affirmative speech and the silence of denial were both essential to God talk. As Being itself (*ipsum Esse subsistens*), God was the source of everything that existed, so all beings made in God's image could tell us something about him. It was also permissible to exploit the exciting new techniques of logic and inference—but with one important proviso. Whenever he made a statement about God, the theologian must realize that it was inescapably inadequate. When we contemplate God, we are thinking of what is beyond thought; when we speak of God, we are talking of what cannot be contained in words. By revealing the inherent limitation of words and concepts, theology should reduce both the speaker and his audience to silent awe. When reason was applied to faith, it must show that what we call "God" was beyond the grasp of the human mind. If it failed to do this, its statements about the divine would be idolatrous.

Even revelation could not tell us anything about God; indeed, its task was to make us realize that God was unknowable. "Man's utmost knowledge is to know that we do not know him," Thomas explained.

> For then alone do we know God truly, when we believe that he is far above all that man can possibly think of God . . . by the fact that certain things about God are proposed to man, which surpass his reason, he is strengthened in his opinion that God is far above what he is able to think.[29]

Even Christ had transcended our conceptual grasp and become unknowable. At his ascension, he was hidden in the cloud that received him, and taken into a realm that is beyond the reach of our intellect. As Saint Paul said, he is "far above . . . any name that can be named."[30] The ascension, therefore, revealed the limits of our knowledge; when Christ left the world, the Word was concealed from us again and would always remain unknowable and unnameable.

Thomas's huge output can be seen as a campaign to counter the tendency to domesticate the divine transcendence. In this he is absolutely true to Denys. But where Denys's theology was based on liturgy, Thomas's apophaticism was rooted in the new metaphysical rationalism. His long and, to a modern sensibility, tortuous analyses should be seen as an intellectual ritual that leads the mind through a labyrinth of thought until it culminates in the final *musterion*. Thomas's influence on Roman Catholic thought has been immense, but he has recently become a laughingstock to atheists (as well as an embarrassment to some theologians) because of the apparent inadequacy of his five "proofs" for the existence of God.

These five "ways" (*viae*), as Thomas preferred to call them, are to be found at the very beginning of the *Summa Theologiae*, his most famous work. This was a teaching manual designed "to introduce beginners to what God taught us as concisely and clearly as the subject matter allows,"[31] and it begins with the most fundamental question of all: Is there a God? This, Thomas believed, needs demonstration, because even though he thought that knowledge of God was innate, it was often vague and even crude. Thomas explicitly dissociated himself from Anselm's "ontological proof": the proposition that "God exists" was not at all self-evident but "needs to be made evident by means of things that are more evident to us, namely, God's effects." Paul had argued that "ever since God created the world his everlasting power and deity—however invisible—have been there for the mind to see in the things that he has made."[32] It was, therefore, possible to argue "from visible effects to hidden causes," because, as Aristotle had made clear, every effect must have a cause, so "God's effects then are enough to prove that God exists." But the doctrine of creation ex nihilo meant that the creatures "are not enough to help us comprehend *what* he is."[33] So before he sets out his "proofs," Thomas tells his students that because of God's absolute unknowability we cannot define what it is that we are trying to prove.

> When we know that something is, it remains to enquire in what *way* it is, so that we may know *what* it is. But since concerning God we cannot know what he is but only what he is not, we cannot consider in what way God is but only in what way he is not. So first we must ask in what way he is not, secondly how he may be known to us, and thirdly how we may speak of him.[34]

We cannot speak about God itself; we can speak only about the contingency of his creatures, which came from nothing.

Having made this crucial apophatic proviso, Thomas briefly—indeed, somewhat perfunctorily—sets forth his five "ways" of arguing from creatures to "what people call God."[35] These five arguments are not original. The first is based on Aristotle's proof of the Prime Mover: all around us, we see things changing, and because every change is caused by something else, the chain of cause and effect must stop somewhere. We thus arrive at the First Cause, itself unchanged by anything. The second proof, closely allied to the first, is based on the nature of causation: we never observe anything causing itself, so there must be an initial Cause, "to which everyone gives the name *God*." The third "way" is based on Ibn Sina's argument for a Necessary Being, which must of itself exist, owes its being "to nothing outside itself," and is "the cause that other things must be." The fourth *via* is a moral argument derived from Aristotle: some things are better, truer, and more exalted than others, and this hierarchy of excellence presupposes an unseen perfection that is best of all. The fifth proof is drawn from Aristotle's belief that everything in the universe has a "Final Cause" that is the "form" of its being. Everything obeys natural laws to attain its proper end and purpose, and the regularity of these laws cannot be accidental. They must be directed "by someone with awareness and understanding," just as the flight of an arrow presupposes an archer—and that "someone is what we call God."

Thomas was not trying to convince a skeptic of God's existence. He was simply trying to find a rational answer to the primordial question: Why does something exist rather than nothing? All the five "ways" argue in one way or another that nothing can come from nothing.[36] At the conclusion of each proof, Thomas rounds the argument off with a variant on the phrase *quod omnes dicunt Deum:* the Prime Mover, the Efficient Cause, the Necessary Being, the Highest Excellence, and the Intelligent Overseer are "what all people call God." It sounds as though everything is done and dusted, but no sooner has Thomas apparently settled the matter than he pulls the rug from under our feet.

He immediately goes on to show that even though we can prove that "what we call God" (a reality that we cannot define) must "exist," we have no idea what the word "exists" can signify in this context. We can talk about God as Necessary Being and so forth, but we do not know what this really means.[37] The same goes for God's attributes. God is Simplicity itself; that means that, unlike all the beings of our experience, "God is not made up of parts." A man, for example, is a composite being: he has a body and soul, flesh, bones, and skin. He has qualities: he is good, kind, fat, and tall. But because God's attributes are identical with his essence, he has no qualities. He is not "good," he *is* goodness. We simply cannot imagine an "existence" like this, so "we cannot know the 'existence' of God any more than we can define him," Thomas explains, because "God cannot be classified as this or that sort of thing." We can get to know mere beings because we can categorize them into species—as stars, elephants, or mountains. God is not a substance, the "sort of thing that can exist independently" of an individual instance of it. We cannot ask whether there is *a* God, as if God were simply one example of a species. God is not and cannot be a "sort of thing."[38]

All the "proofs" have achieved is to show us that there is nothing in our experience that can tell us what "God" means. Because of something that we cannot define, there is a universe where there could have been nothing, but we do not know what we have proved the existence of. We have simply demonstrated the existence of a mystery.[39] But that, for Thomas, is precisely what makes the "five ways" good theology. The question "Why something rather than nothing?" is a good one; human beings keep asking it, because it is in our nature to push our minds to an extreme in this way. But the answer—"what everybody calls 'God' "—is something that we do not, indeed cannot, know. Thomas shared Augustine's view of *intellectus*. In these proofs, we see reason at the end of its tether, asking unanswerable questions and straining toward its "cutting edge," its divine "spark." Pushed to the limit, reason turns itself inside out, words no longer make sense, and we are reduced to silence. Even today, when they contemplate the universe, physicists pit their minds against the dark world of uncreated reality that we cannot fathom. This is the unknowable reality that Thomas is asking his readers to confront by pushing their intellects to a point beyond which they cannot go.

Thomas would say that we know that we are speaking about "God" when our language stumbles and fails in this way. As a modern theologian has pointed out, "This reduction of talk to silence is what is called 'theology.' "[40] Unknowing was not a source of frustration. As Thomas indicates, people can find joy in this subversion of their reasoning powers. Thomas did not expect his students to "believe" in God; he still uses *credere* to mean trust or commitment and defines faith as "the capacity of the intellect to recognize (*assentire*) the genuineness of the transcendent,"[41] to look beneath the surface of life and apprehend a sacred dimension that is as real as—indeed more real than—anything else in our experience. This "assent" did not mean intellectual submission: the verb *assentire* also meant "to rejoice in" and was related to *assensio* ("applause").[42] Faith was the ability to appreciate and take delight in the nonempirical realities that we glimpse in the world.

Like any good premodern theologian, Thomas made it clear that all our language about God can only be analogical, because our words refer to limited, finite categories. We can speak of a good dog, a good book, or a good person and have some idea of what we mean; but when we say that God is not only good but Goodness itself, we lose any purchase on the meaning of what we are saying. Thomas knew that our doctrines about God are simply human constructs.[43] When we say that "God is good" or "God exists," these are not factual statements. They are approximate, because they apply language that is appropriate in one field to something quite different.[44] The statement that "God is the Creator of the world" is also analogical, because we are using the word "creator" outside its normal human context. It is impossible to prove either that the universe was created ex nihilo or that it was uncreated: "there is no proving that men and skies and rocks did not always exist," Thomas insisted, so "it is well to remember this so that one does not try to prove what cannot be proved and give non-believers grounds for mockery, and for thinking the reasons we give are our reasons for believing (*credens*)."[45]

By the thirteenth century, Denys's apophatic method had become central to the Western understanding of God. Theologians and spiritual directors would express it differently, but the essential dynamic would remain the same. Bonaventure (1221–74), an Italian Franciscan who taught in Paris at the same time as Thomas before becoming superior general of his order, seems at first sight to have an entirely different theology.[46] Instead of focusing on the new metaphysics, Franciscan spirituality was based on the life of Christ, with special emphasis on his passion. Its living embodiment was Francis of Assisi, who had tried to reproduce Christ's poverty, humility, and suffering in every detail of his life. Bonaventure saw Francis as an epiphany of the divine, an incarnation of Anselm's ontological proof. Francis had achieved such holiness that it was possible for his disciples, even in this life, "to see and understand that the 'best' is . . . that than which nothing better can be imagined."[47] Bonaventure's theology would be firmly based on this religious experience.

One might expect such an approach to be wholly affirmative. Like most of his contemporaries, Bonaventure saw the entire world as a living symbol of its creator. Like scripture, the "book of Nature" had a spiritual as well as a literal meaning, the latter pointing beyond itself to the former. In his greatest work, *The Journey of the Mind to God,* Bonaventure showed how the disciplines of the university curriculum—the natural sciences, the practical and aesthetic arts, logic, ethics, and natural philosophy—must all contribute to this ascent of mind and heart. But like Augustine, Bonaventure knew that we could not remain focused on the external world. Ultimately we had to "enter into our mind, the image of God—an image which is spiritual and everlasting within us."[48] In that way, we would discover a vision of the divine that shattered our preconceptions and overturned our usual ways of thinking and seeing.

Thomas tended to make negation and affirmation consecutive stages in an argument. He would say something positive about God—and then move on to deny it. But for Bonaventure, negation and affirmation were simultaneous. In the last two chapters of the *Journey,* he invited his readers to meditate on the two highest attributes of God, his existence and his goodness, neither of which we could hope to comprehend. Like Denys and Thomas, Bonaventure made it absolutely clear that it was inaccurate to say that "God exists" because God does not "exist" in the same way as any mere being. But being itself is an attribute that can apply *only* to God.[49] We have no idea what being is: it is not—indeed, it cannot be—an object of thought. We experience being merely as the medium through which we know individual beings, and this makes it very difficult for us to understand how God can be real:

> Thus the mind, accustomed as it is to the opaqueness in
> beings and the phantoms of visible things, appears to be
> seeing nothing when it gazes on the light of Being. It
> cannot understand that this very darkness is the supreme
> illumination of our minds, just as when the eye sees pure
> light, it seems to be seeing nothing.[50]

To counter this, we have to say contradictory things about God in order to break through this conceptual barrier. For Being is "both the first and the last; it is eternal and yet most present; it is most simple and yet the greatest," Bonaventure explained; "it is supremely one and yet omnifarious."[51] At first, each of these attributes appears to cancel out the last, yet on closer examination we see that the apparent contradictions are mutually dependent: God is present in everything *because* being is eternal; multifarious *because* One. In this way, ordinary categories of thought and language break down in a *coincidentia oppositorum*.

The same applied to the contemplation of the Trinity. Like the Cappadocians, Bonaventure instructed his readers to keep their minds in motion between the One and the Three and not attempt to iron out the inherent contradiction: "Take care that you do not believe that you can understand the incomprehensible," he warns.[52] People must use the shock of this irreconcilable complexity to break down their accustomed modes of thinking or they will miss the whole point of Trinitarian *dogma*, which is to "lift you to the heights of admiration."[53]

We even see these apparently diametrically opposed contradictions in the human person of Christ, the supreme revelation of God, who unites "the first and last, the highest and lowest"[54] in such a way that the mind cannot cope:

> The eternal is joined with the time-bound man . . . the most actual is joined with him who suffered supremely and died; the most perfect and immense is joined with the insignificant; he who is both supremely one and supremely omnifarious is joined with an individual who is composite and distinct from others.[55]

Christ, the incarnate Word, does not make the divine any more comprehensible. Quite the reverse: the Word spoken by God segues inexorably into the utter darkness of unknowing, because Christ is not the Terminus of the religious quest, but only the "Way" that leads us to the unknowable Father.[56] Instead of making everything clearer, this supreme revelation plunges us into an obscurity that is a kind of death. For Bonaventure, the suffering and death of Christ the Word incarnates the brokenness and failure of our language about God. There is no clarity, no certainty, and no privileged information. We have to leave these immature expectations behind, as Bonaventure explains in the concluding passage of the *Journey*. We too

> must die and enter this darkness. Let us silence all our care and our imaginings. Let us "pass out of this world to

be with the Father,"[57] so that when the Father is shown
to us, we may say with Philip: "It is enough for us."[58] For
he who loves this death can see God, for it is absolutely
true that "Men shall not see God and live."[59]

Just one generation after Thomas and Bonaventure, however, we can
see a shift in the conception of God. This centered on the controversial figure of John Duns Scotus (1265–1308), the Franciscan philosopher who lectured to packed audiences in Oxford.[60] Scotus criticized
Thomas's theology, which in his view made it impossible to say anything meaningful about God. He was convinced that reason could
demonstrate the existence of anything. It must be possible to arrive at
an adequate understanding of God by our natural powers alone. This
was the governing principle of Scotus's philosophy, the criterion that
determined the truth or falsity of any of his ideas. But this "natural
theology" was feasible only if we knew what we meant when we said
that "God exists." Scotus, therefore, insisted that the word "existence"
was *univocal;* that is, it "had the same basic meaning," whether it
applied to God or to men, women, mountains, animals, or trees.

Thomas, as we know, argued that we could only use words such as
"wisdom," "existence," or "goodness" analogically of God.[61] But that
was not enough for Scotus. There were, he argued, some words, such
as "fat" or "exhausted," that could not apply to God, but if such terms
as "being," "goodness," or "wisdom" were not univocal of God and
creatures, "one could not naturally have any concept of God—which
is false."[62] Pagan and Christian philosophers all agreed that God was
a being of some sort; they simply differed about the kind of being
God was. They both meant the same thing when they said that God
"exists," even though a pagan might believe that God was a fire, while
a Christian would deny this.

Thomas had regarded this type of thinking as potentially idolatrous; if we assumed that God was—in some sense—a mere being, it
was all too easy to project our own ideas onto him and create a deity in
our own image. But Scotus argued that we did in fact derive our
understanding of God from our knowledge of creatures. We know
from experience what a "being" or "wisdom" is, and when we apply it
to God, we simply purge it of all imperfection and limitation. Then

we "ascribe it to the highest perfection and in that sense ascribe it to God."[63] True, God's existence was infinite while the existence of creatures was finite, but this was merely a difference of degree: God simply had a more intensive mode of being, in rather the same way as bright red is more thoroughly red than pink, though both have redness in common. There was no ontological abyss separating God from his creatures. They all "existed," even though God had the largest share of being. Scotus's modern critics have accused him of whittling down God's transcendence and seeing God as merely a bigger or better being than us.[64] Scotus himself tried to counter the objection that he saw God's infinity merely as an extension of the finite by arguing that perfect infinity was not composite and that nothing could be added to it.[65] But in the last resort, he did relinquish the traditional apophatic caution, by insisting that we could know a good deal about God in "a descriptive kind of way."[66] It was the thin end of the wedge. Others would follow Scotus in his desire for a theological language that was clear and distinct, based on certain and demonstrable grounds.

Scotus's preference for a natural, almost scientifically based theology reflected a fundamental change in the training of theologians. In 1277, just four years after Thomas's death, the Catholic hierarchy of France condemned 217 theological propositions, and some of these condemnations were directed against Thomas himself.[67] There was a backlash against the teaching of Aristotle and widespread fear that Aristotelian physics limited God's sovereign power and freedom, because if God had to conform to Aristotle's natural laws, he could not be all-powerful.[68] Clearly people were already beginning to think of God as just another being, another member of the cosmos, for whom such a contradiction would indeed be impossible. The 1277 Condemnations suggest that some theologians were trying to oppose this disturbing idea by claiming that God could indeed do anything he wanted. Even though Aristotle said that nature abhorred a vacuum, God could move the whole cosmos in a straight line, if he chose, and leave a void in its wake; it was not necessary for the earth to be the center of the universe, and God had the power to create an infinite number of other worlds. He could even, argued the English Franciscan William of Ockham (1285–1349), have saved the human race by descending to earth as a donkey.[69]

The university curriculum now required students to study logic, mathematics, and Aristotelian science before they began their theological studies. The younger generation were, therefore, no longer at home with analogical thinking, because the natural sciences required language to be transparent and univocal. Ockham no longer saw doctrines as symbolic; they were literally true and should be subjected to exact analysis and inquiry. Like Scotus, he had no doubt that words like "existence," "power," or "presence" could be used in the same way of God and creatures.[70] Aristotle had insisted that each field of study had its own rationale and that it was dangerous to apply the rules and methods of one science to another. But teachers were beginning to abandon this practice.[71] By the time some students arrived in divinity school, they were so well versed in scientific thinking that they tried to solve theological problems mathematically.[72] They measured free will, sin, and merit according to the laws of proportion and tried to calculate the exact degree of difference between God and creatures, the odds on the possibility of God's creating successively better worlds ad infinitum, and how many angels could sit on the tip of a needle.

The Condemnations of 1277 tried to stop this trend, but they had the opposite effect. The new preoccupation with the idea of God's "power" (conceived simply as a more effective form of the "power" we know) led to a new vogue in hypothetical thinking. Scholars started to dream up all kinds of absurd feats that God should be able to manage, and these were tolerated as long as it was clear that these theories were purely speculative (*secundum imaginationem*). Some became fascinated by the idea of vast, interstellar space,[73] which the French philosopher Nicolas Oresme (1320–82) regarded as a physical manifestation of the immensity of God. Others imagined God creating a vacuum by annihilating material within the cosmos. Would the heavenly spheres surrounding the earth collapse as nature struggled to fill this vacuum? If a stone were thrown into this void, would it move in a straight line? Would people be able to hear and see one another?[74] These philosophers did not believe that they could solve these problems: indeed, their emphasis on God's absolute power militated against it.[75] But, unwittingly, they had prepared the ground for the scientific revolution of the sixteenth and seventeenth centuries, when pioneering geniuses would investigate the mathematical implications of many of the questions raised in the late scholastic period *secundum imaginationem.*[76]

The abstruse speculations of philosophers like Scotus and Ockham led to a rift between theology and spirituality that persists to the present day.[77] During the thirteenth century, some people found the new scholastic theology so dry and off-putting that they began to think that they could reach God only by discarding the intellect altogether. Instead of seeing love and knowledge as complementary, or even fused, in the traditional way, people began to see them as mutually exclusive. Until the fourteenth century, most of the great mystics were also important theologians. The theology of the Cappadocians, Denys, Augustine, Thomas, and Bonaventure was inseparable from their spiritual contemplation (*theoria*) of the divine. But none of the great mystics of the late medieval and early modern periods—Johannes Tauler (1300–61), Henry Suso (c. 1295–1366), Jan van Ruysbroek (1293–1381), Richard Rolle (c. 1290–1348), Julian of Norwich (1343–c. 1416), Margery Kempe (b. 1364), Jean de Gerson (1363–1429), Catherine of Siena (1347–80), Teresa of Ávila (1515–82) and John of the Cross (1542–91)—made any significant contribution to theology.[78]

During the fourteenth and fifteenth centuries, in a complete reversal of former practice, we find people cultivating a privatized type of prayer that was devoted almost exclusively to the achievement of intense emotional states, which they imagined were an "experience" of God. The new spirituality was sometimes aggressively solitary instead of communal, and showed little or no concern for other people.[79] For the English hermit and poet Richard Rolle prayer *was* sensation. "I cannot tell you how surprised I was, the first time I felt my heart begin to warm," he declared disarmingly at the beginning of *The Fire of Love:*

> It was real warmth too, not imaginary, and it felt as if it were actually on fire. I was astonished at the way the heat surged up, and how this new sensation brought great and unexpected comfort. I had to keep feeling my breast to make sure there was no physical reason for it. But once I

> realised that it came entirely from within, that this fire
> had no cause, material or sinful but was the gift of my
> Maker, I was absolutely delighted, and wanted my love
> to be even greater.[80]

This was a spirituality of "urgent longing," "interior sweetness" that set the heart "aglow," "infusion of comfort," and "perfervid love."[81] Rolle heard heavenly music, inaudible to the outward ear, which released a flood of pleasurable feeling that he identified with the love of God. He had no time for theologians, who were "bogged down in their interminable questionings";[82] motivated solely by "vanity," these people should be called "Fool" rather than "Doctor."[83] Rolle regularly insulted anybody who uttered the slightest criticism of his eccentric way of life with a stridency that jars with his lush descriptions of God's love. This emphasis on sensation was strangely parallel to the tendency of the late scholastic theologians, who were increasingly skeptical about the mind's ability to transcend sense data.[84] This new "mysticism" translated the traditionally symbolic discourse of interiority into a literal exploration of observable, quantifiable psychological states, which had become an end in themselves.[85]

Rolle made a great impression on his contemporaries, but many of them were disturbed by this emotional piety, which contravened cardinal principles about the nature of religious experience. As we have seen, contemplatives were supposed to rise above their feelings in order to explore the deeper regions of the psyche. Rolle refused to have a spiritual director who could have instructed him in the special techniques and carefully cultivated attitudes that would enable him to transcend his normal modes of perception. The traditions all insist that a mystic must integrate his spirituality healthily with the demands of ordinary life. Zen practitioners insist that meditation makes them more alert and responsive to their surroundings. But in his writings Rolle alternates between excitable, almost manic exultation and crushing depression. He developed a stammer and found that a job that would once have taken him thirty minutes now took a whole morning. His younger contemporary Catherine of Siena once fell into the fire in an ecstatic swoon while cooking a meal. This unbalanced behavior would become increasingly admired in certain circles. Like Rolle, Catherine refused to submit to spiritual direction that could have helped her to negotiate this perilous psychic hinterland.

Elevated feelings were never supposed to be the end of the spiritual quest: Buddhists insist that after achieving enlightenment, a man or woman must return to the marketplace and there practice compassion for all living beings. This was also true of Christian monks and nuns, who had to serve their communities; even anchorites often acted as counselors for the local laity, who came to them with secular as well as spiritual problems. But Rolle vehemently refused to engage with his fellows, and his contemplation did not lead to kindly consideration and kenotic respect for others—the test of authentic religious experience in all the major faiths. But as the rift between spirituality and theology developed, a flood of pleasurable and consoling emotion would be seen by more and more people as a sign of God's favor.

The Dominican preacher Meister Eckhart (c.1260–1327) was uneasy about this development.[86] Whatever mystics like Rolle believed, the feeling self could not be the end of the religious quest, because when reason fulfills itself in *intellectus,* it has left self behind. For Eckhart, the intellect was still the "place" in the mind where the divine touches the human; in *intellectus,* the "I" ends and "God" begins. We pass over into a state that is "nothing," because it is unlike anything else in our experience. Ultimately, therefore, the intellect was as unnameable as God:

> It is neither this nor that, and yet it is something which is higher above this and that as Heaven above earth. And therefore I give it finer names than I have ever given it before, and yet . . . it is free of all names, it is bare of all forms, wholly empty and free, as God in himself is empty and free. It is so utterly one and simple, as God is one and simple, that man cannot in any way look into it.[87]

The intellect was "nothing" because it had ceased to be itself and had "nothing in common with anything at all . . . it is a strange land and a desert."[88]

Where mystics like Rolle got stuck in the image—the fire, the heat, the "heavenly" harmonies—and seemed obsessed with their personal stories, Eckhart preached a detachment not only from the self but also from the "God," whom Rolle and his like wanted to possess and enjoy.[89] Detachment was the disciplined *kenosis* that would bring us to the "silence" and "desert" of the intellect. We had to eliminate the images, concepts, and experiences that we used to fill our inner emptiness and, as it were, dig out an interior vacuum that would draw God into the self. Eckhart had given a spiritual relevance to the empty space that so fascinated the late scholastics. Nature might abhor a vacuum, but our interior void would attract the Nothingness that was God, since "everything longs to achieve its natural place."[90]

But Eckhart was convinced that all this could be achieved within the normal structures of the Christian life. There was no need for a special lifestyle. People who became attached to one of the privatized spiritual "ways" currently on offer were "finding 'ways' and losing God, who in 'ways' is hidden."[91] The truly detached person did not want an "experience" of the divine presence; indeed, "he does not know or experience or grasp that God lives in him."[92] The discovery of the "intellect" should be a homecoming rather than a bizarre peak experience, since it is a Platonic recollection of a once known but since lost identity. A felt desire for God can be only an ego need, born of the images we use to fill our emptiness. Any "God" we find in this way is an idol that would actually alienate us from ourselves:

> For if you love God as he is God, as he is spirit, as he is person, and as he is image—all this must go! Then how should I love him? You should love him as he is nonGod, a nonspirit, a nonperson, a nonimage, but as he is—pure, unmixed, bright "One" separated from all duality; and in that One we should sink eternally down, out of "something" into "nothing."[93]

Eckhart's exuberant language, which swings so enthusiastically from the affirmative to the apophatic, demonstrates that precisely because this transformation is *not* an emotional "experience," it cannot be described in words.

Despite the new scholasticism, Denys's dialectical method was still ingrained in European theology. We see it in two very different English writers of the fourteenth century. Julian of Norwich, who was not a trained theologian, has a perfect grasp of the apophatic, even at her most affirmative. When she speaks of Christ, for example, she alternates between male and female imagery to push the reader beyond these mundane categories. "In our Mother, Christ, we grow and develop; in his mercy he reforms and restores us; through his passion, death and resurrection he has united us to our being. So does our Mother work in mercy for all his children who respond to him and obey him."[94] And even though the anonymous author of *The Cloud of Unknowing,* who translated Denys' *Mystical Theology* into English, is taking the apophatic tradition in a new, fourteenth-century direction, he still sees it as fundamental to the religious life.[95] If we want to know God, all thoughts about the Trinity, the Virgin Mary, the life of Christ, and the stories of the saints—which are perfectly good in themselves—must be cast under a thick "cloud of forgetting."[96]

At first, the author explains, a beginner would encounter only darkness "and, as it were, a cloud of unknowing."[97] If he asked: "How am I to think of God himself and what is he?" our author replied: "I cannot answer you, except to say 'I do not know!' For with this question you have brought me into the same darkness, the same cloud of unknowing where I want you to be!"[98] We can think about all kinds of things, but "of God himself can no man think."[99] This state of "unknowing" was not a defeat but an achievement; we arrived at this point by ruthlessly paring down all our God talk, until prayer was reduced to a single syllable: "God!" or "Love!" It was not easy. The mind rushed to fill the vacuum we were trying to create within ourselves with "wonderful thoughts of [God's] kindness" and reminded us "of God's sweetness and love, his grace and mercy." But unless we turned a deaf ear to this pious clamor, we would be back where we started.[100] In the meantime, the apprentice must continue with his prayers, liturgy, and *lectio divina* like everybody else. This was not what Eckhart would have called a special spiritual "way" but was a practice that should inform all the routine devotions and spiritual exercises of the Christian life.

If we persevere, the intellect will eventually abdicate and allow love to take over. Here we see the new separation of knowledge from the affections: "Therefore I will leave on one side everything I can think, and choose for my love that which I cannot think!" the author exclaims. "Why? Because [God] may well be loved but not thought. By love he may be caught and held but by thinking never."[101] But the apophatic habit is still so strong that the author immediately starts to deconstruct the notion of "love" and explain what it is *not.* There is no glow, no heavenly music, or interior sweetness in the *Cloud.* In fact the author seems to have Rolle in mind when he comes out strongly against the idea of an intense experience of God's love. He warns beginners to be on their guard against the absurd literalism of this new spirituality. Novices hear talk of all kinds of special feelings—"how a man shall lift up his heart to God and continually long to feel his love. And immediately in their silly minds they understand these words not in the intended spiritual sense but in a physical and material, and they strain their natural hearts outrageously within their breasts!" Some even feel an "unnatural glow."[102] It is impossible to feel for God the love we feel for creatures; the "God" with whom these so-called mystics are infatuated is simply the product of their unhinged imagination.

Clearly this "sham spirituality"[103] was becoming a problem. When novices are told to stop all "exterior" mental activity, the author explains, they don't know what "interior" work means, so "they do it wrong. For they turn their actual physical minds inwards to their bodies, which is an unnatural thing, and they strain as if to see spiritually with their physical eyes."[104] Their antics are painful to behold. They stare into space, looking quite deranged, squat "as if they were silly sheep," and "hang their heads to one side as if they had a worm in their ear."[105] But "interiority" is achieved only by the discipline of "forgetting." That is why the author is not going to tell his disciple to seek God within, and, he adds, "I don't want you to be outside or above, behind, or beside yourself either!"[106] When his disciple retorts in exasperation: "Where am I to be? Nowhere according to you!" our author replies that he is absolutely right: "Nowhere is where I want you! Why, when you are 'nowhere' physically, you are 'everywhere' spiritually."[107] There were no words to describe this kind of love. A person who has not put himself through the process of "forgetting" will see a dichotomy between "inner" and "outer," "nowhere" and "everywhere." But "nowhere" is not a "place" within the psyche; it is off the map of our secular experience.

> So let go this "everywhere" and "everything" for this "nowhere" and this "nothing." Never mind if you cannot fathom this nothing, for I love it so much the better. It is so worthwhile in itself that no thinking about it will do it justice.[108]

This "nothing" might seem like darkness, but it is actually "overwhelming spiritual light that blinds the soul that is experiencing it."[109] So the apprentice must be prepared to "wait in the darkness as long as is necessary," aware only of "a simple, steadfast intention reaching out towards God."[110]

*Kenosis* is at the heart of the *Cloud*'s spirituality. Instead of seeking special raptures, the author tells his disciple to seek God for himself and not "for what you can get out of him."[111] But the discipline of self-emptying was becoming a thing of the past. Theologians were becoming more self-important, and "mystics" more self-indulgent. The new polarity was resulting in thinking theologians and loving mystics. Denys the Carthusian, an extremely learned Flemish monk of the fifteenth century, was disturbed by this change. The old mystical theology, he recalled, had been accessible to all the faithful, no matter how uneducated they were; it had been grounded in the ordinary routines of liturgy, community life, and the practice of charity. But the theology of Scotus and Ockham was incomprehensible to all but a few experts. The theology of unknowing had encouraged humility; the new speculations of the schoolmen seemed to inflate their conceit and could be imparted to anybody who had the intelligence to follow it, regardless of his moral stature.[112] Theology was not only becoming aridly theoretical; without the discipline of the apophatic, it was in danger of becoming idolatrous. Europe was on the brink of major social, cultural, political, and intellectual change. As it entered the modern world, spirituality was at a low ebb, and Europeans might find it difficult to respond creatively to the challenge.

# PART II

---

# The Modern God

(1500 CE TO THE PRESENT)

# SEVEN

# Science and Religion

It is often said that the modern period began in the year 1492, when Christopher Columbus crossed the Atlantic in the hope of finding a new sea route to India and discovered the Americas instead. This voyage would have been impossible without such scientific discoveries as the magnetic compass and the latest insights in astronomy. The people of Western Europe were on the brink of a new world that would give them unprecedented control over their environment, and Christian Spain was in the vanguard of this change. Columbus's patrons were the Catholic monarchs Ferdinand and Isabella, whose marriage had united the Iberian kingdoms of Aragon and Castile. Spain was in the process of becoming a modern, centralized state. This was an age of transition. Columbus himself was certainly conversant with the new scientific ideas that were eagerly discussed in the Spanish universities, but he was still rooted in the older religious universe. A devout Christian, he had been born into a family of converted Jews and retained an interest in the Kabbalah, the mystical tradition of Judaism. He also regarded himself as a latter-day Crusader: once he reached India, he intended to establish a military base for the recovery of Jerusalem.[1] The people of Europe had started their journey to modernity, but the traditional myths of religion still gave meaning to their rational and scientific explorations.

On January 2, 1492, Columbus had been present at the conquest of Granada, the last Muslim stronghold in Europe, by the armies of Ferdinand and Isabella. On March 31, the monarchs signed the Edict of Expulsion that forced the Jews of al-Andalus to choose between baptism and deportation; in 1499, the Muslim inhabitants of Spain would be given the same choice. Many of the Spanish Jews were so attached to their homeland that they converted to Christianity, but about eighty thousand crossed the border into Portugal and another fifty thousand fled to the new Ottoman Empire.[2] Modernity had its own intransigence. Some would find the modern age liberating and enthralling; but for others it would be experienced as coercive, invasive, and destructive. Ferdinand and Isabella were creating the kind of absolute government that was essential to the economy of early modern Europe. They could no longer tolerate such autonomous, self-governing institutions as the guild, the corporation, or the Jewish community, so the victory of Granada was followed by an act of ethnic cleansing.

As part of their unification of kingdoms that had hitherto been independent and had their own unique ethos, Ferdinand and Isabella had established the Spanish Inquisition in 1483. Its aim was to enforce ideological conformity as a base for the new Spanish identity. In a pattern that would be repeated in later secular states, inquisitors sought out dissidents and forced them to abjure their "heresy," a word deriving from the Greek *airesis,* "to go one's own way." The Spanish Inquisition was not an archaic attempt to preserve a bygone religious world; it was a modernizing institution devised by the monarchs to create national unity.[3] Its chief victims were the Jewish and Muslim *conversos,* who had opted for baptism rather than deportation and were suspected of backsliding. Many conversos became committed Catholics, but there were rumors of an underground movement of dissidents who practiced their old faith in secret. The inquisitors were instructed to torture anybody who lit candles on Friday night or refused to eat pork, in order to force them to recant and to name other renegades. Not surprisingly, some of these "new Christians" were not only alienated from Catholicism but became skeptical about religion itself.

The Jews who had fled to Portugal were tougher; they had preferred exile rather than abjuring their faith. Initially, they were welcomed by King João II, but when Manuel I succeeded to the throne in 1495, Ferdinand and Isabella, his parents-in-law, forced him to baptize all the Jews in Portugal. Manuel compromised by granting them immunity from the Inquisition for fifty years. Known as Marranos ("pigs"), a term of abuse that Portuguese Jews adopted as a badge of pride, they had time to organize a successful Jewish underground. For generations, closet Jews tried to practice their faith to the best of their ability, but they labored under huge difficulties. Cut off from the rest of the Jewish world, they had no access to Jewish literature and no synagogues and were able to perform only a few of the major rituals. Because they had received a Catholic education, their minds were filled with Christian symbols and doctrines, so inevitably, as the years passed, their faith was neither authentically Jewish nor truly Christian.[4]

Others, as we shall see, would become the first atheists and free-thinkers in modern Europe. Deprived of the observances that made the Torah a living reality, Marrano religion became distorted. In the Portuguese universities, the Marranos had studied logic, physics, medicine, and mathematics, but they had no expertise in the more intuitive disciplines of Jewish practice. Relying perforce on reason alone, their theology bore no relation to traditional Judaism.[5] Their God was the First Cause of all being, who did not intervene directly in human affairs; there was no need for the Torah, because the laws of nature were accessible to everybody. This is the kind of God that, left to itself, human reason tends to create, but in the past Jews had found the rational God of the philosophers religiously empty. Like many modern people—and for many of the same reasons—some of the Marranos would find this God alien and incredible.

The Jews who migrated to the Ottoman Empire had an entirely different experience. Their exile, a spiritual as well as a physical dislocation, had inflicted a deep psychic wound; everything seemed to be in the wrong place.[6] Some Spanish Jews settled in Safed in Palestine, where they met Isaac Luria (1534–72), a frail northern European Jew who had developed a form of Kabbalah that spoke directly to their predicament. Kabbalists had always felt at liberty to interpret the first chapters of Genesis allegorically, transforming them into an esoteric account of the inner life of God. In this tradition, Luria had created an entirely new creation myth that bore no resemblance to the orderly cosmogony of Genesis and that began with an act of *kenosis*. Because God was omnipresent, there was no space for the world, no place where God was not. So En Sof, the inscrutable and unknowable Godhead, as it were, shrank into itself in a voluntary *zimzum* ("withdrawal"), a self-diminishment that made itself less. The creation continued in a series of cosmic accidents, primal explosions, and false starts, which seemed a more accurate depiction of the arbitrary world that Jews now inhabited. Sparks of divine light had fallen into the Godless abyss created by *zimzum*. Everything was exiled from its rightful place, and the Shekhinah wandered through the world, yearning to be reunited with the Godhead.[7]

Nobody understood this strange story literally; like any creation myth, it was primarily therapeutic, speaking figuratively of a timeless rather than a historical reality. It became authoritative because it was such a telling description of the exiles' experience, at the same time showing them that their tragedy was not unique but was in tune with fundamental laws of existence. Instead of being outcasts, Jews were central actors in the process that would redeem the universe, because their careful observance of Torah could end this universal displacement and effect the "restoration" (*tikkun*) of the Shekhinah to the Godhead, the Jews to the Promised Land, and the rest of the world to its rightful state.[8] By 1650, Lurianic Kabbalah had become a mass movement in the Jewish world from Poland to Iran, the only Jewish theology at this time to win such wide acceptance.[9]

Without the special rituals devised by Luria, this myth would have remained a senseless fiction. Weeping and rubbing their faces in the dust, Kabbalists made night vigils in order to confront their sorrow; they lay awake all night, calling out to God in their abandonment, and took long hikes in the Galilean countryside to act out their sense of homelessness. But there was no wallowing: Kabbalists were required to work through their pain in a disciplined, stylized manner until it gave way to a measure of joy. Vigils always finished at dawn with a meditation on the end of humanity's estrangement from the divine. Kabbalists practiced disciplines of concentration (*kawwanoth*) that evoked from the farthest reaches of the psyche a wonder and delight that they had not known they possessed. Compassion was a crucial Lurianic virtue, and there were severe penances for faults that injured others: Jews who had suffered so much themselves must not increase the sum of grief in the world.[10] After the disaster of 1492, many Jews had retreated from the *falsafah* that had been so popular in Spain and found that the new *mythos* and its rituals enabled them to make contact with the deeper roots of their grief and to discover a source of healing.[11] But in the new world that was coming into being in Europe, this type of creative *mythos* would soon be a thing of the past.

Other European countries were in the throes of the same transformation as Spain, even though at this early stage few were aware of its magnitude. By the sixteenth century, the people of the West had started to create an entirely new and unprecedented type of civilization that depended on a radical change in the economic base of society. Instead of relying, like every premodern economy, on a surplus of agricultural produce with which they could trade in order to fund their cultural achievements, the modern economy rested on the technological replication of resources and the constant reinvestment of capital, which provided a source of wealth that could be renewed indefinitely. This freed it from many of the constraints of premodern societies, where the economy could not expand beyond a certain point and eventually outran its resources. Consequently, these agrarian societies tended to be conservative, because they simply could not afford the constant replication of the infrastructure that has come to characterize modernity. Original thought was not encouraged, because it could lead to frustration and social unrest, since fresh ideas could rarely be implemented and projects that required too large a financial outlay were usually shelved. It seemed preferable, therefore, to concentrate on preserving what had already been achieved.[12] Now, however, Western people were gradually acquiring the confidence to look to the future instead of the past. Where the older cultures had taught men and women to remain within carefully defined limits, pioneers such as Columbus were encouraging them to venture beyond the confines of the known world, where they discovered that, thanks to their modern technology, they not only survived but prospered.

By the sixteenth century, therefore, a complex process was at work in Europe that was slowly changing the way people thought and experienced the world. Inventions were occurring simultaneously in many different fields; none seemed particularly momentous at the time, but their cumulative effect would be decisive.[13] Specialists in one discipline found that they benefited from discoveries made in others. Scientists and explorers, for example, both relied on the increased efficiency of instrument makers. By 1600, innovations were occurring on such a scale and in so many areas at once that progress seemed irreversible and set to continue indefinitely. But in the early sixteenth century, the Great Western Transformation was only in its infancy. Spain may have been the most advanced country in Europe, but it was not the sole model of a modern state. In the course of their struggle against Spanish hegemony, the Netherlands deliberately developed a more liberal ideology to counter Spanish autocracy. There were thus two rival versions of modernity: one open and tolerant, the other exclusive and coercive.

And as society altered to accommodate these developments, religion would also have to change. At this point, faith still pervaded the whole of life and had not yet been confined to a distinct sphere. But secularization was beginning. A centralized state was crucial to productivity and, like Ferdinand and Isabella, rulers all over Europe began the difficult process of welding separate kingdoms into modern nation-states. Princes, such as Henry VII of England (1457–1509) and Francis I of France (1494–1547), adopted policies designed to reduce the influence of the Church and subordinate it to their own political goals. The increasing role of banks, stock companies, and stock exchanges, over which the Church had no control, also eroded its power. This steadily unstoppable trend, which pushed religion into a separate, marginal place in society, would be felt in all kinds of obscure ways that were never fully articulated. Secularization would be accelerated by three crucial and formative sixteenth-century movements: the Renaissance, the Reformation, and the Scientific Revolution. These were not disconnected or rival projects. They influenced one another in the same way as the other innovations of the period; all three reflected the emerging early modern zeitgeist and were pervaded by the religious ethos.

The reduced role of the Church did not mean that people were becoming disenchanted with their faith; on the contrary, they were probably more religious than they had been in the medieval period. Religion was involved in the modernization process at every level and would affect and be affected by the escalating spiral of social, political, and scientific change. The humanism of the Renaissance, for example, was deeply religious. The Dutch humanist Desiderius Erasmus

(1466–1536) wanted to read the scriptures in the original languages and translate them into a more elegant Latin, and his textual work was of immense importance to the reformers. Renaissance art benefited from the anatomical drawings of Andreas Vesalius (1515–64). Other painters exploited the new mathematical understanding of space: in their own field, they were striving for a vision that was as rational as the dawning scientific ethos. The technical inventions of the period helped artists achieve an empirical accuracy and fidelity to nature that was unprecedented, based on the depiction of objects viewed from a single, objective perspective and placed in relation to one another in a unified space.[14] But this "objectivity" did not mean an abandonment of the transcendent: this "scientific art" achieved a numinous vision, just as early modern scientists sought a solution that was elegant, aesthetic, and redolent of the divine.[15]

Renaissance religion recoiled from the arid theology of the late scholastics and had absorbed the personalized emphasis of much fourteenth-century spirituality. Lorenzo Valla (1405–57) had already stressed the futility of mixing sacred truth with "tricks of dialectics" and "metaphysical quibbles."[16] The humanists wanted the kind of emotive religion described by the Italian poet Francesco Petrarch (1304–74), who had argued that "theology is actually poetry, poetry concerning God," effective not because it "proved" anything but because it reached the heart.[17] The humanists' textual study of the New Testament was part of their attempt to return, like any premodern reformers, *ad fontes,* to the "wellsprings" of their tradition, shaking off the medieval legacy in order to rediscover the gospels and the fathers of the Church. They were particularly drawn to the affective spirituality of Paul and Augustine, whom they revered not as doctrinal authorities, but as individuals like themselves, who had embarked on a highly personal and emotional quest. The humanists were largely responsible for creating the concept of the individual that would be crucial to the modern ethos. Only a person free of communal, social, or dogmatic shibboleths could innovate freely, experiment boldly, reject established authority, and risk the possibility of error. The hero of the early modern period was the explorer, who could penetrate new realms of thought and experience independently but was ready to cooperate with others.

Even though they were conscious of their great achievements, the humanists nevertheless retained a traditional sense of the limitations of the human mind; their study of the early Christian writers and the classical authors of Greece and Rome, whose world had been so different from their own, had made them aware not only of the diversity of human affairs but of the way all ideas and attitudes—including their own—were indelibly influenced by historical and cultural conditions.[18] Current norms could never be absolute.[19] The reports of explorers, who brought back tales of civilizations that were based on quite different premises, had also enlarged their sympathies. The humanists had a passionate interest in rhetoric, fine speech, and the arts of persuasion, and Aristotle had taught them to examine the particular context of any given argument. Instead of simply concentrating on *what* was said, it was essential to understand how local circumstances affected any truth. Here humanists represented the more liberal ethos of modernity.

But in their emphatic rejection of Scotus, Ockham, and the medievals, they also represented the intolerant strain of the modern spirit.[20] As philosophy, science, and technology progressed, the rejection of the recent past would seem essential to the discovery of new truth. Rapid economic and technological changes, the challenge of bringing order to the new nation-states, and the fluctuations of distant markets, as well as reports of the exotic New World, all encouraged people to put tradition to one side and seek wholly novel solutions to their unprecedented problems. But this could also lead to a wholesale dismissal of apparently outmoded ideas and attitudes. The humanists were convinced they were on the side of progress, and they were right. "Everything that surrounds us is our own work, the work of man," said the fifteenth-century biblical scholar Gionozo Manetti, "and when we see these marvels, we realise that we are able to make better things, more beautiful things, better adorned, more perfect than those we have made until now."[21] It did not follow, however, that the medieval approach to art, literature, or religion had been entirely misguided; it had just reflected a different world. In religious matters, the modern tendency to wipe the slate clean to begin again, while understandable, would ultimately be detrimental.

The three great Protestant reformers, Martin Luther (1483–1546), Huldrych Zwingli (1484–1531), and John Calvin (1509–64), all exemplified this vehement rejection of the immediate past. Like the

Renaissance humanists, they had no time for the natural theology of the late scholastics and wanted a more personal and immediate faith. Zwingli and Calvin, indeed, remained humanists throughout their lives, their religious reform largely inspired by the Renaissance zeitgeist. At this time of massive change, there was a good deal of religious uncertainty. People were not able to be religious in the same way as the medievals. But where could they hear the authentic voice of Christianity?[22] The reformers were trying to articulate a religious mood that was strongly felt but had not yet been adequately conceptualized. Their Reformation was just one expression of the Great Western Transformation.[23] Instead of being regarded as the instigator of change, Luther should rather be seen as the spokesman of a current trend.

Historians used to think that the Reformation was primarily a reaction to the corruption of the Church, but there seems to have been a spiritual revival in Europe at this time, especially among the laity, who now felt empowered to criticize abuses that had previously passed without comment. As society changed, ideas and rituals that had been religiously viable before the advent of modernity became suddenly abhorrent.[24] Instead of giving people a sense of life's transcendent possibilities, they caused only anxiety. Luther memorably expressed this alienation from older practices.

> Although I lived a blameless life as a monk, I felt that I was a sinner with an uneasy conscience before God. I also could not believe that I had pleased him with my works. . . . I was a good monk, and kept my order so strictly that if ever a monk could get to heaven by monastic discipline, I was that monk. All my companions in the monastery would confirm this. . . . And yet my conscience did not give me certainty, but I always doubted and said, "You didn't do that right. You weren't contrite enough. You left that out of your confession."[25]

In the past, the monastic life had encouraged a spirituality that was essentially communal. Monks had listened to the scriptures together during the liturgy. *Lectio divina* had been a ruminative, unanxious, and even enjoyable method of appropriating the truths of religion. But the new emphasis on the individual made Luther so obsessed with his own spiritual performance that he had become mired in the ego that he was supposed to transcend. None of the medieval rites and practices could touch what he called the *tristitia* ("sorrow") that filled him with an acute terror of death and a conviction of abject impotence.[26] In addition, he had expressed the yearning for absolute certainty that would also characterize religion in the modern period.

Luther found salvation in the doctrine of justification by faith alone. Human beings could not save themselves by performing meritorious deeds and rituals; if we had faith, Christ would clothe us in his own righteousness. Our good deeds were, therefore, the result rather than the cause of God's favor. This was not an original idea; it was already a perfectly respectable Catholic position.[27] But while he was studying Paul's letter to the Romans, it broke upon Luther with the overwhelming power of a new revelation when he came across the words: "The just man lives by faith."[28] They "made me feel as though I had been born again, and as though I had entered through the open gates of paradise itself," he would recall later.[29] The precise conclusion that Luther drew from this one sentence would probably have surprised Paul, but it spoke to the unconscious needs of a generation that found traditional practices empty and unproductive.[30]

The profound societal changes of early modernity caused many to feel disoriented and lost. Living in medias res, they could not see the direction that their society was taking but experienced its slow transformation in isolated, incoherent ways. As the old mythology that had given structure and significance to their ancestors crumbled in this new situation, many seem to have experienced the sense of powerlessness that had afflicted Luther. Before their own conversions to fresh religious vision, Zwingli and Calvin had also experienced a paralyzing helplessness before the trials of human existence and were convinced that they could contribute nothing toward their own salvation. Consequently, all the reformers emphasized the unqualified divine sovereignty that would not only characterize the modern God but also help to shape the Scientific Revolution.[31]

The emphasis on God's absolute power meant that God alone could change the course of events, so human beings, who were essentially impotent, must rely on his unconditional might. When the young Zwingli had contracted the plague that wiped out 25 percent of the population of Zurich, he knew there was nothing he could do to save himself. "Do as you will for I lack nothing," he prayed. "I am your vessel to be restored or destroyed."[32] The young Calvin had felt so in thrall to the institutional Church that he was both unwilling and unable to break free, and it had taken what seemed a divine initiative to shift him: "At last God turned my course in a different direction by the hidden bridle of his providence . . . by a sudden conversion to docility, he tamed a mind too stubborn for its years."[33]

When Luther spoke of the faith that could justify men and women he did not, of course, mean "belief" in our modern sense but an act of total trust in the absolute power of God. "Faith," he explained in one of his sermons, "does not require information, knowledge and certainty, but a free surrender and joyful bet on his unfelt, untried and unknown goodness."[34] Luther had no time for the "false theologian," who "looks upon the invisible things of God as though they were clearly perceptible in those things that have actually happened."[35] Far from giving a clear vision, faith brought "a sort of darkness that can see nothing."[36] Alienated from the natural theology of Scotus and Ockham, he did not imagine for one moment that the investigation of the cosmos or natural reasoning could bring us true knowledge of God. It was not only pointless but could even be dangerous to try to prove God's existence, because too much speculation about God's inconceivable might in governing the universe could cause human beings to fall into a state of abject despair and terror.[37] But despite its religious motivation, this deliberate desacralization of the cosmos was a secularizing idea that would encourage scientists to approach the world independently of the divine.[38]

Luther's reliance on "scripture alone" would lead to a theology that was more dependent than hitherto on the word. The success of the reformers was due in large part to the invention of the printing press, which not only helped to propagate the new ideas but also changed people's relationship to the text. The word would now replace the image and the icon in people's thinking, and this would make theology more verbose.[39] Ritual was also downgraded; ritual acts of piety designed, so the reformers assumed, to acquire merit, were at best futile and at worst blasphemous.[40] Lutheran churches maintained many of the customary vestments, paintings, altarpieces, and ceremonies; organ music and hymns survived, and the German Reformation would inspire a new tradition of church music that would reach its apogee in the work of J. S. Bach (1685–1750). It would give a transcendent dimension to the often prosaic words of the vernacular. But in the Calvinist tradition, pictures and statues vanished, church music was ruthlessly simplified, and ceremony was abandoned in favor of extempore worship.

Printing helped to secularize the relationship of the reader to the truth that he was trying to acquire.[41] In the past, the Church had—to an extent—been able to supervise the flow of ideas and information, but the proliferation of books and pamphlets after the middle of the sixteenth century made this censorship far more difficult. As the printed book began to replace oral methods of communication, the information it provided was depersonalized and, perhaps, became more fixed and less flexible than in the old days, when truth had developed in dynamic relation between master and pupil. The printed page itself was an image of precision and exactitude, a symptom of the mental outlook of the early modern commercial ethos. Inventors, merchants, and scientists were discovering the importance of accuracy; their knowledge was oriented to this world and to concrete, practical results. Efficiency was becoming the watchword of modernity. It was no longer desirable to reach for nebulous truth: things had to work effectively on the ground. As people were forced to pit their wits against extraordinary challenges occurring simultaneously on so many different fronts, a more systematic and pragmatic approach to knowledge was becoming essential.

This would inevitably affect the way people thought about religion. In premodern society, men and women had experienced the sacred in earthly objects, so that symbol and the sacred had been inseparable. The Eucharistic bread and wine had been identical with the transcendent reality to which they directed attention. Now the reformers declared that the Eucharist was "only" a symbol and the Mass no longer a symbolic reenactment of Calvary but a simple memorial. They were beginning to speak about the myths of religion as though they were *logoi,* and the alacrity with which people seized upon these new teachings suggests that many Christians in Europe were losing the older habits of thought.

The theological quarrels between Rome and the reformers and, later, among the reformers themselves were giving more importance to the exact formulation of abstruse doctrines. The Protestant reformers and their Catholic opponents all used the printing press, council, and synod to draw ever finer dogmatic distinctions as they struggled to express their differences from one another. From the 1520s, the reformers started to issue "catechisms," dialogues of stereotyped questions and answers, to ensure that their congregations accepted a particular interpretation of the creed. Correct faith was gradually becoming a matter of accepting the proper teachings. The Protestant reliance on "scripture alone" dispensed with the Catholic notion of "tradition" that saw each generation deepening its understanding of the sacred text in a cumulative "bricolage." Instead of trying to get beyond language, Protestants would be encouraged to focus on the precise, original, and supposedly unchanging word of God in print. Instead of reading the sacred text in a communal setting, they would wrestle with its obscurities on their own. Slowly, in tune with the new commercial and scientific spirit, a distinctively "modern" notion of religious truth as logical, unmediated, and objective was emerging in the Western Christian world.[42]

As the Reformation proceeded, Protestantism began to morph into a bewildering number of sects, each with its own doctrinal bias, its own interpretation of the Bible, and each convinced that it alone had a monopoly on truth.[43] There was now a clamor of religious opinion in Europe. When Luther had battled with the Catholic authorities, other intellectually minded clergy either did the same or took vociferous issue with his ideas. Preachers began to air their disagreements in public and urged the laity to join the debate. Zwingli argued that lay folk should feel empowered to question official dogma and should not need to wait on the decisions of a synod. "Calvinists" started to articulate doctrines to distinguish themselves from "Lutherans." Inevitably, this orgy of acrimonious doctrinal debate would affect the traditional notion of "belief," pushing intellectual orthodoxy to the fore.

Catholics also found it necessary to reformulate their faith, but they maintained to a greater degree the older notion of religion as practice. The Spaniards, still in the vanguard of modernization, took the lead in the Catholic reformation initiated by the Council of Trent (1545–63), which made the Church a more centralized body on the model of the absolute monarchy. The Council reinforced the power of pope and hierarchy, issued a catechism to ensure doctrinal conformity, ensured that the clergy were educated to a higher standard, and rationalized liturgical and devotional practices, jettisoning those that were either corrupt or no longer effective. Trent set up programs of education and parish organization to ensure that the new intellectual style spread to the laity.[44] But even though the Council fathers went to such lengths to enforce dogmatic orthodoxy, their prime concern was to promote regular liturgical observance to enable the laity to transform the old external, communal rites into genuinely interior devotion. Catholics were certainly drifting toward the new conception of "belief," but they would never identify it so completely with doctrinal assent as Protestants.[45]

Other Spanish reformers, such as Teresa of Ávila and John of the Cross, modernized the religious orders, attempting to weed out the more dubious and superstitious devotions and make the spiritual quest more systematic and less dependent on the whims of inadequate advisers. Mystics of the new age should know what to expect, learn how to deal with the pitfalls and dangers of the interior life, and husband their spiritual energies productively. The former soldier Ignatius of Loyola (1491–1556), founder of the Society of Jesus, perfectly embodied the efficiency and effectiveness of the early modern West. His *Spiritual Exercises* provided a systematic, time-efficient, thirty-day retreat—a sort of crash course in mysticism, designed to make each Jesuit a dynamic force in the world. Like the Iberian explorers, Jesuit missionaries were dispatched all over the world: Francis Xavier (1506–52) to Japan, Robert di Nobili (1577–1656) to India, and Matteo Ricci (1552–1610) to China.

The reformed Catholic Church and the new Protestant denominations all succumbed to the iconoclasm of modernity, which would forever feel obliged to destroy what had been personally superseded. The positive achievements of the Catholic reformation were balanced by the horrors of the Inquisition. Protestants used the Old Testament ban on images as a mandate to trash statues and frescoes. Luther raged against the pope, Turks, Jews, women, and rebellious peasants. The Protestant reformers may have demanded that Christians be free to read and interpret the Bible as they chose, but there was no toleration for anybody who opposed their own teachings. Luther believed that all "heretical" books should be burned, and both Calvin and Zwingli were prepared to execute dissidents. Despite its intense religiosity, the divisions effected by the Protestant Reformation also helped to accelerate the process of secularization and the growth of nationalism. In order to maintain order, the princes had to separate themselves from the turmoil engendered by the squabbling churches and denominations, whose political power therefore diminished. As an infant nation struggled for political independence from Rome, it built a distinct identity, opting for Catholic or Protestant affiliation, and nonconformists were often persecuted as political dissidents and traitors.

As it entered the modern period, therefore, the West was torn between a frequently strident dogmatism on the one hand, and a more liberal humility that recognized the limits of knowledge on the other. The plays of William Shakespeare (1564–1616) explored the myriad possibilities of the human personality. He shared the Renaissance understanding of the importance of context; ideas, customs, and behavior were inextricably combined with a particular set of circumstances, so it was impossible to judge them from a purely objective, theoretical point of view. Human affairs were not motivated primarily by rational considerations. People were often caught unawares by unconscious or emotional impulses that were neither pragmatic nor efficient but sometimes worked against their own interests. *Hamlet* depicted the tortured consciousness of a hero with whom everybody somehow identified turning ceaselessly yet fruitlessly upon itself, unable to understand its motivation or achieve any degree of certainty about the most pressing and practical matters. In *Othello,* the apparently "motiveless malignancy" of Iago militated against simplistic ideas of good and evil. Shakespeare made his audiences aware that human beings were mysterious to themselves and others, and that it was disastrous and counterproductive to either attempt to manipulate them or expect them to act in a certain way.

In his own distinctive way, the French essayist Michel de Montaigne (1533–92) expressed a similar spirit, and was skeptical of any human attempt to attain absolute truth. In the famous "Apology of Raymond Sebond," written, tongue-in-cheek, largely to please his father, Montaigne had marveled at Sebond's intellectual confidence. This sixteenth-century Spanish philosopher had argued that we could derive all the information we required about God, salvation, and human life from a study of the natural world. But for Montaigne, reason was so blind and lame that nothing was certain or even probable. If an argument was sufficiently attractive, human beings could be persuaded to believe almost anything. But, far from being cast down by this unknowing, Montaigne was able to live quite happily with this modest assessment of the human intellect and seemed to enjoy the diversity and complexity of early modern life. Like the Renaissance humanists, he had no wish to pass judgment on a world that was daily becoming more difficult to assess. He regarded himself as a loyal Catholic but, in light of the new discoveries that constantly revealed the limits of human understanding, judged the attempt to impose any kind of orthodoxy as arrogant, futile, and dishonest.

It would be a mistake to imagine that the entire population absorbed the new ideas instantaneously. The vast majority probably felt obscurely perplexed at the sudden fragmentation of Christendom without any clear understanding of what was going on. For at least two hundred years, old mental habits of thought persisted, sometimes jostling uneasily with the new values, and we can see this at work even in the scientific revolution. In 1530, Nicolaus Copernicus (1473–1543), the Polish-born canon of the cathedral of Frauenburg in Prussia, completed *De revolutionibus,* a thesis that argued that the sun was the center of the universe. A typical Renaissance man, Copernicus had studied mathematics, optics, and perspective at Kraków, canon law in Bologna, and medicine at Padua and had lectured on astronomy in Rome. In Frauenberg, working at different times as a church administrator, bailiff, military governor, judge, and physician, he had continued his study of the stars. Copernicus knew that most of the population would find the idea of a heliocentric, or sun-centered, universe impossible either to understand or to accept, so he did not publish his treatise but circulated the manuscript privately. Nevertheless, *De revolutionibus* was widely read in both Catholic and Protestant countries and inspired a good deal of interest.

Since the twelfth century, Europeans had adopted a cosmology based on Aristotelian physics and popularized by the Egyptian astronomer Ptolemy (c. 90–168).[46] The Earth was firmly at the center of the universe, encased like an onion in eight spherical shells composed of an invisible substance called ether. These spheres revolved in a uniform manner around the Earth, and embedded in the ether of each of the first seven spheres was one of the heavenly bodies: Moon, Mercury, Venus, Sun, Mars, Jupiter, and Saturn. The fixed stars occupied the eighth sphere at the outermost rim of the universe and gave stability to the whole. The Ptolemaic system was the most accurate account of the data that had been accumulated in the ancient world, when techniques of observation had, of course, been limited and inadequate. The medievals also found it morally satisfying. The Earth may have been the center of the universe but it was also the lowest point of creation. On Earth all was change and decay. But as one moved past the waxing and waning moon to the more constant sun and, finally, reached the fixed stars, everything became more reliable, until beyond the eighth sphere was the immutable world of heaven. Even though Ptolemy's system was spiritually uplifting, however, it was cumbersome scientifically. Because the circle was universally regarded as the symbol of perfection, it was taken for granted that the planetary orbits described a perfect circle. But observers had noted that some planets appeared to move erratically and seemed brighter at some times than at others. Ptolemy tried to account for these irregularities by an intricate mathematical device that had the planets revolving in small "epicycles" around a central point, which itself described a perfectly circular course around the Earth. When viewed from the Earth, he explained, the center of the epicycle *seemed* to move irregularly, but if it were possible to observe it from an off-center point, it would be seen to move in a wholly uniform manner.

Copernicus turned the whole system inside out.[47] Even though his thesis would spark an intellectual revolution, he still retained a foothold in the old mythical world, finding it impossible to abandon the heavenly spheres or the symbolism of the circular planetary orbits. Copernicus, the church administrator, scanned the heavens in order to fix the dates of the religious festivals, but, as a Renaissance man, he was disturbed by the inelegance of Ptolemaic cosmology. How could the Creator have devised such an unwieldy and aesthetically unpleasing cosmos? Looking back *ad fontes* to classical antiquity, he found that in the third century BCE, Aristarchus of Samos had suggested that the planets revolved around the sun and that the Earth revolved on its own axis. He discovered that the Pythagoreans believed that mathematics rather than physics was the key to any understanding of the natural world, and that Philolaus, one of Pythagoras's pupils, thought that the Earth, planets, and sun all revolved around a central, cosmic fire.

But none of these Greek *phusikoi* had worked out the mathematical implications of their theories. Copernicus proceeded to do so and produced a radically new hypothesis. If, for the sake of argument, we supposed that the Earth revolved daily on its own axis and *also* described an annual revolution around the sun, we could account for all known celestial phenomena just as accurately as Ptolemy did but in a far more elegant manner. The daily revolution of the celestial bodies and the annual motion of the sun that we *thought* we observed could be explained by the Earth's diurnal rotation on its axis and its annual orbit around the sun. The heavenly movements we observed were simply a projection of the Earth's motion in the opposite direction.

Copernicus's theory was roundly criticized, not because he could not prove it, but because it contravened basic principles of Aristotelian physics. The mathematics worked beautifully, but—according to the traditional academic hierarchy—mathematics was supposed to defer to physics, the superior science. It is not surprising that most people found the idea of a sun-centered universe incredible. It contradicted not only the standard scientific explanation but also basic common sense. Copernicus was asking his colleagues to believe that the Earth, which *seemed* static, was actually moving very fast indeed and that the planets only *appeared* to be in motion around us because of a mistaken projection. Copernican theory demanded that people no longer trust the evidence of their senses and accept on faith the counterintuitive theories of an eccentric mathematician.

There were at first few specifically religious objections. Even though some biblical texts implied that the sun moved in the heavens and that the Earth was stable,[48] Catholics were not obliged to interpret them literally. They still followed Augustine's principle of accommodation, which had ruled that a scriptural text should be reinterpreted if it clashed with science. Copernicus had offered his hypothesis *sub imaginationem* in the traditional way, and when he read his treatise in the Vatican in 1534, the pope gave it cautious approval. When *De revolutionibus* was finally published in 1543, Copernicus was on his deathbed and his editor Andreas Osiander (1498–1552) took it upon himself to write a preface to protect the dying man from harassment: because astronomy could not prove any of its hypotheses, we should depend on divine revelation for reliable information about the cosmos.[49]

Neither Copernicus nor the handful of people who were able to entertain the idea of a heliocentric universe regarded themselves as religious rebels. Luther is reported to have remarked irritably in his *Table Talk* that Copernicus was a "fool" who wanted "to turn the whole art of astronomy upside down" but seemed more concerned about scientific orthodoxy than its religious implications.[50] Luther was not a biblical literalist; his disciple Philipp Melanchthon (1497– 1560) was initially hostile to Copernicus, but mathematics and astronomy figured prominently in the curricula he devised for Protestant universities. Calvin never mentioned Copernicus, but he held fast to Augustine's principle of accommodation. He was not surprised to hear that the biblical description of the cosmos differed from the latest discoveries of learned philosophers. In Genesis, for example, Moses had described the sun and moon as the largest of the heavenly bodies, but modern astronomers claimed that Saturn was bigger. "Here lies the difference; Moses wrote in a popular style things which, without instruction, all ordinary persons, endued with common sense, are able to understand; but astronomers investigate with great labour whatever the sagacity of the human mind can comprehend."[51] The Bible had nothing to say about astronomy. "He who would learn astronomy and other recondite arts, let him go elsewhere," Calvin instructed emphatically. Science was "very useful" and must not be impeded "because some frantic persons are wont boldly to reject whatever is unknown to them."[52]

Intrigued by Copernicus's hypothesis, some scientists tried to develop his ideas. In his observatory on the island of Hveen in the Swedish Sound, the Danish astronomer, mathematician, and imperial astrologer Tycho Brahe (1546–1601) corrected outstanding inaccuracies in the astronomical table and discovered a new star in Cassiopeia. He rejected Copernicus's theory, however, and suggested a compromise with the Ptolemaic system: the planets rotated round the sun, which revolved around the stationary Earth. The English astronomer William Gilbert (1540–1603) thought that the Earth might have an inner magnetism that caused it to turn daily on its axis. In Italy, the Dominican friar Giordano Bruno (1548–1600) left his religious order in 1576 and inveighed against the inadequacies of Aristotelian physics. Fascinated by the ancient hermetic religion of Egypt, Bruno was convinced that esoteric spiritual exercises could give the philosopher direct access to the divine life that lay hidden behind the veil of physical reality.[53] This, he claimed, was the real meaning of heliocentric theory, which Copernicus—a mere jobbing mathematician—had not fully understood.

Arguably the most brilliant of these pioneering scientists was the German astronomer Johannes Kepler (1571–1630),[54] who had corresponded with Brahe, helped him in his work, and succeeded him in the post of imperial astrologer. Like Copernicus, Kepler was convinced that mathematics was the key to understanding the cosmos and that the scientist's task was to test his mathematical theories against rigorous empirical observation. In 1609, he published *Mysterium cosmographicum,* the first public attempt to justify and refine Copernicus's heliocentric theory, which had been unnecessarily complicated by Copernicus's retention of the circular planetary orbits; there were also outstanding problems with his hypothesis. What kept terrestrial objects from flying off the earth as it traveled through space at such high speed? After struggling for ten years to find a way of confirming the idea that the planets moved in perfect circles, Kepler was finally persuaded by Brahe's remarkably accurate observations to jettison it and, basing his calculations on Euclidean geometry, formulated the first "natural laws"—precise, verifiable statements about particular phenomena that were universally applicable.[55]

First: the planets moved in elliptical rather than circular orbits, traveling at speeds that varied proportionately according to their distance from the sun. Second: while in orbit, the planet would sweep out equal areas of the ellipse in equal intervals of time. Third: the ratio of the squares of the orbital periods was exactly equal to the ratio of the cubes of their average distance from the sun.[56] Kepler also suggested that instead of being moved by the automatic motion of the spheres, the planets were moved by mathematical forces. Extending Gilbert's theory of the earth's magnetism to all celestial bodies, he suggested that the elliptical orbits of the planets were created by the moving force (*anima motrix*) of the sun, combined with its own magnetism and that of the planets. The universe was, therefore, a self-regulating machine and ran on the same principles that governed dynamics here on earth.[57]

In reaching these groundbreaking conclusions, Kepler had depended not only on mathematics and empirical observation but on the same kind of hermetic mystical speculations as Bruno. He too was convinced that Copernicus had not understood the full implications of his theory, which he had stumbled upon "like a blind man, leaning on a stick as he walks."[58] But with the aid of theology, he, Kepler, would show that it was no accident that the universe took the form it did.[59] Geometry was God's language; like the Word that had existed with God from before the creation, it was identical with God.[60] So the study of geometry was the study of God, and by studying the mathematical laws that inform all natural phenomena, we commune with the divine mind.[61] Because he was convinced that God had impressed his image on the cosmos, Kepler saw the Trinity everywhere. The Trinity was the "form and archetype" of the only three stationary things in the universe: the sun, the fixed stars, and the space between the heavenly bodies.[62] The planets rotated in their orbits because of a mystic force, emanating from the sun in the same way as the Father creates through the Son and sets things in motion through the Spirit.[63] The solar system did not merely remind Kepler of the Trinity; he insisted that the Trinity had in part prompted his discoveries. But he was not entirely swept away by religious enthusiasm. He knew that the theological truth he found in the cosmos was dependent upon mathematics, empirical observation, and measurement. "If they do not agree, the whole of the preceding work has undoubtedly been a delusion."[64]

Today it is often assumed that modern science has always clashed with religion. Kepler, a mathematician of extraordinary genius, reminds us that early modern science was rooted in faith. These pioneering scientists had no desire to get rid of religion. Instead, they would develop a secular theology, written by and for laymen, because their discoveries made them think differently about God. During the sixteenth and seventeenth centuries, science, philosophy, and religion were tightly welded together. Kepler was convinced that during his mathematical exploration of the universe, he had "followed with sweat and panting the footprints of the Creator."[65] Scientists had to cast aside everything they thought they knew and confront the unknown—in rather the same way as their contemporary John of the Cross encountered the unknown God, telling his readers: "To come to the knowledge you have not, you must go by a way in which you know not."[66] If they did not have the courage to move beyond the safety of received ideas, mystic and scientist alike would become trapped in theories that were no longer adequate.

At the end of the sixteenth century, however, the intolerant strain of modernity came to the fore in Italy, the home of the Renaissance. The Protestant Reformation had been traumatic for all Catholics, but Italians had also witnessed the sack of Rome by German mercenary troops in 1527, the collapse of the republic of Florence in 1536, and, finally, the Spanish domination of the Italian peninsula. Put on the defensive, the Catholic hierarchy became fanatically intent on achieving absolute control over their subjects—many of whom were willing in these fearful times to trade the burden of freedom for the consolations of certainty. The theology of Thomas Aquinas and the philosophy and science of Aristotle, transformed beyond all recognition into a rigid system of dogma, became Catholic orthodoxy; all other schools of thought were regarded with deep suspicion. In 1559, Pope Paul IV had issued the first official Index of Prohibited Books and Pope Pius V (1566–72) set up the Congregation of the Index to supervise the Vatican program of censorship. As a result, at the turn of the seventeenth century, there was a spate of condemnations. It was now extremely dangerous to criticize Aristotelian cosmology. The work of the Italian philosopher Bernardino Telesio (1509–88) and the Dominican Tommaso Campanella (1568–1639) was condemned because of their opposition to Aristotle, and Campanella was imprisoned for twenty-seven years. Francesco Patrizi (1529–97) was forced to abjure the now "subversive" philosophy of Platonism and was condemned for teaching the infinity of interstellar space; Francesco Pucci (1543–97) was executed for his heterodox views on Original Sin; and in 1600, Giordano Bruno was burned at the stake for preaching the occult heresy that the stars had souls and that there existed an infinite number of worlds.[67]

It was in this grim political climate that the Italian astronomer Galileo Galilei (1564–1642) announced that he had proved Copernicus right. Unlike Kepler and Bruno, Galileo had no interest in the occult; instead of seeing the universe as a numinous reflection of the divine mystery, he described it as a cosmic mechanism ruled by mathematical laws. By observing the oscillation of a swinging lamp in the cathedral of Pisa, he had inferred the value of a pendulum for the exact measurement of time. He had invented a hydrostatic balance, written a treatise on specific gravity, and proved mathematically that all falling bodies, whatever their size, descended to earth at the same velocity. One of his most famous achievements was to perfect the refracting telescope, through which in 1609 he observed the craters of the moon, sunspots, the phases of Venus, and the four moons of Jupiter. The spots on the sun and the pitted surface of the moon proved that these were not the perfect bodies described by Aristotle. It was now clear that Jupiter was a moving planet and was circled by satellites similar to our own moon. All this, Galileo concluded, was proof positive of the Copernican hypothesis. In 1610, he published *The Sidereal Messenger* to immediate acclaim. All over Europe, people made their own telescopes and scanned the heavens themselves. When Galileo visited Rome the following year, the Jesuits publicly confirmed his discoveries and, to enormous applause, Prince Federico Cesi made him a member of the Accademia dei Lincei.

The case of Galileo has become a cause célèbre, emblematic of what is thought to be the eternal and inherent conflict between science and religion. But, in fact, Galileo was a victim not of religion per se but of the post-Tridentine Catholic Church at a time when it felt an endangered species. Pope Urban VIII (1568–1644) made an appalling error when he silenced Galileo, but Galileo also made mistakes. Each represented the intolerance of modernity, which was beginning to overtake the more open, liberal, and healthily skeptical spirit of the Renaissance.

Galileo exemplified the precision and practical orientation of the emerging modern spirit. He insisted that it was impossible to understand a single word of the Book of Nature without knowing the language of mathematics. First the scientist should isolate the phenomenon he was observing—the swinging pendulum or the falling body. Next he must translate the problem into mathematical theorems, axioms, and propositions. Finally, his mathematical conclusions must be tested to ensure that they were an accurate fit with the physical phenomenon that had sparked the investigation. Instead of losing himself in mystical theories, the scientist should concentrate on an object's measurable, quantitative characteristics—its size, shape, number, weight, or motion. Other qualities— taste, color, texture, or smell, which was what a nonspecialist would notice first—were irrelevant, because they were merely subjective impressions.[68] Scientists were beginning to develop an entirely different way of contemplating the world. When he looked at an object, Galileo bypassed its sensual properties—whether it was "white or red, bitter or sweet, sounding or mute, of a pleasant or non-pleasant odour"—and explored instead the abstract, mathematical principles that accounted for it.[69] A scientist could believe in something that did not exist in his actual experience and could never be realized in the physical world, because his mathematical calculations had given him absolute confidence in its existence. Galileo was no longer content to speak hypothetically. Hypotheses were mere conjectures, matters of opinion, and it was the task of science to provide unequivocal certainty. Convinced that the sun-centered universe was a physical fact that could be established empirically, he committed himself to finding an incontrovertible proof that was "necessary," that is, self-evident, irrefutable, and backed up by carefully observed physical evidence.[70] If a scientist's conclusions left any room for doubt, they were not, in his view, scientific.[71]

But of course it was not possible to prove religious truth in this way. To his dying day, Galileo adhered to the traditional relationship of *mythos* and *logos* and insisted that his theories did not in any way contradict religion. Mechanics (the study of motion) had nothing to say about theology. They were two entirely distinct disciplines, each with its own sphere of competence. Other early modern scientists would find it necessary to invoke God as an explanation for their theories, but not Galileo. In his famous "Letter to the Grand-Duchess Christina," which set forth his views on the relationship of science and religion, he wholeheartedly endorsed Augustine's principle of accommodation. Science focused on the material world, theology on God. The two disciplines should be kept separate and must not encroach upon each other's domain. God was the author of both the Book of Nature and the Bible, and "two truths cannot contradict one another."[72] If scientists made statements about religion and if the devout claimed that scripture gave infallible information about the hidden structures of nature, there could only be the worst kind of confusion.[73] Copernicus had understood this perfectly: he had always limited his remarks to "physical conclusions based above all on sensory experience and very accurate observations."[74] But in cases where there was no conclusive proof, Galileo argued that we should bow to the authority of the Bible: "I have no doubt at all that, where human reason cannot reach, and where consequently one cannot have a science, but only opinion and faith, it is appropriate piously to conform absolutely to the literal meaning of scripture."[75]

What Galileo did not seem to have realized was that the political climate had changed. The Vatican no longer regarded theology as a speculative science but was systematically reducing the teachings of Aristotle and Aquinas to an inflexible set of propositions formulated in such a way as to end all discussion and maximize certainty.[76] In 1605, the Jesuit cardinal Robert Bellarmine (1542–1621), who epitomized this new attitude, had become papal theologian. For Bellarmine, the task of theology was simply to organize doctrines into neat systems that could be marshaled effectively against the enemies of the Church. The execution of Bruno had made it horribly clear that papal officials were ready to enforce the new orthodoxy using the same coercive methods as any early modern monarchy.

Galileo was not a lone voice; he belonged to a "family" of Catholic progressives who supported his Copernican ideas but constantly advised him not to tangle with the Vatican authorities.[77] And yet despite his conviction that theology and science were entirely separate disciplines, he seemed perversely intent on reconciling his discoveries with scripture. In his *Letters on Sunspots* (1612), he produced biblical quotations proving that his theory was "most agreeable to the truths of holy writ"[78] and was furious when the papal censors insisted that he delete them. When opposed, Galileo could be just as scornful and impatiently self-righteous as any cardinal. But why, given his clearly stated views, had he included the quotations in the first place? Hypothetical thinking had been acceptable to Copernicus and would continue to be essential to scientific procedure. Was Galileo's insistence on absolute certainty another sign of the dogmatism of the age?

In 1615, the learned Carmelite friar Paolo Foscarini arrived in Rome to make a calm but forceful plea for the heliocentric universe. In the Bible, Foscarini argued, God revealed only those truths that could not be discovered by natural reason and had left the rest to human beings. When Bellarmine read his treatise, he replied that as far as he knew there was no definitive proof of the Copernican theory. If there were, it would be a different matter: "Then we would have to use great care in explaining the passages of scripture that seem contrary. . . . But I cannot believe that there is such a demonstration until someone shows it to me."[79] Galileo immediately pointed out that the Council of Trent upheld the authority of the Bible only in matters of faith and morals and that heliocentric theory fell under neither category. It did not seem to have occurred to him that it was probably unwise to correct Bellarmine, the principal spokesman of reformed Catholicism, about the Council's rulings. He then further muddied the waters by overstating his case, arguing that his experiments *had* provided the definitive proof that Bellarmine declared to be missing.[80] But this was not the case: Galileo's observations on sunspots, the phases of Venus, and the tides were suggestive but not conclusive. On both sides, there was a clash of misplaced certainty.[81]

Galileo was right to argue that poetical remarks in the Bible should not be read as definitive scientific observations; this had been standard exegetical practice in the West since the time of Augustine, and in failing to recognize this, Bellarmine was theologically at fault. But Galileo had not been able to meet his own high standards of scientific verification and had not fully appreciated the importance of hypothetical and probable reasoning in science. In mixing science and religion, he had violated his own principles and entered the now dangerous minefield of scriptural interpretation.[82] If he had presented his view as the probable theory it actually was, he could have remained at peace with the Church. Instead, he insisted that he was in possession of a proof that he had not achieved. In 1616, Copernicus's *De revolutionibus* and Foscarini's treatise were put on the Index. Galileo himself was not threatened, and Bellarmine even gave him a certificate stating that he had not been asked to recant any of his theories.[83]

But in 1623, Galileo entered the lists again when his old friend Maffeo Barberini became Pope Urban VIII. When they met in Rome, Urban feted Galileo and agreed that he could write what he chose about heliocentric theory, as long as he presented his theories as hypothetical in the usual way. Galileo returned to Florence to work on his *Dialogues on the Two World Systems*. But after this promising beginning, two of Galileo's patrons were implicated in Spanish political intrigues at the papal court and were disgraced, and Galileo was damaged by association.[84] To make matters worse, he had added a final paragraph to the *Dialogues*. "Simplicio," the character who represented the new Aristotelian orthodoxy and performed throughout the dialogue as the "fall guy," argued that Copernican theory was "neither true nor conclusive" and that it "would be excessive boldness for anyone to limit and restrict the divine power and wisdom to one particular fancy of his own."[85] These words were a direct quotation of published remarks by Urban himself, who would not have been pleased to see them on the lips of Simplicio, whose name was an insult in itself. On April 12, 1633, Galileo was summoned to the Holy Office and was judged guilty of disobedience. On June 22, he was forced to recant on his knees, and returned to Florence, where he was confined to his country estate.

When Copernicus had presented his ideas in the Vatican, the pope had given his approval; ninety years later, *De revolutionibus* was placed on the Index. In 1605, Francis Bacon (1561–1626), counselor to King James I of England, had declared that there could be no conflict between science and religion. But that openness was giving way to dogmatism and suspicion. There would soon be no place in the new Europe for the skepticism of Montaigne or the psychological agnosticism of Shakespeare. By the beginning of the seventeenth century, the notion of truth had begun to change. Thomas Aquinas would not have recognized his theology in its post-Tridentine guise. His apophatic delight in unknowing was being replaced by a strident lust for certainty and a harsh dogmatic intolerance. The spirituality of silence was giving way to wordy debate; the refusal to *define* (a word that literally means "to set limits upon") was being superseded by aggressive definitions of ineffable dogma. Faith was beginning to be identified with "belief" in man-made opinions—and that would, eventually, make faith itself difficult to maintain.

The first modern Western atheists, however, were not Christians who had been alienated by the terrible convictions of their clergy but Jews living in the most liberal country in Europe. Their experience tells us a good deal about our current religious predicament. By the early seventeenth century, while the rest of Europe was in the grip of severe economic recession, the Dutch were enjoying a golden age of prosperity and expansion. They did not share the new sectarian dogmatism. Toward the end of the sixteenth century, some of the

Marrano Jews had been permitted to leave Portugal and migrated to Venice, Hamburg, London, and, above all, Amsterdam, which became their New Jerusalem. In Holland, Jews were not confined to ghettos, as they were elsewhere in Europe; they became successful businessmen and mingled freely with gentiles. When they arrived in Amsterdam, the Marranos were eager for the opportunity to practice their faith fully.

But they found conventional religious life bewildering. For decades the Iberian Jews had lived without communal religious life and had no experience of ritual observance. The Dutch rabbis had the difficult task of guiding them back into the fold, making allowances for their problems without compromising tradition, and it is a tribute to them that most of the Marranos were able to make the transition.[86] But initially their reaction was similar to that of people today who find the "beliefs" of religion arbitrary and incredible because they have not fully participated in its transformative rites. The abstruse laws of diet and purification must have seemed barbaric and meaningless to the Marrano sophisticates, who found it difficult to accept the rabbis' explanations because they were used to thinking things out rationally for themselves. According to Isaac Orobio de Castro, a philosophy professor who had lived in Iberia for years as a closet Jew, some of them had become "unspeakable atheists":[87] they were "full of vanity, pride and arrogance," loved to display their learning "by contradicting what they do not understand," and felt that their expertise in the modern sciences put them above "those who are indeed educated in the sacred laws."[88]

A tiny minority of the Marranos found the transition to full cultic observance impossible. One of the most tragic cases was that of Uriel da Costa, who had experienced Portuguese Christianity as oppressive, cruel, and composed of rules and doctrines that bore no relation to the gospels.[89] He had formed his own idea of Jewish religion by reading the Bible, but when he arrived in Amsterdam he was shocked to find that contemporary Judaism was just as far removed from scripture as Catholicism. Outraged, he published a treatise attacking the Torah and declaring that he believed only in human reason and the laws of nature. He caused such ferment that the rabbis were forced to excommunicate him. There was as yet no notion in Europe of a "secular Jew," and as an excommunicate da Costa was shunned by Jews and Christians alike; children jeered at him in the street. In despair, he returned to the synagogue, but he still could not adapt to a faith that seemed incomprehensible. In 1640, he committed suicide.

In 1655 Juan da Prado, who had been a committed member of the Jewish underground in Portugal for twenty years, arrived in Amsterdam. He too had found that without the spiritual exercises that produced them, the ideas of conventional religion lacked substance and had succumbed to Marrano deism, seeing God as identical with the laws of nature.[90] He too was shocked by his first encounter with a fully functioning Jewish community and was loud in his complaints. Why did the Jews think they were God's chosen people? Was it not degrading to imagine that the First Cause was a Personality? Two years after his arrival, Prado was excommunicated and became more extreme in his views, arguing that all religion was rubbish and that reason, not "revelation," was the sole arbiter of truth. We have no idea how he ended his days.

The unhappy stories of Prado and da Costa show that the *mythos* of confessional religion is unsustainable without spiritual exercises. Reason alone can produce only an attenuated deism that is easily abandoned, as its God is remote, abstract, and ultimately incredible. And yet at the same time as the Jewish community in Amsterdam was being torn apart by these conflicts, the Christians of Europe had begun to develop their own form of deism; like Prado, they too would regard scientific rationality as the only route to truth and would seek a rational certainty that Jewish, Christian, and Muslim philosophers had long held to be impossible in matters of faith.

# EIGHT

# Scientific Religion

In 1610, the English poet John Donne (1572–1631) lamented the state of the world, which he thought was entering its final phase. A deeply conservative man, Donne was a casualty of the Reformation. Born into a devout Catholic family, he had abjured his faith after his brother had died in prison for sheltering a Catholic priest and had become bitterly hostile to the new Catholicism. He was profoundly disturbed by the recent scientific discoveries that seemed wantonly to have destroyed the old cosmic vision of perfection and harmony. These were hard times. Europe was in the throes of economic recession and the social unrest attendant on modernization, and yet in the midst of this confusion, the "new Philosophy"* called "all in doubt."

> 'Tis all in peeces, all cohaerence gone;
> All just supply, and all Relation.[1]

It was as though the universe had suffered a massive earthquake. New stars had been sighted in the firmament, and others had disappeared. The heavens no longer enjoyed their "Sphericall . . . round proportion embracing all," and planets were said to wander in "Eccentrique parts" that violated the "pure forme" that men had observed for so long.[2] When these fundamentals had shifted, how could anybody be certain of the truth?

Donne was not alone in his pessimism. That same year Henry IV

---

* The term "philosophy" was synonymous with "science."

of Navarre, who had seemed the only monarch capable of stemming the tide of denominational violence that was threatening to engulf the whole of Europe, had been assassinated by a Catholic fanatic. This was immediately recognized as a tragic turning point and had the same kind of impact in seventeenth-century Europe as did the assassination of President John F. Kennedy in twentieth-century America.[3] Henry had been determined to contain the religious passions that were becoming murderously divisive in France and had followed a policy of strict neutrality. He had granted civil liberties to French Protestants, and when the *parlement* expelled the Jesuits, Henry had reinstated them. His death, which shocked moderate Catholics and Protestants alike, sent a grim message: a policy of toleration had been tried but it had failed. By 1600, England was drifting into a civil war and the principalities of Germany were struggling to achieve independence from the Holy Roman Empire and form nation-states. Sweden supported the Protestant princes, and the Austrian Hapsburgs the Catholics. In 1618, this strife escalated into the full-scale Thirty Years' War, which killed 35 percent of the population of central Europe, which was reduced to a charnel house. Religion was clearly incapable of bringing the warring parties together. The more Roman Catholic zealots gloried in the slaughter of Protestants and the more Protestants exultantly burned Catholic strongholds to the ground, the more people of moderation and goodwill despaired of a solution.

But not everybody shared Donne's misgivings about the "new Philosophy." The Flemish Jesuit Leonard Lessius (1554–1623), one of the most distinguished theologians in Europe, shows that not all Catholics had developed the tunnel vision of the Vatican.[4] Lessius was committed to the Catholic Reformation, had studied in Rome under Bellarmine, and on his return to the University of Louvain had introduced the works of Aquinas in their new guise into the curriculum. But he was also a Renaissance man, open to all the changing intellectual currents of the early modern world. He had studied jurisprudence and economics, and had been one of the first to appreciate the altered role of money in the nascent capitalist economy. In 1612, just two years after Galileo had published *The Sidereal Messenger,* Lessius not only applauded his discoveries but was able to confirm them, because he too had observed the pitted surface of the moon and the satellites of

Jupiter through his telescope and was filled with "immense admiration" when he beheld this evidence of "God's wisdom and power."[5]

These remarks were included in Lessius's most important work, *Divine Providence and the Immortality of the Soul* (1612), a treatise directed "against atheists and politicians." There had been some concern in recent years about the emergence of "atheism," though at this date the term did not yet mean an outright denial of God's existence. It usually referred to any belief that the writer deemed incorrect. For Lessius, "atheism" was a heresy of the past: the only "atheists" he could name were the ancient Greek philosophers. He was especially concerned about the "atomists"—Democritus, Epicurus, and the Roman poet Lucretius (c. 95–55 BCE)—who had believed that the universe had come into being by chance. Democritus had imagined innumerable particles, so tiny that they were "indivisible" (*atomos*), careering round empty space, colliding periodically to form the material bodies of our world. There was a new interest in atomism in Europe at this time; it certainly troubled John Donne.[6] Democritus's infinite cosmic space suited the Copernican universe very well, now that it had been shorn of the celestial spheres. But Democritus had seen no need for an overseeing God, and Lessius could not accept this. Citing the Stoic philosophy of Cicero, he argued that the intricate design of the natural world required an intelligent Creator. It would be as absurd to deny the hand of divine providence as to imagine that a "faire, sumptuous and stately palace" had been put together "only by a suddain mingling and meeting together of certaine peeces of stones into this curious and artificiall forme."[7]

The French mathematician and Franciscan friar Marin Mersenne (1588–1648) was a committed scientist and had supported Galileo when it was not politically expedient to do so.[8] But in *The Impiety of Deists, Atheists and Libertines of Our Time,* he had no difficulty in identifying modern "atheists."[9] None of them denied the existence of God: some, like the devout Parisian priest Pierre Charron (1541–1603) or the Paduan philosopher Geronimo Cardano (1501–76), were merely skeptical about the ability of human reason to arrive at any final truth. Mersenne was particularly disturbed by the hermetic philosophy of Bruno, another of his "atheists," who had believed that nature had its own divine powers and needed no supervision. To counter this, Mersenne developed a Christian version of atomism, which added a supervising Creator God to Democritus's universe.[10] The atoms had neither intelligence nor purpose, so nature had no occult power of its own and was entirely dependent upon *le grand moteur de la universe*. It is significant that in combating "atheism," both Lessius and Mersenne turned instinctively to the science and philosophy of antiquity rather than to their own theological tradition. Thomas Aquinas had insisted that we could not learn anything about the nature of God from the created world; now the complexity that scientists were discovering in the universe had persuaded theologians that God must be an Intelligent Designer. Denys and Thomas would not have approved.

Mersenne was present at a conference in Paris in November 1628, when a distinguished group of philosophers listened to a spirited critique of scholasticism in the presence of Cardinal Pierre de Bérulle (1575–1629), the papal nuncio. Also present was the philosopher and scientist René Descartes (1596–1650), who refused to join the applause. The assembly, Descartes explained, had made a fundamental error in being satisfied with knowledge that was merely probable. But he had developed a philosophical method based on the mathematical sciences that yielded absolute certainty. It was not easy, but if followed diligently over a long period of time, it could be applied effectively to any field of knowledge, including theology. After the conference, Bérulle took Descartes aside and told him that he had a duty—indeed, a divine mission—to publish this method, if he thought that it could pull Europe back from the abyss.

Descartes had been educated at the Jesuit college of La Flèche in Anjou, founded by Henry IV, where he was encouraged to read widely. He had been overwhelmed with excitement when he read Galileo for the first time and had also been fascinated by the skepticism of Montaigne, though as time went on he became convinced that this was not the right message for a world torn apart by warring dogmatisms that seemed unable to find a truth to bring people together. Descartes' philosophy was marked by the horror of his time. He had been present when the heart of Henry IV, martyr of tolerance, had been enshrined in the cathedral at La Flèche. Throughout his life, he was convinced that both Catholics and Protestants could hope for heaven. His goal was to find a truth on which everybody—Catholics, Protestants, Muslims, deists, and "atheists"—could agree so that all people of good will could live together in peace.

Descartes' ideas were formed on the battlefields of the Thirty Years' War. On leaving school, he had joined the army of Maurice, Count of Nassau (1567–1625), and traveled Europe as a gentleman soldier, meeting some of the most important mathematicians and philosophers of the day. He claimed afterward that he had learned far more in the army than he would have at a university. As he witnessed the war at first hand, he became convinced that it was essential to find a way out of the theological and political impasse that seemed to be destroying civilization itself; everything seemed to be falling apart. The only way forward was to go back to first principles and start all over again. In 1619, Descartes transferred to the army of Maximilian I of Bavaria. As he was journeying to take up his new post, a heavy snowfall forced him to put up in a small *poêle,* a stove-heated room, near Ulm on the Danube. For once, he had time for serious, solitary reflection, and it was during this retreat that he devised his method. He experienced three luminous dreams, commanding him to lay the foundations of a "marvellous science" that would bring together all the disciplines—theology, arithmetic, astronomy, music, geometry, optics, and physics—under the mantle of mathematics. Descartes had been haunted by Montaigne's challenge at the end of the "Apology of Raymond Sebond": unless we could find one thing about which we were *completely* certain, we could be sure of nothing. In the *poêle*, Descartes turned Montaigne's skepticism on its head and made the experience of doubt the foundation of certainty.

First, he insisted, the thinker must empty his mind of everything that he thought he knew. He must, he told himself, "accept nothing as true which I did not clearly recognize to be so: that is to say, carefully to avoid precipitation and prejudice in judgments, and to accept in them nothing more than what was presented in my mind so clearly and distinctly that I could have no occasion to doubt it."[11] It was a rationalized version of Denys's way of denial.[12] A scientist must empty his mind of the truths of revelation and tradition. He could not trust the evidence of his senses, because a tower that looked round from a distance might really be square. He could not even be certain that the objects in his immediate environment were real: How did we know that we were not dreaming when we saw, heard, or touched them? How could we prove that we were awake? His aim was to find ideas that were immediately self-evident; only "clear" and "distinct" truths could provide a basis for his Universal Mathematics.

Eventually, Descartes found what he was looking for. "I noticed that whilst I wished to think all things false, it was absolutely essential that the 'I' should be somewhat," he concluded.

> Remarking that this truth, *"I think, therefore I am"* was so certain and so assured that all the most extravagant suppositions brought forward by the sceptics were incapable of shaking it, I came to the conclusion that I could receive it without scruple as the first principle of the philosophy for which I was seeking.[13]

This was the one certain thing that answered Montaigne's challenge. The internal experience of doubt itself revealed a certainty that nothing in the external world could provide. When we experience ourselves thinking and doubting, we become aware of our existence. The ego rose ineluctably from the depths of the mind by the disciplined ascesis of skepticism:[14] "What then am I? A thing which thinks [*res cogitans*]. What is a thing that thinks? It is a thing which doubts, understands, conceives, affirms, denies, wills, refuses, which also imagines and feels."[15] Descartes' famous maxim *"Cogito ergo sum"* ("I think, therefore I am") neatly reversed traditional Platonic epistemology: "I think, therefore there is that which I think." The modern mind was solitary, autonomous, and a world unto itself, unaffected by outside influence and separate from all other beings.

From this irreducible nub of certainty, Descartes went on to prove the existence of God and the reality of the external world. Because the material universe was lifeless, godless, and inert, it could tell us nothing about God. The only animate thing in the entire cosmos was the thinking self, and it was here that we should look for incontrovertible proof. Descartes was clearly influenced by Augustine and Anselm. Doubt reveals the imperfection of the thinker, because when we doubt we become acutely aware that something is missing. But the experience of imperfection presupposes a prior notion of perfection, because it is a relative term, comprehensible only in terms of its absolute. It was impossible that a finite being could by its own efforts conceive the idea of perfection, so it must follow "that it had been placed in me by a Nature which was really more perfect than mine could be, and which even had within itself all the perfections of which I could form any idea—that is to say, to put it in a word, which was God."[16] How else could we know that we doubted and desired—that we lacked something and were not, therefore, perfect—if we did not have within ourselves an innate idea that enabled us to recognize the defects of our own nature?

Most medieval theologians had rejected Anselm's ontological proof because, despite its apophatic dynamic, he had called God a "thing" (*aliquid*) that must "exist." But now Descartes claimed that God was a "clear and distinct" idea in the human mind and was entirely happy to apply the word "existence" to God. Where Thomas had said that God was not a "sort of thing," Descartes found no difficulty in calling God *a* being, albeit the "first and a sovereign Being."[17] Like Anselm, he saw existence as one of the perfections. "For it is not within my power to think of God without existence (that is of a supremely perfect Being devoid of a supreme perfection) though it is in my power to imagine a horse either with wings or without wings."[18] This truth was as clear as—if not clearer than—Pythagoras's theorem of the right-angled triangle. "Consequently it is at least as certain that God, who is a Being so perfect, is, or exists, as any demonstration of geometry can possibly be."[19]

God was absolutely necessary to Descartes' philosophy and his science, because without God he had no confidence in the reality of the external world.[20] Because we could not trust our senses, the existence of material things was "very dubious and uncertain." But a perfect being was truth itself and would not allow us to remain in error on such a fundamental matter:

> On the sole ground that God is not a deceiver and that consequently He has not permitted any falsity to exist in my opinion which He has not likewise given me the faculty of correcting, I may assuredly hope to conclude that I have within me the means of arriving at the truth even here.[21]

What we know about the external world, we know in exactly the same way as God knows it; we could have the same "clear" and "distinct" ideas as God himself.

Once Descartes was confident that the material world existed, he could proceed with the second part of his project: the creation of a single scientific method that could bring a world that was spinning out of control under the rule of reason. In his desire to master reality, Descartes could not accept the idea that the cosmos had come into being by accident. His cosmos was an intricate, well-oiled machine, set in motion and sustained by an all-powerful God. Like Mersenne, Descartes revived ancient Greek atomism, but with the crucial addition of an overseeing Creator. At the moment of creation, God had imposed his mathematical laws upon the atoms, so that when an atom collided with another, this was not a matter of chance but achieved by divinely implanted principles.[22] Once everything had been set in motion, no further divine action was necessary, and God was able to retire from the world and allow it to run itself.

In a time of frightening political turbulence, a universe that ran as regularly as clockwork seemed profoundly attractive. Descartes, a devout Catholic all his life, had experienced his "method" as a God-given revelation and in gratitude—extraordinary as this may seem—vowed to make a pilgrimage to the shrine of Our Lady of Loreto. Yet Descartes' philosophy was profoundly irreligious: his God, a clear idea in his mind, was well on the way to becoming an idol, and his meditation on the thinking self did not result in *kenosis* but in the triumphant assertion of the ego. There was no awe in Descartes' theology: indeed, he believed that it was the task of science to dispel wonder. In the future people should look, for example, at the clouds, "in such a way that we will no longer have occasion to wonder at anything that can be seen of them, or anything that descends from them."[23]

When he dedicated his *Meditations on First Philosophy* to "The Most Illustrious Dean and Doctors of the Sacred Faculty of Theology in Paris," Descartes made an astonishing claim: "I have always considered that the two questions respecting God and the soul were the chief of those that ought to be demonstrated by philosophical [i.e., "scientific"] rather than theological argument."[24] In the clear expectation that they would agree with him, Descartes calmly informed the most distinguished body of theologians in Europe that they were not competent to discuss God. Mathematics and physics would do the job more effectively.[25] And the theologians were all too happy to agree. It was a fateful move. Henceforth, theology would increasingly be translated into a "philosophical" or "scientific" idiom that was alien to it.

Even those who could see flaws in Descartes' Universal Mathematics were excited by the idea of a mechanical universe, ruled at all times and in all places by the same unequivocal laws.[26] Increasingly, the mechanical universe would be seen as a model for society. Citizens should submit to a rational government in the same way as the different parts of the cosmos obeyed the rational laws of the scientific God. People were also intrigued by the idea of a single method that would lead infallibly to wisdom and certainty and make the existence of God as necessary and lucid as one of Euclid's theorems. Doubt and perplexity would soon be things of the past.

In the years after the Thirty Years' War, when religion seemed so badly compromised, it was thought that reason alone could create the conditions of a sustainable peace. The German philosopher Gottfried Wilhelm Leibniz (1646–1716) was also a diplomat who worked tirelessly to bring the new nation-states of Europe together.[27] One of his chief projects was the construction of a universal language based on mathematical principles that would enable people to converse clearly and distinctly. The English philosopher John Locke (1632–1704) was convinced that the religious intolerance that had rent Europe apart was simply the result of an inadequate idea of God. If people were allowed to use their rational powers freely, they would discover the truth for themselves, because the natural world gave ample evidence for God. There was no further need for revelation, ritual, prayer, or superstitious doctrines. Where premodern theologians had been continually alert to the danger of God becoming an idolatrous projection, Locke argued that "when we would frame an *Idea,* the most suitable we can to the Supreme Being, we enlarge every one of these [Simple *Ideas*] with our *Idea* of Infinity, and so putting them together, make our complex *Idea of God.*"[28]

But the French mathematician Blaise Pascal (1623–62), a passionately religious man, returned to the older idea that God was hidden in nature and that it was no use trying to find him there.[29] In fact, the mechanical universe was godless, frightening, and devoid of meaning:

> When I see the blind and wretched state of man, when I
> survey the whole universe in its deadness and man left to
> himself with no light, as though lost in this corner of the

universe without knowing who put him there, what he
has to do, what will become of him when he dies, incapable of knowing anything, I am moved to terror, like a
man transported in his sleep to some terrifying desert
island, who wakes up quite lost with no means of escape.
Then I marvel that so wretched a state does not drive
people to despair.[30]

Certainty did not come from the rational contemplation of "clear"
and "distinct" ideas but from the "heart," the inner core of the human
person. In the "Memorial" stitched into the lining of his doublet, Pascal recorded an experience that had filled him with "certainty, certainty, heartfelt joy, peace." It had come from the God of Abraham,
Isaac, and Jacob, not the God "of philosophers and scholars."[31]

Pascal could see that Christianity was about to make a serious mistake. Theologians were eager to embrace the modern ethos and make
their teaching conform to the "clear and distinct" ideas currently in
vogue, but how far should the new science impinge upon religion? A
God who was merely "the author of mathematical truths and of the
order of the elements" could bring no light to the darkness and pain
of human existence. It would only cause people to fall into atheism.[32]
Pascal was one of the first people to see that atheism—meaning a radical denial of God's existence—would soon become a serious option.[33]
A person who had not engaged himself with the rituals, exercises,
and practices of religion would not be convinced by the arguments of
the philosophers; for such a person, faith could only be a wager, a leap
in the dark. Pascal had developed his rational powers more than
most: by the age of eleven, he had worked out for himself the first
twenty-three propositions of Euclid; at sixteen he had published a
remarkable treatise on geometry; and he went on to invent a calculat-
ing machine, a barometer, and a hydraulic press. But he knew that
reason could not produce religious conviction; "the heart" had its own
reasons for faith.[34]

In the Netherlands, a Jewish philosopher had developed an atheistic
vision that was at once more radical yet also more religious than
either Descartes' or Locke's.[35] In 1655, shortly after Prado had arrived
in Amsterdam, the young Baruch Spinoza (1632–77) stopped attend-

ing services and began to voice serious doubts about traditional Judaism. Spinoza had been born in Amsterdam of parents who had lived as Marranos in Portugal but had successfully adapted to Orthodox Judaism. He had always had access to the intellectual life of the gentile world and had received a traditionally Jewish education, as well as studying mathematics, astronomy, and physics. But, living in a Marrano environment, he was accustomed to the idea of an entirely rational religion and argued that what we call "God" was simply the totality of nature itself. Eventually, on July 27, 1656, the rabbis pronounced the sentence of excommunication on Spinoza too, and he was glad to go. As a genius with powerful friends and patrons, he could survive outside a religious community in a way that his predecessors could not, and he became the first thoroughgoing secularist to live beyond the reach of established religion. Yet he remained an isolated figure, since Jews and gentiles both found his pantheistic philosophy shocking and "atheistic."

Spinoza shared the Marrano disdain for revealed religion, though he agreed with Descartes that the very idea of "God" contains a validation of God's existence. But this was not the personalized God of Judeo-Christianity. Spinoza's God was the sum and principle of natural law, identical with and equivalent to the order that governs the universe. God was neither the Creator nor the First Cause, but was inseparable from the material world, an immanent force that welded everything into unity and harmony. When human beings contemplated the workings of their minds, they opened themselves to the eternal and infinite reality of the God active within them. Spinoza experienced his philosophical study as a form of prayer; the contemplation of this immanent presence filled him with awe and wonder. As he explained in his *Short Treatise on God* (1661), the deity was not an object to be known but the principle of our thought, so the joy we experienced when we attained knowledge *was* the intellectual love of God. A true philosopher should cultivate intuitive knowledge, flashes of insight that suddenly fused all the information he had acquired discursively into a new and integrated vision, an *ekstatic* perception that Spinoza called "beatitude."

Most Western thinkers would not follow Spinoza. Their God was becoming increasingly remote, and those who adopted an immanent view of the divine were often regarded as rebels against the established order. The Peace of Westphalia (1648) had brought the Thirty Years' War to an end and set up a system of sovereign nation-states, but this new polity could not be established overnight. As the modern market economy developed, it became essential to change the political structures of society. To enhance the wealth of the nation, more and more people had to be brought into the productive process—even at a quite humble level, as printers, factory hands, and office workers. They would, therefore, need a modicum of education in the modern ethos, and, inevitably, they began to demand a share in the decision making of their government. Democracy was found to be essential to the nation-state and the capitalist economy. Countries that democratized forged ahead; those that tried to confine their wealth and privilege to the aristocracy fell behind. No elite group gives up power willingly, of course. The democratization of Europe was not a peaceful process but was achieved in a series of bloody revolutions, civil wars, the assassination of the nobility, militant dictatorships, and reigns of terror.

During the 1640s and 1650s, for example, England had seen a violent civil war, the execution of King Charles I (1649), and a period of republican rule under the Puritan government of Oliver Cromwell (1599–1658). Levelers, Quakers, Diggers, and Muggletonians had developed their own revolutionary piety.[36] If God dwelled in nature— if, as some said, God *was* nature—there was no need for clerics and churches, and everybody should share the nation's prosperity. George Fox (1624–91), founder of the Society of Friends, taught Christians to seek their own inner light and "make use of their own understanding without direction from another";[37] in the scientific age, religion should be "experimental," every one of its doctrines tested empirically against each person's experience.[38] For Richard Coppin, the God within was the only true authority. Because God informed all things, Jacob Bauthumely regarded the worship of a distinct, separate God as blasphemous, while Laurence Clarkson called upon the omnipresent God to empower the people to bring the aristocracy down.

This fervid piety was not quelled by the restoration of the monarchy in 1660 under King Charles II; it simply went underground. The next thirty years were a time of extreme anxiety, since people feared another violent revolution.[39] A flourishing market economy was developing in London and the southeast, but the poor resented the affluence of the new commercial classes, the authority of the recently established Church of England, and the privileges of the landed gentry. In Cambridge, the mathematician and clergyman Isaac Barrow (1630–77) developed a liberal Anglicanism that he hoped would help to build an orderly society, modeled on the cosmos, in which all people kept to their proper orbits and worked together harmoniously for the common good. A regular member of these discussion groups was the young Isaac Newton (1642–1727).[40]

Like Descartes, Newton aspired to create a universal science capable of interpreting the whole of human experience. Where Descartes' quest had been solitary, Newton understood the importance of cooperation in science. He wanted to build on the achievements of his great predecessors, and felt, as he wrote to his friend Robert Hooke, as though he were "standing on the shoulders of giants."[41] But these giants had left some unanswered questions: What kept the planets in their orbits? Why did terrestrial objects always fall to the ground? In a series of lectures, published in 1687, Newton argued that the universal science was not mathematics, as Descartes had believed, but mechanics, "which accurately proposes and demonstrates the art of measuring."[42] His Universal Mechanics would start by measuring the motions of the universe and then, on the basis of these findings, go on to explain all other phenomena.[43]

Newton achieved a magnificent synthesis that brought together in a single theory Cartesian physics, Kepler's laws of planetary motion, and Galileo's laws of terrestrial movement. Gravity proved to be the fundamental force that accounted for all celestial and earthly activity. In order to maintain their orbits around the sun at their relative speeds and distances, the planets were pulled toward the sun by an attractive force that decreased inversely as the square of the distance from the sun. The moon and the oceans were drawn toward the earth by the same law. For the first time, all the disparate facts observed in the cosmos had been brought together into a comprehensive theory. At last the solar system had become intelligible. Everything—the annual orbits of the planets, the rotation of the earth, the motions of the moon, the tidal movement of the seas, the precession of the equinoxes, a stone falling to the ground—could now be explained by gravity. Gravity caused all bodies to incline mutually toward one another; it prevented the planets from flying off into space and enabled them to maintain their stable orbits at the relative speeds and distances specified by Kepler.

If it was to be truly universal, the Universal Mechanics must account for *all* phenomena. Because gravity could not explain how the solar system came about, Newton had to find its original cause. "Though these bodies may, indeed, continue in their orbits by the mere laws of gravity," he argued, "yet they could by no means have at first derived the regular position of the orbits by themselves from these laws."[44] The sun, planets, and comets had been positioned so precisely that they "could only proceed from the counsel and domination of an intelligent and powerful Being."[45] Like most seventeenth-century scientists, Newton was convinced that matter was inert: it was unable to move or develop unless acted upon by an outside force. So God was essential to the entire system. There could be no question of excluding God from science. "Thus much concerning God," Newton concluded, "to discourse of whom from the appearances of things does certainly belong to natural philosophy."[46]

Indeed, Newton explained in a later work, the discussion of God was a matter of priority in science:

> The main Business of natural Philosophy is to argue from Phaenomena without feigning Hypotheses, and to deduce Causes from Effects, till we come to the very first Cause, which certainly is not mechanical; and not only to unfold the Mechanism of the World, but chiefly to resolve these and such like Questions.[47]

In a letter to the classicist Richard Bentley (1662–1742), Newton confessed that from the outset he had hoped to provide a scientific proof for God's existence. "When I wrote my treatise about our Systeme, I had an eye upon such Principles as might work with considering men for the beleife in a Deity and nothing can rejoyce me more then to find it usefull for that purpose."[48] When he had considered the mathematical balance of the solar system, he was "forced to ascribe it to ye counsel and contrivance of a voluntary Agent," who was obviously "very well skilled in Mechanicks and Geometry."[49] Gravity could not explain everything. It "may put ye planets into motion but without ye divine powers, it could never put them into such Circulating motion as they have about ye sun."[50] Gravity could not account for the superb design of the cosmos. The earth rotated on its axis every day at a speed of about a thousand miles an hour at the equator; if this speed were reduced to a hundred miles per hour, day and night would be ten times as long, the heat of the sun would shrivel vegetation by day, and everything would freeze during the long nights. The motions that Newton had observed were conserved by inertial force, but originally they "must have required a divine power to impress them."[51]

At a stroke, Newton overturned centuries of Christian tradition. Hitherto leading theologians had argued that the creation could tell us nothing about God; indeed, it proved to us that God was unknowable. Thomas Aquinas's "five ways" had shown that though one could prove that "what all men call God" had brought something out of nothing, it was impossible to know what God was. But Newton had no doubt that his Universal Mechanics could explain all God's attributes. The Oxford orientalist Edward Pococke (1604–91) had told him that the Latin *deus* was derived from the Arabic *du* ("lord").[52] In the laws of gravity that held the universe together, Newton saw evidence of this divine "dominion" (*dominatio*), the overwhelming force that masters and controls the cosmos. It was the fundamental divine attribute: "It is the dominion of a spiritual being that constitutes a God."[53] But this domineering God was very different from Luria's self-emptying En Sof or the kenotic God of the Trinity. Having established "Dominion" as the divine quality par excellence, it was possible to infer other attributes. A study of the universe proved that the God who created it must have intelligence, perfection, eternity, infinity, omniscience, and omnipotence: "That is, he continues from age to age, and is present from infinity to infinity; he rules all things and he knows what happens and what is able to happen."[54]

God had been reduced to a scientific explanation and given a clearly definable function in the cosmos. God was actually "omnipresent not *virtually* only but *substantially*" in the universe, acting on matter in the same way as the will acts on the body.[55] By 1704, Newton had come to believe that all the animating forces of nature were physical manifestations of this divine presence, though he expressed this conviction only in private to close friends.[56] Not a single natural power worked independently of God. God was immediately present in the laws that he had devised; gravity was not simply a force of nature but the activity of God himself, he explained to Bentley. Gravity was the "Agent acting constantly according to certain laws that makes bodies move *as though* they attract each other."[57]

> Did blind chance know that there was light, and what was its refraction, and fit the eyes of all creatures after the most conscious manner, to make use of it? These, and such like considerations, always have and ever will prevail with mankind, to believe that there is a Being who made all things, and has all things in his power and who is therefore to be feared.[58]

God's existence was now a rational consequence of the world's intricate design.

Newton was convinced that this "beleife," a word that he habitually used in its modern sense, had prompted the primordial religion of humanity. While he was working on the *Principia*, he began to write a treatise entitled *The Philosophical Origins of Gentile Theology*, which argued that Noah had founded a faith based on the rational contemplation of nature. There had been no revealed scriptures, no miracles, and no mysteries.[59] Noah and his sons had worshipped in temples that were replicas of the heliocentric universe and taught them to see nature itself as "the true Temple of ye great God they worshipped." This primordial faith had been "the true religion till ye nations corrupted it." Science was the *only* means of arriving at a proper understanding of the sacred: "For there is no way (wth out revelation)* to come to ye knowledge of a Deity but by ye frame of nature."[60] Scientific rationalism, therefore, was what Newton called the "fundamental religion." But it had been corrupted with "Monstrous Legends, false miracles, veneration of reliques, charmes, ye doctrine of Ghosts or Daemons, and their intercession, invocation & worship and other such heathen superstitions."[61] Newton was particularly incensed by the doctrines of the Trinity and the Incarnation, which, he argued, had been foisted on the faithful by Athanasius and other unscrupulous fourth-century theologians.

---

* In the manuscript, the words in parentheses have been added as an afterthought above the line.

Thomas Aquinas's contemplation of the cosmos had revealed the existence of a mystery. But Newton hated mystery, which he equated with sheer irrationality: "'Tis the temper of the hot and superstitious part of mankind in matters of religion," he wrote irritably, "ever to be fond of mysteries & for that reason to like best what they understand least."[62] It was positively dangerous to describe God as a mystery, because this "conduces to the rejection of his existence. It is of concern to theologians that the conception [of God] be made as easy and as agreeable as possible, so as not to be exposed to cavils and thereby called into question."[63] For the early modern rationalist, truth could not be obscure, so the God that was Truth must be as rational and plausible as any other fact of life.

Newton's scientific theology quickly became central to the campaign against "atheism." During these anxious years, people saw "atheists" everywhere, but they were still using the term to describe anybody they disapproved of, regardless of his or her beliefs; "atheism" thus functioned as an image of deviancy that helped people to place themselves on the shifting moral spectrum of early modernity.[64] In the 1690s, an "atheist" could be recognized by his drunkenness, fornication, or unsound politics. It was not yet possible to sustain unbelief. Certainly people experienced doubts from time to time. John Bunyan (1628–88) described the "storms," "flouds of Blasphemies," "confusion and astonishment" that descended on him when he wondered "whether there were in truth a God or no."[65] But it was well-nigh impossible to maintain such skepticism on a permanent basis, because the conceptual difficulties were insurmountable.[66] The doubter would find no support in the most advanced thought of the time, which insisted that the natural laws brilliantly uncovered by the scientists required a Lawgiver.[67] Until there was a body of cogent reasons, each based on another cluster of scientifically verified truths, outright atheistic denial could only be a personal whim or passing impulse.

But the fear of "atheism" persisted, and when theologians tried to counter the "heresies" of Spinoza or the Levelers, they turned instinctively to the new scientific rationalism. The French priest and philosopher Nicholas de Malebranche (1638–1715) based his anti-atheistic riposte on Descartes. Others followed Newton. The Irish physicist and chemist Robert Boyle (1627–91), founding member of the Royal Society, was convinced that the intricate motions of the mechanistic universe proved the existence of a divine Engineer. He commissioned a series of lectures designed to counter atheism and superstition by presenting the public with the discoveries of the new science. Christian leaders, such as John Tillotson, archbishop of Canterbury (1630–94), were eager to embrace this scientific religion, because they regarded reason as the most reliable path to truth. The Boyle lecturers were all ardent Newtonians, and Newton himself gave his support to the venture.[68]

In his Boyle lectures, Richard Bentley argued that the efficient machinery of the cosmos required an all-powerful and wholly benign Designer. Samuel Clarke (1675–1729), who delivered the lectures in 1704, maintained that "almost everything in the World demonstrates to us this great Truth; and affords undeniable Arguments, to prove that the World and all Things therein, are the Effects of an Intelligent and Knowing Cause."[69] Only mathematics and science could counter the arguments of atheists like Spinoza, so there could only be "One only Method or Continued Thread of Arguing."[70] Newton's Universal Mechanics had proved what the scriptures had long maintained: "He is the Great One, above all his works, the awe-inspiring Lord, stupendously great."[71] Newton had finally refuted those skeptics who believed that "all the Arguments of Nature are on the side of Atheism and Irreligion."[72]

Largely as a result of his Boyle lectures, which made a huge impression, Clarke was hailed as the most important theologian of the day. His God was tangible: "There is no such thing as what men call the course of nature or the power of nature. [It] is nothing else but the will of God producing certain effects in a continued regular, constant and uniform manner."[73] God had become a mere force of nature. Theology had thrown itself on the mercy of science. At the time this seemed a good idea. After the disaster of the Thirty Years' War, a rational ideology that could control the dangerous turbulence of early modern religion seemed essential to the survival of civilization. But the new scientific religion was about to make God incredible. In reducing God to a scientific explanation, the scientists and theologians of the seventeenth century were turning God into an idol, a mere human projection. Where Basil, Augustine, and Thomas had insisted that the natural world could tell us nothing about God, Newton, Bentley, and Clarke argued that nature could tell us everything we needed to know about the divine. God was no longer transcendent, no longer beyond the reach of language and concepts. As Clarke had shown, his will and attributes could be charted, measured, and definitively proven in twelve clear and distinct propositions. People were starting to become dependent upon the new science. But what would happen when a later generation of scientists found another ultimate explanation for the universe?

# NINE

# Enlightenment

For many of the educated elite, the eighteenth century was exhilarating. The Thirty Years' War was now a distant but salutary memory, and people were determined that Europe should never again fall prey to such destructive bigotry. As Locke had argued, scientists had shown that the natural world gave sufficient evidence for a creator, so there was no further need for churches to force their teachings down the throats of their congregants. For the first time in history, men and women would be free to discover the truth for themselves.[1] A fresh generation of scientists seemed to confirm Newton's faith in the grand design of the universe. The invention of the magnifying lens opened up yet another new world that gave further evidence of divine planning and design. The Dutch microscopist Anton van Leeuwenhoek (1632–73) had for the first time observed bacterial spermatozoa, the fibrils and striping of muscle, and the intricate structure of ivory and hair. These marvels all seemed to point to a supreme Intelligence, which could now be discovered by the extraordinary achievements of unaided human reason.

The new learning spread quickly from Europe to the American colonies, where the prolific author and clergyman Cotton Mather (1663–1728), whose father, Increase (1639–1723), had been a friend of Robert Boyle's, undertook his own microscopic investigations and was the first to experiment with plant hybridization. He kept up eagerly with European science and, in 1714, was actually admitted to the Royal Society. In 1721, he published *The Christian Philosopher,* the first book on science available in America for the general reader. Significantly, it was also a work of religious apologetics. Science, Mather insisted, was a "wondrous *Incentive* to *Religion*";[2] the entire universe could be seen as a temple, "*built* and *fitted* by that Almighty Architect."[3] This "Philosophical" faith, which could be accepted by Christian and Saracen alike, would transcend the murderous doctrinal quarrels of the sects and heal class divisions:

> Behold, a *Religion,* which will be found *without Controversy;* a *Religion,* which will challenge all possible Regards from the *High,* as well as the *Low,* among the People; I will resume the Term, a Philosophical Religion; and yet how *Evangelical*![4]

It was indeed a proclamation (*evangelion*) of "good news." Newton's laws had revealed the great design in the universe, which pointed directly to the Creator God; by this religion, "atheism is now for ever hissed and chased out of the world."[5]

Yet Mather showed how easily old beliefs could coexist with the new. During the 1680s, he had warned his congregations that Satan regarded New England as his own province and had fought a bitter campaign against the colonists. Satan himself was responsible for the Indian Wars, the smallpox epidemics, and the decline in piety that had caused such anxiety in the Puritan community. In his *Memorable Providences Relating to Witchcraft and Possessions* (1689), Mather did much to fan the fears that exploded in the infamous Salem witch trials (1692), in which he took a leading role. His faith in scientific rationality had not been able to assuage his own inner demons or his conviction that evil spirits lurked everywhere, poised to overthrow the colony.

But despite the explosion of irrationality in Salem, educated Americans were able to participate in the philosophical movement known as the Enlightenment. In both Europe and the American colonies, an elite group of intellectuals was convinced that humanity was beginning to leave superstition behind and was on the brink of a glorious new era. Science gave them greater control over nature than had ever been achieved before; people were living longer and felt more confident about the future. Already some Europeans had begun to insure their lives.[6] The rich were now prepared to reinvest capital systematically on the basis of continuing innovation and in the firm expectation that trade would continue to improve.

In order to keep abreast of these exciting developments, religion would have to change, so Enlightenment philosophers developed a new form of theism, based entirely on reason and Newtonian science, which they called Deism. It is not true that Deism was a halfway house to an outright denial of God.[7] Deists were passionate about God and almost obsessed with religion. Like Newton, they believed that they had discovered the primordial faith that lay beneath the ancient biblical account. They spread their rational religion with near-missionary zeal, preaching salvation through knowledge and education. Ignorance and superstition had become the new Original Sins. The theologians Matthew Tindal (1655–1733) and John Toland (1670–1722) in the British Isles, the philosopher Voltaire (1694–1778) in France, and the scientist, statesman, and philosopher Benjamin Franklin (1706–90) and the statesman Thomas Jefferson (1743–1826) in America all sought to bring faith under the control of reason. The Enlightenment philosophes wanted every single person to grasp the truths unveiled by science and learn to reason and discriminate correctly.[8] Inspired by Newton's vision of a universe ruled by immutable laws, they were offended by a God who intervened erratically in nature, working miracles and revealing "mysteries" that were not accessible to our reasoning powers.

Voltaire defined Deism in his *Philosophical Dictionary* (1764). Like Newton, he thought that true religion should be "easy," its truths clearly discernible, and, above all, it should be tolerant.

> Would it not be that which taught much morality and
> very little dogma? That which tended to make men just
> without making them absurd? That which did not order
> one to believe in things that are impossible, contradic-
> tory, injurious to divinity, and pernicious to mankind,
> and which dared not menace with eternal punishment
> anyone possessing common sense? Would it not be that
> which did not uphold its belief with executioners, and
> did not inundate the earth with blood on account of
> unintelligible sophism? Which taught only the worship
> of one god, justice, tolerance, and humanity?[9]

Scarred by the theological wrangling and violence of the Reformation and the Thirty Years' War, European Deism was marked by anticlericalism but was by no means averse to religion itself. Deists needed God. As Voltaire famously remarked, if God did not exist, it would be necessary to invent him.

The Enlightenment was the culmination of a vision that had been long in the making. It built on Galileo's mechanistic science, Descartes' quest for autonomous certainty, and Newton's cosmic laws, and by the eighteenth century, the philosophes believed that they had acquired a uniform way of assessing the whole of reality. Reason was the only path to truth. The philosophes were convinced that religion, society, history, and the workings of the human mind could all be explained by the regular natural processes discovered by science. But their rational ideology was entirely dependent upon the existence of God. Atheism as we know it today was still intellectually inconceivable. Voltaire regarded it as a "monstrous evil," but was confident that because scientists had found definitive proofs for God's existence, there were "fewer atheists today than there have ever been."[10] For Jefferson, it was impossible that any normally constructed mind could contemplate the design manifest in every atom of the universe and deny the necessity of a supervising power.[11] "If *Men* so much admire Philosophers, because they *discover* a small Part of the *Wisdom* that made all things," Cotton Mather argued, "they must be stark blind, who do not admire that *Wisdom* itself."[12] Science could not explain its findings without God; God was a scientific as well as a theological necessity. Disbelief in God seemed as perverse as refusing to believe in gravity. Giving up God would mean abandoning the only truly persuasive scientific explanation of the world.

This emphasis on proof was gradually changing the conception of belief. Jonathan Edwards (1703–58), the New England Calvinist theologian, was thoroughly conversant with Newtonian science and was moving away so radically from the idea of an interventionist God that he denied the efficacy of petitionary prayer. Yet he continued to defend the older view of belief, which, he insisted, involved far more than merely "confirming a thing by testimony." It was not simply a matter of weighing the evidence: faith involved "esteem and affection" for the truths of religion as well as intellectual submission.[13] There could be no true belief unless a person was emotionally and morally involved in the religious quest. But others disagreed. Jefferson defined belief as "the assent of the mind to an intelligible proposition."[14] Jonathan Mayhew, pastor of West Church in Boston from 1747 to 1766, warned his parishioners that they must suspend their belief or disbelief in God until they had "impartially examined the matter, and [could] see the evidence on one side or the other."[15]

But like Mather, Mayhew was not always consistent. He preached hellfire sermons and the importance of personal intimacy with a God who would respond to one's prayers and intervene in one's life, and this Deism with an admixture of traditional *mythos* was more typical than the austere faith of such radicals as Toland. Only a few could sustain a totally consistent Deist faith. Most people retained traditional Christian beliefs but did their best to purge them of "mystery." During the eighteenth century, a somewhat paradoxical theology was developing. In the supernatural realm, God remained a mysterious and loving Father, active in the lives of his worshippers. But in the natural world, God had been forced to retreat: he had created it, sustained it, and established its laws, but after that the mechanism worked by itself and God made no further direct interventions. In the past, Brahman had been identical with the atman of each being; *intellectus* had been the cutting edge of human reason. "Nature" and "supernature" had not been hermetically distinct; now they were beginning to seem opposed.[16] Philosophers were discovering other natural laws that governed human life without any reference to God. Adam Smith (1723–90) expounded the laws of the economy that determined the wealth of nations, Voltaire regarded morality as a purely social development, and the scientific history of Edward Gibbon (1737–94) dealt only with natural causation. The polarity of natural versus supernatural was just one of the dualisms—mind/matter, church/state, reason/emotion—that would characterize modern consciousness as it struggled to master the paradoxes of reality.

Enlightenment thinking involved a relatively small number of people. Not everybody was convinced by the new scientific religion. The nonconformist ideology of the Levelers, Quakers, and Diggers lingered on among the literate English underclass as part of a principled opposition to the establishment.[17] The scientific assumption that matter was inert and passive and could be set in motion only by a higher power was associated with policies that sought to deprive the "lower orders" of independent, autonomous action. The literate, convict settlers who had rebelled against industrialized England and were deported to Australia took this commonwealth ideal with them and called themselves Diggers. There was considerable opposition to Newtonian theology among the "Tory" or "country" wing of the Church of England, which may have been more widespread than historians have appreciated.[18] John Hutchinson (1674–1737), its principal spokesman, had a very large following. The eminent doctor George Cheyne (1671–1743) had been an ardent Newtonian in his youth, but later became disenchanted with liberal, scientifically based Anglicanism and the new science, with its emphasis on induction and calculation. He became a disaffected anti-establishment Methodist. George Horne (1730–92), bishop of Norwich, complained in his private diary that the followers of Hutchinson got no preferment, that the liberal clergy had invented a natural religion that was a mere simulacrum of authentic Christianity, and that Deism had "darkened the sun."[19] Mathematics could not provide the same certainty as revealed truth, and natural religion was simply a ploy to keep people in line. It had made "Christianity good for nothing but to keep societies in order, the better that there should be no Christ than that it should disturb societies."[20]

Sadly, many saw Newtonian ideology as indissolubly linked with coercive government. As if in reaction against this rational faith, a host of fervent pietistic movements flourished during the Age of Reason. The German religious leader Nicholas Ludwig von Zinzendorf (1700–60) insisted that faith was "not in thoughts nor in the head, but in the heart."[21] God was not an objective fact that could be proved logically but "a presence in the soul."[22] Traditional doctrines were not purely notional truths; if they were not expressed practically in daily life, they would become a dead letter. Academics amuse themselves by "chattering about the mysteries of the Trinity," but the significance of the doctrine lay in spiritual exercises; the Incarnation was not a historical fact in the distant past but expressed the mystery of new birth in the individual.[23]

Pietists who opted for the "religion of the heart" were not in revolt from reason; they were simply refusing to reduce faith to merely intellectual conviction. John Wesley (1703–91) was fascinated by the Enlightenment and tried to apply a scientific and systematic "method" to spirituality: his Methodists followed a strict regimen of prayer, scripture study, fasting, and good works. But he insisted that religion was not a doctrine in the head but a light in the heart. "We do not lay the main stress of our religion on any opinions, right or wrong," he explained. "Orthodoxy or right opinion is at best but a very slender part of religion, if it can be allowed to be any part of it at all."[24] If the rational evidence for Christianity became "clogged and encumbered, this could be a blessing in disguise, as it would compel people "to look into themselves" and "attend to that same light."[25] Pietism shared many of the Enlightenment ideals: it mistrusted external authority, ranged itself with the moderns as against the ancients, shared the emphasis on liberty, and was excited by the possibility of progress.[26] But it refused to relinquish the older patterns of religion in favor of a streamlined, rationalized piety.

But without discipline, the "religion of the heart" could easily degenerate into sentimentality and even hysteria. We have seen that Eckhart, the author of the *Cloud,* and Denys the Carthusian had all been concerned about a religiosity that confused affective states with the divine presence. The Enlightenment tendency to polarize heart and head could mean that a faith that was not capable of intelligent self-appraisal degenerated into emotional indulgence. This became clear during the religious revival known as the First Great Awakening that erupted in the American colony of Connecticut in 1734. The sudden deaths of two young people in the community of Northampton plunged the town into a frenzied religiosity, which spread like a contagion to Massachusetts and Long Island. Within six months, three hundred people had experienced "born-again" conversions, their spiritual lives alternating between soaring highs and devastating lows when they fell prey to intense guilt and depression. When the revival burned itself out, one man committed suicide, convinced that the loss of ecstatic joy must mean that he was predestined to hell. In premodern spirituality, rituals such as the Eleusinian mysteries had been skillfully crafted to lead people through emotional extremity to the other side. But in Northampton, the new American cult of liberty meant that there was no such supervision, that everything was spontaneous and free, and that people were allowed to run the gamut of their emotions in a way that for some proved fatal.

There was a paradox in the Enlightenment.[27] Philosophers insisted that individuals must reason for themselves, and yet they were only permitted to think in accordance with the scientific method. Other more intuitive ways of arriving at different kinds of truth were now belittled in a manner that would prove highly problematic for religion. Again, revolutionary leaders in France and America preached the doctrine of untrammeled liberty with immense passion and enthusiasm, but their doctrine of nature was rigorously mechanical: the motion and organization of every single component of the universe was completely determined by the interaction of its particles and the iron rule of nature's law. In England, Newton's cosmology would be used to endorse a social system in which the "lower" orders were governed by the "higher," while in France, Louis XIV, the Sun King, presided over a court in which his courtiers revolved obsequiously around him, each in his allotted orbit. Central to this political vision and Newtonian science was the doctrine of the passivity of matter, which needed to be activated and controlled by a higher power. People who challenged this orthodoxy were associated with radical movements and often found themselves in bad odor with the establishment.[28]

In rather the same way as Spinoza, John Toland believed that God was identical with nature and that matter was, therefore, not inert but vital and dynamic: he died in abject poverty. Locke thought it possible that some material substances might be able to "think" and perform rational procedures. He had a radical past: because he was involved in the turbulence preceding the Glorious Revolution of 1688, he had been forced to flee to Holland, where he lived in exile for six years as "Mr. van der Linden." The Presbyterian minister and chemist Joseph Priestley (1733–1804), who remained an outsider all his life—educated in Daventry instead of Oxford and exercising his ministry in the provinces—argued that Newtonian theory was not in fact dependent upon the inertia of matter. When he spoke in support of the French Revolution in 1789, a Birmingham mob burned his house to the ground and he migrated to America.

Others questioned the idea that there was only one method of arriving at truth. Giambattista Vico (1668–1744), professor of rhetoric at the University of Naples, argued that the historical method was as reliable as the scientific but rested on a different intellectual foundation.[29] The study of rhetoric showed that it was just as important to know who a philosopher was addressing and to understand the context of his discourse as to master its content. Mathematics was crucial to the new science; it claimed to yield clear and distinct results that could be applied to all fields of study. But mathematics, Vico argued, was essentially a game that had been devised and controlled by human beings. If you applied the mathematical method to material that was separate from the human intellect—to cosmology, for instance—there was not the same "fit." Because nature operated independently of us, we could not understand it as intimately as something that we had created ourselves. But we could know history in this way, because our civilizations were human artifacts. So why did modern philosophers expend all their energies on "the study of the world of nature, which, since God made it, he alone knows?"[30]

The study of history depended on what Pascal had called the "heart." Instead of logical, deductive thought, Vico pointed out, the historian had to use his imagination (*fantasia*) and enter empathically into the world of the past. When a historian studied the past, he had to turn within, recollect the phases of his own development, and thus sympathetically reconstruct the stages of the evolution of a particular culture. By examining its metaphors and imagery, he discovered the preconceptions that drew a society together, "a judgment without reflection, universally felt by an entire group, an entire people, a whole nation."[31] By this process of introspection, the historian was able to grasp an internal, integrating principle that enabled him to appreciate the uniqueness of each civilization. Truths were not absolute; what was true in one culture was not so for another; symbols that worked for one people would not speak to others. We understand the rich variety of human nature only when we learn to enter imaginatively and compassionately into the context in which a proposition or doctrine is developed.

Vico seemed to sense that a gap had opened between science and the humanities that had not existed before.[32] The scientific method taught the observer to be detached from what he was investigating, because it was essential to science that the result of an experiment be the same, whoever performed it. Objective truth aspires to be independent of historical context and is assumed to be the same in any period or culture. Such an approach tends to canonize the present, so that we project what *we* believe and find credible back onto the past or onto a civilization whose symbols and presuppositions might be different from our own. Vico referred to this uncritical assessment of alien societies and remote historical periods as the "conceit" of scholars or rulers: "It is another property of the human mind that wherever men can form no idea of distant or unknown things, they judge them by what is familiar and at hand."[33]

Vico had put his finger on an important point. The scientific method has dealt brilliantly with objects but is less cogent when applied to people or the arts. It is not competent to assess religion, which is inseparable from the complex human beings who practice it and, like the arts, cultivates a perception based on imagination and empathy. A scientist will first form a theory and then seek to prove it experimentally; religion works the other way around, and its insights come from practical experience. Where science is concerned with facts, religious truth is symbolic and its symbols will vary according to context; they will change as society changes, and the reason for these changes must be understood. Like the arts, religion is transformative. Where the scientist is supposed to remain detached from the object of his investigation, a religious person must be changed by the encounter with the symbols of his or her faith—in rather the same way as one's outlook can be permanently transformed by the contemplation of a great painting.

As the Enlightenment intensified, Jean-Jacques Rousseau (1712–78), the Genevan philosopher, educationist, and essayist who had settled in Paris, came to many of the same conclusions as Vico. He did not share the philosophes' optimistic vision of improvement. Science, he believed, was divisive, because very few people could participate in the scientific revolution and most were left behind. As a result, people were living in different intellectual worlds. Scientific rationalism, which cultivated a dispassionate objectivity, could obscure "the natural repugnance to see any sensitive being perish or suffer."[34] Knowledge, Rousseau believed, had become cerebral; instead we should listen to the "heart." For Rousseau the "heart" was not equivalent to emotion; it referred to a receptive attitude of silent waiting—not unlike Greek *hesychia*—that was ready to listen to the instinctive impulses that precede our conscious words and thoughts. Instead of attending to reason alone, we should learn to hear this timid voice of nature as a corrective to the aggressive reasoning of those philosophers who sought to master the emotions and bring the more unruly elements of life under control.[35]

In his novel *Émile* (1762), Rousseau tried to show how an individual could be educated in this attitude. The self-emptying of *kenosis* was a crucial part of his program. It was *amour propre* ("self-love") that imprisoned the soul within itself and corrupted our reasoning powers with selfishness and arrogance. So before he attained the age of reason, a child should be taught not to dominate others; instead of receiving a purely theoretical education, he must cultivate the virtue of compassion by means of disciplined action. As a result of this training, when his reasoning powers finally developed, they would not be distorted by egotism. In the novel, Émile is able to persuade Sophie, who represents Wisdom, to marry him only when he is prepared to forgo his attachment to her: "The fear of losing everything will prevent you from possessing everything."[36] Rousseau had no time for Christianity, whose God, he felt, had become a mere projection of human desires. He was looking for the "God" that transcended the old doctrines, a deity that would be discovered by *kenosis*, compassion, and the humble contemplation of the majesty of the universe.


Rousseau nurtured the revolutionary passion that would make the French Enlightenment more radical and political. This would not be the case in America. Unlike the French Revolution, the American War of Independence against Britain (1775–83) had no antireligious dimension. Its leaders—George Washington (1732–99), John Adams (1725–1826), Jefferson, and Franklin—experienced the revolution as a secular, pragmatic struggle against an imperial power. The Declaration of Independence, drafted by Jefferson, was a modernizing Enlightenment document based on Locke's notion of human rights and appealing to the modern ideals of autonomy, independence, and equality in the name of the God of Nature. The vast majority of the colonists could not relate to the Deism of their leaders and developed a form of revolutionary Calvinism that enabled them to join the struggle.[37] When their leaders spoke of liberty, they thought of Saint

Paul's freedom of the Sons of God;[38] they recalled the heroic struggle of their Puritan forebears against tyrannical Anglicanism in old England; and some believed that as a result of the revolution, Jesus would shortly establish the Kingdom of God in America.[39] This Christian ideology was a Calvinist version of Adams's belief that the settlement of America was part of God's plan for the enlightenment of the whole of humanity[40] and the conviction of Thomas Paine (1737–1809) that "we have it in our power to begin the world again."[41] Unlike Europeans, Americans did not regard religion as oppressive but found it a liberating force that was enabling them to respond creatively to the challenge of modernity and come to the Enlightenment ideals in their own way.

In France, however, religion was part of the ancien régime that needed to be swept away. There was even an incipient atheism that denied God's existence. In 1729, Jean Meslier, an exemplary parish priest, died weary of life, leaving his few meager possessions to his parishioners. Among his papers, they discovered the manuscript of his *Memoire* in which he declared that Christianity was a hoax. He had never dared to say this openly during his lifetime, but now he had nothing to fear. Religion was simply a device to subdue the masses. The gospels were full of internal contradictions, and their texts were corrupt. The miracles, visions, and prophecies that were supposed to "prove" divine revelation were themselves incredible, and the doctrines of the church manifestly absurd. So too were the "proofs" of Descartes and Newton. Matter did not require a God to set it in motion; it was dynamic and moved by its own momentum, and its existence depended on nothing other than itself. Voltaire circulated the manuscript privately, though he doctored it in order to make Meslier a respectable Deist. But in the *Memoire* we find the germ of much of the atheistic critique of the future. It shows that the new fashion for proving the existence of God could easily backfire; it also shows a connection between the desire for social change and the theory of dynamic matter.

In France as in England, people outside the establishment were becoming critical of the orthodox Enlightenment belief in the inertia of matter. In 1706, Jean Pigeon (1654–1739), a self-educated military man with a flair for mechanical physics, had presented Louis XIV with a model of the Copernican system that he had made himself.[42]

But he found that the experience of constructing his own universe, as it were, took all the wonder out of creation; God suddenly seemed little more than a craftsman like himself. He also came to believe that matter was not passive after all. Pigeon's son-in-law André-Pierre Le Guay de Prémontval (1716–64) continued to preach the gospel of dynamic matter and a downsized God to large audiences until he was forced to flee to Holland. Julien Offray de La Mettrie (1709–51) had also taken refuge in the Netherlands, where he published *Man, a Machine* (1747) which ridiculed Cartesian physics and argued that intelligence was inherent in the material structure of organisms. For La Mettrie, God was simply an irrelevance.[43] He included the record of a conversation with a fellow skeptic, who yearned for the destruction of religion.

> No more theological wars, no more soldiers of religion—such terrible soldiers! Nature infected with sacred poison would repair its rights and purity. Deaf to all other voices, tranquil mortals will follow only the spontaneous dictates of their own being, the only commands which can never be despised with impunity, and which alone can lead us to happiness through the pleasant paths of virtue.[44]

People were sick of the intolerant behavior of the churches. But few were prepared to break with religion entirely. La Mettrie himself was careful to distance himself from the opinions of the "wretch" he quoted.

But in 1749, the novelist Denis Diderot (1713–84) was imprisoned in Vincennes for writing an atheistic tract. As a young man, he had been intensely religious and even considered becoming a Jesuit. When his adolescent ardor faded, Diderot threw in his lot with the philosophes and studied biology, physiology, and medicine, but he had not yet given up on religion. In his *Pensées philosophiques,* like any good Deist, he sought rational evidence from Descartes and Newton to combat atheism, and was increasingly drawn to microscopic biology, which claimed to find evidence for the existence of God in the minutiae of nature. But he was not wholly convinced. Diderot passionately believed that even our most cherished beliefs must be subjected to rigorous critical scrutiny, and started to attend the lectures of

Pigeon's circle, where he learned of some disturbing new experiments. In 1741, the Swiss zoologist Abraham Trembley discovered that a hydra could regenerate itself if cut in two. In 1745, John Turberville Needham, a Catholic priest, found that minute creatures generated spontaneously in putrefying gravy and that a whole world of infinitesimally small organisms inhabited a single drop of water, coming into being and passing away only to be replaced by others within the span of a few minutes. Perhaps, Diderot could not help reflecting, the whole cosmos was like that drop of water, endlessly creating and re-creating itself without the intervention of a Creator.

In 1749, Diderot published *A Letter on the Blind for the Use of Those Who See,* the treatise that put him in prison, which took the form of a fictional dialogue between Nicolas Sanderson, the blind Cambridge mathematician, and Gervase Holmes, an Anglican minister who represented Newtonian orthodoxy.[45] Sanderson is on his deathbed and can find no consolation in Newton's proof for God's existence, because he cannot see any of the marvels that so impressed Holmes. Sanderson has been forced to rely on ideas that could be tested mathematically, and this has led him into an outright denial of God's existence. At the very beginning of time, Sanderson believes, there had been no trace of God—only swirling particles in an empty void. The evolution of our world was probably a good deal more arbitrary and messier than the tidy, purposive process described by Newton. Here, remarkably, Diderot makes Sanderson envisage a process of brutal natural selection. The "design" we see in the universe is simply due to the survival of the fittest. Only those animals survived "whose mechanism was not defective in any important particular and who were able to support themselves,"[46] while those born without heads, feet, or intestines perished. But such aberrations still occur. "Look at me, Mr Holmes," Sanderson cries. "I have no eyes. What have we done, you and I, to God, that one of us has this organ—while the other has not?"[47] It is no good relying on God to find a solution to such insoluble problems: "My good friend, Mr Holmes," Sanderson concludes, "confess your ignorance."[48]

When Voltaire wrote a letter of reproach to him in prison, Diderot replied that these were not his own opinions. "I believe in God," he wrote, "but I live very well with the atheists." Actually, however, it made very little difference to him whether God existed or not. God had become a sublime but useless truth. "It is very important not to mistake hemlock for parsley but to believe or not to believe in God is not important at all."[49] After his release, Diderot was invited to edit Ephraim Chambers's *Cyclopaedia* (1728) but completely transformed it, making the *Encyclopédie* a major weapon in his campaign to enlighten society. All the major philosophes contributed, and even though Diderot was constantly threatened with exile or prison, he managed to produce the final volume in 1765.

One of his editors was Paul Heinrich Dietrich, Baron d'Holbach (1723–89), who presided over a salon in the Rue Royale that had the reputation of being a hotbed of atheism, even though only three of the regular members actually denied God's existence. In 1770, d'Holbach, with Diderot's help, published *The System of Nature*, which brought together the discussions of the salonistes. D'Holbach was passionately antitheistic and wanted to replace religion with science. There was no final cause, no higher truth, and no grand design. Nature had generated itself and preserved itself in motion, performing all the tasks traditionally attributed to God.

> Nature is not a work; she has always been self-existent; it is in her bosom that everything is operated; she is an immense laboratory, provided with the materials, and makes instruments of which she avails herself to act. All her works are the effects of her own energy, and of these agents or causes which she makes, which she contains, which she puts into action. Eternal, uncreated, indestructible elements, always in motion, in combining themselves variously, give birth to all the phenomena which our eyes behold.[50]

Enlightened human beings had learned to examine the world rationally, rid their minds of the God delusion, and think for themselves. Science alone could validate morality, religion, politics, and even the arts.[51]

For d'Holbach, religion was born of weakness, fear, and superstition; people had created gods to fill the gaps in their knowledge, so religious belief was an act of intellectual cowardice and despair. First, men and women had personified the forces of nature, creating divinities in their own image, but eventually they had merged all these godlings into a massive deity that was simply a projection of their own fears and desires. Their God was "nothing but a gigantic, exaggerated man," rendered incredible and unintelligible "by dint of keeping together incompatible qualities."[52] God was an incomprehensible chimera, a mere negation of human limitations.[53] His infinity, for example, simply meant that he had no spatial boundaries, but such a being was utterly inconceivable. How could you reconcile the goodness of an omnipotent God with human suffering? This incoherent theology was bound to disintegrate in the Age of Reason. Descartes, Newton, Malebranche, and Clarke, who had all tried to save God, were simply atheists in disguise. Clarke, for example, had assumed that matter could not have brought itself into existence, but recent research had proved that he was mistaken. Even the great Newton had succumbed to the prejudices of his infancy. His Dominion was nothing but a deified despot, created in the image of a powerful man.[54] If only these philosophers had realized that they need look no higher than Nature, their philosophy would have come out correctly.

*The System of Nature* has been called the bible of the "scientific naturalism" or "scientism" that has continued to fuel the assault on faith. Its central belief is that the natural, material world is the only reality; it needs no external Cause because it is self-originating. There is no God, no soul, and no afterlife, and, although human beings can live useful and creative lives, the world itself has neither point nor purpose of its own. It just *is*. Science alone can give us a reliable understanding of all reality, including human intelligence and behavior. Because there can be no evidence for God's existence, all rational, educated individuals must repudiate religion altogether.

In relying so heavily on modern science, the churches had made themselves vulnerable to exactly this type of attack, which undermined the very scientists who had been the champions of religion. The assembly of French clergy commissioned the leading theologian Abbé Nicolas-Sylvestre Bergier to write a riposte; but his two-volume *Examen de materialisme* (1771) fell into the old trap, arguing that scientists had proved the inertia of matter and that, as a result, "we are forced to believe that there is in the universe, a substance of different nature, an active being to which movement must be attributed as to the First Cause, a Motor."[55] Newtonian religion was Bergier's only resource; he seemed unaware of the traditional premodern conviction that the natural world could indeed tell us nothing about God. The apophatic method was so alien to him that he apparently found nothing amiss in speaking of God as *a* being and *substance* located *in* the universe.

The French Revolution (1789), with its call for liberty, equality, and fraternity, seemed to embody the principles of the Enlightenment and promised to usher in a new world order, but in the event, it was only a brief, dramatic interlude: in November 1799, Napoléon Bonaparte (1769–1821) replaced the revolutionary government with a military dictatorship. The revolution made a profound impression on Europeans who were hungry for social and political change, but like other modernizing political movements, it was compromised by cruelty and intransigence. Fought in the name of freedom, it had used systematic violence to suppress dissidence; it produced the Reign of Terror (1793–94) as well as the Declaration of the Rights of Man, and the storming of the Bastille on July 14, 1789, was followed three years later by the September Massacres.

After the September Massacres, the militantly atheistic leader Jacques Hébert (1757–94) had enthroned the Goddess of Reason on the high altar of Notre Dame Cathedral, demoted saints in favor of revolutionary heroes, abolished the Mass, and ransacked the churches. But the general public was not yet ready to get rid of God, and when Maximilien Robespierre (1758–94) seized control, he replaced the Cult of Reason with the more anodyne Deist Cult of the Supreme Being, dispatching Hébert to the guillotine, only to follow him a few months later. When he became First Consul, Napoléon reinstated the Catholic Church. But the symbolism of God's dramatic abdication in favor of Reason linked the idea of atheism with revolutionary change. Henceforth in Europe—though not in the United States—atheism would be indissolubly associated with the hope for a more just and equal world.

Meanwhile, a different strand of Enlightenment thought undermined the tenets of both the Enlightenment and its science-based religion. Some scientists and philosophers had started to investigate the human mind and developed a critical epistemology that cast doubt on the competence of the intellect to achieve any kind of certainty.[56] The physicist Pierre-Louis Moreau de Maupertuis (1698–1759), a committed Newtonian in his youth, had become highly skeptical of any attempt to prove God's existence: philosophers, churchmen, and physicists were finding evidence of God's hand in "wings of butterflies and in every spider's web," though these things could have come about by chance. Future scientists could easily find a natural explanation for the apparent "design" in nature, and then what would happen to a faith that depended on scientific theory?[57] It was pointless to try to deduce God's existence from nature, argued the physicist Jean Le Rond d'Alembert (1717–83), because our knowledge of the universe was incomplete: we could observe it only at a given moment of time. There was also plenty of natural evidence to suggest that far from being a loving Creator, God might in truth be willful and irresponsible. The brilliant mathematician Marie-Jean Caritat, Marquis de Condorcet (1743–94) thought that scientists should concentrate on the study of psychology; we might find that we were incapable of understanding the natural laws we thought we had observed, which would make the vogue for natural theology a waste of time.[58]

The Scottish philosopher David Hume (1711–76) wittily disposed of Descartes' clear and distinct ideas. We could never achieve objective knowledge and absolute certainty, because the human mind imposed its own order on the chaotic mass of sense data. All our knowledge was, therefore, inescapably subjective, because it was shaped and determined by human psychology. Our metaphysics was pure fantasy, and the so-called natural laws merely reflected a human prejudice. The "proofs" for God's existence should be greeted with profound skepticism. Science, which was based on observation and experiment, could give us no information about God, one way or the other. But Hume had gone too far. Violating fundamental scientific and religious presuppositions, he seemed to invalidate the entire scientific enterprise that was now essential to the way people thought. Dismissed as a mischievous eccentric, he found few disciples in his lifetime. Other eighteenth-century Scottish philosophers opposed him by claiming that truth was indeed objective and available to any human being of sound "common sense."

Some thirty years later, however, the German philosopher Immanuel Kant (1724–1804) read Hume and felt as though he had been roused from a dogmatic slumber. In the *Critique of Pure Reason* (1781), he agreed that our understanding of the natural world was deeply conditioned by the structure of our minds and that it was impossible to achieve any knowledge of the reality we call God, which lay beyond the reach of the senses. We could neither prove nor disprove God's existence, because we had no reliable means of verification. Even though Kant regarded the Enlightenment as a liberating movement, his philosophy in effect imprisoned people within their own subjective thought processes. But Kant agreed that it was natural for human beings to have ideas that exceeded the grasp of their minds. He once reassured his servant that he had "only destroyed dogma to make room for faith,"[59] and yet he had no time for the rituals and symbols of religion that made faith viable.

On August 8, 1802, Napoléon visited Pierre-Simon de Laplace (1749–1827), the leading physicist of his generation.[60] A protégé of d'Alembert and an admirer of Kant, Laplace shared their modest assessment of the powers of human reason. When discussing scientific matters, he did not mention God at all—not because he was hostile to religion but because he saw God as irrelevant to physics. This indifference to faith was a new departure: the pioneering scientists of early modernity—Copernicus, Kepler, Galileo, Descartes, and Newton—had all been deeply preoccupied with faith, and some had found God essential to their science. But when he developed his "nebular hypothesis," Laplace showed how fatally easy it would be to oust God as the ultimate explanation. In a note added to later editions of his popular *Exposition du système du monde* (1796), he suggested that the solar system had been produced by a gaseous cloud that covered the sun and condensed to form the planets; the mechanical laws of nature did the rest. During his visit to Laplace, Napoléon, filled with wonder at the marvels of the cosmos, is said to have cried rhetorically: "And who is the Author of all this?" Calmly, Laplace replied: "I have no need of that hypothesis."[61]

It was an emblematic moment, but few people were able either to take it in or grasp its implications. In the very same year as Napoléon made his visit to Laplace, the British churchman Archdeacon William Paley (1743–1805) published *Natural Theology* (1802), which achieved instant success and recognition in the English-speaking world. Like

Lessius a century earlier, Paley reached instinctively for the argument from design as irrefutable proof for the existence of God. Just as the intricate machinery of a watch found in a desert place bespoke the existence of a watchmaker, the exquisite adaptations of nature revealed the necessity of a Creator. Only a madman would imagine that a machine came about by chance, and it was equally ludicrous to doubt that the wonders of the natural world—the intricate structure of the eye, the minute hinges of an earwig's wing, the regular succession of the seasons, or the intermeshing muscles and ligaments of the hand—pointed to a divine plan, in which every detail had its unique place and purpose. Paley was not suggesting that the universe was simply *like* a machine; it *was* a mechanism that had been directly contrived by the Creator. There had been no change or development. God had created every species of plant and animal in its present form—just as Genesis described.

Paley's image was attractive at a time when the Industrial Revolution had inspired a new interest in machinery. It made the idea of God as "easy" as Newton believed that it should be: it was not difficult to understand; it gave a clear, rational explanation; and the vision of a universe operating as regularly as clockwork was a comforting antidote to the terrifying tales of the French Revolution. Throughout the nineteenth century, *Natural Theology* was required reading for Cambridge undergraduates and was accepted as normative by leading British and American scientists for over fifty years. The young Charles Darwin (1809–82) found it deeply persuasive.

But it did not please everybody. The Romantic movement had already started to rebel against Enlightenment rationalism. The English poet, mystic, and engraver William Blake (1757–1827) believed that human beings had been damaged during the Age of Reason. Even religion had gone over to the side of a science that alienated people from nature and from themselves. Newtonian science had been exploited by the establishment, who used it to support a social hierarchy that suppressed the "lower orders," and in Blake's poetry Newton, albeit unfairly, became a symbol of the oppression, aggressive capitalism, industrialization, and exploitation of the modern state.[62] The true prophet of the industrial age was the poet, not the scientist. He alone could recall human beings to values that had been lost during the scientific age, which had tried to master and control the whole of reality:

> *Calling the lapsed Soul*
> *And weeping in the evening dew*
> *That might controll*
> *The starry pole*
> *And fallen, fallen light renew.*[63]

The Enlightenment had created a God of "fearful symmetry," like the Tyger, remote from the world in "distant deeps and skies."[64] The God of Newton must undergo a *kenosis,* return to earth, die a symbolic death in the person of Jesus,[65] and become one with humanity.[66]

In 1812, the revolutionary young aristocrat Percy Bysshe Shelley (1792–1822) was expelled from University College, Oxford, for writing an atheistic tract, but "The Necessity of Atheism" simply argued that God was not a necessary consequence of the material world. Shelley did not want to get rid of the divine altogether. Like his older contemporary William Wordsworth (1770–1850), he had a strong sense of a "Spirit," an "unseen Power" that was integral to nature and inherent in all its forms.[67] Unlike the philosophes, the Romantics were not averse to the mysterious and indefinable. Nature was not an object to be tested, manipulated, and dominated but should be approached with reverence as a source of revelation. Far from being inactive, the material world was imbued with a spiritual power that could instruct and guide us.

Since childhood, Wordsworth had been aware of a "Spirit" in nature. He was careful not to call it "God" because it was quite different from the God of the natural scientists and theologians; it was rather

> *A presence that disturbs me with the joy*
> *Of elevated thoughts; a sense sublime*
> *Of something far more deeply interfused*
> *Whose dwelling is the light of setting suns,*
> *And the round ocean and the living air,*
> *And the blue sky, and in the mind of man:*
> *A motion and a spirit, that impels*
> *All thinking things, all objects of all thought*
> *And rolls through all things.*[68]

Always concerned with accuracy of expression, Wordsworth deliberately called this presence "something," a word often used as a substitute for exact definition. He refused to give it a name, because it did not fit any familiar category. It bore little resemblance to the arid God of the scientists that had retreated from nature but was strongly reminiscent of the immanent force of being that people in the ancient world had experienced within themselves and in animals, plants, rocks, and trees.

The Romantic poets revived a spirituality that had been submerged in the scientific age. By approaching nature in a different way, they had recovered a sense of its numinous mystery. Wordsworth was wary of the "meddling intellect" that "murders to dissect," pulling reality apart in its rigorous analysis. Unlike the scientists and rationalists, the poet did not seek to master nature but to acquire a "wise passiveness" and "a heart that watches and receives."[69] He could then hear the silently imparted lessons that had been impressed upon him by the streams, mountains, and groves of the Lake District during his infancy.[70] Since reaching adulthood, both Wordsworth and Shelley had felt estranged from this living presence; the receptive, listening attitude had been educated out of them. But by assiduously cultivating this "wise passiveness," Wordsworth had recovered an insight that was not dissimilar to that achieved by yogins and mystics. It was a

> *blessed mood,*
> *In which the burthen of the mystery,*
> *In which the heavy and the weary weight*
> *Of all this unintelligible world,*
> *Is lightened:—that serene and blessed mood,*
> *In which the affections gently lead us on,—*
> *Until, the breath of this corporeal frame*
> *And even the motion of our human blood*
> *Almost suspended, we are laid asleep*
> *In body, and become a living soul:*
> *While with an eye made quiet by the power*
> *Of harmony and the deep power of joy,*
> *We see into the life of things.*[71]

Like some of the philosophes, Wordsworth was fascinated by the workings of the human mind; he understood that the mind deeply

affected our perception of the external world but was convinced that this was a two-way process. The external world silently informed our mental processes; the human psyche was receptive as well as creative, "working but in alliance with the works which it beholds."[72]

Wordsworth's younger contemporary John Keats (1795–1821) used the term "Negative Capability" to describe the *ekstatic* attitude that was essential to poetic insight. It occurred "when a man is capable of being in uncertainties, Mysteries, doubts, without any irritable reaching after fact & reason."[73] Instead of seeking to control the world by aggressive reasoning, Keats was ready to plunge into the dark night of unknowing: "I am however young writing at random—straining at particles of light in the midst of a great darkness—without knowing the bearing of any one assertion, of any one opinion."[74] He claimed gleefully that he had no opinions at all, because he had no self. A poet, he believed, was "the most unpoetical of any thing in existence; because he has no Identity."[75] True poetry had no time for "the egotistical sublime,"[76] which forced itself on the reader:

> We hate poetry that has a palpable design upon us—and
> if we do not agree, seems to put its hands in its breeches
> pocket. Poetry should be great & unobtrusive, a thing
> which enters into one's soul, and does not startle it or
> amaze it with itself but with its subject.—How beautiful
> are the retired flowers! how they would lose their beauty
> were they to throng into the highway crying out "admire
> me I am a violet! dote on me I am a primrose!"[77]

Where the philosophes had been wary of the imagination, Keats saw it as a sacred faculty that brought new truth into the world: "I am certain of nothing but of the holiness of the heart's affections and the truth of Imagination—What the imagination seizes as Beauty must be truth—whether it existed before or not—for I have the same Idea of all our Passions as of Love they are all in their Sublime creative of essential Beauty."[78]

The German theologian Friedrich Schleiermacher (1768–1834), who was greatly influenced by the Romantic movement, was also in retreat from Newtonian religion. He too sought a presence in "the mind of man." In *On Religion: Speeches to Its Cultured Despisers* (1799), he argued that the religious quest should not begin with an analysis of the cosmos but in the depths of the psyche.[79] A religion of this kind would not be an alienating force but involved with what was "highest and dearest" to us.[80] God was to be found in the "depths of human nature," in "the ground of its actions and thought."[81] The essence of religion lay in the feeling of "absolute dependence" that was fundamental to human experience.[82] This did not mean abject servility toward a distant, externalized God. Crucial aspects of our lives—our parentage, genetic inheritance, and the time and manner of our death—were entirely beyond our control. We experienced life, therefore, as "given," something that we received. This "dependence" was not merely something that had been implanted by God; it *was* God, the source and "whence" of our being.[83] Yet this theology was somewhat reductive: for Schleiermacher, the human being had become the center, origin, and goal of the religious quest. Instead of being the ultimate explanation of the universe, God was a necessary consequence of human nature, a device that enabled us to understand ourselves.

The German philosopher Georg Wilhelm Friedrich Hegel (1770–1831) remained fully committed to the Enlightenment ideal of objective knowledge but would have agreed with Blake that the externalized God must lose its lonely isolation and immerse itself in mundane reality. Human beings had thoughts and aspirations that exceeded their rational grasp, and they had traditionally expressed these in the mythos of religion. But it was now possible to reformulate these philosophically. In *The Phenomenology of Mind* (1807), Hegel argued that the ultimate reality, which he called *Geist* ("Spirit" or "Mind"), was not *a* being but "the inner being of the world, that which essentially is."[84] It was, therefore, being itself. Hegel developed a philosophical vision that recalled Jewish Kabbalah. It was a mistake to imagine that God was outside our world, an addition to our experience. Spirit was inextricably involved with the natural and human worlds and could achieve fulfillment only in finite reality. This, Hegel believed, was the real meaning of the Christian doctrine of incarnation. Conversely, it was only when human beings denied the alienating idea of a separate, externalized God that they would discover the divinity inherent in their very nature, because the universal Spirit was most fully realized in the human mind.

Hegel's vision articulated the optimistic, forward-thrusting spirit of modernity. There could be no harking back to the past. Human beings were engaged in a dialectical process in which they ceaselessly cast aside ideas that had once been sacred and incontrovertible. Every state of being brings forth its opposite; these opposites clash, are integrated, and create a new synthesis. Then the whole process begins again. The world was thus continuously re-creating itself. The structures of knowledge were not fixed but were simply stages in the unfolding of a final, absolute truth. Hegel's dialectic expressed the modern compulsion to discard recent orthodoxy. Religion, he believed, was one of those phases that human beings would leave behind as they progressed toward their ultimate fulfillment. In what with hindsight we can see to be a sinister move, Hegel identified the alienating religion that we had to reject with Judaism. Apparently unaware of the similarity of his philosophy to the Kabbalah, he blamed the Jewish people for transforming the immanent Spirit into a tyrannical external God that had estranged men and women from their own nature. In a way that would become habitual in the modern critique of faith, he had presented a distorted picture of "religion" as a foil for his own ideas, selecting one strand of a complex tradition and arguing that it represented the whole.

Even though Hegel stressed the relentlessly progressive movement of reality, he, like the Romantic poets, had actually recast older ideas in a modern form. As modernization proceeded, Western people were about to enter a world that was at once enthralling and disturbing. To keep pace with these fundamental changes, they had been forced to change their religion, their methods of education, and the social and political structures of their society. As they struggled to adapt to their radically altered world, they had abandoned traditional attitudes that seemed, however, to be embedded in the structure of humanity. As the Enlightenment proper drew to an end, some of these were beginning to resurface. Poets, philosophers, and theologians were urging people to recover a more receptive attitude to life. They were questioning the modern dichotomy between the natural and the supernatural and countering the distant Newtonian God with the image of an immanent Spirit. They had revived the idea of mystery. Condorcet, Hume, and Kant had suggested that unknowing was an inescapable part of our response to the world. The Age of Reason was not over, however. Only an elite group of intellectuals had been able to participate in the Enlightenment proper. But a religious movement was about to bring many of its basic assumptions into the mainstream so that they would become essential to the Western outlook.

# TEN

# Atheism

In 1790, the Reverend Jedidiah Morse descended on Boston from the rural outreaches of Massachusetts and launched a crusade against Deism, which had just attained the peak of its development in the United States. Hundreds of preachers joined this assault, and by the 1830s, Deism had been marginalized and a new version of Christianity had become central to the faith of America.[1] Known as "Evangelicalism," its objective was to convert the new nation to the "good news" of the Gospel. Evangelicals had no time for the remote God of the Deists; instead of relying on natural law, they wanted a return to biblical authority, to personal commitment to Jesus, and to a religion of the heart rather than the head. Faith did not require learned philosophers and scientific experts; it was a simple matter of felt conviction and virtuous living.

On the frontiers, nearly 40 percent of Americans felt slighted by the aristocratic republican government, which did not share their hardships but taxed them as heavily as the British and bought land for investment without any intention of leaving the comforts of the eastern seaboard. Frontiersmen and frontierswomen were ready to listen to a new kind of preacher who stirred up a wave of revivals known as the Second Great Awakening (1800–35). This Awakening was more politically radical than the first. The ideals of its prophets seemed very different from those of the founding fathers. They were not educated men, and their rough, populist Christianity seemed light-years away from the Deism of Adams, Franklin, and Jefferson. Yet they too belonged to the modern world and were able to convey the ideals of the republic to the people in a way that their political leaders could not.

With his wild, flowing hair, Lorenzo Dow looked like a latter-day John the Baptist; he still saw a storm as a direct act of God, and yet he would often begin a sermon with a quotation from Jefferson or Paine and constantly urged his congregations to cast superstition aside and think for themselves. When Barton Warren Stone left the Presbyterians to found a more democratic church, he called his secession a "declaration of independence." James O'Kelly who had fought in the Revolution and been thoroughly politicized, left mainstream Christianity to found his own church of "Republican Methodists." These men have been called "folk geniuses."[2] They were able to translate modern ideals such as freedom of speech, democracy, and equality into an idiom that the less privileged could understand and make their own. Drawing on the radical strain in the gospels, they insisted that the first should be last and the last first, that God favored the poor and unlettered. Jesus and his disciples had not had a college education, so people should not be in thrall to a learned clergy; they had the common sense to figure out the plain meaning of the scriptures for themselves.[3] These prophets mobilized the population in nationwide mass movements, making creative use of popular music and the new communications media. Instead of imposing modernity from above, as the founding fathers had intended, they created a grassroots rebellion against the rational establishment. They were highly successful. The sects founded by Smith, O'Kelly, and others amalgamated later to form the Disciples of Christ, which by 1860 had become the fifth-largest Protestant denomination in the United States with some two hundred thousand members.[4]

Rooted in eighteenth-century Pietism, Evangelical Christianity led many Americans away from the cool ethos of the Age of Reason to the kind of populist democracy, anti-intellectualism, and rugged individualism that still characterizes American culture. Preachers held torchlight processions and mass rallies, and the new genre of the gospel song transported the audience to ecstasy, so that they wept and shouted for joy. Like some of the fundamentalist movements today, these congregations gave people who felt disenfranchised and exploited a means of making their voices heard by the establishment.

But the Evangelical movement was not confined to the frontiers.

Christians in the developing cities of the Northeast had also become disillusioned with the Deist establishment, whose revolution had signally failed to inaugurate a better world. Many of the denominations were anxious to create a "space" that was separate from the federal government. They had been deeply perturbed by the fearful stories of the French Revolution, which seemed to epitomize the dangers of untrammeled rationality, and were appalled that Thomas Paine, who had supported their own war for liberty, had published *The Age of Reason* (1794) when the Terror was at its height. If their democratic society was to avoid the dangers of mob rule, the people must become more Godly. "If you wish to be free indeed, you must be virtuous, temperate, well-instructed," insisted Lyman Beecher (1775–1863), a leading Evangelical pastor of Cincinnati.[5] America was the new Israel, insisted Timothy Dwight, president of Yale; its expanding frontier was a sign of the coming Kingdom, so to be worthy of their calling, Americans must become more religious.[6] Deism was now regarded as a satanic foe, responsible for the inevitable failures of the infant nation: giving to nature the honor due to Jesus Christ, Deism would promote atheism and materialism.[7]

Yet despite their apparently visceral recoil from the Enlightenment, Evangelicals were eager to embrace its natural theology. They remained deeply dependent upon Scottish Common Sense philosophy and Paley's argument from design and saw Newton's God as essential to Christianity. The natural laws that scientists had discovered in the universe were tangible demonstrations of God's providential care and provided the faith of Jesus Christ with unshakable, scientific certainty. At the same time as he called for a religion of the heart, Lyman Beecher also insisted that Evangelical Christianity was "eminently a rational system."[8] And by this he meant the rationality of science.[9] In the same spirit, James McCosh (1811–94), president of Princeton, argued that theology was a "science" that, "from an investigation of the works of nature, would rise to a discovery of the character and will of God." Any theologian, he declared, must proceed

> in the same way as he does in every other branch of investigation. He sets out in search of facts; he arranges and coordinates them, and rising from the phenomena which present themselves to their cause, he discovers, by the

ordinary laws of evidence, a cause of all subordinate causes.[10]

God functioned in exactly the same way as any natural phenomenon; in the modern world, there was only one path to truth, so theology must conform to the scientific method.

During the 1840s, Charles Grandison Finney (1792–1875), a pivotal figure in American religion, brought the rough, democratic Christianity of the frontiers to the urban middle classes.[11] Finney used the wilder techniques of the older prophets but addressed professionals and businessmen, urging them to experience Christ directly without the mediation of the establishment, to think for themselves, and to rebel against academic theologians. Christianity was a strictly rational faith; its God was the Creator and Governor of Nature who worked through the laws of physics. Every natural event revealed God's providence. Even the emotions engendered by the revivals were not directly inspired by God (as Jonathan Edwards had supposed); instead these pious passions showed that God worked through the skill of the preacher, who knew how to use natural psychological means to elicit these responses.

The Evangelicals brought natural theology, hitherto a minority pursuit, into the mainstream. Even though they continued to insist on the transcendence of God, they believed paradoxically that he could be known through science as a matter of common sense. Wary of learned experts, they wanted a plain-speaking religion with no abstruse theological flights of fancy. They read the scriptures with an unprecedented literalism, because this seemed more rational than the older allegorical exegesis. Like scientific discourse, religious language should be univocal, clear, and transparent. The Evangelicals also brought the Enlightenment concept of "belief" as intellectual conviction to the center of Protestant religiosity and perpetuated the Enlightenment separation of the natural from the supernatural. Finally, in an attempt to ground their faith in something tangible, they followed the philosophes in making the practice of morality central to religion. They wanted a rationalized God who shared their own moral standards and behaved like a good Evangelical.[12] In the past, moral and compassionate behavior had introduced people to transcendence; now people were declaring that God was "good" in exactly the same way as a human being. Interestingly, he shared their enthusiasm for the virtues that ensured success in the marketplace: thrift, sobriety, self-discipline, diligence, and temperance. This God was clearly in danger of becoming an idol.

Yet again American religion was proving to be a modernizing force but this time it supported the capitalist ethos while at the same time articulating a healthy criticism of the system. During the 1820s, Evangelicals threw themselves into moral crusades to hasten the coming of the Kingdom, campaigning against slavery, urban poverty, exploitation, and liquor, and fighting for penal reform, the education of the poor, and the emancipation of women. There was an emphasis on the worth of each human being, egalitarianism, and the ideal of inalienable human rights. These Christian reform groups were among the first to channel the efficiency, energy, and bureaucratic skills of capitalism into nonprofit enterprises, teaching people to plan, organize, and pursue a clearly defined goal.[13] There was a widespread conviction that the technological improvements in transport, machinery, public health, gaslight, and communications that were giving Americans such control over their environment would also lead to moral improvement.

By the middle of the nineteenth century, largely, perhaps, because of the Evangelical initiative, Americans were more religious than ever before. In 1780, there were only about 2,500 congregations in the United States; by 1820, there were 11,000, and by 1860 a phenomenal 52,000—an almost twenty-one-fold increase. In comparison, the population of the United States rose from about 4 million in 1780 to 10 million in 1820 and 31 million in 1860—a less than eightfold increase.[14] In America, Protestantism empowered the people against the establishment, and this tendency still continues, so that today it is difficult to find a popular movement in the United States that is not associated with religion in some way. By the 1850s, Christianity in America had taken what it wanted from the Enlightenment and, confident in a certainty derived from science, seemed perfectly attuned to the modern world.

By contrast, a new type of atheism was emerging in Europe that was different from the "scientism" of Diderot and d'Holbach.[15] Americans were wary of intellectualism and, appalled by the French Revolution, had used Christianity to promote social reform. But Germans were inspired by the French Revolution, which had translated the intellectual ideals of the Enlightenment into a program for justice and equity. The social and political situation in Germany ruled out revolutionary activity, and after the experience of France, it seemed better to try to change the way people thought than resort to violence and terror, so during the 1830s, an anti-establishment intellectual cadre had emerged in the universities.

Many of these revolutionary intellectuals were theologically literate. In Germany, theology was an advanced and progressive discipline: two out of every five graduates had a theological degree and knew that they were in the vanguard of religious change. At the end of the eighteenth century, German scholars such as Johann Eichhorn (1752–1827), Johann Vater (1771–1826), and Wilhelm DeWette (1780–1849) had pioneered a new method of reading the Bible, applying to scripture the modern historical-critical methodology used to study classical texts. As a result, they had discovered that the Pentateuch had not been authored by Moses but was composed of at least four different sources, and were beginning to look at revelation and religious truth in an entirely different way. Other young men became disciples of Schleiermacher and Hegel and were eager to accelerate the dialectical progress that Hegel had described by abolishing reactionary ideologies and institutions. They were particularly incensed by the social privileges of the clergy and regarded the Lutheran Church as a bastion of conservatism.

The new European atheism was a product of this hunger for radical social and political change. As part of the corrupt old regime, the churches had to go, together with the God who had supported the system.[16] As modernization intensified, rapid industrialization and population growth during the 1840s led to severe social deprivation. Food riots were brutally suppressed. It was in this climate that Ludwig Feuerbach (1804–72), pupil of Schleiermacher and Hegel, published *The Essence of Christianity* (1841), which was avidly read, not simply as a theological statement but as a revolutionary tract. Feuerbach had taken Hegel's call for a God and religion of this world to its logical conclusion.[17] If the idea of a remote, external God was so alienating, why not get rid of him altogether? God, Feuerbach argued, was simply an oppressive human construct. People had projected their own human qualities onto an imaginary being that was merely a reflection of themselves. So "man's belief in God is nothing other than his belief in himself. . . . In his God he reveres and loves nothing other than his own being."[18] Hegel had been right. God was not external to humanity; the goodness, power, and love that were attributed to him were human qualities and should be revered for their own sake.[19] The idea of God had deprived Christians of self-confidence,[20] encouraging them to think that "*in the face of God, the world and man are nothing.*"[21] The people must realize that *they* were the only "gods" that existed and understand that any authority rooted in the idea of God was nothing more than an expression of blatant self-interest.

The declaration of the Second Republic in France in 1848 led to widespread hopes that something similar could be achieved in Germany, and there were calls for constitutional rule. Hoping that this agitation would spread to the rest of Europe, Karl Marx (1818–83) published his *Communist Manifesto,* but a year later it was clear that the revolutionary movement had failed. Marx took it for granted that God did not exist, so he did not bother to justify his atheism philosophically; his sole aim was to alleviate human misery. Born into a middle-class Jewish family at Trier, Marx had studied with Hegel in Berlin, where he had met some of the most controversial theologians of the day. Failing to get an academic post in Germany, he worked as a journalist in Paris until he was expelled for his political activities and settled in London, where he began work on *Das Kapital,* his monumental analysis of capitalism.

While Feuerbach's analysis was quite sound, Marx conceded, it did not go far enough. The time for theory was past. "The philosophers have only *interpreted* the world," he insisted emphatically; "the point, however, is to *change* it."[22] Instead of meditating on Hegel's dialectic, a committed revolutionary must make it happen; he must bring the underlying contradictions of capitalist society into the open, thus accelerating the emergence of the forces that would negate them. Of course God was a projection of human needs—that went without saying—but these needs were created by material and social factors that conditioned the way people thought and lived. The injustice of capitalism had produced a God that was simply a consoling illusion:

> *Religious* distress is at the same time an *expression* of real
> distress and a *protest* against real distress. Religion is the
> sigh of the oppressed creature, the heart of a heartless
> world, just as it is the spirit of a spiritless situation. It is
> the *opium* of the people.[23]

When men and women were no longer reduced by an oppressive system to a "debased, enslaved, abandoned, despicable essence," the idea
of God would simply wither away.[24] Atheism was not an abstract theory but a project. It was a program that was essential to the well-being
of humanity: "The *abolition* of religion as the *illusory* happiness of the
people is *required* for their real happiness."[25]

Others were beginning to argue that it was science, which for so long
had been its willing handmaid, that would eliminate religion. In
his six-volume *Cours de philosophie positive* (1830–42), the French
philosopher Auguste Comte (1798–1857) presented the intellectual
history of humanity in three stages. In its primitive theological phase,
people had seen gods as the ultimate causes of events; then these
supernatural beings had been transformed into metaphysical abstractions; and in the final and most advanced "positivist" or scientific
phase, the mind no longer dwelled on the inner essences of things,
which could not be tested empirically, but focused only on facts.
Western culture was now about to enter this third, positivist phase.
There was no way back. We could not regress into the theological or
metaphysical consolations of the past but were compelled by the inexorable laws of history to move forward into the age of science.

Science was becoming more rigorous and in the process had
started to undermine popular religious certainties. In 1830, Charles
Lyell (1797–1875) had published the first volume of his *Principles of
Geology,* which argued that the earth's crust was far older than the six
thousand years suggested in the Bible; moreover, it had not been
shaped directly by God but was formed by the slow, incremental
effects of wind and water.[26] Lyell, a liberal-minded Christian, refused
to discuss the theological implications of his findings, because science
"ought to be conducted as if the scriptures were not in existence."[27]
He was intensely irritated by the unprofessional work of some of his

colleagues, who attached "transcendent importance" to "every point of supposed discrepancy or coincidence between the phenomena of nature and the generally-received interpretations of the Hebrew text."[28] He thus enunciated his own version of the ancient distinction between *mythos* and *logos*. Science and theology were different disciplines, and it was dangerous to mix the two.

Scientists no longer considered their discipline a branch of "philosophy," which had always been interested in metaphysics, and they no longer saw themselves as gentlemen scholars but as professionals. By the middle of the nineteenth century, it was not only physicists but geologists, botanists, and biologists who formulated their insights in the exact language of mathematics. As part of their new professional ethos, they were beginning to insist on a "positivist" assessment of truth that excluded anything that was not quantifiable.[29] The Cambridge geologist Adam Sedgwick (1785–1873) defined science as "the consideration of all subjects, whether of a pure or mixed nature, capable of being reduced to measurement and calculation."[30] Clearly this could not include God. Because of the marvelous advances in technology, scientists were held in higher esteem than ever before. Science seemed the avatar of progress. It was definite, precise, and accurate; it accumulated truth in a methodical, purposeful manner, proved its theories, corrected earlier mistakes, and moved fearlessly into the future. Impressed by this new professional rigor and eager to share science's prestige, people in other disciplines were increasingly influenced by its positivist standard of truth.

But Lyell's revelations gave many believers, who were used to thinking that science was on their side, a salutary jolt. In America, after a brief but intense panic, Evangelical churchmen started to pull back from their strict biblical literalism. But they still relied on the argument from design, and few were aware of the disturbing new evidence that life itself—not merely the earth's crust—had evolved from "lower" to "higher" forms. The fossil record showed that innumerable species had failed to survive; instead of a neat design, the geologists were uncovering a natural history of pain, death, and racial extinction. In 1844, the popular Scottish writer Robert Chambers (1802–71) published *Vestiges of the Natural History of Creation,* arguing that scientists would soon prove that there was a purely natural explanation for the development of life. But others tried to "baptize" these new discoveries. For the Swiss American Harvard professor Louis Agassiz (1807–73) this struggle had been part of God's grand design;[31] God had simply been preparing the earth for its human inhabitants. Agassiz saw evidence of the divine Mind in the symmetry of nature, in which patterns were repeated in every vertebrate. This could not have been accidental: an "intelligent and intelligible connection between the facts of nature must be looked upon as a direct proof of the existence of a thinking God."[32]

But a seed of doubt had been sown. The English poet Alfred Tennyson (1809–92) gave moving expression to the buried anxiety that was eroding the faith of his contemporaries. The instant popular success of *In Memoriam* (1850) showed that he had voiced the unspoken fears of many. For two hundred years, Western Christians had been encouraged to believe that the scientific investigation of the natural world endorsed their faith. But now, it appeared, if there had been a divine plan, it had been cruel, callously prodigal, and wasteful. As Tennyson memorably put it, Nature was "red in tooth and claw." Because the scientific proof on which people had been taught to depend had been radically called into question, we could only "faintly trust the larger hope":[33]

> That nothing walks with aimless feet
> That not one life shall be destroy'd
> Or cast as rubbish to the void
> When God hath made the pile complete.[34]

But "trust" seemed vague and insubstantial beside the confident, precise, and certain knowledge of science. Incapable of verification, religious truth now appeared "futile" and "frail":[35]

> Behold, we know not anything;
> I can but trust that good shall fall
> At last—far off—at last, to all,
> And every winter change to spring.
>
> So runs my dream: but what am I?
> An infant crying in the night:
> An infant crying for the light:
> And with no language but a cry.[36]

The Victorians had been encouraged to see themselves as invincible; they had believed that science would conduct them into a world of spiritual and moral progress. But, it seemed, stripped of the faith that made it possible to endure the sorrow of life, instead of coming of age, humanity was still afflicted by the terror and bewilderment of its infancy.

Some theologians had persistently stood out against the canonization of a scientifically based natural theology. Horace Bushnell (1802–76), the notorious Congregationalist pastor of Hartford, Connecticut, was denounced as a heretic for pointing out that theology had more in common with poetry than with science.[37] Religious language *had* to be vague and imprecise, because what we called "God" lay beyond the scope of the rational intellect. Statements about God "always affirm something which is false, or contrary to the truth intended," because "they impute form to that which is really out of form."[38] "Fixed forms of dogma" invariably distorted truth, because such "definitions are, in fact, only changes of symbol, and if we take them to be more, they will infallibly lead us to error."[39] Remarks that would once have been commonplace were now greeted with fury. Western Christians had become addicted to scientific proof and were convinced that if God was not an empirically demonstrable fact, there was no sense in which religion could be true.

On December 27, 1831, Charles Darwin, naturalist on board the HMS *Beagle,* had embarked on a five-year scientific survey of South American waters to study the flora, fauna, and geology of Tenerife, the Cape Verde Islands, Buenos Aires, Valparaiso, the Galapagos, Tahiti, New Zealand, Tasmania, and finally the Keeling (Cocos) Islands. The evidence he gathered forced him to deny Paley's argument from design. God had certainly not created the world exactly as we knew it. Instead, it seemed clear that the species had evolved slowly over time, as they adapted to their immediate environment. During this process of natural selection innumerable species had indeed perished. In November 1859, Darwin published *The Origin of Species by Means of Natural Selection*. Later, in *The Descent of Man* (1871), he suggested even more controversially that *Homo sapiens* had developed from the progenitor of the orangutan, gorilla, and chimpanzee. Human beings were not the pinnacle of a purposeful creation; like everything else, they had evolved by trial and error, and God had had no direct hand in their making.

The evolutionary hypothesis shattered so many fundamental preconceptions that initially few could absorb it in its entirety. Even Alfred Russel Wallace (1823–1913), who had made a significant contribution to Darwin's work, could not accept the lack of a controlling Intelligence.[40] The American botanist Asa Gray (1810–88), a convinced evolutionist as well as a dedicated Christian, used the evolutionary hypothesis in his study of plant life but could not accept the absence of an overall divine plan.[41] Darwinian theory not only undermined the design-based theology that had become the mainstay of Western Christian belief, but repudiated central principles of the Enlightenment.

Darwin, however, had no desire to destroy religion. His faith ebbed and flowed over the years, especially after the tragic death of his daughter Annie, but his chief problem with Christianity was not natural selection; rather, it was the doctrine of eternal damnation—a reaction, doubtless, to hellfire sermons. He told Asa Gray that it was absurd to doubt that "a man may be an ardent theist and an evolutionist," adding, "I have never been an atheist in the sense of denying the existence of a God. I think that generally (and more and more as I grow older) but not always, that agnostic would be the most correct description of my state of mind."[42] But as a result of his researches, God was no longer the only scientific explanation of the universe. Not only was there no scientific proof for God; natural selection had shown that such proof was impossible. If Christians wanted to believe that the evolutionary process was somehow supervised by God—and many did—this would henceforth be a matter of personal choice. Darwin's discoveries accelerated the already growing tendency to exclude theology from scientific discussion. By the end of the 1860s, most scientists were still Christians, but qua scientists they had stopped talking about God. As the American physicist Joseph Henry (1797–1878) said, scientific truth demanded stringent, physical evidence; it must enable us to "explain, to predict, and in some cases to control the phenomena of nature."[43] Wholly dependent on concrete, measurable fact, science now rejected any hypothesis that was not based on the human experience of the natural world and could not, therefore, be tested.

One of the first people to understand how this would impact natural theology was Charles Hodge, Princeton professor of theology, who wrote the first sustained religious attack on Darwinism in 1874. He noted that scientists had become so immersed in the study of nature that they believed *only* in natural causes and did not appreciate that religious truth was also factual and must be respected as such.[44] Hodge could see what would happen to Christian faith once scientists no longer accepted God as the ultimate explanation. He was correct to announce that religion, as he knew it, "has to fight for its life against a large class of scientific men."[45] But this would not have been the case had not Christians allowed themselves to become so dependent upon a scientific method that was entirely alien to it. Hodge himself took issue with Darwin on supposedly scientific grounds. Stuck in the early modern model of scientific procedure, he still saw science as the systematic collection of facts and did not understand the value of hypothetical thinking. He concluded that because Darwin had not proved his theory, it was unscientific. For Hodge it was impossible "to any ordinarily constituted mind" to believe that the intricate structure of the eye, for example, was not the result of design.[46]

But in opposing Darwin on religious grounds, Hodge was a lone voice. Most Christians, unable to appreciate the full implications of natural selection, were still willing to accommodate evolution. Darwin was not yet the bogeyman that he would later become. During the late nineteenth century, conservative Christians were far more troubled by an entirely different issue.

In 1860, the year after the publication of *Origin,* seven Anglican clergymen published *Essays and Reviews,* a series of articles that made the German Higher Criticism of the Bible available to the unsuspecting general public, who now learned to their astonishment that Moses had not written the first five books of the Bible, King David was not the author of the Psalms, and biblical miracles were little more than a literary trope. At this time, German clerics were far better educated than their counterparts in Britain and America, who were ill-equipped either to follow German scholarship themselves or to explain it to their flocks.[47] But by the 1850s, British nonconformists, who were not allowed to study at either Oxford or Cambridge, had started to attend German universities, and they brought the Higher Criticism back home with them. There had already been clashes between these "Germanized" scholars and their colleagues in colleges and seminaries.

*Essays and Reviews* caused a sensation. It sold twenty-two thousand copies in two years (more than *Origin* in the first twenty years of its publication), went through thirteen editions in five years, and inspired some four hundred books and articles in response.[48] Three of the authors belonged to a circle of progressive clergymen and scientists at Oxford and Cambridge who kept one another abreast of developments in their fields:[49] Baden Powell, Savilian professor of geometry at Oxford; Benjamin Jowett, classicist and later master of Balliol College; and Mark Pattison, rector of Lincoln College. The essays were of variable quality: they discussed the nature of predictive prophecy, the interpretation of miracle stories, and the authorship of Genesis. But by the far the most important article was Jowett's essay "On the Interpretation of Scripture," which argued that the Bible should be subjected to the same rigorous scholarship as any other ancient text. Evangelical Protestants, who had been taught to look for the plain sense of scripture and had in the process lost any understanding of the nature of mythology, found these ideas deeply disturbing. In 1888, the English novelist Mrs. Humphry Ward published *Robert Elsmere,* which told the story of a clergyman whose faith was destroyed by the Higher Criticism. At one point his wife complains: "If the Gospels are not true in fact, as history, I cannot see how they are true at all, or of any value."[50] The novel became a best seller, indicating that many readers shared her dilemma.

The hierarchy was equally disturbed by these new theories. Immediately after the publication of *Essays and Reviews,* a letter to *The Times,* cosigned by the Archbishop of Canterbury and twenty-five other bishops, threatened to bring the authors to the ecclesiastical courts. Two were indeed tried for heresy, convicted (though the ruling was later overturned), and lost their posts, and Jowett was temporarily suspended from clerical duties. Bishops, theologians, and professors collaborated on major symposia to counter *Essays and Reviews,* and, in an unlikely alliance, Anglo-Catholics joined forces with Evangelicals in a statement that affirmed the divine inspiration of the Bible. Seven hundred seventeen scientists (of minor status) also signed a strongly worded protest, and some of the signatories established the Victoria Institute to defend the literal truth of scripture.[51]

The more progressive theologians who adopted the new historical-critical method often found that their staunchest supporters were scientists who, like themselves, were at the cutting edge of their field.[52] When, for example, John William Colenso (1814–83), missionary bishop of Natal, was ostracized for his critical study of the Pentateuch, Lyell introduced him to his club and gave him financial help and the two became firm friends. When the Reverend Frederic William Farrar (1831–1903) wrote an article on the Flood, arguing, on evidence provided by the Higher Criticism and geological science, that the deluge had not in fact covered the entire earth, his essay was rejected by the editors of William Smith's *Dictionary of the Bible*. But Darwin supported Farrar's candidacy for the Royal Society, and Farrar was one of the bearers of Darwin's coffin and preached a moving eulogy beside his grave.[53]

In the United States, the more liberal Christians were open to the Higher Criticism. Henry Ward Beecher (1813–87), Lyman's son, believed that doctrine and belief should take second place to charitable work and argued that it was unchristian to penalize somebody for holding a different theological opinion. The liberals were also willing to "christen" Darwinism, arguing that God was at work in the process of natural selection and that humanity was gradually evolving to a greater spiritual perfection: soon men and women would find that no gulf separated them from God and that they were able to live at peace with one another. But a rift was developing between the liberals and conservatives. In dedicated opposition to the Higher Criticism, Charles Hodge insisted that every single word of the Bible was divinely inspired and infallibly true. His son Archibald wrote a classic defense of the literal truth of the Bible with his younger colleague Benjamin Warfield. All the stories and statements of the Bible were "absolutely errorless and binding for faith and obedience." Everything in scripture was unqualified "truth to the facts."[54]

In 1886, the revivalist preacher Dwight Lyman Moody (1837–99) founded the Moody Bible Institute in Chicago to combat the Higher Criticism, his aim to create a cadre to oppose the false ideas that, he argued, would bring the nation to destruction. Similar colleges were founded by William B. Riley in Minneapolis in 1902 and by the oil magnate Lyman Stewart in Los Angeles in 1907. For some, the Higher Criticism was becoming a symbol of everything that was wrong in the modern world. "If we have no infallible standard," argued the Methodist clergyman Alexander McAlister, "we may as well have no standard at all"; once biblical truth had been unraveled, all decent values would disappear.[55] For the Methodist preacher Leander W. Mitchell, the Higher Criticism was to blame for the drunkenness and infidelity now widespread in the United States,[56] while the Presbyterian M. B. Lambdin saw it as the cause of the rising divorce rate, graft, corruption, crime, and murder.[57] But the stridency of these claims reflects an anxiety. Christians had been taught to regard the truths of religion as well within the grasp of their minds and to treat the plain sense of scripture as factual. This attitude was becoming more and more difficult to maintain.

After Darwin, it was possible to deny God's existence without flying in the face of the most authoritative scientific evidence. For the first time, unbelief was a viable and sustainable intellectual option. But people were still wary of the term "atheist." The English social reformer George Holyoake (1817–1906) preferred to call himself a "secularist," because atheism still had overtones of immorality.[58] Charles Bradlaugh (1833–91), who refused to take the parliamentary oath with its invocation of God when he took up his seat in the House of Commons, was proud to call himself an atheist—but immediately qualified his position: "I do not say that there is no God; and until you tell me what you mean by God I am not mad enough to say anything of the kind." But he knew that God was not *"something* [a word he deliberately italicized] entirely distinct and different in substance" from the world we know.[59]

The British biologist Thomas H. Huxley (1825–95) felt that outright atheism was too dogmatic, because it made metaphysical claims about God's nonexistence on insufficient physical evidence.[60] It was probably Huxley who coined the term "agnostic" (a word based on the Latin *agnosco:* "I do not know") sometime in the 1860s. For Huxley, agnosticism was not a belief but a method. Its requirement was simple: "In matters of the intellect, do not pretend that conclusions are certain which are not demonstrated and demonstrable." Because they had all maintained this principled reticence, refusing the luxury of absolute certainty, Socrates, Paul, Luther, Calvin, and Descartes had all been agnostics, and agnosticism was now "the fundamental principle of modern science."[61] But Huxley also saw scientific rationalism as a new secular religion that demanded conversion and total commitment. People would have to choose between the myths of religion and the truths of science. There could be no compromise: "one or the other would have to succumb after a struggle of unknown duration."[62]

Huxley clearly felt that he had a fight on his hands. While science was the symbol of irreversible progress, religion seemed part of the old world that was doomed to disappear.[63] For Robert G. Ingersoll (1833–99), lawyer, orator, and state attorney general who became a leading spokesman of American agnosticism, humanity would soon outgrow God: one day everybody would recognize that religion was an extinct species.[64] For the American poet and novelist Charles Eliot Norton (1827–1908), "the loss of religious faith among the most civilized portions of the race is a step from childishness to maturity."[65] By the 1870s, this conviction had hardened into a new myth that saw religion and science as locked in eternal and inevitable conflict. The champions of science constructed a revisionist history of the relations between the two, floridly told, that cast the heroes of "progress"— Bruno, Galileo, Luther—as the hapless victims of evil cardinals and fanatical puritans. For the American propagandist Joel Moody, religion was the "science of evil."

> Men of generous culture or of great learning and women of eminent piety and virtue from the humble cottage to the throne have been led out for matters of conscience or butchered before a mindless rabble lusting after God. The limbs of men and women have been torn from their bodies, their eyes gouged out, their flesh mangled and slowly roasted, their children barbarously tortured before their eyes, because of religious opinion.[66]

For Ingersoll, human history had been scarred by "a deadly conflict" in which the brave, lonely champions of truth, "straining against fear and mental slavery, prejudice and martyrdom," had dragged humanity "inch by inch" closer to the truth.[67]

In 1871, John William Draper (1811–82), head of the department of medicine at New York University, published *The History of the Conflict Between Religion and Science,* which went through fifty printings and was translated into ten languages. While Religion clung timidly to the unchangeable truths of revelation, Science forged expansively ahead, giving us telescopes, barometers, canals, hospitals, sanitation, schools, the telegraph, calculus, sewing machines, rifles, and warships. Only Science could liberate us from the tyranny of Religion (Draper habitually capitalized these terms so that they seemed like characters in a morality play). "The ecclesiastic must learn to keep himself within the domain he has chosen, and cease to tyrannize over the philosopher, who, conscious of his own strength and the purity of his motives, will bear such interference no longer."[68]

Ultimately, however, Draper's polemic was marred by his blatantly anti-Catholic prejudice. Less immediately popular but more influential long-term was *A History of the Warfare of Science and Theology in Christendom* (1896) by the ardent secularist Andrew Dixon White (1832–1918), first president of Cornell University.

> *In all modern history, interference with science in the supposed interest of religion, no matter how conscientious such interference may have been, has resulted in the direst evils both to religion and science—and invariably. And, on the other hand, all untrammelled scientific investigations no matter how dangerous to religion some of its stages may have seemed, for the time, has invariably resulted in the highest good of religion and of science.*[69]

The two were implacably opposed. One of these protagonists was beneficial to humanity; the other, evil and dangerous. Ever since Augustine had insisted on the "absolute authority of scripture," all theologians "without exception, have forced mankind away from the truth, and have caused Christendom to stumble for centuries into abysses of error and sorrow."[70]

In reality, the relations between science and faith had been more complex and nuanced. But this overblown polemic has remained the stock-in-trade of the atheist critique of religion and is widely accepted as a matter of fact. White's misrepresentation of Augustine's view of scripture is just one example of his bias. One of the most persistent of the apocryphal tales that developed at this time is the story of Huxley's encounter with Samuel Wilberforce, bishop of Oxford (1805–73). In June 1860, shortly after the publication of *Origin,* they took part in a debate at a meeting of the British Association. Wilberforce is said to have played to the gallery and, having shown that he had absolutely no understanding of evolution, concluded by facetiously asking Huxley whether he claimed descent from a monkey through his grandmother or grandfather. Huxley retorted that he would rather be descended from an ape than a man like Wilberforce, who used his great talents to obscure the truth. It is a story that brilliantly encapsulates the "warfare" myth in its depiction of intrepid science victoriously triumphing over complacent, ignorant religion. But, as scholars have repeatedly demonstrated, there is no record of this exchange until the 1890s. It is not mentioned in contemporary accounts of the meeting. In fact, Wilberforce was entirely conversant with Darwinian theory; his speech at the British Institution summarized the recent review that he had written of *Origin,* which Darwin himself, acknowledging that Wilberforce had pointed out serious omissions in his argument that he would have to address, had considered "uncommonly clever."[71]

Closely allied to the "warfare" myth in atheistic polemic was the view that belief in itself was immoral, which has also become an essential ingredient of atheist ideology. It dates from the publication of *Ethics of Belief* (1871) by William Kingdon Clifford (1845–79), professor of mathematics at University College, London, who argued that it was not only intellectually but morally perverse to accept any opinion—religious, scientific, or ethical—without sufficient evidence. He illustrated his thesis with the story of a shipowner who knew that his ship needed extensive repairs but decided to spare himself the expense, reflecting that it had survived many voyages and that God would not allow it to sink with so many passengers on board. When the ship went down in midocean, he was able to collect the insurance.

Clifford's book struck an instant chord. By the late 1860s, widespread veneration for science as the only path to truth had made the idea of "belief" without verification offensive not only intellectually but morally. For the American sociologist Lester Ward (1841–1913), superstition (a term that he applied indiscriminately to any religious idea) led to neurological softening of the brain and weakened moral fiber. Once you had accepted the idea that some matters lay beyond human comprehension, you would swallow anything.[72] For the English philosopher John Stuart Mill (1806–73), the delusions of faith "would sanction half the mischievous illusions recorded in history."[73] Credulity was an act of abject cowardice: "Give me the storm and tempest of thought and action, rather than the dead calm of ignorance and faith!" Ingersoll protested with his usual bravura, "Banish me from Eden if you will; but first let me eat of the fruit of the tree of knowledge!"[74]

Today we are so used to the idea that science and religion are at loggerheads that these ideas no longer surprise us. But in the late nineteenth century, most churchmen still looked up to science; they had not yet fully appreciated how thoroughly Darwinism had undermined the natural theology on which their "belief" was based. At this time, it was not the religious who were fueling the antagonism between the two disciplines but the advocates of science. Most scientists had no interest in bashing religion; they were content to get on quietly with their research and objected only when theologians tried to obstruct their inquiries.[75] It was the popularizers of Darwin who went on the offensive in an antireligious crusade. During the last decades of the nineteenth century, Karl Vogt (1817–95), Ludwig Büchner (1824–99), and Ernst Haeckel (1834–1919) toured Europe, lecturing enthusiastically to packed audiences.[76] Vogt was a good scientist (though some of his colleagues feared that he reached his conclusions too hastily) but was so vehemently anticlerical that when he discussed religion, he lost all perspective. His method was to present faith at its most simplistic—inveighing fiercely against the myth of Noah's Ark, for example, as though it were a real impediment to scientific advance—and then to devote a disproportionate amount of time and energy to attacking the straw dog he had set up.

When they turned their attention to religion, all three were liable to depart from the precision that characterized their discussion of science, so their critique was marred by wild generalizations. When he read Haeckel's best seller *The Riddle of the Universe,* the philosopher Friedrich Paulsen said that he burned with shame to think that it had been written by a German scholar in the land of scholarship.[77] Haeckel had, for example, argued that at the Council of Nicaea, the bishops had compiled the New Testament by simply picking the four gospels at random from a pile of forged documents—information he had acquired from an exceptionally scurrilous English pamphlet. He even got the date of Nicaea wrong. When he discussed science, Haeckel was careful, methodical, and accurate; none of these qualities was in evidence when he wrote about religion.

Huxley had little time for this polemic, because he understood that no investigation of the physical world could provide evidence for or against God. He thought Draper a bore, Vogt a fool, and utterly despised Büchner's best-selling *Force and Matter,* which argued that the universe had no purpose, that everything had derived from a single cell, and that only an idiot could believe in God. Pascal had explained that "the heart has its reasons" for beliefs that were not accessible to our reasoning powers, and this also seems true of late-nineteenth-century unbelief. The proselytizing atheists did not exemplify the precision, objectivity, and impartial examination of the evidence that was now characteristic of the scientific rationalism they glorified. Nevertheless, their emotional diatribes attracted huge crowds. There had always been an intolerant strain in modernity; it had long seemed necessary to abjure recent orthodoxy as a condition for the creation of new truth. Atheism was still a minority passion, but people who nurtured subterranean doubts yet were not ready to let their faith go may have found this passionate critique vicariously cathartic.

Others relinquished their faith with sorrow and felt no Promethean defiance, no heady liberation. In "Dover Beach," the British poet Matthew Arnold (1822–88) heard the "melancholy, long, withdrawing roar" of faith as it receded, bringing "the eternal note of sadness in." Human beings could only cling to one another for comfort, for the world that once seemed

> So various, so beautiful, so new,
> Hath really neither joy, nor love, nor light,
> Nor certitude, nor peace, nor help for pain;
> And we are here as on a darkling plain
> Swept with confused alarms of struggle and flight,
> Where ignorant armies clash by night.[78]

At its best, religion had helped people to build within themselves a haven of peace that enabled them to live creatively with the sorrow of life; but during the scientific age, that interiorized security had been exchanged for an unsustainable certainty. As their faith ebbed, many Victorians sensed the void that it left behind.

When the German philosopher Friedrich Nietzsche (1844–1900) looked into the hearts of his contemporaries, he found that God had already died, there, but as yet very few people were aware of this.[79] In *The Gay Science* (1882), he told the story of a madman who ran one morning into the marketplace, crying: "I seek God!" In mild amusement, the sophisticated bystanders asked him if God had run away or emigrated. "Where has God gone?" the madman demanded. "We have killed him—you and I! We are all his murderers!"[80] The astonishing progress of science had made God quite irrelevant; it had caused human beings to focus so intently on the physical world that they would soon be constitutionally unable to take God seriously. The death of God—the fact that the Christian God had become incredible—was "beginning to cast its first shadows over Europe." The tiny minority who were able to understand the implications of this unprecedented event were already finding that "some sun seems to have set and profound trust has been turned to doubt."[81]

By making "God" a purely notional truth attainable by the rational and scientific intellect, without ritual, prayer, or ethical commitment, men and women had killed it for themselves. Like the Jewish Marranos, Europeans were beginning to experience religion as tenuous, arbitrary, and lifeless. The madman longed to believe in God but he could not. The unthinkable had happened: everything that the symbol of God had pointed to—*absolute* goodness, beauty, order, peace, truthfulness, justice—was being slowly but surely eliminated from European culture. Morality would no longer be measured by reference to an ultimate value that transcended human interests but simply by the needs of the moment. For Marx the death of God had been a project—something to be achieved in the future; for Nietzsche it had already occurred: it was only a matter of time before "God" would cease to be a presence in the scientific civilization of the West. Unless a new absolute could be found to take its place, everything would become unhinged and relative: "What were we about when we uncoupled this earth from the sun?" the madman demanded.

"Where is the earth moving to now? Are we falling continuously? And backwards and sideways and forwards in all directions? Is there still an above and below? Do we not stray, as though through an infinite nothingness?"[82] Nietzsche was, of course, familiar with the philosophical and scientific arguments for the denial of God, but he did not bother to rehearse them. God had not died because of the critique of Feuerbach, Marx, Vogt, and Büchner. There had simply been a change of mood. Like the ancient Sky God, the remote modern God was retreating from the consciousness of his former worshippers.

The century that had begun with a conviction of boundless possibility was giving way to a nameless dread. But, Nietzsche believed, human beings could counter the danger of nihilism by making themselves divine. They must become the new absolute and take the place of God. The God they had projected outside themselves could be born within the human spirit as the *Übermensch* ("Superman") who would provide the universe with ultimate meaning. To achieve this, we had to rebel against the Christian God who had marked the limit of human aspiration, estranged us from our bodies and passions, and enfeebled us with the ideal of compassion. As an incarnation of its will to power, the *Übermensch* would push the evolution of the species into a new phase so that humanity would finally become supreme. But what would happen when human beings did indeed imagine that they were the highest reality and a law unto themselves? What if the ideal of *kenosis* was replaced by the naked lust for empowerment, backed by the immense capacity of scientific technology?

Sigmund Freud (1856–1939), founder of the science of psychoanalysis, illustrates the shift in mood that Nietzsche had diagnosed.[83] Although he grew up in a Jewish household that took religion very seriously—or, perhaps, *because* of his religious upbringing—God was indeed dead for Freud. He did not become an atheist as a result of his study of psychology; he was a psychoanalyst because he was an atheist. For Freud, the idea of God was simply untenable. In 1875, he had discovered the writings of Feuerbach, who had fallen into eclipse since the 1840s, and believed implicitly in the "warfare" myth: in this seemingly interminable conflict, religion must be eliminated.[84] Science alone could ensure the physical and mental health of humanity, and, in fact, its victory was inevitable. Human rationality was coming into its own, gradually breaking the fetters that had impeded its development. "The voice of the intellect is a soft one," he wrote, and it would eventually succeed in quashing religion, but only in "a distant, distant future."[85] It was dangerous to force people into atheism prematurely, as this could lead to unhealthy denial.

Freud had studied medicine at the University of Vienna but always had a deep interest in religion and philosophy. His religious studies, however, were conducted in light of the death of God in his heart. There was no need to justify his atheism, because its truth was self-evident. The idea of God was "so patently infantile, so foreign to reality, that to anyone with a friendly attitude to humanity, it is painful to think that the great majority of mortals would never be able to rise above this view of life."[86] Observing the similarity between religious rites and the obsessive rituals of some of his patients, Freud concluded that religion was a neurosis that bordered on insanity. The desire for God sprang from the infant's experience of helplessness and his yearning for a protector; it reflected the child's passion for justice and fairness and his longing for life to continue forever.

Freud had already worked out his theory of the origins of faith before he began to study religion. He simply selected texts, which he interpreted somewhat eccentrically, that supported his conviction that religion sprang from psychological pressures reflecting our evolutionary development. He had been influenced by the theories of Jean-Baptiste Lamarck (1744–1829), who thought all living creatures had an innate urge to adapt to their environment. To reach the leaves on a high branch, a giraffe learned how to stretch its neck and passed this acquired characteristic to the next generation. In a Lamarckian theory, since dismissed as simplistic, Freud suggested that religion was an acquired trait of this kind, which had developed in response to a specific event. At a very early stage of human history, he suggested in *Totem and Taboo* (1913), the patriarch had exclusive rights to the females of the tribe. This aroused the hostility and resentment of his sons, who overthrew and killed him but later, tormented by remorse, invented rituals to assuage their guilt. In *Moses and Monotheism* (1938), Freud argued that Moses had been killed by the Israelites in the wilderness during a ritual reenactment of this primal murder.

His definition of religion in *The Future of an Illusion* (1927) is also reductive: religion is wish fulfillment of instinctual, unconscious desires, a fantasy that was once consoling but is now doomed to failure, because its myths and rituals belong to such a primitive stage of human evolution. It was time to allow science to allay our fears and provide a new basis for morality. These explanations won respect because they were rooted in science, but Freud's critique was flawed by a rather unscientific view of the female as *homme manqué*: religion was a female activity, while atheism represented the postreligious, healthy masculine human being.[87] His view of religion as rooted in the infant's veneration of the father also prompts the question of whether Freud's rejection of God did not spring from an unconscious hostility to his own father.

Freud has been called the last of the philosophes. In one sense, psychoanalysis can be seen as the culmination of the Enlightenment project to bring the whole of reality under the control of reason. Thanks to Freud's pioneering work, dreams could be interpreted, subconscious impulses brought to light, and the hidden meaning of ancient myths laid bare. But Freud also diminished the Enlightenment ideal by demonstrating that reason comprised only the outermost rind of the human mind and was a superficial crusting on a seething melting pot of primitive instincts over which we had little control. Where Darwin had revealed that nature was "red in tooth and claw," Freud showed that the mind was a battlefield on which we struggled endlessly with the unconscious forces of our own psyche, with little hope of final resolution.

Freud brought to light a darker strand of the fin de siècle when he suggested that human beings were as strongly motivated by a death wish as by the lust for procreation. But at the end of the nineteenth century, many Christians believed that human beings were evolving to a new and more perfect state. For their part, agnostics were convinced that the world would be a better place without God. Ingersoll looked forward to a future in which "man, gathering courage from a succession of victories over the obstructions of nature, will attain to a serene grandeur unknown to the disciples of any superstition."[88] Doubt was "the womb and cradle of progress."[89] The idea that a "personal God does all" had bred "idleness, ignorance and misery,"[90] but now people could channel the energies that had been sapped by religion into the creation of a more just and equal world. "A battle is going on, in which the humblest human creature is not incapable of taking some part, between the powers of good and those of evil," wrote John Stuart Mill. The task of this generation was to promote "the very slow and often almost insensible progress by which good is gradually being ground from evil."

> To do something during life, on even the humblest scale
> if nothing more is within reach, towards bringing this
> consummation ever so little nearer, is the most animating
> and invigorating thought which can inspire a human
> nature.[91]

This rather than any belief in the supernatural was the religion of the future; working for their fellow human beings would fill the void described by Nietzsche.

But this vision of hope required an act of faith. The American Civil War (1861–65) and the Franco-Prussian War (1870–71) had both revealed the horror of warfare in the industrial age, when the exact sciences were applied to weaponry to devastating effect. Yet the nation-states of Europe seemed in thrall to Freud's death wish. After the Franco-Prussian War, they began an arms race that led to the carnage of the First World War (1914–18), apparently regarding warfare as a Darwinian necessity in which only the fittest would survive. At whatever cost to itself or others, the modern state must build the biggest army and create the most destructive weapons. The British writer I. F. Clarke has shown that between 1871 and 1914, it was unusual to find a single year in which a novel or story looking forward to a terrifying future war did not appear in some European country.[92] The "next great war" loomed as a fearful but unavoidable ordeal, from which the nation would emerge with renewed strength and vigor.

As the nineteenth century drew to a close, the British poet and novelist Thomas Hardy (1840–1928) poignantly expressed the modern predicament. In "The Darkling Thrush," dated December 31, 1900, he expressed the bleak desolation of the human spirit excluded from traditional ways of arriving at a sense of life's meaning. He described the "sharp features" of the wintry landscape as "the century's corpse"; it seemed to Hardy that "every spirit upon earth seemed fervourless as I." Suddenly, an aged thrush—"frail, gaunt and small"—began to sing, flinging his soul upon the growing gloom. As he listened to this "full hearted evensong," Hardy could only reflect, with a calm, sad acceptance:

> So little cause for carolings
>      Of such ecstatic sound
> Was written on terrestrial things
>      Afar or nigh around,
> That I could think there trembl'd through
>      His happy good-night air
> Some blessed Hope, whereof he knew
>      And I was unaware.[93]

# ELEVEN

# Unknowing

At the Second International Congress of Mathematicians in Paris in 1900, the German mathematician David Hilbert (1862–1943) confidently predicted a century of unparalleled scientific progress. There were just twenty-three outstanding problems in the Newtonian system, and once these had been solved, our knowledge of the universe would be complete. There appeared to be no limit to the modern Western achievement. In nearly all fields, artists, scientists, and philosophers seemed to anticipate a brave new world. "In or about December 1910, human nature changed," wrote the British novelist Virginia Woolf (1882–1941) after visiting the startling exhibition of French postimpressionist painters. Artists deliberately flouted their viewers' expectations, tacitly proclaiming the need for a new vision in a new world. Old certainties were evaporating. Some wanted to contemplate irreducible fundamentals, cut out the peripheral, and focus on the essential in order to construct a different reality: scientists searched for the atom or the particle; sociologists and anthropologists reverted to primeval societies and primitive artifacts. People wanted to break the past asunder, split the atom to make something new. Pablo Picasso (1881–1973) either dismembered his subjects or viewed them simultaneously from different perspectives. The novels of Woolf and James Joyce (1882–1941) abandoned the traditional narratives of cause and effect, throwing their readers into the chaotic stream of their characters' consciousness, so that they were uncertain about what actually was happening or how they should judge the action.

But the First World War revealed the self-destructive nihilism that, despite its colossal attainments, lurked at the heart of modern Western civilization. It has been described as the collective suicide of Europe: by slaughtering a generation of young men, the war so damaged European society at its core that arguably it has never fully recovered. The utter futility of trench warfare, fought as it was for no adequate social, ideological, or humanitarian cause, defied the rationalism of the scientific age. The most advanced and civilized countries in Europe had crippled themselves and their opponents with their new military technology simply to serve the national ego. The war itself seemed a terrible parody of the mechanical ideal: once the intricate mechanism of conscription, troop transportation, and the manufacture of weapons had been switched on, it seemed to acquire its own momentum and proved almost impossible to stop. After the armistice, the economy of the West seemed in terminal decline, and the 1930s saw the Great Depression and the rise of fascism and communism. By the end of the decade, the unthinkable had happened and the world was embroiled in a second global war. It was now difficult to feel sanguine about the limitless progress of civilization. Modern secular ideologies were proving to be as lethal as any religious bigotry. They revealed the inherent destructiveness of all idolatry: once the finite reality of the nation had become an absolute value, it was compelled to overcome and destroy all rival claimants.

Modern science had been founded on the belief that it was possible to achieve objective certainty. Hume and Kant had cast doubt on this ideal by suggesting that our understanding of the external world was merely a reflection of human psychology. But even Kant believed that the fundamental categories of Newtonian science—space, time, substance, and causality—were beyond question. Yet within a generation of Hilbert's confident prediction that all physicists had to do was add the final touches to Newton's great "Systeme," it had been superseded. Already in the late nineteenth century, the Scottish physicist James Clerk Maxwell (1831–79) had developed the theory of electromagnetic radiation, showing that physicists were beginning to understand time quite differently from the way we experience it, since a radio wave could be received before it had been sent. The puzzling experiments on ether drift and the speed of light conducted by the American scientists Albert Michelson (1852–1931) and Edward

Morley (1838–1923) suggested that the relative velocities of light from the sun were the same in the direction of the earth's rotation as when opposed to it, which was entirely inconsistent with Newtonian mechanics. There followed the discovery of radioactivity by Alexander-Edmond Becquerel (1820–91) and the isolation of quantum phenomena by Max Planck (1858–1947). Finally, Albert Einstein (1879–1955) applied Planck's quantum theory to light, and formulated his theories of special (1905) and general (1916) relativity. Relativity was able to accommodate the Michelson-Morley findings by merging the concepts of space and time, regarded as absolutes by Newton, into a space-time continuum. Building on Einstein's breakthrough, Niels Bohr (1885–1962) and Werner Heisenberg (1901–76) developed quantum mechanics, an achievement that contradicted nearly every major postulate of Newtonian physics.

So much for the traditional assumption that knowledge would proceed incrementally, as each generation improved on the discoveries of its forebears. In the bewildering universe of quantum mechanics, three-dimensional space and unidimensional time had become relative aspects of a four-dimensional space-time continuum. Atoms were not the solid, indestructible building blocks of nature but were found to be largely empty. Time passed at different rates for observers traveling at different speeds: it could go backward or even stop entirely. Euclid's geometrical laws no longer provided the universal and necessary structure of nature. The planets did not move in their orbits because they were drawn to the sun by gravitational force operating at a distance but because the space in which they moved was actually curved. Subatomic phenomena were particularly baffling because they could be observed as both waves and particles of energy. "All my attempts to adapt the theoretical foundation of physics to this knowledge failed me," Einstein recalled. "It was as if the ground had been pulled out from under me, with no firm foundation to be seen anywhere upon which one could have built."[1]

If these discoveries were bewildering to scientists, they seemed utterly impenetrable to the layman. A curved space, finite and yet unbounded; objects that were not things but merely processes; an expanding universe; phenomena that took no definite shape until they were observed—all defied any received presupposition. Newton's grand certainties had been replaced by a system that was ambiguous, shifting, and indeterminate. Despite Hilbert, we seemed no closer to understanding the universe. Human beings, randomly produced minutiae whose existence was probably ephemeral, still appeared to be cast adrift in a vast, impersonal universe. There was no clear answer as to what had preceded the "big bang" that had given birth to the universe. Even physicists did not believe that the equations of quantum theory described what was actually there; these mathematical abstractions could not be put into words, and our knowledge was confined to symbols that were mere shadows of an indescribable reality. Unknowing seemed built into the human condition. The revolution of the 1920s had overturned traditional scientific orthodoxy, and if that had happened once, it could happen again.

Some Christians believed that the new physics was friendly to faith, even though Einstein always insisted that relativity was a scientific theory and had no bearing on religion. They seized eagerly on his famous remark in a debate with Bohr in Brussels (1927) that although quantum mechanics was "certainly imposing," an "inner voice tells me that it . . . does not bring us any closer to the secret of the Old One. I, at any rate, am convinced that He does not throw dice."[2] But Einstein was not referring to the personal God; he had simply used the "Old One" (a medieval Kabbalistic image) to symbolize the impersonal, intelligible, and immanent order of what exists. The British astronomer Arthur Stanley Eddington, however, saw relativity as evidence for the existence of mind in nature; Canon Arthur F. Smethurst regarded it as a manifestation of the Holy Spirit;[3] others saw the new conception of time as validating the afterlife;[4] big bang theory was thought to substantiate the Genesis account;[5] and some even managed to see the indeterminacy of quantum mechanics as support for God's providential control of the world.[6] This type of speculation was ill-conceived. Inured to their need for scientific proof, these apologists were still interpreting the ancient biblical symbols in too literal a manner. Max Planck had a more sage view of the relations between science and religion. The two were quite compatible: science dealt with the objective, material world and religion with values and ethics. Conflict between them was based "on a confusion of the images and parables of religion with scientific statement."[7]

After Einstein, it became disturbingly clear that not only was science unable to provide us with definitive certainty but its findings were inherently limited and provisional too. In 1927, Heisenberg formulated the principle of indeterminacy in nuclear physics, showing that it was impossible for scientists to achieve an objective result because the act of observation itself affected their understanding of the object of their investigation. In 1931, the Austrian philosopher Kurt Gödel (1906–78) devised a theorem to show that any formal logical or mathematical system must contain propositions that are not verifiable within that system; there would always be propositions that could be proved or disproved only by input from outside. This completely undercut the traditional assumption of systematic decidability. In his 1929 Gifford Lectures in Edinburgh, the American philosopher John Dewey (1859–1952) argued that Descartes' quest for certainty could no longer be the goal of modern philosophy. Heisenberg had liberated us from seventeenth-century mechanics, when the universe had seemed like a giant machine made up of separate components, whereas this new generation of scientists was revealing the deep interconnectedness of all reality.

Apparently our brains were incapable of achieving a complete worldview or incontrovertible proof. Our minds were limited, and some problems, it seemed, would remain insoluble. As the American physicist Percy Bridgman (1882–1961) explained:

> The structure of nature may eventually be such that our processes of thought do not correspond to it sufficiently to permit us to think about it at all. . . . The world fades out and eludes us. . . . We are confronted with something truly ineffable. We have reached the limit of the great pioneers of science, the vision, namely, that we live in a sympathetic world in that it is comprehensible to our minds.[8]

Scientists were beginning to sound like apophatic theologians. Not only was God beyond the reach of the human mind, but the natural world was also terminally elusive. It seemed that a degree of agnosticism was endemic to the human condition.

Yet however unsettling this new scientific revolution, physicists did not seem unduly dismayed.[9] Einstein had declared that if his theory of relativity was correct, it was possible to make three predictions:

it would account for the apparently eccentric precession of the planet Mercury; it would be possible to calculate the exact deflection of a beam of light by the gravitational mass of the sun; and because the mass of the sun would reduce the velocity of light, this would have an effect on the light it emitted. Within ten years, the first two predictions were confirmed by experimental data. But the third was not established until the 1960s, because the reduction of the speed of light was minute and scientists lacked the technology to measure it. In principle, Einstein could be proved wrong. He himself was not perturbed: when asked what would happen if his theories were not vindicated in the laboratory, he retorted, "So much the worse for the experiments; the theory is right!" Scientific theory did not seem to depend wholly on ratiocination and calculation: intuition and a sense of beauty and elegance were also important factors. And during these forty years, physicists were content to work as though relativity were true. They had what religious people would call "faith" in it. It was finally rewarded when a new spectroscopic technique became available and scientists could finally observe the effect Einstein had predicted. In science, as in theology, human beings could make progress on unproven ideas, which worked practically even if they had not been demonstrated empirically.

The scientific revolution of the 1920s clearly influenced the work of the Austrian philosopher Karl Popper (1902–94). In his seminal book *The Logic of Scientific Discovery* (1934), he upheld the rationality of science and its commitment to rigorous testing and principled neutrality, but argued that it did not, as commonly thought, proceed by the systematic and cumulative collection of empirically verified facts. It moved forward when scientists came up with bold, imaginative guesses that could never be perfectly verified and were no more reliable than any other "belief," because testing could show only that a hypothesis was *not* false. Popper was often heard to say: "We don't know anything." According to the British philosopher Bryan Magee, he believed that this was "the most important philosophical insight there is, which ought to inform all our philosophical activity."[10] Human beings never achieve perfect knowledge, because anything we know at any given moment is invariably revised later. But far from being depressed by this, Popper found his constant engagement with insoluble problems an endless delight. "One of the many great sources of happiness," he explained in his memoir, "is to get a glimpse, here and there, of a new aspect of the incredible world we live in, and of our incredible role in it."[11]

This was also Einstein's experience. The new science was no longer averse to mystical wonder and mystery. As Einstein explained:

> The most beautiful emotion we can experience is the mystical. It is the sower of all true art and science. He to whom this emotion is a stranger . . . is as good as dead. To know that what is impenetrable to us really exists, manifesting itself to us as the highest wisdom and the most radiant beauty, which our dull faculties can comprehend only in their most primitive forms—this knowledge, this feeling is at the centre of all true religiousness. In this sense, and in this sense only, I belong to the ranks of devoutly religious men.[12]

Einstein emphatically did not subscribe to the personalized modern God. But many of the theologians whose work we have considered—Origen, the Cappadocians, Denys, and Aquinas—would have understood exactly what he meant.

Not everybody was ready to abandon the quest for certainty. During the 1920s, a group of philosophers in Vienna met to discuss, among other topics, the ideas of the Austrian mathematician Ludwig Wittgenstein (1889–1951). The goal of his extremely complex *Tractatus logico-philosophicus* (1921) was to show the utter futility of speaking of ideas that lay beyond clear facts based on empirical sense data: "Whereof one cannot speak," he said famously, "thereof one must be silent."[13] It was quite legitimate to say "It is raining," because this statement was easy to verify. But it was pointless to discuss anything hypothetical or ineffable—in philosophy, ethics, aesthetics, logic, or mathematics—so this type of speculation should be scrapped. True to his principles, Wittgenstein had left his university in 1918 to become a village schoolmaster until 1930, when he accepted a Cambridge fellowship.

The Vienna Circle agreed that because we could make meaningful statements only about matters that could be tested and verified by sense experience, the natural sciences alone were a reliable source of knowledge.[14] Emotive language was meaningless, because it was equipped simply to arouse feeling or inspire action and could not be proved one way or the other. Obviously the concept of "God" had no meaning at all; indeed, atheism and agnosticism were also incoherent positions, because there was nothing to be agnostic or atheistic about.[15] Like other intellectuals at this time, the logical positivists—as these philosophers became known—were attempting to return to irreducible fundamentals. Their stringent position also revealed the intolerant tendency of modernity that would characterize other types of fundamentalism. Their narrow definition of truth entailed a wholesale dismissal of the humanities and a refusal to entertain any rival view.[16] Yet human beings have always pondered questions that are not capable of definitive solutions: the contemplation of beauty, mortality, and suffering has been an essential part of human experience, and to many it seems not only arrogant but unrealistic to dismiss it out of hand.

At the other extreme of the intellectual spectrum, a form of Christian positivism developed that represented a grassroots rebellion against modern rationalism. On April 9, 1906, the first congregation of Pentecostalists claimed to have experienced the Spirit in a tiny house in Los Angeles, convinced that it had descended upon them in the same way as upon Jesus's disciples on the Jewish festival of Pentecost, when the divine presence had manifested itself in tongues of fire and given the apostles the ability to speak in strange languages.[17] When they spoke in "tongues," Pentecostalists felt they were returning to the fundamental nub of religiosity that existed beneath any logical exposition of the Christian faith. Within four years, there were hundreds of Pentecostal groups all over the United States, and the movement had spread to fifty other countries.[18] At first they were convinced that their experience heralded the Last Days: crowds of African Americans and disadvantaged whites poured into their congregations in the firm belief that Jesus would soon return and establish a more just society. But after the First World War had shattered this early optimism, they saw their gift of tongues as a new way of speaking to God: Had not Saint Paul explained that when Christians found prayer difficult, "the Spirit itself intercedes for us with groans that exist beyond all utterance"?[19]

In one sense, this was a distorted version of apophatic spirituality:

Pentecostalists were reaching out to a God that existed beyond the scope of speech. But the classical apophaticism of Origen, Gregory of Nyssa, Augustine, Denys, Bonaventure, Aquinas, and Eckhart had been suspicious of this type of experiential spirituality. At a Pentecostal service, men and women fell into tranced states, were seen to levitate, and felt that their bodies were melting in ineffable joy. They saw bright streaks of light in the air and sprawled on the ground, felled by a weight of glory.[20] This was a form of positivism, because Pentecostalists relied on the immediacy of sense experience to validate their beliefs.[21] But the meteoric explosion of this type of faith indicated widespread unhappiness with the modern rational ethos. It developed at a time when people were beginning to have doubts about science and technology, which had shown their lethal potential during the Great War. Pentecostalists were also reacting against the more conservative Christians who were trying to make their Bible-based religion entirely reasonable and scientific.

As A. C. Dixon, one of the founding fathers of Protestant fundamentalism, explained in 1920, "I am a Christian because I am a Thinker, a Rationalist, a Scientist." His faith depended upon "exact observation and correct thinking." Doctrines were not theological speculations but facts.[22] Evangelical Christians still aspired to the early modern ideal of absolute certainty based on scientific verification. Yet fundamentalists would also see their faith experiences—born-again conversions, faith healing, and strongly felt emotional conviction—as positive verification of their beliefs. Dixon's almost defiant rationalism indicates, perhaps, a hidden fear. With the Great War, an element of terror had entered conservative Protestantism in the United States. Many believed that the catastrophic encounters at the Somme and Passchendaele were the battles that, according to scripture, would usher in the Last Days; many Christians were now convinced that they were on the front line of an apocalyptic war against Satan. The wild propaganda stories of German atrocities seemed proof positive that they had been right to fight the nation that had spawned the Higher Criticism.[23] But they were equally mistrustful of democracy, which carried overtones of the "mob rule" and "red republic" that had erupted in the atheistic Bolshevik revolution (1917).[24] These American Christians no longer saw Jesus as a loving savior; rather, as the leading conservative Isaac M. Haldeman proclaimed, the Christ of Revelation "comes forth as one who no longer seeks either friendship or love. . . . He descends that he may shed the blood of men."[25]

Every single fundamentalist movement that I have studied in Judaism, Christianity, and Islam is rooted in profound fear.[26] For Dixon and his conservative Protestant colleagues, who were about to establish the first fundamentalist movement of modern times, it was a religious variation of the widespread malaise that followed the Great War, and it made them distort the tradition they were trying to defend. They were ready for a fight, but the conflict might have remained in their own troubled minds had not the more liberal Protestants chosen this moment to launch an offensive against them. The liberals were appalled by the apocalyptic fantasies of the conservatives. But instead of criticizing them on biblical and doctrinal grounds, they hit quite unjustifiably below the belt. Their assault reflected the acute anxieties of the postwar period and, at this time of national trauma, was calculated to elicit outrage, fury, and a determination to retaliate.

Fundamentalism—be it Jewish, Christian, or Muslim—nearly always begins as a defensive movement; it is usually a response to a campaign of coreligionists or fellow countrymen that is experienced as inimical and invasive. In 1917, during a particularly dark period of the war, liberal theologians in the Divinity School of the University of Chicago launched a media offensive against the Moody Bible Institute on the other side of town.[27] They accused these biblical literalists of being in the pay of the Germans and compared them to atheistic Bolsheviks. Their theology was, according to the *Christian Register,* "the most astounding mental aberration in the field of religious thinking."[28] The conservatives responded in kind, retorting that, on the contrary, it was the pacifism of the liberals that had caused America to fall behind in the arms race;[29] it was they who had been in league with the Germans, since the Higher Criticism that the liberals admired had caused the collapse of decent values in Germany.[30] For decades, the Higher Criticism had been surrounded with a nimbus of evil. This type of symbolism, which takes the debate beyond the realm of logic and dispassionate discussion, is a persistent feature of fundamentalist movements.

In 1920, Dixon, Reuben A. Torrey, and William B. Riley officially established the World's Christian Fundamentals Association to fight for the survival of both Christianity and the world. That same year, at a meeting of the Northern Baptist Convention, Curtis Lee Lewis defined the "fundamentalist" as a Christian who fought to regain territory already lost to the Antichrist and "to do battle royal for the fundamentals of the faith."[31] The movement spread. Three years later, the fundamentalists were riding high, and it seemed as if they would succeed in gaining the upper hand in most of the Protestant denominations. But then a new campaign caught their attention, which brought fundamentalism, at least for a few decades, into disrepute.

In 1920 the Democratic politician William Jennings Bryan (1860–1925) launched a crusade against the teaching of evolution in schools and colleges; almost single-handedly, Bryan was responsible for ousting the Higher Criticism from the top of the fundamentalist agenda and putting Darwinism in its place.[32] He saw the two issues as indissolubly linked but regarded evolution as by far the more dangerous. Two books—*Headquarter Nights* (1917) by Vernon L. Kellogg and *The Science of Power* (1918) by Benjamin Kidd—had made a great impression on him. The authors reported interviews with German soldiers, who had testified to the influence that Darwinian ideas had played in Germany's determination to declare war. This "research" convinced Bryan that evolutionary theory heralded the collapse of morality and decent civilization. His ideas were naive, simplistic, and incorrect, but people were beginning to be suspicious of science and he found a willing audience. When Bryan toured the United States, his lecture "The Menace of Darwinism" drew large crowds and got extensive media coverage. But an unexpected development in the South threw the campaign into even greater prominence.

At this date, the fundamentalist movement was chiefly confined to the northern states, but southerners had become concerned about evolution. In 1925, the state legislatures of Florida, Mississippi, Tennessee, and Louisiana passed laws to prohibit the teaching of evolution in the public schools. In response, John Scopes, a young teacher in Dayton, Tennessee, decided to strike a blow for free speech, confessed that he had broken the law, and in July 1925 was brought to trial. The new American Civil Liberties Union (ACLU) sent a team of lawyers to defend him, headed by the rationalist campaigner

Clarence Darrow (1857–1938). When Bryan agreed to speak in defense of the anti-evolution law, the trial ceased to be about civil liberties and became a contest between religion and science.

Like many fundamentalist disputes, the Scopes trial was a clash between two incompatible points of view.[33] Both Darrow and Bryan represented core American values: Darrow, of course, stood for intellectual liberty and Bryan for the rights of the ordinary folk, who were traditionally leery of learned experts, had no real understanding of science, and felt that sophisticated elites were imposing their own values on small-town America. In the event, Bryan was a disaster on the stand and Darrow was able to argue brilliantly for the freedom that was essential to the scientific enterprise. At the end of the trial, Darrow emerged as the hero of lucid rational thought, while Bryan was seen as a bumbling, incompetent anachronism who was hopelessly out of touch with the modern world: he compounded the symbolism by dying a few days later. Scopes was convicted, the ACLU paid his fine, but Darrow and science were the real victors at Dayton.

The press had a field day. Most notably, the journalist H. L. Mencken (1880–1956) denounced the fundamentalists as the scourge of the nation. How appropriate it was, he crowed, that Bryan, who loved simple country people, including the "gaping primates of the upland villages," had ended his days in a "one-horse, Tennessee village." Fundamentalists were everywhere: they are "thick in the mean streets behind the gas works. They are everywhere learning is too heavy a burden for mortal minds to carry, even the vague pathetic learning on tap in the little red schoolhouse." They were the enemies of science and freedom and had no legitimate place in the modern world.[34] The author Maynard Shipley argued that if the fundamentalists seized control of the denominations and imposed their bigoted views on the people, America would be dragged back to the Dark Ages.[35]

At Dayton, the liberals had felt threatened when the rights of free speech and free inquiry were in jeopardy. These rights were sacred, not because they were "supernatural" but because they were now central to the modern identity, and as such inviolable and nonnegotiable. Take these rights away, and everything would be awry. For the fundamentalists, who feared modernity and knew that some of its most vocal exponents had vowed to destroy religion, the new doctrine of biblical inerrancy was sacred, not just because of its supernatural sanction but because it provided the sole guarantee of certainty in an increasingly uncertain world. There would in the future be similar clashes between people at different stages of the modernization process who had competing notions of the sacred. The religious had struck a blow for a value that they felt was imperiled, and the liberals had struck back, hard. And at first the liberal assault appeared to have paid off. After the Scopes trial, the fundamentalists went quiet and seemed suitably vanquished. But they had not gone away. They had simply withdrawn defensively, as fundamentalists of other traditions would do in the future, and created an enclave of Godliness in a world that seemed hostile to religion, forming their own churches, broadcasting stations, publishing houses, schools, universities, and Bible colleges. In the late 1970s, when this countercultural society had gained sufficient strength and confidence, the fundamentalists would return to public life, launching a counteroffensive to convert the nation to their principles.

During their time in the political wilderness, the fundamentalists became more radical, nursing a deep grievance against mainstream American culture.[36] Subsequent history would show that when a fundamentalist movement is attacked, it almost invariably becomes more aggressive, bitter, and excessive. Rooted as fundamentalism is in a fear of annihilation, its adherents see any such offensive as proof that the secular or liberal world is indeed bent on the elimination of religion. Jewish and Muslim movements would also conform to this pattern. Before Scopes, Protestant fundamentalists tended to be on the left of the political spectrum, willing to work with socialists and liberals in the disadvantaged areas of the rapidly industrializing cities. After Scopes, they swung to the far right, where they have remained.

The ridicule of the press proved to be counterproductive, since it made the fundamentalists even more militant in their views. Before Scopes, evolution had not been an important issue; even such ardent literalists as Charles Hodge knew that the world had existed for a lot longer than the six thousand years mentioned in the Bible. Only a very few subscribed to so-called creation science, which argued that Genesis was scientifically sound in every detail. Most fundamentalists were Calvinists, though Calvin himself had not shared their hostility to scientific knowledge. But after Dayton, an unswerving biblical literalism became central to the fundamentalist mind-set and creation science became the flagship of the movement. It would become impossible to discuss the issue rationally, because evolution was no longer merely a scientific hypothesis but a "symbol," indelibly imbued with the misery of defeat and humiliation. The early history of the first fundamentalist movement in the modern era proved to be paradigmatic. When attacking religion that seems obscurantist, critics must be aware that this assault is likely to make it more extreme.

The Second World War (1939–45) revealed the terrifying efficiency of modern violence. The explosion of atomic bombs over Hiroshima and Nagasaki laid bare the nihilistic self-destruction at the heart of the brilliant achievements of *Homo technologicus*. Our ability to harm and mutilate one another had kept pace with our extraordinary economic and scientific progress, and we seemed to lack either the wisdom or the means to keep our aggression within safe and appropriate bounds. Indeed, the shocking discovery that six million Jews had been systematically slaughtered in the Nazi camps, an atrocity that had originated in Germany, a leading player in the Enlightenment, called the whole notion of human progress into question.

The Holocaust is sometimes depicted as an eruption of premodern barbarism; it is even seen as an expression of religious impulses that had been repressed in secular society. But historians and social critics have challenged this view.[37] It is certainly true that Christian anti-Semitism had been a chronic disease in Europe since the time of the Crusades; and while individual Christians protested against the horror and tried to save their Jewish neighbors, many of the denominations were largely and shamefully silent. Hitler had never officially left the Catholic Church and should have been excommunicated; Pope Pius XII neither condemned nor distanced himself from the Nazi programs.

But to blame the entire catastrophe on religion is simply—and perhaps even dangerously—inaccurate. Far from being in conflict with the rational pursuit of well-organized, goal-oriented modernity, the hideous efficiency of the Nazis was a supreme example of it. Rulers had long initiated policies of ethnic cleansing when setting up their modern, centralized states. In order to use all the human resources at their disposal and to maintain productivity, governments had found it necessary to bring out-groups such as the Jews into the mainstream, but the events of the 1930s and 1940s showed that this tolerance was merely superficial and the old bigotry still lurked beneath. To carry out their program of genocide, the Nazis relied on the technology of the industrial age: the railways, the advanced chemical industry, and rationalized bureaucracy and management. The camp replicated the factory, the hallmark of industrial society, but what it mass-produced was death. Science itself was implicated in the eugenic experiments carried out there. The modern idolatry of nationalism had so idealized the German *volk* that there was no place for the Jews: born of the new "scientific" racism, the Holocaust was the ultimate in social engineering in what has been called the modern "garden culture," which simply eliminated weeds—the supreme, perverted example of rational planning in which everything is subordinated to a single, clearly defined objective.[38]

Perhaps the Holocaust was not so much an expression as a perversion of Judeo-Christian values.[39] As atheists had been eager to point out, the symbol of God had marked the limit of human potential. At the heart of the Nazi ideology was a romantic yearning for a pre-Christian German paganism that they had never properly understood, and a negation of the God who, as Nietzsche had suggested, put a brake on ambition and instinctual "pagan" freedom. The extermination of the people who had created the God of the Bible was a symbolic enactment of the death of God that Nietzsche had proclaimed.[40] Or perhaps the real cause of the Holocaust was the ambiguous afterlife of religious feeling in Western culture and the malignant energies released by the decay of the religious forms that had channeled them into more benign, productive outlets.[41] In Christian theology, hell had traditionally been defined as the absence of God, and the camps uncannily reproduced the traditional symbolism of the inferno: the flaying, racking, whipping, screaming, and mocking; the distorted bodies; the flames and stinking air all evoked the imagery of hell depicted by the artists, poets, and dramatists of Europe.[42] Auschwitz was a dark epiphany, providing us with a terrible vision of what life is like when all sense of the sacred is lost and the human being—whoever he or she may be—is no longer revered as an inviolable mystery.

The Holocaust survivor and Nobel Prize winner Elie Wiesel believed that God died in Auschwitz. During his first night in the camp, he had watched the black smoke curling into the sky from the crematorium where the bodies of his mother and sister were being consumed. "Never shall I forget those moments," he wrote years later, "which murdered my God and my soul and turned my dreams to dust."[43] He relates how one day the Gestapo hanged a child with the face of a "sad-eyed angel" who was silent and almost calm as he climbed the gallows. It took the child nearly an hour to die in front of the thousands of spectators who were forced to watch. Behind Wiesel, one of the prisoners muttered: "Where is God? Where is He?" And Wiesel heard a voice within him saying in response: "Where is He? Here He is—He is hanging here on this gallows."[44]

This story can also be seen as an outward sign of the death of God announced by Nietzsche. How do we account for the great evil we see in a world supposedly created and governed by a benevolent deity? For the Jewish writer Richard Rubenstein this conception of God is no longer viable. Because Jews so narrowly escaped extermination, Rubenstein does not believe that they should jettison their religion, as this would cut them off from their past. But the nice, moral God of liberal Jews seems too anodyne and antiseptic: it ignores life's inherent tragedy in the hope that things will improve. Instead, Rubenstein is drawn to the self-emptying God of Isaac Luria, who had not been able to control the world he had brought into being. The mystics had seen God as Nothingness; Auschwitz had revealed the abysmal emptiness of life, and the contemplation of Luria's En Sof was a way of entering into the primal Nothingness from which we came and to which we all return.[45] The British theologian Louis Jacobs, however, believed that Luria's impotent God could not give meaning to human existence. He preferred the classic solution that God is greater than human beings can conceive and that his ways are not our ways. God may be incomprehensible, but people have the option of putting their trust in this ineffable God and affirming a meaning, even in the midst of meaninglessness.

Another Auschwitz story shows people doing precisely that. Even in the camps, some of the inmates continued to study the Torah and to observe the festivals, not in the hope of placating an angry deity but because they found, by experience, that these rituals helped them to endure the horror. One day a group of Jews decided to put God on trial. In the face of such inconceivable suffering, they found the conventional arguments utterly unconvincing. If God was omnipotent, he could have prevented the Shoah; if he could not stop it, he was impotent; and if he could have stopped it but chose not to, he was a monster. They condemned God to death. The presiding rabbi pronounced the verdict, then went on calmly to announce that it was time for the evening prayer. Ideas about God come and go, but prayer, the struggle to find meaning even in the darkest circumstances, must continue.

The idea of God is merely a symbol of indescribable transcendence and has been interpreted in many different ways over the centuries. The modern God—conceived as powerful creator, first cause, supernatural personality realistically understood and rationally demonstrable—is a recent phenomenon. It was born in a more optimistic era than our own and reflects the firm expectation that scientific rationality could bring the apparently inexplicable aspects of life under the control of reason. This God was indeed, as Feuerbach suggested, a projection of humanity at a time when human beings were achieving unprecedented control over their environment and thought they were about to solve the mysteries of the universe. But many feel that the hopes of the Enlightenment also died in Auschwitz. The people who devised the camps had imbibed the classical nineteenth-century atheistic ethos that commanded them to think of themselves as the only absolute; by making an idol of their nation, they felt compelled to destroy those they viewed as enemies. Today we have a more modest conception of the powers of human reason. We have seen too much evil in recent years to indulge in a facile theology that says—as some have tried to say—that God knows what he is doing, that he has a secret plan that we cannot fathom, or that suffering gives men and women the opportunity to practice heroic virtue. A modern theology must look unflinchingly into the heart of a great darkness and be prepared, perhaps, to enter into the cloud of unknowing.

After the Second World War, philosophers and theologians all struggled with the idea of God, seeking to rescue it from the literalism that had made it incredible. In doing so, they often revived older, premodern ways of thinking and speaking about the divine. In his later years, Wittgenstein changed his mind. He no longer believed that language should merely state facts but acknowledged that words also issued commands, made promises, and expressed emotion. Turning his back on the early modern ambition to establish a single method of arriving at truth, Wittgenstein now maintained that there were an infinite number of social discourses. Each one was meaningful—but only in its own context. So it was a grave mistake "to make religious belief a matter of evidence in the way that science is a matter of evidence,"[46] because theological language worked "on an entirely different plane."[47] Positivists and atheists who applied the norms of scientific rationality and common sense to religion and those theologians who tried to prove God's existence had all done "infinite harm,"[48] because they implied that God was an external fact—an idea that was intolerable to Wittgenstein. "If I thought of God as another being outside myself, only infinitely more powerful," he insisted, "then I would regard it as my duty to defy him."[49] Religious language was essentially symbolic; it was "disgusting"[50] if interpreted literally, but symbolically it had the power to manifest a transcendent reality in the same way as the short stories of Tolstoy. Such works of art did not argue their case or produce evidence but somehow called into being the ineffable reality they evoked. But because the transcendent reality was ineffable—"wonderful beyond words"[51]—we would never come to know God merely by talking about him. We had to change our behavior, "try to be helpful to other people," and leave egotism behind.[52] If, Wittgenstein believed, he would one day be capable of making his entire nature bow down "in humble resignation to the dust," then, he thought, God would, as it were, come to him.[53]

The German philosopher Martin Heidegger had no time for the modern, personalized God but saw *Sein* ("Being") as the supreme reality. It was not *a* being, so bore no relation to any reality that we knew; it was wholly other and should more accurately be called Nothing. And yet, paradoxically, Being was *seiender* ("being-er"), more complete than any particular being. Despite its utter transcendence, we can gain some understanding of it—but not through the aggressive thrust of scientific investigation. Instead, we had to cultivate what Heidegger called "primordial thinking," a listening, receptive attitude characterized by silence. This was not a logical process, and it was not something that we *did*. Instead, it was something that happened within us, a lighting up—almost a revelation. Being was not a fact that we could grasp once and for all, but an apprehension that we built up over time, repetitively and incrementally. We had to immerse ourselves in this cast of mind again and again, in rather the same way as a historian projects himself repeatedly into a historical figure or era.

Theologians, Heidegger believed, had reduced God to a mere being. God had become Someone Else and theology a positive science. In his early work, therefore, Heidegger insisted that it was essential systematically to dismantle faith in this "God" so that we might recover a sense of Being. The God of the philosophers, a typically modern invention, was as good as dead: it was impossible to pray to such a god. This was a time of great depletion; the technological domination of the earth had brought about the nihilism foretold by Nietzsche, because it had made us forgetful of Being. But in his later work, Heidegger found it heartening that God had become incredible. People were becoming conscious of a void, an absence at the heart of their lives. By practicing meditative "thinking," we could learn to experience what Heidegger called "the return of the holy." No longer hopelessly mired in mere beings, we should cultivate that primordial waiting in which Being could, as it were, "speak" to us directly.[54]

Many were dismayed by Heidegger's apparent refusal to condemn National Socialism after the war. But his ideas were extremely evocative and influenced a generation of Christian theologians. Rudolf Bultmann (1884–1976) insisted that God must be de-objectified and that the scriptures did not convey factual information but could be understood only if Christians involved themselves existentially with their faith. "To believe in the cross of Christ does not mean to concern ourselves . . . with an objective event," he explained, "but rather to make the cross our own."[55] Europeans had lost the sense that their doctrines were mere gestures toward transcendence. Their literalist approach showed a complete misunderstanding of the purpose of myth, which is "not to present an objective picture of the world as it is. . . . Myth should be interpreted not cosmologically but . . . existentially."[56] Biblical interpretation could not even begin without personal engagement, so scientific objectivity was as alien to religion as to art. Religion was possible only when people were "stirred by the question of their own existence and can hear the claim that the text makes."[57] A careful examination of the Gospels showed that Jesus did not see God as "an object of thought or speculation" but as an existential demand, a "power that constrains man to decision, who confronts him in the demand for good."[58] Like Heidegger, Bultmann understood that the sense of the divine was not something to be comprehended once and for all; it came to us repetitively, by constant attention to the demands of the moment. He was not speaking of an exotic mystical experience. Having lived through the Nazi years, Bultmann knew how frequently, in such circumstances, men and women are confronted by an internal requirement that seems to come from outside themselves and which they cannot reject without denying what is most authentic to them. God was, therefore, an absolute claim that drew people beyond self-interest and egotism into transcendence.

Paul Tillich (1886–1965) was born in Prussia and served as an army chaplain in the trenches during the First World War, after which he suffered two major breakdowns. Later he became a professor of theology at the University of Frankfurt but was expelled by the Nazis in 1933 and emigrated to the United States. He saw the modern God as an idolatry that human beings must leave behind.

> The concept of a "Personal God," interfering with natural events, or being "an independent cause of natural events" makes God a natural object beside others, an object among others, a being among beings, maybe the highest, but nevertheless, *a* being. This indeed is not only the destruction of the physical system but even more the destruction of any meaningful idea of God.[59]

A God who interfered with human freedom was a tyrant, not so different from the human tyrants who had wrought such havoc in recent history. A God envisaged as a person in a world of his own, an "ego" relating to a "thou," was simply *a* being. Even the Supreme Being was just another being, the final item in the series. It was, Tillich insisted, an "idol," a human construction that had become absolute. As recent history had shown, human beings were chronically predisposed to idolatry. The "idea that the human mind is a perpetual manufacturer of idols is one of the deepest things which can be said about our thinking of God," Tillich remarked. "Even orthodox theology is nothing other than idolatry."[60] An atheism that passionately rejected a God that had been reduced to a mere being was a religious act.

For centuries, symbols such as "God" or "providence" enabled people to look through the ebb and flow of temporal life to glimpse Being itself. This helped them to endure the terror of life and the horror of death, but now, Tillich argued, many had forgotten how to interpret the old symbolism and regarded it as purely factual. Hence, these symbols had become opaque; transcendence no longer shone through them. When this happened they died and lost their power, so when we spoke of these symbols in a literal manner, we made statements that were inaccurate and untrue. That was why, like so many premodern theologians, Tillich could state without qualification: "God does not exist. He is being itself beyond essence and existence. Therefore to argue that God exists is to deny him."[61] This was not, as many of his contemporaries believed, an atheistic statement:

> We can no longer speak of God easily to anybody,
> because he will immediately question: "Does God exist?"
> Now the very asking of that question signifies that the
> symbols of God have become meaningless. For God, in
> the question, has become one of the innumerable objects
> in time and space which may or may not exist. And this is
> not the meaning of God at all.[62]

God could never be an object of cognition, like the objects and people we see all around us. To look through the finite symbol to the reality—the God beyond "God" that lies beyond theism—demands courage; we have to confront the dead symbol to find *"the God who appears when God has disappeared in the anxiety of doubt."*[63]

Tillich liked to call God the ground of being. Like the atman in the Upanishads, which was identical with the Brahman as well as being the deepest core of the individual self, what we call "God" is fundamental to our existence. So a sense of participation in God does not alienate us from our nature or the world, as the nineteenth-century atheists had implied, but returns us to ourselves. Like Bultmann, however, Tillich did not regard the experience of being as an exotic state. It was not distinguishable from any of our other affective or intellectual experiences, because it pervaded and was inseparable from them, so it was inaccurate to say "I am now having a 'spiritual' experience." An awareness of God did not have a special name of its own but was fundamental to our ordinary emotions of courage, hope, or despair. Tillich also called God the "ultimate concern"; like Bultmann, he believed that we experience the divine in our absolute commitment to ultimate truth, love, beauty, justice, and compassion—even if it requires the sacrifice of our own life.

The Jesuit philosopher Karl Rahner (1904–84), who had been Heidegger's pupil, dominated Catholic thought in the mid-twentieth century. He insisted that theology was not a set of dogmas handed down mechanically as self-evidently true. These teachings must be rooted in the actual conditions in which men and women lived, reflecting the manner in which they knew, perceived, and experienced reality. People did not come to know what God was by solving doctrinal conundrums, proving God's existence, or engaging in an abstruse metaphysical quest, but by becoming aware of the workings of their own nature. Rahner was advocating a version of what the Buddha had called "mindfulness." When we struggle to make sense of the world, we constantly go beyond ourselves in our search for understanding. Thus every act of cognition and every act of love is a transcendent experience because it compels us to reach beyond the prism of selfhood. Constantly, in our everyday experience, we stumble against something that takes us beyond ourselves, so transcendence is built into the human condition.

Rahner stressed the importance of mystery, which was simply an aspect of humanity. The transcendent is not an add-on, something separate from normal existence, because it simply means "to go beyond." When we know, choose, and love other beings in this world, we have to go outside ourselves; when we try to get beyond all particular beings, we move toward what lies beyond words, concepts, and categories. That mystery, which defies description, is God. Religious doctrines were not meant to explain or define the mystery; they were simply symbolic. A doctrine articulates our sense of the ineffable and makes us aware of it. A dogmatic statement, therefore, is "merely the means of expressing a being referred beyond itself and anything imaginable."[64]

Bernard Lonergan (1904–84), a Canadian Jesuit, rejected the positivists' belief that all reliable knowledge was derived from external sense data. In *Insight: A Study of Human Understanding* (1957), he argued that knowledge required more than simply "taking a look." It demanded *in*-sight, an ability to see into an object and contemplate it in its various modes: mathematical, scientific, artistic, moral, and finally metaphysical. Continually we find that something eludes us: it urges us to move on further if we wish to become wise. In all cultures, humans have been seized by the same imperatives—to be intelligent, responsible, reasonable, and loving, and, if necessary, to change. All this pulls us into the realm of the transcendental, the Real and Unconditioned, which in the Christian world is called "God." But this demonstration of the ubiquity of God does not force acceptance. Lonergan concluded by pointing out that his book had merely been a set of signs that readers must appropriate and make their own, a task that each person could complete only for him- or herself.

Since the scientific revolution of the 1920s, there has been a growing conviction that unknowing is an ineradicable part of our experience. In 1962, the American intellectual Thomas Kuhn (1922–96) published *The Structure of Scientific Revolutions,* which criticized Popper's theory of the systematic falsification of existing scientific theories but also undermined the older conviction that the history of science represented a linear, rational, and untrammeled progress toward an ever more accurate achievement of objective truth. Kuhn believed that the cumulative testing of hypotheses was only part of the story. During "normal" periods, scientists did indeed research and test their theories, but instead of reaching out toward new truth, they were, in fact, simply seeking confirmation of the scientific paradigm of the day. Teachers and texts all worked to support the prevailing orthodoxy and tended to ignore anything that challenged it; they could advance no farther than the current paradigm, which thus acquired a conviction and rigidity not unlike theological dogma. But then—as had occurred during the 1920s—the "normal" period was succeeded by a dramatic paradigm shift. The accumulating uncertainties and puzzling results of experiments became irresistible, and scientists contended with one another to find a new paradigm. This was not a rational process; it consisted of imaginative and unpredictable flights into the unknown, all influenced by metaphors, imagery, and assumptions drawn from other fields. Kuhn seemed to suggest that aesthetic, social, historical, and psychological factors were also involved, so that the ideal of "pure science" was a chimera. Once the fresh paradigm had been established, a new "normal" period would begin in which scientists worked to endorse the new model, disregarding hints that it was not impregnable, until the next major breakthrough.

It seemed that the scientific knowledge that had come upon the early modern world with the force of a new revelation was not, after all, fundamentally different from the understanding we derived from the humanities. In *Knowing and Being*, Michael Polyani (1891–1976), a chemist and philosopher of science, argued that all knowledge was tacit rather than objectively and self-consciously acquired. He drew attention to the role of practical knowledge, which had been greatly overlooked in the modern emphasis on theoretical understanding. We learn how to swim or dance without being able to explain precisely how it is done. We recognize a friend's face without being able to specify exactly what it is that we recognize. Our perception of the external world is not a mechanical, straightforward absorption of data. We integrate a vast number of things into a focal awareness, subjecting them to an interpretive framework that is so deeply rooted that we cannot make it explicit. The speed and complexity of this integration easily outstrips the relatively ponderous processes of logic or inference. Indeed, knowledge is of little use to us until it has been made tacit. Once we have learned how to drive a car, "the text of the manual is shifted to the back of the driver's mind and transported almost entirely to the tacit operations of a skill."[65]

When we learn a skill, we literally dwell in the innumerable muscular actions we perform without fully knowing how we achieve them. All understanding, Polyani claimed, is like this. We interiorize a language or a poem "and make ourselves dwell in them. Such extensions of ourselves develop new faculties in us; our whole education operates in this way; as each of us interiorises the cultural heritage, she grows into a person seeing the world and experiencing life in terms of this outlook."[66] This, it has been pointed out, is not dissimilar to the Cappadocians' insistence that the knowledge of God was acquired not merely cerebrally but by the physical participation in the liturgical tradition of the Church, which initiated people into a form of knowing that was silent and could not be clearly articulated.[67]

Polyani argued that the scientific method is not simply a matter of progressing from ignorance to objectivity; as in the humanities, it is more likely to consist of a more complex movement from explicit to tacit knowledge. In order for their investigations to work, scientists often have to believe things that they know will be later proved wrong—though they can never be sure which of their current convictions will be so jettisoned. Because there is so much that cannot be proven, there will always be an element of what religious people call "faith" in science—the kind of faith that physicists showed in Einstein's theory of relativity in the absence of empirical proof.

Scientific rationalism consists largely of problem solving, an approach that does lead to systematic advance: after a problem has been solved, it can be laid aside and scientists can move on to tackle the next. But the humanities do not function in this way, because the problems they confront, such as mortality, grief, evil, or the nature of happiness, are not capable of a once-and-for-all solution. It can take a lifetime's engagement with a poem before it reveals its full depth. This type of contemplation may function differently from ratiocination, but it is not for that reason irrational; it is like the "thinking" Heidegger prescribed: repetitive, incremental, and receptive.[68] The French philosopher Gabriel Marcel (1889–1973) distinguished between a *problem*, "something met which bars my passage" and "is before me in its entirety," and a *mystery*, "something in which I find myself caught up, and whose essence is not before me in its entirety."[69] We have to remove a problem before we can proceed, but we are compelled to participate in a mystery—rather as the Greeks flung themselves into the rites of Eleusis and grappled with their mortality. "A mystery is something in which I am myself involved," Marcel continued, "and it can therefore only be thought of as *a sphere where the distinction between what is in me and what is before me loses its meaning and its essential validity.*"[70] It is always possible—and perhaps a modern temptation—to turn a mystery into a problem and try to solve it by applying the appropriate technique. It is significant that today a detective story based on such problem solving is popularly known as a "mystery." But for Marcel this is a "fundamentally vicious proceeding" that could be symptomatic of a "corruption of the intelligence."[71]

Philosophers and scientists were beginning to return to a more apophatic approach to knowledge. But the tradition of Denys,

Thomas, and Eckhart had been so submerged during the modern period that most religious congregations were unaware of it. They tended still to think about God in the modern way, as an objective reality, "out there," that could be categorized like any other being. During the 1950s, for example, I learned by heart this answer to the question "What is God?" in the Roman Catholic catechism: "God is the supreme spirit, who alone exists of himself and is infinite in all perfections." Denys, Anselm, and Aquinas were probably turning in their graves. The catechism had no hesitation in asserting that it was possible simply to draw breath and *define,* a word that literally means "to set limits upon," a transcendent reality that must exceed all words and concepts.

Not surprisingly, many thoughtful people were unable to believe in this remote and abstractly conceived deity. By the middle of the twentieth century, it was commonly imagined that secularism was the coming ideology and that religion would never again play a role in public life. But atheism was still not perceived as an easy option. Jean-Paul Sartre (1905–80) spoke of a God-shaped hole in human consciousness where the sacred had always been. The desire for what we call God is intrinsic to human nature, which cannot bear the utter meaninglessness of the cosmos. We have invented a God to explain the inexplicable; it is a divinized humanity. But even if God existed, Sartre claimed, it would be necessary to reject him, since this God negates our freedom. This was not a comfortable creed. It demanded a bleak acceptance of the fact that our lives had no meaning—a heroic act that brought an apotheosis of freedom but also a denial of an intrinsic part of our nature.

Albert Camus (1913–60) could no longer subscribe to the nineteenth-century dream of a deified humanity. Our lives were rendered meaningless by our mortality, so any philosophy that tried to make sense of human existence was a delusion. We had to do without God and pour all our loving solicitude and care upon the world. But this would bring no liberation. In *The Myth of Sisyphus* (1942), Camus showed that the abolition of God required a lifelong and hopeless struggle that it was impossible to rationalize. In his passion for life and hatred of death, Sisyphus, king of ancient Corinth, had defied the gods, and his punishment was to spend eternity engaged in a futile task: each day he had to roll a boulder up a mountainside; but when he reached the summit, the rock rolled downhill, so the next day he had to begin all over again. This was an image of the absurdity of human life, from which even death offered no release. Can we be happy in the knowledge that we are defeated before we even begin? If we make a heroic effort to create our own meaning in the face of death and absurdity, Camus concludes that happiness is possible:

> I leave Sisyphus at the foot of the mountain! One always finds one's burden again. But Sisyphus teaches the higher fidelity that negates the gods and raises rocks. He too concludes that all is well. This universe henceforth without a master seems to him neither sterile nor futile. Each atom of that stone, each mineral flake of that night-filled mountain in itself forms a world. The struggle itself toward the heights is enough to fill a man's heart. One must imagine Sisyphus happy.[72]

By the middle of the twentieth century, many found it impossible to imagine that getting rid of God would lead to a brave new world; there was no serene Enlightenment optimism in the rationality of human existence. Camus had embraced the state of unknowing. He did not know for certain that God did not exist; he simply chose to believe this. We have to live with our ignorance in a universe that is silent in the face of our questioning.

Within a decade of Camus' death, though, the world had drastically changed. There was a rebellion against the ethos of modernity; new forms of religiosity, a different kind of atheism, and, despite the fact that unknowing seemed built into our condition, a strident lust for certainty.

# TWELVE

# Death of God?

During the 1960s, Europe experienced a dramatic loss of faith. After a rise in religious observance during the austerity years immediately after the Second World War, for example, British people stopped going to church in unprecedented numbers and the decline has steadily continued.[1] A recent poll has estimated that only about 6 percent of Britons attend a religious service regularly. In both Europe and the United States, sociologists proclaimed the triumph of secularism. In 1965, *The Secular City*, a best seller by the American theologian Harvey Cox, claimed that God was dead and that henceforth religion must center on humanity rather than a transcendent deity; if Christianity failed to absorb these new values, the churches would perish. The decline of religion was just one sign of major cultural change during this decade, when many of the institutional structures of modernity were pulled down: censorship was relaxed, abortion and homosexuality were legalized, divorce became easier, the women's movement campaigned for gender equality, and the young railed against the modern ethos of their parents. They called for a more just and equal society, protested against the materialism of their governments, and refused to fight in their nation's wars or to study in its universities. They created an "alternative society" in revolt against the mainstream.

Some saw the new wave of secularism as the fulfillment of the rational ethos of the Enlightenment. Others saw the 1960s as the beginning of the end of the Enlightenment project and the start of "postmodernity."[2] Truths hitherto regarded as self-evident were called into question: the teachings of Christianity, the subordination of women, and the structures of social and moral authority. There was a new skepticism about the role of science, the modern expectation of continuous progress, and the Enlightenment ideal of rationality. The modern dualities of mind/body; spirit/matter, and reason/ emotion were challenged. Finally, the "lower orders," who had been marginalized and even subjugated during the modern period— women, homosexuals, blacks, indigenous populations, colonized peoples—were demanding and beginning to achieve liberation.

Atheism was no longer regarded as a term of abuse. As Nietzsche had predicted, the idea of God had simply died, and for the first time ordinary folk, who were not pioneering scientists or philosophers, were happy to call *themselves* atheists.[3] They did not spend time examining the scientific and rational arguments against God's existence: for many Europeans, God had simply become *otiosus* ("superfluous"). As the political philosophers Antonio Negri and Michael Hardt have explained:

> Modern negativity is located not in any transcendent realm but in the hard reality before us: the fields of patriotic battles in the First and Second World Wars, from the killing fields at Verdun to the Nazi furnaces and the swift annihilation of thousands in Hiroshima and Nagasaki, the carpet bombing of Vietnam and Cambodia, the massacres from Setif and Soweto to Sabra and Shatila, and the list goes on and on. There is no Job who can sustain such suffering.[4]

Belief had emerged as the enemy of peace. John Lennon's song "Imagine" (1971) looked forward to a world where there was no heaven and no hell—"above us only sky." The elimination of God would solve the world's problems. This was a simplistic belief, since many of the conflicts that had inspired the peace movement were caused by an imbalance of political power, secular nationalism, and the struggle for world domination. But religion had been implicated in many of these atrocities: in Northern Ireland and the Middle East it had served as a tribal or ethnic marker, it was used rhetorically by politicians, and it was clear that it had signally failed in its mandate of saving the world.

In the United States, a small group of theologians created a form of "Christian atheism" that tried to engage with the "hard reality" of world events and enthusiastically proclaimed the death of God. In *The Gospel of Christian Atheism* (1966), Thomas J. J. Altizer (b. 1927) announced the "good news": God's demise had freed us from slavery to a tyrannical, transcendent deity. Altizer spoke in mystical, poetic terms of the dark night of the soul, the pain of abandonment, and the silence that must ensue before what we mean by "God" can become meaningful once more. Our former notions of divinity had to die before theology could be reborn. In *The Secular Meaning of the Gospel* (1963), Paul Van Buren (1924–98) argued that science and technology had invalidated traditional mythology. Even the sophisticated theology of Bultmann or Tillich was still immersed in the old, unviable ethos. We must give up God and focus on Jesus of Nazareth, the liberator, who "defines what it is to be a man."[5] William Hamilton (b. 1924) saw Death of God theology as a twentieth-century way of being Protestant in *Radical Theology and the Death of God* (1966): just as Luther had left his cloister and gone out into the world, the modern Christian must walk away from the sacred place where God used to be; he would find the man Jesus in the world of technology, power, money, sex and the city. Human beings did not need God; they must find their own solution to the world's problems.

The Death of God movement was flawed: it was essentially a white, middle-class, affluent, and—sometimes offensively—Christian theology. Like Hegel, Altizer saw the Jewish God as the alienating deity that had been negated by Christianity. Black theologians asked how white people felt able to affirm freedom through God's death when they had enslaved people in God's name. But despite its limitations, Death of God theology was a prophetic voice calling for a critique of contemporary idols (which included the modern idea of God) and urging a leap from familiar certainties into the unknown that was in tune with the spirit of the sixties.

But despite its vehement rejection of the authoritarian structures of institutional religion, sixties youth culture was demanding a more religious way of life. Instead of going to church, the young went to Kathmandu or sought solace in the meditative techniques of the Orient. Others found transcendence in drug-induced trips, or personal transformation in such techniques as the Erhard Seminars Training (est). There was a hunger for *mythos* and a rejection of the scientific rationalism that had become the new Western orthodoxy. Much twentieth-century science had been cautious, sober, and highly conscious in a disciplined, principled way of its limitations and areas of competence. But since the time of Descartes, science had also been ideological and had refused to countenance any other method of arriving at truth. During the sixties, the youth revolution was in part a protest against the illegitimate domination of rational discourse and the suppression of *mythos* by *logos*. But because the understanding of the traditional ways of arriving at more intuitive knowledge had been neglected in the West during the modern period, the sixties quest for spirituality was often wild, self-indulgent, and unbalanced.

It was, therefore, premature to speak of the death of religion, and this became evident in the late 1970s, when confidence in the imminent arrival of the Secular City was shattered by a dramatic religious resurgence. In 1978–79, the Western world watched in astonishment as an obscure Iranian ayatollah brought down the regime of Shah Muhammad Reza Pahlavi (1919–80), which had seemed to be one of the most progressive and stable in the Middle East. At the same time as governments applauded the peace initiative of President Anwar al-Sadat of Egypt (1918–81), observers noted that young Egyptians were donning Islamic dress, casting aside the freedoms of modernity, and engaging in a takeover of university campuses in order to reclaim them for religion—in a way that was paradoxically reminiscent of student rebellions during the sixties. In Israel, an aggressively religious form of Zionism (which had originally been a defiantly secular movement) had risen to political prominence, and the ultra-Orthodox parties, which David Ben-Gurion (1886–1973), Israel's first prime minister, had confidently predicted would fade away once the Jewish people had their own secular state, were gathering strength. In the United States, Jerry Falwell (1933–2007) founded the Moral Majority in 1979, urging Protestant fundamentalists to get involved in politics and to challenge any state or federal legislation that pushed a "secular humanist" agenda.

This militant religiosity, which would emerge in every region where a secular, Western-style government had separated religion and politics, is determined to drag God and/or religion from the sidelines to which they have been relegated in modern culture and back to center field. It reveals a widespread disappointment in modernity. Whatever the pundits, intellectuals, or politicians thought, people all over the world were demonstrating that they wanted to see religion more clearly reflected in public life. This new form of piety is popularly known as "fundamentalism," but many object to having this Christian term foisted on their reform movements. They do not in fact represent an atavistic return to the past. These are essentially innovative movements and could have taken root at no time other than our own. Fundamentalisms too can be seen as part of the postmodern rejection of modernity. They are not orthodox and conservative; indeed, many are actually anti-orthodox and regard the more conventional faithful as part of the problem.[6]

These movements have mushroomed independently, and even those that have emerged within the same tradition do not have an identical vision. However, they bear what has been called a "family resemblance," and seem instinctively to follow the pattern set by American Protestant fundamentalism, the earliest of these movements. All are initially defensive movements rooted in a profound fear of annihilation, which causes them to develop a paranoid vision of the "enemy." They begin as intrafaith movements, and only at a secondary stage, if at all, do they direct their attention to a foreign foe.

Protestant fundamentalism was chiefly exercised by theological questions that had been challenged by the new scientific discoveries. Fundamentalisms in other traditions have been sparked by entirely different problems and are not preoccupied with "belief" in the same way. In Judaism, the state of Israel has inspired every one of the Jewish fundamentalisms, because this has been the form in which secularism has chiefly impacted on Jewish religious life. Some are passionately *for* the state of Israel and regard its army, political institutions, and every inch of the Holy Land as sacred; others are either vehemently *opposed* to the notion of a secular state or adopt a deliberately neutral stance toward it. In the Muslim world, the political state of the *ummah,* the "community," has become an Achilles' heel. The Qur'an insists that the prime duty of a Muslim is to build a just and decent society, so when Muslims see the *ummah* exploited or even terrorized by foreign powers and governed by corrupt rulers, they can feel as religiously offended as a Protestant who sees the Bible spat upon. Islam has traditionally been a religion of success: in the past, Muslims were always able to surmount disaster and use it creatively to rise to new spiritual and political heights. The Qur'an assures them that if their society is just and egalitarian, it will prosper—not because God is tweaking history on their behalf but because this type of government is in line with the fundamental laws of existence. But Muslims have been able to make little headway against the secular West, and some have found this as threatening as Darwinism seems to fundamentalist Christians. Hence there have been ever more frantic efforts to get Islamic history back on track.

Because fundamentalists feel under threat, they are defensive and unwilling to entertain any rival point of view, yet another expression of the intolerance that has always been part of modernity. Christian fundamentalists take a hard line on what they regard as moral and social decency. They campaign against the teaching of evolution in public schools, are fiercely patriotic but averse to democracy, see feminism as one of the great evils of the day, and conduct a crusade against abortion. Some extremists have even murdered doctors and nurses who work in abortion clinics. Like evolution, abortion has become symbolic of the murderous evil of modernity. Christian fundamentalists are convinced that their doctrinal "beliefs" are an accurate, final expression of sacred truth and that every word of the Bible is literally true—an attitude that is a radical departure from mainstream Christian tradition. They believe that miracles are an essential hallmark of true faith and that God will give the believer anything he asks for in prayer.

Fundamentalists are swift to condemn people whom they regard as the enemies of God: most Christian fundamentalists see Jews and Muslims as destined for hellfire, and some regard Buddhism, Hinduism, and Daoism as inspired by the devil. Jewish and Muslim fundamentalists take a similar stance, each seeing their own tradition as the only true faith. Muslim fundamentalists have toppled governments, and some extremists have been guilty of terrorist atrocities. Jewish fundamentalists have founded illegal settlements in the West Bank and the Gaza Strip with the avowed intention of driving out the Arab inhabitants, convinced that they are paving the way for the Messiah; others throw stones at Israelis who drive their cars on the Sabbath.

In all its forms, fundamentalism is a fiercely reductive faith. In their anxiety and fear, fundamentalists often distort the tradition they are trying to defend. They can, for example, be highly selective in their reading of scripture. Christian fundamentalists quote extensively from the book of Revelation and are inspired by its violent End-time vision but rarely refer to the Sermon on the Mount, where Jesus tells his followers to love their enemies, to turn the other cheek, and not to judge others. Jewish fundamentalists rely heavily on the Deuteronomist sections of the Bible and seem to pass over the rabbis' injunction that exegesis should lead to charity. Muslim fundamentalists ignore the pluralism of the Qur'an, and extremists quote its more aggressive verses to justify violence, pointedly disregarding its far more numerous calls for peace, tolerance, and forgiveness. Fundamentalists are convinced that they are fighting for God, but in fact this type of religiosity represents a retreat from God. To make purely human, historical phenomena—such as "family values," "the Holy Land," or "Islam"—sacred and absolute is idolatry, and, as always, their idol forces them to try to destroy its opponents.

But it is essential for critics of religion to see fundamentalism in historical context. Far from being typical of faith, it is an aberration. The fundamentalist fear of annihilation is not a paranoid delusion. We have seen that some of the most formative creators of the modern ethos have indeed called for the abolition of religion—and they continue to do so. All these movements begin with what is perceived to be an attack by liberal coreligionists or a secularist regime, and further assaults simply make them more extreme. We have seen how this occurred in the United States after the media harassment in the wake of the Scopes trial. In the Jewish world, fundamentalism took two major steps forward: first, after the Shoah, when Hitler had tried to exterminate European Jewry; and second, after the October War of 1973, when the Arab armies took Israel by surprise and made a much better showing on the battlefield.

The same pattern is observable in the Muslim world. It would be a grave mistake to imagine that Islam caused Muslims to recoil instinctively from the modern West. At the turn of the twentieth century, every single leading Muslim intellectual, with the exception of the Iranian ideologue Jamal al-Din al-Afghani (1839–97), was in love with the West, recognized it at a profound level, and wanted his country to look just like Britain and France.[7] Muhammad Abdu

(1849–1905), grand mufti of Egypt, hated the British occupation of his country, but he felt entirely at home with Western culture, had studied the modern sciences, and read Guizot, Tolstoy, Renan, Strauss, and Herbert Spencer. After a trip to France, he is said to have made this deliberately provocative statement: "In Paris, I saw Islam but no Muslims; in Egypt, I see Muslims but no Islam." His point was that their modernized economies had enabled Europeans to promote conditions of justice and equity that came closer to the spirit of the Qur'an than was possible in a partially modernized society. At about the same time in Iran, leading mullahs campaigned alongside secular intellectuals for representational government and constitutional rule. After the Constitutional Revolution of 1906, they got their parliament, but two years later the British discovered oil in Iran and had no intention of allowing the parliament to scupper their plans to use this oil to fuel the British navy. Yet immediately after the revolution, hopes were high. In his *Admonition to the Nation and Exposition to the People* (1909), Sheikh Muhammad Husain Naini (1850–1936) argued that representative government was the next best thing to the coming of the Hidden Imam, the Shiite Messiah who would inaugurate a role of justice and equity in the last days. The constitution would limit the tyranny of the shah and should therefore be endorsed by every Muslim.[8]

It is important to emphasize this early enthusiasm for modernity, because too many Westerners regard Islam as inherently fundamentalist, atavistically opposed to democracy and freedom, and chronically addicted to violence. But Islam was the last of the three monotheisms to develop a fundamentalist strain; it did not do so until the late 1960s, after the Arabs' catastrophic defeat by Israel in the Six-Day War of 1967, when the Western ideologies of nationalism and socialism, which had little grassroots support, appeared to have failed. Religion seemed a way of returning to the precolonial roots of their culture and regaining a more authentic identity. Western foreign policy has also hastened the rise of fundamentalism in the Middle East. The coup organized by the CIA and British Intelligence in Iran (1953) that displaced the nationalist, secular ruler Muhammad Mosaddeq (1880–1967) and put the exiled shah Muhammad Reza Pahlavi (1878–1944) back on the throne left Iranians with a sense of bitter humiliation, betrayal, and impotence. The failure of the international community to alleviate the plight of the Palestinians has led others to despair of a conventional political solution. Western support for such rulers as the shah and Saddam Hussein, who denied their people basic human rights, has also tarnished the democratic ideal, since the West seemed proudly to proclaim its belief in freedom while inflicting dictatorial regimes on others. It has also helped to radicalize Islam, since the mosque was often the only place where people could express their discontent.

The rapid secularization of some of these countries has often taken the form of an assault on religion. In Europe and the United States, secularism developed gradually over a long period, and the new ideas and institutions had time to trickle down naturally to all members of the population. But many Muslim countries had to adopt the Western model in a mere fifty years or so. When KemalAtatürk (1881–1938) secularized Turkey, he closed down all the madrassas and abolished the Sufi orders. The shahs made their soldiers go through the streets tearing off women's veils with their bayonets and ripping them to pieces. These reformers wanted their countries to *look* modern, even though only a small elite sector was familiar with the Western ethos. In 1935, Shah Reza Pahlavi ordered his soldiers to shoot at a crowd of unarmed demonstrators who were peacefully protesting against obligatory Western dress in Mashhad, one of the holiest shrines in Iran. Hundreds of Iranians died that day. In such a context, secularism does not appear a liberating option.

Sunni fundamentalism developed in the concentration camps in which President Gamal Abdel Nasser (1918–70) interred thousands of members of the Muslim Brotherhood without trial. Many of them had done nothing more incriminating than handing out leaflets or attending a meeting. In these vile prisons they were subjected to mental and physical torture and became radicalized.[9] Sayyid Qutb (1906–66) entered the camp as a moderate, but as a result of his imprisonment—he was tortured and finally executed—he evolved an ideology that is still followed by Islamists today.[10] When he heard Nasser vowing to confine Islam to the private sphere, secularism did not seem benign. In his landmark book *Milestones,* we see the paranoid vision of the fundamentalist who has been pushed too far: Jews, Christians, communists, capitalists, and imperialists were all in league against Islam. Muslims had a duty to fight against the barbarism (*jahiliyyah*) of their day, starting with so-called Muslim rulers like Nasser.

This was an entirely new idea. In making *jihad,* understood as armed conflict, central to the Islamic vision, Qutb had distorted the faith that he was trying to defend. He was not the first to do so; he had been influenced by the writings of the Pakistani journalist and politician Abu Ala Mawdudi (1903–79), who feared the effects of Western imperialism in the Muslim world.[11] In order to survive, Mawdudi believed, Muslims must be prepared for revolutionary struggle. This *jihad* could take many forms: some would fight with the pen, others would engage in politics, but in the last resort every able-bodied Muslim must be prepared for war. No major Muslim thinker had ever made "holy war" a central tenet of the faith before; Mawdudi was well aware that he was making a highly controversial claim but was convinced that this radical innovation was justified by the present political emergency. Qutb took the same view: when asked how he could reconcile his hard line with the emphatic warning in the Qur'an that there must be no compulsion in matters of religion,[12] he explained that Qur'anic tolerance was impossible when Muslims were subjected to such violence and cruelty. There could be toleration only *after* the political victory of Islam and the establishment of a truly Muslim *ummah.*[13]

This *jihadi* ideology was not returning to the "fundamental" ideas of Islam, even though Qutb in particular based his revolutionary program on a distorted version of the life of Muhammad. He was preaching an Islamic liberation theology similar to that adopted by Catholics fighting brutal regimes in Latin America. Because God alone was sovereign, no Muslim was obliged to obey any ruler who contravened the Qur'anic demand for justice and equity. In rather the same way, when the revolutionary Iranian leader Ayatollah Ruhollah Khomeini (1902–89) declared that only a *faqih,* a cleric versed in Islamic jurisprudence, should be head of state, he was breaking with centuries of Shiite tradition, which since the eighth century had separated religion and politics as a matter of sacred principle. It was as shocking to some Shiite sensibilities as if the pope should abolish the Mass. But after decades of secularism as interpreted by the shahs, Khomeini believed that this was the only possible way forward. Khomeini also preached a modern third-world theology of liberation. Islam, he declared, was "the religion of militant individuals who are committed to freedom and independence. It is the school of those who struggle against imperialism."[14]

Many forms of what we call "fundamentalism" should be seen as essentially political discourse—a religiously articulated form of nationalism or ethnicity. This is clearly true of Zionist fundamentalism in Israel, where extremists have advocated the forcible deportation of Arabs and the illegal settlement of territories occupied during the 1967 war. On February 25, 1994, Baruch Goldstein, a follower of the late Rabbi Meir Kahane, who had advocated the expulsion of Arabs from Israel, shot twenty-nine Palestinian worshippers in the Cave of the Patriarchs in Hebron; and on November 4, 1995, Yigal Amir, a religious Zionist, assassinated Prime Minister Yitzak Rabin for signing the Oslo Accords. Islamic fundamentalism is also politically motivated. The Palestinian party Hamas began as a resistance movement, and developed only after the secular policies of Yassir Arafat and his party, Fatah, appeared to have become both ineffective and corrupt. Hamas's reprehensible killing of Israeli civilians is politically rather than religiously inspired, and its goals are limited. Hamas is not attempting to force the entire world to submit to Islam, has no global outreach, and targets only Israelis. Any military occupation is likely to breed resistance, and when an occupation has lasted for over forty years, this resistance is likely to take a violent form.

Critics of Islam believe that the cult of murderous martyrdom is endemic in the religion itself. This is not the case. Apart from the brief incident of the so-called assassin movement at the time of the Crusades—for which the Ismaili sect responsible was universally reviled in the Muslim world—it has not been a feature of Islamic history until modern times. The American scholar Robert Pape has made a careful study of suicide attacks between 1980 and 2004, including the al-Qaeda atrocities of September 11, 2001, and concluded:

> Overwhelmingly suicide-terrorist attacks are not driven by religion as much as they are by a clear strategic objective: to compel modern democracies to withdraw military forces from the territory that the terrorists view as their homeland. From Lebanon to Sri Lanka, to Chechnya to Kashmir, to the West Bank, every major suicide-

terrorist campaign—more than 95 percent of all the inci-
dents—has had as its major objective to compel a democratic state to withdraw.[15]

Osama Bin Laden, for example, cited the presence of American
troops in his native Saudi Arabia and the Israeli occupation of Palestinian land high on his list of complaints against the West.

Terrorism undoubtedly threatens our global security, but we need
accurate intelligence that takes all the evidence into account. It will
not help to utter sweeping and ill-founded condemnations of "Islam."
In a recent Gallup poll, only 7 percent of the Muslims interviewed in
thirty-five countries believed that the 9/11 attacks were justified.
They had no intention of committing such an atrocity themselves, but
they believed that Western foreign policy had been largely responsible for these heinous actions. Their reasoning was entirely political:
they cited such ongoing problems as Palestine, Kashmir, Chechnya,
and Western interference in the internal affairs of Muslim countries.
But the majority of Muslims who condemned the attacks all gave religious reasons, quoting, for example, the Qur'anic verse that states
that the taking of a single life is equivalent to the destruction of the
entire world.[16]

Since 9/11, Western politicians have assumed that Muslims hate
"our way of life, our democracy, freedom, and success." But when
asked what they most admired about the West, the politically radicalized and the moderates both listed Western technology; the Western
ethic of hard work, personal responsibility, and the rule of law; as
well as Western democracy, respect for human rights, freedom of
speech, and gender equality. And, interestingly, a significantly higher
percentage of the politically radicalized (50 percent versus 35 percent
of moderates) replied that "moving toward greater governmental
democracy would foster progress in the Arab/Muslim world."[17]
Finally, when asked what they resented most about the West, its "dis-
respect for Islam" ranked high on the list of both the politically radicalized and the moderates. Most see the West as inherently intolerant:
only 12 percent of radicals and 17 percent of moderates associated
"respecting Islamic values" with Western nations. What could Muslims do to improve relations with the West? Again, among the top
responses from both radicals and the moderates was "improve the

presentation of Islam to the West, present Islamic values in a positive manner."[18] There are 1.3 billion Muslims in the world today; if the 7 percent (91 million) of the politically radicalized continue to feel politically dominated, occupied, and culturally and religiously disrespected, the West will have little chance of changing their hearts and minds.[19] Blaming Islam is a simple but counterproductive answer; it is far less challenging than examining the political issues and grievances that resonate in so much of the Muslim world.

A form of secular fundamentalism has recently developed in the Western world that in style and strategy is similar to the atheism of Vogt, Büchner, and Haeckel. While physicists have felt comfortable with the unknowing that seems to be an essential component of intellectual advance, some biologists, whose discipline has not yet experienced a major reversal, have remained confident of their capacity to discover absolute truth and some, abandoning the agnostic restraint of Darwin and Huxley, have started to preach a militant form of atheism. In 1972, the French biochemist Jacques Monod (1910–76), Nobel Prize winner and professor of molecular biology at the College de France, published *Chance and Necessity,* which argued for the absolute incompatibility of theism and evolutionary theory. Change is the result of chance and is propagated by necessity. It is therefore impossible to speak of purpose and design in the universe: we must accept the fact that we humans have come into being by accident; that there is no benign Creator, no divine Friend that shapes our lives and values; and that we are alone in the immense and impersonal cosmos. Like Clifford, Monod maintained that it was not only intellectually but also *morally* wrong to accept any ideas that were not scientifically verifiable. But he admitted that there was no way of proving that this ideal of objectivity was in fact true: it was an ideal that was essentially arbitrary, a claim for which there was insufficient evidence.[20] He thus tacitly admitted that even the scientific quest began with an act of faith.

Monod's ideas were not always accessible to those not steeped in French culture, and some of the first popular expositions of the implications of evolution in the English-speaking world were written, with great brilliance and clarity, by the Oxford biologist Richard

Dawkins. In *The Blind Watchmaker* (1986), he explained that while Paley's argument for an Intelligent Designer had been perfectly acceptable in the early nineteenth century, Darwin had shown that the *appearance* of design occurred quite naturally in the process of evolutionary development. The "Blind Watchmaker" was natural selection, a blind, purposeless process that could not plan intelligently; nor could it deliberately produce the "contrivance" that Paley had found in nature. For Dawkins, atheism is a necessary consequence of evolution. He has argued that the religious impulse is simply an evolutionary mistake, a "misfiring of something useful";[21] it is a kind of virus, parasitic on cognitive systems naturally selected because they had enabled a species to survive.

Dawkins is an extreme exponent of the scientific naturalism, originally formulated by d'Holbach, that has now become a major worldview among intellectuals. More moderate versions of this "scientism" have been articulated by Carl Sagan, Steven Weinberg, and Daniel Dennett, who have all claimed that one has to choose between science and faith. For Dennett, theology has been rendered superfluous, because biology can provide a better explanation of why people are religious. But for Dawkins, like the other "new atheists"—Sam Harris, the young American philosopher and student of neuroscience, and Christopher Hitchens, critic and journalist—religion is the cause of all the problems of our world; it is the source of absolute evil and "poisons everything."[22] They see themselves in the vanguard of a scientific/rational movement that will eventually expunge the idea of God from human consciousness.

But other atheists and scientists are wary of this approach. The American zoologist Stephen Jay Gould (1941–2002) followed Monod in his discussion of the implications of evolution. Everything in the natural world could indeed be explained by natural selection, but Gould insisted that science was not competent to decide whether God did or did not exist, because it could work only with natural explanations. Gould had no religious ax to grind; he described himself as an atheistically inclined agnostic but pointed out that Darwin himself had denied he was an atheist and that other eminent Darwinians—Asa Gray, Charles D. Walcott, G. G. Simpson, and Theodosius Dobzhansky—had been either practicing Christians or agnostics. Atheism did not, therefore, seem to be a necessary consequence of accepting evolutionary theory, and Darwinians who held forth dog-matically on the subject were stepping beyond the limitations that were proper to science.

Gould also revived, in new form, the ancient distinction and com-plementarity of *mythos* and *logos* in what he called NOMA (Non-Overlapping Magisteria). A "magisterium," he explained, was "a domain where one form of teaching holds the appropriate tools for meaningful discourse and resolution."[23] Religion and science were separate magisteria and should not encroach on each other's domain:

> The magisterium of science covers the empirical realm: what is the universe made of (fact) and why does it work this way (theory)? The magisterium of religion extends over questions of ultimate meaning and moral value. These two magisteria do not overlap, nor do they encom-pass all inquiry.[24]

The idea of an inherent conflict between religion and science was false. They were two distinct magisteria that "hold equal worth and necessary status for any complete human life; and . . . remain logically distinct and fully separate in lines of inquiry."[25]

But the new atheists will have none of this, and in his somewhat immoderate way, Dawkins denounces Gould as a quisling. They adhere to a hard-line form of scientific naturalism that mirrors the fundamentalism on which they base their critique: atheism is always a rejection of and parasitically dependent on a particular form of the-ism. The work of the new atheists has been exhaustively criticized, notably by John F. Haught, Alister McGrath, and John Cornwell.[26] Like all religious fundamentalists, the new atheists believe that they alone are in possession of truth; like Christian fundamentalists, they read scripture in an entirely literal manner and seem never to have heard of the long tradition of allegoric or Talmudic interpretation or indeed of the Higher Criticism. Harris seems to imagine that biblical inspiration means that the Bible was actually "written by God."[27] Hitchens assumes that faith is entirely dependent upon a literal read-ing of the Bible, and that, for example, the discrepancies in the gospel infancy narratives prove the falsity of Christianity: "Either the gospels are in some sense literal truth, or the whole thing is essentially a fraud and perhaps a moral one at that."[28] Like Protestant fundamentalists, Dawkins has a simplistic view of the moral teaching of the Bible, taking it for granted that its chief purpose is to issue clear rules of conduct and provide us with "role models," which, not surprisingly, he finds lamentably inadequate.[29] He also presumes that since the Bible claims to be inspired by God it must also provide scientific information. Dawkins's only point of disagreement with the Protestant fundamentalists is that he finds the Bible unreliable about science while they do not.

It is not surprising that Dawkins is incensed with American creationists who are campaigning against the teaching of evolution, and the proponents of a new, quasi-scientific philosophy that has tried to revive the theory of intelligent design (ID). These include Philip E. Johnson, professor of law at Berkeley and author of *Darwin on Trial* (1991); the biochemist Michael Behe, author of *Darwin's Black Box* (1996); and the philosopher William Dembski, author of *The Design Inference* (1998). These theists do not all posit God as the Designer, but they do argue that ID is a viable alternative to Darwinism and cite a supernatural agency in creation as if it were scientific evidence. But as Dennett points out, the ID theorists have not devised any experiments or made any empirical observations that challenge modern evolutionary thinking. ID, he concludes, is therefore not science.[30] ID is also theologically incorrect to make scientific statements. *Mythos* and *logos* have different fields of competence, and, as we have seen, when they are confused you have bad science and inadequate religion. But while Dawkins's irritation with creationists and ID theorists is understandable, he is not correct to assume that fundamentalist belief either represents or is even typical of either Christianity or religion as a whole.

This type of reductionism is characteristic of the fundamentalist mentality. It is also essential to the critique of Dawkins, Hitchens, and Harris to present fundamentalism as the focal core of the three monotheisms. They have an extremely literalist notion of God. For Dawkins, religious faith rests on the idea that *"there exists a superhuman, supernatural intelligence, who deliberately designed and created the universe and everything in it."*[31] Having set up this definition of God as Supernatural Designer, Dawkins only has to point out that there is in fact no design in nature in order to demolish it. But he is mistaken to assume that this is "the way people have generally understood the term" God.[32] He is also wrong to claim that God is a scientific hypothesis, that is, a conceptual framework for bringing intelligibility to a series of experiments and observations.[33] It was only in the modern period that theologians started to treat God as a scientific explanation and in the process produced an idolatrous God concept.

The new atheists all equate faith with mindless credulity. Harris wrote *The End of Faith* immediately after 9/11, insisting that the only way to rid our world of terrorism was to abolish all faith. Like Dawkins and Hitchens, he defines faith as "Belief without Evidence,"[34] an attitude that he regards as morally reprehensible. It is not surprising, perhaps, that he should confuse "faith" with "belief" (meaning the intellectual acceptance of a proposition) because the two have become unfortunately fused in modern consciousness. But like other atheists and agnostics before him, Harris goes on to declare that faith is the root of all evil. A belief might *seem* innocent enough, but once you have blindly accepted the dogma that Jesus "can be eaten in the form of a cracker,"[35] you have made a space in your mind for other monstrous fictions: that God desires the destruction of Israel, the ethnic cleansing of Palestinians, or the 9/11 massacres. Everybody must stop believing in anything that cannot be verified by the empirical methods of science. It is not enough to get rid of extremists, fundamentalists, and terrorists. "Moderate" believers are equally guilty of the "inherently dangerous" crime of faith and must share responsibility for the terrorist atrocities.[36]

Our civic toleration of faith must therefore be eliminated. "As long as we respect the principle that religious faith must be respected simply because it is real faith," Dawkins insists, "it is hard to withhold respect for Usama bin Laden and the suicide bombers." The obvious and self-evident alternative is to "abandon the principle of automatic respect for religious faith," because "the teachings of 'moderate religion,' though not extremist in themselves, are an open invitation to extremism."[37] This rejection of the Enlightenment principle of toleration is new. It is, surely, itself extremist. "The very idea of religious tolerance," Harris maintains, "is one of the principal forces driving us toward the abyss."[38] In this lack of tolerance, they are again at one with the religious fundamentalists, even though they must be aware that the absence of respect for difference has led to some of the worst atrocities in modern times. It is hard to hear talk of elimination without recalling the Nazi camp and the Gulag.

As its critics have already pointed out, there is an inherent contradiction in the new atheism, especially in its emphasis on the importance of "evidence" and the claim that science always proves its theories empirically. As Popper, Kuhn, and Polyani have argued, science itself has to rely on an act of faith. Even Monod acknowledged this. Dawkins's hero Darwin admitted that he could not prove the evolutionary hypothesis but he had confidence in it nonetheless, and for decades, as we have seen, physicists were happy to have faith in Einstein's theory of relativity, even though it had not been definitively verified. Even Harris makes a large act of faith in the ability of his own intelligence to arrive at objective truth—a claim that Hume or Kant would have found questionable.

All three of these proselytizing atheists present religion at its absolute worst. It is very important to remember the evils committed in the name of religion, and they are right to bring them to our attention. All too often, people of faith like to enumerate the sins of other traditions while ignoring the stains on their own. Christians, for example, are often eager to criticize Islam for its intolerance, showing not only an embarrassing ignorance of Muslim history but total myopia toward the crusades, persecutions, and inquisitions conducted by their own coreligionists. But claiming that religion has *only* been evil is inaccurate. Science is the child of *logos* and we should, therefore, be able to rely on scientists, with their finely honed reasoning powers, to sift the evidence in a balanced, impartial way. But Harris, for example, finds it quite acceptable to assert emphatically that *"most Muslims are utterly deranged by their religious faith."*[39] This type of remark is just as biased and untrue as some of the religious rhetoric he condemns.

It is also misleading to insist that all the problems of the modern world are entirely due to religion, if only because at this perilous moment in human history we need clear heads and accurate intelligence. At the beginning of his book, Dawkins asks us to imagine, with John Lennon, a world without religion.

Imagine no suicide bombers, no 9/11, no 7/7, no Crusades, no witch-hunts, no Gunpowder Plot, no Indian partition, no Israeli/Palestinian wars, no Serb/Croat/ Muslim massacres, no persecution of Jews as "Christ killers," no Northern Ireland "troubles," no "honour killings," no shiny-suited bouffant-haired televangelists fleecing gullible people of their money.[40]

But not all these conflicts are wholly due to religion. The new atheists show a disturbing lack of understanding of or concern about the complexity and ambiguity of modern experience, and their polemic entirely fails to mention the concern for justice and compassion that, despite their undeniable failings, has been espoused by all three of the monotheisms.

Religious fundamentalists also develop an exaggerated view of their enemy as the epitome of evil. This makes the critique of the new atheists too easy. They never discuss the work of such theologians as Bultmann or Tillich, who offer a very different view of religion and are closer to mainstream tradition than any fundamentalist. Unlike Feuerbach, Marx, and Freud, the new atheists are not theologically literate. As one of their critics has remarked, in any military strategy it is essential to confront the enemy at its strongest point; failure to do so means that their polemic remains shallow and lacks intellectual depth.[41] It is also morally and intellectually conservative. Unlike Feuerbach, Marx, Ingersoll, or Mill, these new atheists show little concern about the poverty, injustice, and humiliation that have inspired many of the atrocities they deplore; they show no yearning for a better world. Nor, like Nietzsche, Sartre, or Camus, do they compel their readers to face up to the pointlessness and futility that ensue when people lack the means of creating a sense of meaning. They do not appear to consider the effect of such nihilism on people who do not have privileged lives and absorbing work.

Dawkins argues that we are moral beings because the virtuous behavior of our ancestors probably helped to ensure their survival. Altruism was, therefore, not divinely inspired but simply the result of an accidental genetic mutation that programmed our forebears to behave more generously and cooperatively than others. But, he continues, there are many such "blessed" evolutionary misfirings in human behavior, one of which is "the urge to kindness—to altruism, to generosity, to empathy, to pity."[42] Many theologians would have no difficulty with this view. It is surely characteristic of our humanity to take something basic and instinctual and transform it in such a way that it transcends the purely pragmatic. Cooking, for example, probably began as a useful survival skill, but we have gone on to develop haute cuisine. We acquired the ability to run and jump in order to get away from predators, and now we have ballet and athletics. We cultivated language as a useful means of communication and have created poetry. The religious traditions have done something similar with altruism. As Confucius pointed out, they have found that when they practiced it "all day and every day," it elevated human life to the realm of holiness and gave practitioners intimations of transcendence.

In the past, theologians have found it useful to have an exchange of views with atheists. The ideas of the Swiss theologian Karl Barth (1886–1968) were enhanced by the writings of Feuerbach; Bultmann, Tillich, and Rahner were all influenced by Heidegger.[43] But it is difficult to see how theologians could dialogue fruitfully with Dawkins, Harris, and Hitchens because their theology is so rudimentary. We should, however, take careful note of what we might call the Dawkins phenomenon. The fact that these intemperate antireligious tracts have won such wide readership not only in secular Europe but also in religious America suggests that many people who have little theological training have problems with the modern God. Some believers are still able to work creatively with this symbol, but others are obviously not. They get little help from their clergy, who may not have had an advanced theological training and whose worldview may still be bounded by the modern God. Modern theology is not always easy reading. Theologians should try to present it in an attractive, accessible way to enable congregants to keep up with the latest discussions and the new insights of biblical scholarship, which rarely reach the pews.

Our world is already dangerously polarized, and we do not need another divisive ideology. The history of fundamentalism shows that when these movements are attacked, they nearly always become more extreme. The atheist assault is likely to drive the fundamentalists to even greater commitment to creationism, and their contemptuous dismissal of Islam is a gift to Muslim extremists, who can use it to argue that the West is indeed intent on a new Crusade.[44]

Typical of the fundamentalist mind-set is the belief that there is only one way of interpreting reality. For the new atheists, scientism alone can lead us to truth. But science depends upon faith, intuition, and aesthetic vision as well as on reason. The physicist Paul Dirac has argued that "it is more important to have beauty in one's equations than to have them fit experiment."[45] The mathematician Roger Penrose believes that the creative mind "breaks through" into a Platonic realm of mathematical and aesthetic forms: "Rigorous argument is usually the *last* step! Before that, one has to make many guesses, and for these aesthetic convictions are enormously important."[46] There are many circumstances in which human beings have to lay aside an objectivist analysis, which seeks in some way to master what it contemplates.[47] When confronted with a work of art, we have to open our minds and allow it to carry us away. If we seek to relate intimately to another person, we have to be prepared to make ourselves vulnerable—as Abraham did when he opened his heart and home to the three strangers at Mamre.

As Tillich pointed out, men and women continually feel drawn to explore levels of truth that go beyond our normal experience. This imperative has inspired the scientific as well as the religious quest. We seek what Tillich called an "ultimate concern" that shapes our life and gives it meaning. The ultimate concern of Dawkins and Harris appears to be reason; this has seized and taken possession of them. But their idea of reason is very different from the rationality of Socrates, who used his reasoning powers to bring his dialogue partners into a state of unknowing. For Augustine and Aquinas, reason became *intellectus,* opening naturally to the divine. Today, for many people, reason no longer subverts itself in this way. But the danger of this secularization of reason, which denies the possibility of transcendence, is that reason can become an idol that seeks to destroy all rival claimants. We hear this in the new atheism, which has forgotten that unknowing is a part of the human condition, so much so that, as the social critic Robert N. Bellah has pointed out: "Those who feel they are . . . most fully objective in their assessment of reality are most in the power of deep, unconscious fantasies."[48]

Modern physicists, as we have seen, are not wary of unknowing: their experience of living with apparently insoluble problems evokes awe and wonder. In the 1970s, string theory became the Holy Grail of science, the final theory that would unify force and matter in a model integrating gravity and quantum mechanics. There is some skepticism about string theory: Richard Feynman, for example, dismissed it as "crazy nonsense,"[49] but some string theorists have admitted that their discoveries cannot be either proven or refuted experimentally and have even claimed that no adequate experiment can be devised to test what is a mathematical explanation of the universe.[50] The wonder of modern cosmology seems derived in no small measure from the physicists' inherent inability to answer all its questions.[51] They know that the terms they use to describe these natural mysteries—big bang, dark matter, black holes, dark energy—are metaphors that cannot adequately translate their mathematical insights into words. Unlike Newton, of course, modern physicists are not introducing God or the supernatural into their cosmos. But the obviously mythical character of these terms is a reminder that what they point to is not readily comprehensible; they are straining at the limits of scientific investigation, and these terms should carry an air of mystery because they name what cannot yet be investigated.

Today many physicists sense that they are on the brink of another major paradigm shift.[52] Even Stephen Hawking is no longer so certain that a theory of everything, which will enable humans to look into the "mind of God," is readily available. They have learned that what seemed incontrovertible could be replaced overnight by an entirely different scientific model, and are at home with unknowing. Thus the cosmologist Paul Davies speaks of his delight in science with its unanswered and, perhaps, unanswerable questions:

> Why did we come to exist 13.7 billion years ago in a Big Bang? Why are the laws of electromagnetism or gravitation as they are? Why these laws? What are we doing here? And, in particular, how come we are able to understand the world? Why is it that we're equipped with intellects that can unpick all this wonderful cosmic order and make sense of it? It's truly astonishing.[53]

Davies has confessed: "It may seem bizarre, but in my opinion, science offers a surer path to God than religion."[54] He is still asking the primordial question: Why is there something rather than nothing?

Modern physicists have more information than our ancestors could have dreamed of, but unlike Dawkins, they do not all dismiss this query as redundant or pointless. Human beings seem framed to pose problems for themselves that they cannot solve, pit themselves against the dark world of uncreated reality, and find that living with such unknowing is a source of astonishment and delight.

Philosophy, theology, and mythology have always responded to the science of the day, and a philosophical movement has developed since the 1980s that has embraced the indeterminacy of the new cosmology. Postmodern thinking is heir to Hume and Kant in its assumption that what we call reality is constructed by the mind and that all human understanding is therefore interpretation rather than the acquisition of accurate, objective information. From this it follows that no single vision can be sovereign; that our knowledge is relative, subjective, and fallible rather than certain and absolute; and that truth is inherently ambiguous. Received ideas that are the products of a particular historical and cultural milieu must, therefore, be stringently deconstructed. But this analysis must not be based on any absolute principle, and there is no assurance that we will ever arrive at—or even approximate—a wholly accurate version of the truth. Fundamental to postmodern thought is the conviction that instead of ideologies mirroring external conditions, the world is profoundly affected by the ideology that human beings impose upon it. We are not forced by sense data to adopt a particular worldview, so we have a choice in what we affirm—as well as an immense responsibility.

Postmodernists are particularly suspicious of Big Stories. They regard Western history as scarred by the ceaseless compulsion to impose a totalizing system on the world. Sometimes this has been theological and has resulted in crusade and persecution, but the "stories" have also been scientific, economic, ideological, and political, resulting in the technological domination of nature and the sociopolitical subjection of others in slavery, genocide, colonialism, anti-Semitism, and the oppression of women and other minorities. So, like Nietzsche, Freud, and Marx, postmodernists seek to deflate such beliefs but without attempting to substitute an absolute "story" of their own. Postmodernism is iconoclastic, therefore. As one of its early luminaries, Jean-François Lyotard (1924–98), explained, it can be defined as "the incredulity towards grand narratives (*grands récits*)." Top of the list of such *récits* is the modern "God," who is omnipotent and omniscient and keeps watch over the world, working all things to his own purposes. But postmodernism is also averse to an atheism that makes absolute, totalistic claims. As Jacques Derrida (1930–2004) cautioned, we must also be alert to "theological prejudices" not only in religious contexts, where they are overt, but in all metaphysics—even those that profess to be atheist.[55] Like any postmodern philosopher, Derrida was deeply suspicious of the fixed, binary polarities that characterize modern thought, and the atheist/theist divide was, he believed, too simple. Atheists have reduced the complex phenomena of religion to formulas that suit their own ideologies—as Marx did when he called religion an opiate of the oppressed or Freud when he saw it as oedipal terror. A fixed and final denial of God on metaphysical grounds was for Derrida as culpable as any dogmatic religious "theology" (his term for a *grand récit*). Derrida himself, a secularized Jew, said that though he might pass for an atheist, he prayed all the time, had a messianic hope for a better world, and inclined to the view that, since no absolute certainty is within our grasp, we should for the sake of peace hesitate to make declarative statements of either belief or unbelief.

Some orthodox believers and most fundamentalists will be repelled by this unabashed relativism, but there are aspects of Derrida's thought that recall earlier theological attitudes. His theory of deconstruction, which denies the possibility of finding a single, secure meaning in any text, is positively rabbinical. He has also been called a "negative" theologian and was greatly interested in Eckhart. What he called *différance* is neither a word nor a concept but a quasi-transcendental possibility—a "difference" or "otherness"—that lies within a word or idea such as "God." For Eckhart, this *différance* was the God beyond God, a new but unknowable metaphysical ground that was inseparable from the human self. But for Derrida, *différance* was only quasi-transcendental; it is a potential, something that we cannot see but that makes us aware that we may have to qualify or even unsay anything we say or deny of God.

In his later work, Derrida seemed haunted by the potential and lure of an open future. He affirmed what he calls the "undeconstructible," which is not another absolute, because it does not exist, and yet we weep and pray for it. As he explained in his lecture "The Force of Law" (1989), justice is an undeconstructible "something" that is never fully realized in the actual circumstances of daily life but that informs all legal speculation. Justice is not what exists; it is what we desire. It calls us; it seems sometimes within our grasp but ultimately eludes us. And yet we go on trying to incarnate it in our legal systems. Derrida later went on to discuss other "undeconstuctibles": gift, forgiveness, and friendship. He loved to talk of the "democracy to come": we yearn for democracy but we never fully achieve it; it remains an incessant hope for the future. And in the same way, "God," a term often used in the past to set a limit to human thought and endeavor, becomes for the postmodern philosopher the desire beyond desire, a memory and a promise that is, by its very nature, indefinable.

Some postmodern thinkers have applied these ideas to theology. Significantly, they are usually philosophers rather than theologians. Reversing the trend begun by such philosophes as Diderot, d'Holbach, and Freud, their interest heralds a change in the intellectual atmosphere of academe. At the time of the Death of God movement in the 1960s, God's days seemed numbered, but now God seems alive and well. Postmodern theology challenges the assumption that secularism is irreversible; some have suggested that we are now entering a "postsecular" age but have also made it clear that the religion being revitalized must be different from "modern" faith. The first to apply Derrida's ideas to theology was Mark C. Taylor in *Erring: A Postmodern A/theology* (1984); the slash in the subtitle was designed to mark a Derridian hesitation before settling for either God or Godlessness. Taylor saw a link between deconstruction and the 1960s Death of God movement, but criticized Altizer for being stuck in the modern dialectic in which things were either dead or alive, absent or present. In his view, religion was present even when it seemed absent—so much so that he was criticized for allowing religion in his later work to be entirely swallowed up in other discourses.

Those philosophers who focused on Derrida's later work have been more successful. The Italian postmodernist Gianni Vattimo argues that from the very first religion had recognized that it was an essentially interpretive discourse: it had traditionally proceeded by endlessly deconstructing its sacred texts, so that from the start it had the potential to liberate itself from metaphysical orthodoxy. Vattimo is anxious to promote what is called "weak thought" to counter the aggressively triumphalist certainty that characterizes a good deal of modern religion and atheism. Metaphysics is dangerous because it makes absolute claims for either God or reason. "Not all metaphysics have been violent," Vattimo admits, "but all violent people of great dimensions have been metaphysical."[56] Hitler, for example, was not content to hate only the Jews in his vicinity but created a *grand récit* that made metaphysical claims about Jews in general. "When someone wants to tell me the absolute truth," Vattimo remarks shrewdly, "it is because he wants to put me under his control."[57] Both theism and atheism make such claims, but there are no absolute truths anymore—only interpretations.[58]

Modernity, Vattimo believes, is over; when we contemplate history, we cannot now see the future as an inevitable and unilinear progression toward emancipation. Freedom no longer lies in the perfect knowledge of and conformity to the necessary structure of reality, but in an appreciation of multiple discourses and the historicity, contingency, and finitude of all religious, ethical, and political values—including our own.[59] Vattimo wants to bring down "walls," including the walls that separate theists and atheists. Even though he believes that society will reembrace religion, he does not want to abandon secularization, because he regards the Church-state alliance set up by Constantine as a Christian aberration. The ideal society should be based on charity rather than truth. In the past, Vattimo recalls, religious truth generally emerged from people interacting with others rather than by papal edict. Vattimo recalls Christ's saying "When two or three are gathered together in my name, I will be in the midst of them," and the classic hymn "Where there is love, there is also God."[60]

The American philosopher John D. Caputo has been influenced by Heidegger and the postmodern thinker Gilles Deleuze (1925–95) as well as by Derrida. He too advocates "weak thought" and transcendence of the warring polarities of atheism and theism. He sees the limitations of the old Death of God movement but fully endorses the desire of Altizer and Van Buren to deconstruct the modern God. Although he appreciates Tillich's emphasis on the essentially symbolic nature of religious truth, he is, however, wary of calling God the "ground of being," since this sets brakes on the process of endless flux and becoming that is essential to life by stabilizing a grounding center of our being.[61] Atheist and theist alike should abandon the modern appetite for certainty. One of the problems of the original Death of God movement was that its terminology was too final and absolute. No state of affairs is permanent, and we are now witnessing the death of the Death of God. The atheistic ideas of Nietzsche, Marx, and Freud are "perspectives . . . constructions, and fictions of grammar."

> Enlightenment secularism, the objectivist reduction of religion to something other than itself—say, to a distorted desire for one's mommy, or to a way of keeping the ruling authorities in power—is one more story told by people with historically limited imaginations, with contingent conceptions of reason and history, of economics with labour, of nature and human nature, of desire, sexuality, and women, and of God, religion, and faith.[62]

The Enlightenment had its own rigors. Postmodernity should be "a more enlightened Enlightenment, that is, no longer taken in by the dream of Pure Objectivity."[63] It should open doors "to another way of thinking about faith and reason" in order to achieve "a redescription of reason that is more reasonable than the transhistorical Rationality of the Enlightenment."[64]

So how does Caputo see God? Following Derrida, he would describe God as the desire beyond desire.[65] Of its very nature, desire is located in the space between what exists and what does not; it addresses all that we are and are not, everything we know and what we do not know. The question is not "Does God exist?" any more than "Does desire exist?" The question is rather "What do we desire?" Augustine understood this when he asked, "What do I love when I love my God?" and failed to find an answer. Like Denys and Aquinas, Caputo does not see negative theology as a deeper, more authoritative truth. It simply emphasizes unknowing—"in the sense that we really don't know!"[66] For Caputo, "religious truth is truth without knowledge."[67] He has adapted Derrida's *différance* to create his "theology of the event," distinguishing between a *name*, such as "God," "Justice," or "Democracy," and what he calls the *event,* that which is "astir" in that name, something that is never fully realized. But the "event" within the name inspires us, turns things upside down, making us weep and pray for what is "to come."

The name is a kind of provisional formulation of an
event, a relatively stable, if evolving structure, while the
event is ever restless, on the move, seeking new forms to
assume, seeking to get expressed in still unexpressed
ways.[68]

We pray for what is "to come," not for what already exists. The
"event" does not require "belief" in a static, unchanging deity who
"exists" but inspires us to make what is "astir" in the name "God"—
absolute beauty, peace, justice, and selfless love—a reality in the
world.

Religion as described by these postmodern philosophers may
sound alien to much "modern" religion, but it evokes many of the
insights of the past. Both Vattimo and Caputo insist that these are primordial, perennial ideas with a long pedigree. Vattimo's claim that
religion is essentially interpretive recalls the maxim of the rabbis:
"What is Torah? It is the interpretation of Torah." When he affirms
the primacy of charity and the communal nature of religious truth,
we recall the rabbis' repeated insistence that "when two or three
study Torah together, the Shekhinah is in their midst," the story of
Emmaus, and the communal experience of liturgy. Caputo also sees
Anselm's "ontological proof" as "autodeconstructive":

Whatever it is you say God is, God is more. The very
constitution of the idea is deconstructive of any such construction . . . the very formula that describes God is that
there is no formula with which God can be described.[69]

When Caputo argues that the "event" requires a response rather than
"belief," he echoes the rabbis' definition of scripture as *miqra,* a summons to action.

Above all, both Caputo and Vattimo stress the importance of the
apophatic. All these perceptions that were once central to religion
tended to be submerged in the positivist discourse of modernity, and
the fact that they have surfaced again in a different form suggests that
this type of "unknowing" is inherent in our very humanity. The distinctively modern yearning for purely notional, absolute, and empirically proven truth may have been an aberration. Caputo himself
suggests as much. Noting that atheism is always a rejection of a par-

ticular conception of the divine, he concludes: "If modern atheism is the rejection of a modern God, then the delimitation of modernity opens up another possibility, less the resuscitation of premodern theism than the chance of something beyond both the theism and the atheism of modernity."[70]

It is an enticing prospect. If atheism was a product of modernity, now that we are entering a "postmodern" phase, will this too, like the modern God, become a thing of the past? Will the growing appreciation of the limitations of human knowledge—which is just as much a part of the contemporary intellectual scene as atheistic certainty—give rise to a new kind of apophatic theology? And how best can we move beyond premodern theism into a perception of "God" that truly speaks to all the complex realities and needs of our time?

# Epilogue

We have become used to thinking that religion should provide us with information. Is there a God? How did the world come into being? But this is a modern preoccupation. Religion was never supposed to provide answers to questions that lay within the reach of human reason. That was the role of *logos*. Religion's task, closely allied to that of art, was to help us to live creatively, peacefully, and even joyously with realities for which there were no easy explanations and problems that we could not solve: mortality, pain, grief, despair, and outrage at the injustice and cruelty of life. Over the centuries people in all cultures discovered that by pushing their reasoning powers to the limit, stretching language to the end of its tether, and living as selflessly and compassionately as possible, they experienced a transcendence that enabled them to affirm their suffering with serenity and courage. Scientific rationality can tell us why we have cancer; it can even cure us of our disease. But it cannot assuage the terror, disappointment, and sorrow that come with the diagnosis, nor can it help us to die well. That is not within its competence. Religion will not work automatically, however; it requires a great deal of effort and cannot succeed if it is facile, false, idolatrous, or self-indulgent.

Religion is a practical discipline, and its insights are not derived from abstract speculation but from spiritual exercises and a dedicated lifestyle. Without such practice, it is impossible to understand the truth of its doctrines. This was also true of philosophical rationalism. People did not go to Socrates to learn anything—he always insisted that he had nothing to teach them—but to have a change of mind. Participants in a Socratic dialogue discovered how little they knew and that the meaning of even the simplest proposition eluded them. The shock of ignorance and confusion represented a conversion to the philosophic life, which could not begin until you realized that you knew nothing at all. But even though it removed the last vestiges of the certainty upon which people had hitherto based their lives, the Socratic dialogue was never aggressive; rather, it was conducted with courtesy, gentleness, and consideration. If a dialogue aroused malice or spite, it would fail. There was no question of forcing your interlocutor to accept your point of view: instead, each offered his opinion as a gift to the others and allowed them to alter his own perceptions. Socrates, Plato, and Aristotle, the founders of Western rationalism, saw no opposition between reason and the transcendent. They understood that we feel an imperative need to drive our reasoning powers to the point where they can go no further and segue into a state of unknowing that is not frustrating but a source of astonishment, awe, and contentment.

Religion was not an easy matter. We have seen the immense effort made by yogins, hesychasts, Kabbalists, exegetes, rabbis, ritualists, monks, scholars, philosophers, and contemplatives, as well as laypeople in regular liturgical observance. All were able to achieve a degree of *ekstasis* that, as Denys explained, by introducing us to a different kind of knowing, "drives us out of ourselves." In the modern period too, scientists, rationalists, and philosophers have experienced something similar. Einstein, Wittgenstein, and Popper, who had no conventional religious "beliefs," were quite at home in this hinterland between rationality and the transcendent. Religious insight requires not only a dedicated intellectual endeavor to get beyond the "idols of thought" but also a compassionate lifestyle that enables us to break out of the prism of selfhood. Aggressive *logos,* which seeks to master, control, and kill off the opposition, cannot bring this transcendent insight. Experience proved that this was possible only if people cultivated a receptive, listening attitude, not unlike the way we approach art, music, or poetry. It required *kenosis,* "negative capability," "wise passiveness," and a heart that "watches and receives."

The consistency with which the various religions have stressed the importance of these qualities indicates that they are somehow built into the way men and women experience their world. If the religious lose sight of them, they are revived by poets, novelists, and philosophers. My last chapter concluded with postmodern theology, not because this represents the pinnacle of the Western theological tradition but because it has rediscovered practices, attitudes, and ideals that were central to religion before the advent of the modern period. That is not to say, of course, that all faiths are the same. Each tradition formulates the sacred differently, and this will certainly affect the way people experience it. There are important differences between Brahman, Nirvana, God, and Dao, but that does not mean that one is right and the others wrong. On this matter, nobody can have the last word. All faith systems have been at pains to show that the ultimate cannot be adequately expressed in any theoretical system, however august, because it lies beyond words and concepts.

But many people today are no longer comfortable with this apophatic reticence. They feel that they know exactly what they mean by God. The catechism definition I learned at the age of eight—"God is the Supreme Spirit, who alone exists of himself and is infinite in all perfections"—was not only dry, abstract, and rather boring; it was also incorrect. Not only did it imply that God was a fact that it was possible to "define," but it represented only the first stage in Denys's threefold dialectical method. I was not taught to take the next step and see that God is *not* a spirit; that "he" has *no* gender; and that we have *no* idea what we mean when we say that *a* being "exists" who is "infinite in all perfections." The process that should have led to a stunned appreciation of an "otherness" beyond the competence of language ended prematurely. The result is that many of us have been left stranded with an incoherent concept of God. We learned about God at about the same time as we were told about Santa Claus. But while our understanding of the Santa Claus phenomenon evolved and matured, our theology remained somewhat infantile. Not surprisingly, when we attained intellectual maturity, many of us rejected the God we had inherited and denied that he existed.

Paul Tillich pointed out that it is difficult to speak about God these days, because people immediately ask you if *a* God *exists*. This means that the symbol of God is no longer working. Instead of pointing beyond itself to an ineffable reality, the humanly conceived construct that we call "God" has become the end of the story. We have seen that during the early modern period the idea of God was reduced to a scientific hypothesis and God became the ultimate explanation of the universe. Instead of symbolizing the ineffable, God was in effect reduced to a mere *deva,* a lowercase god that was a member of the cosmos with a precise function and location. When that happened, it was only a matter of time before atheism became a viable proposition, because scientists were soon able to find alternative explanatory hypotheses that rendered "God" redundant. This would not have been a disaster had not the churches come to rely on scientific proof. Other paths to knowledge had been downgraded in the modern world, and scientific rationality was now regarded as the only acceptable path to truth. People had grown accustomed to thinking of God as a "clear," "distinct," and self-evident idea. Had not Descartes, founder of modern philosophy, told them that the existence of God was even clearer and more obvious than one of Euclid's theorems? Did not the great Newton insist that religion should be "easy"?

Above all, many of us forgot that religious teaching was what the rabbis called *miqra.* It was essentially and crucially a program for action. You had to *engage* with a symbol imaginatively, become ritually and ethically *involved* with it, and allow it to effect a profound change in you. That was the original meaning of the words "faith" and "belief." If you held aloof, a symbol would remain opaque and implausible. Many people today can work with the symbolism of the modern God in this way; backed up by ritual and compassionate, self-emptying practice, it still introduces them to the transcendence that gives meaning to their lives. But not everybody is able to do this. Because "faith" has come to mean intellectual assent to a set of purely notional doctrines that make no sense unless they are applied practically, some have given up altogether. Others, reluctant to abandon religion, are obscurely ashamed of their "unbelief" and feel uncomfortably caught between two sets of extremists: religious fundamentalists, whose belligerent piety they find alienating, on the one hand, and militant atheists calling for the wholesale extermination of religion, on the other.

Idolatry has always been one of the pitfalls of monotheism. Because its chief symbol of the divine is a personalized deity, there is an inherent danger that people would imagine "him" as a larger, more powerful version of themselves, which they could use to endorse their own ideas, practices, loves, and hatreds—sometimes to lethal effect. There can be only one absolute, so once a finite idea, theology, nation, polity, or ideology is made supreme, it is compelled to destroy anything that opposes it. We have seen a good deal of this kind of idolatry in recent years. To make limited historical phenomena—a particular idea of "God," "creation science," "family values," "Islam" (understood as an institutional and civilizational entity), or the "Holy Land"—more important than the sacred reverence due to the "other" is, as the rabbis pointed out long ago, a sacrilegious denial of everything that "God" stands for. It is idolatrous, because it elevates an inherently limited value to an unacceptably high level. As Tillich pointed out, if it assumes that a man-made idea of "God" is an adequate representation of the transcendence toward which it can only imperfectly gesture, a great deal of mainstream theology is also idolatrous. Atheists are right to condemn such abuses. But when they insist that society should no longer tolerate faith and demand the withdrawal of respect from all things religious, they fall prey to the same intolerance. Some atheists are unhappy about this militancy. For Julian Baggini, atheism means "open-hearted commitment to truth and rational enquiry," so that "hostile opposition to the beliefs of others combined with a dogged conviction of the certainty of one's own beliefs . . . is antithetical to such values."[1]

During the early modern period, Western people fell in love with an ideal of absolute certainty that, it seems, may be unattainable. But because some are reluctant to relinquish it, they have tended to overcompensate, claiming certitude for beliefs and doctrines that can only be provisional. This has perhaps contributed to the aggressive tenor of a great deal of modern discourse. There are very few Socratic "philosophers" these days who know that they lack wisdom. Too many people assume that they alone have it and, in matters secular as well as religious, appear unwilling even to consider a rival point of view or seriously assess evidence that might qualify their case. The quest for truth has become agonistic and competitive. When debating an issue in politics or in the media, in the law courts or academe, it is not enough to establish what is true; we also have to defeat—and even humiliate—our opponents. Even though we hear a great deal about the importance of "dialogue," it is rare to hear a genuinely Socratic exchange of views. It is often obvious in public debates that instead of listening receptively to other participants, panelists simply use others' remarks as grist for a brilliant point of their own that will deliver the coup de grâce. Even when the issues debated are too complex and multifaceted for a simple solution, these discussions rarely end in a realistic Socratic *aporia* or an acknowledgment that the other side may also have merit.

This too is part of our democratic heritage, and in practical matters it may be the fairest way of getting things done. This was the kind of discussion that was going on in the Athenian assemblies from which Socrates carefully dissociated his own dialogic technique. Unfortunately, much of the current debate about faith is conducted in this antagonistic spirit and it is not helpful. We badly need to consider the nature of religion and discover where and how it goes wrong. But if dialogue lacks either compassion or *kenosis,* it cannot lead to truly creative insight or enlightenment. Religious truth has always developed communally and orally; in the past, when two or three sat down together and reached out toward the "other," they experienced transcendence as a "presence" among them. But it was essential that religious debates be conducted "in the most kindly manner," to quote the Qur'an. A vicious polemic is likely to exacerbate already existing tensions. We have seen that when they feel under attack, fundamentalists almost invariably become more extreme. Hitherto Muslims had little problem with Darwin, but a new hostility toward evolutionary theory is now developing in the Muslim world as a direct response to Dawkins's attack. In a world that is already so dangerously polarized, can we really afford yet another divisive discourse?

In the past, theologians found that extended dialogue with atheists helped them to refine their own ideas. An informed atheistic critique should be welcomed, because it can draw our attention to inadequate or idolatrous theological thinking. The written discussion of the atheistic philosopher J. J. C. Smart and his theist colleague J. J. Haldane is a model of courtesy, intellectual acumen, and integrity and shows how valuable such a debate can be—not least in making it clear that it is impossible to settle either the existence or nonexistence of God by rational arguments alone.[2] A scientific critique of conventional "beliefs" can also be helpful in revealing the limitations of the literalistic mind-set that is currently blocking understanding. Instead of arguing that an ancient *mythos* is factual, perhaps it would be better to study the original meaning of the ancient cosmologies and apply it analogically to our own situation. Instead of clinging to a literal reading of the first chapter of Genesis, it could be helpful to face up to the implications of the Darwinian vision of nature "red in tooth and claw." This could become a meditation on the inescapable suffering of life, make us aware of the inadequacy of any neat theological solution, and give us a new appreciation of the First Noble Truth of Buddhism, "Existence is suffering (*dukkha*)"—an insight that in nearly all faiths is indispensable for enlightenment.

There is much to be learned from older ways of thinking about religion. We have seen that far from regarding revelation as static, fixed, and unchanging, Jews, Christians, and Muslims all knew that revealed truth was symbolic, that scripture could not be interpreted literally, and that sacred texts had multiple meaning, and could lead to entirely fresh insights. Revelation was not an event that had happened once in the distant past but was an ongoing, creative process that required human ingenuity. They understood that revelation did not provide us with infallible information about the divine, because this would always remain beyond our ken. We have seen that the doctrine of creation ex nihilo made it clear to Christians that the natural world could tell us nothing about God, and that the Trinity taught them that they could not think of God as a simple personality. Even the supreme revelation of Christ, the incarnate Word, showed that the reality that we call "God" was as elusive as ever. Jewish, Christian, and Muslim scholars all insisted on the paramount importance of intellectual integrity and thinking for oneself. Instead of clinging nervously to the insights of the past, they expected people to be inventive, fearless, and confident in their interpretation of faith. Religion must not be allowed to impede progress but should help people embrace the uncertainties of the future. There could be no question of a clash between science and theology, because these disciplines had different spheres of competence; science, Calvin insisted, must not be obstructed by the fears of a few ignorant and "frantic persons." If a biblical text appeared to contradict current scientific discoveries, the exegete must interpret it differently.

We must not idealize the past. Every age has its bigots, and there have always been people who were less theologically skilled than others and interpreted the truths of religion in a prosaic, factual manner.

When as a young nun I was being especially obtuse, my superior used to tell me that I was "a literal-minded blockhead." There have always been such. But the theologians who promoted a more apophatic approach to God were not marginal thinkers. The Cappadocians, Denys, and Thomas; the rabbis, the Kabbalists, and Maimonides; al-Ghazzali, Ibn Sina, and Mulla Sadra were all major carriers of tradition. Before the modern period, this was the orthodox position. We now have such a different view of faith that this may be difficult to accept, because it is always hard to transcend the limitations of our own time. We cannot, perhaps, ever become fully aware of our own cultural mood precisely because we are *in* that mood, and as a result we tend to absolutize it. Today we assume that because *we* rationalize faith and regard its truths as factual, this is how it was always done. But this involves a double standard. "The *past* is relativised, in terms of this or that socio-historical analysis. The *present,* however, remains strangely immune to relativisation," the American scholar Peter Berger has explained. "The New Testament writers are seen as afflicted with a false consciousness rooted in *their* time, but the analyst takes the consciousness of *his* time as an unmixed intellectual blessing."[3] We tend to assume that "modern" means "superior," and while this is certainly true in such fields as mathematics, science, and technology, it is not necessarily true of the more intuitive disciplines—especially, perhaps, theology.

We now understand basic religious terms differently and in a way that has made faith problematic. "Belief" no longer means "trust, commitment, and engagement" but has become an intellectual assent to a somewhat dubious proposition. Religious leaders often spend more time enforcing doctrinal conformity than devising spiritual exercises that will make these official "beliefs" a living reality in the daily lives of the faithful. Instead of using scripture to help people to move forward and embrace new attitudes, people quote ancient scriptural texts to prevent any such progress. The words "myth" and "mythical" are now often synonymous with untruth. "Mystery" no longer refers to a ritualized initiation but has been routinely decried as mental laziness and incomprehensible mumbo jumbo. The Greek fathers used the word *dogma* to describe a truth that could not be put readily into words, could be understood only after long immersion in ritual, and, as the understanding of the community deepened, changed from one generation to another. Today in the West "dogma" is defined as "a body of opinion formulated and authoritatively stated," while a "dogmatic" person is one who "asserts opinions in an arrogant and authoritative manner."[4] We no longer understand Greek *theoria* as the activity of "contemplation" but as a "theory," an idea in our heads that has to be proved. This neatly demonstrates our modern understanding of religion as something that we think rather than something that we do.

In the past, religious people were open to all manner of different truths. Jewish, Christian, and Muslim scholars were ready to learn from pagan Greeks who had sacrificed to idols, as well as from one another. It is simply not true that science and religion were always at daggers drawn: in England, the Protestant and Puritan ethos were felt to be congenial to early modern science and helped its advance and acceptance.[5] Mersenne, who belonged to a particularly austere branch of the Franciscan order, took time off from his prayers to conduct scientific experiments, and his mathematical ideas are still discussed today. The Jesuits encouraged the young Descartes to read Galileo and were fascinated by early modern science. Indeed, it has been said that the first scientific collective was not the Royal Society but the Society of Jesus.[6] But as modernity advanced, confidence dimmed and attitudes hardened. Thomas Aquinas had taught Aristotelian science when it was controversial to do so and had studied Jewish and Muslim philosophers while most of his contemporaries reflexively supported the Crusades. But the defensive post-Tridentine Church interpreted his theology with a rigidity that he would have found repugnant. The modern Protestant doctrine of the literal infallibility of scripture was first formulated by Hodge and Warfield in the 1870s, when scientific methods of biblical criticism were undermining "beliefs" held to be factually true. Like the new and highly controversial Catholic doctrine of papal infallibility, defined in 1870, it expressed a yearning for absolute certainty at a time when this was proving to be a chimera.

Today, when science itself is becoming less determinate, it is perhaps time to return to a theology that asserts less and is more open to silence and unknowing. Here, perhaps, dialogue with the more thoughtful Socratic forms of atheism can help to dismantle ideas that have become idolatrous. In the past, people were often called "atheists" when society was in transition from one religious perspective to another: Euripides and Protagoras were accused of "atheism" when they denied the Olympian gods in favor of a more transcendent theology; the first Christians and Muslims, who were moving away from traditional paganism, were persecuted as "atheists" by their contemporaries. When we have eaten a strong-tasting dish in a restaurant, we are often offered a sorbet to cleanse our palate so that we can taste the next course properly. An intelligent atheistic critique could help us to rinse our minds of the more facile theology that is impeding our understanding of the divine. We may find that for a while we have to go into what mystics called the dark night of the soul or the cloud of unknowing. This will not be easy for people used to getting instant information at the click of a mouse. But the novelty and strangeness of this negative capability could surprise us into awareness that stringent ratiocination is not the only means of acquiring knowledge. It is not only a poet like Keats who must, while waiting for new inspiration, learn to be "capable of being in uncertainties, Mysteries, doubts, without any irritable reaching after fact & reason."

But is there no way of grounding commitment to the unknown and indefinable God? Are we doomed to the perpetual regression of postmodern thought? Perhaps the only viable "natural theology" lies in religious experience. By this, of course, I do not mean fervid emotional piety. We have seen that in the past scholars and spiritual directors had little time for this religious positivism. Instead of seeking out exotic raptures, Schleiermacher, Bultmann, Rahner, and Lonergan have all suggested that we should explore the normal workings of our minds and notice how frequently these propel us quite naturally into transcendence. Instead of looking for what we call God "outside ourselves" (*foris*) in the cosmos, we should, like Augustine, turn within and become aware of the way quite ordinary responses segue into "otherness." We have seen how the inherent finitude of language was regularly exploited by teachers like Denys to make the faithful aware of the silence we encounter on the other side of speech. It has been well said that music, which, as we saw at the beginning of this book, is a "definitively" rational activity, is itself a "natural theology."[7] In music the mind experiences a pure, direct emotion that transcends ego and fuses subjectivity and objectivity.

As Basil explained, we can never know the ineffable *ousia* of God but can glimpse only its traces or effects (*energeiai*) in our time-bound, sense-bound world. It is clear that the meditation, yoga, and rituals that work aesthetically on a congregation have, when practiced assiduously over a lifetime, a marked effect on the personality—an effect that is another form of natural theology. There is no dramatic "born-again" conversion but a slow, incremental, and imperceptible transformation. Above all, the habitual practice of compassion and the Golden Rule "all day and every day" demands perpetual *kenosis*. The constant "stepping outside" of our own preferences, convictions, and prejudices is an *ekstasis* that is not a glamorous rapture but, as Confucius's pupil Yan Hui explained, is itself the transcendence we seek. The effect of these practices cannot give us concrete information about God; it is certainly not a scientific "proof." But something indefinable happens to people who involve themselves in these disciplines with commitment and talent. This "something" remains opaque to those who do not undergo these disciplines, however, just as the Eleusinian "mystery" sounded trivial and absurd to somebody who remained obstinately outside the cult hall and refused to undergo the initiation.

Like the ancient Sky Gods, the remote God of the philosophers tends to fade from people's minds and hearts. The domineering God of modern "scientific religion" overexternalized the divine and pushed it away from humanity, confining it, like Blake's Tyger, to "distant deeps and skies." But premodern religion deliberately humanized the sacred. The Brahman was not a distant reality but was identical with the atman of every single creature. Confucius refused to define *ren* (later identified with "benevolence") because it was incomprehensible to a person who had not yet achieved it. But the ordinary meaning of *ren* in Confucius's time was "human being." *Ren* is sometimes translated into English as "human-heartedness." Holiness was not "supernatural," therefore, but a carefully crafted attitude that, as a later Confucian explained, refined humanity and elevated it to a "godlike" (*shen*) plane.[8] When Buddhists contemplated the tranquillity, poise, and selflessness of the Buddha, they saw him as the avatar of the otherwise incomprehensible Nirvana; this was what Nirvana looked like in human terms. They also knew that this state was natural to human beings and that if they put the Buddhist method into practice they too could achieve it. Christians had a similar experience when their imitation of Christ brought them intimations of *theos* ("deification").

Certain individuals became icons of this enhanced, refined humanity. We think of Socrates approaching his execution without recrimination but with openhearted kindness, cheerfulness, and serenity. The gospels show Jesus undergoing an agonizing death and experiencing the extremity of despair while forgiving his executioners, making provision for his mother, and having a kindly word for one of his fellow victims. Instead of becoming stridently virtuous, aggressively orthodox, and contemptuous of the ungodly, these paradigmatic personalities became more humane. The rabbis were revered as avatars of the Torah, because their learning and practice enabled them to become living, breathing, and human embodiments of the divine imperative that sustained the world. Muslims venerate the Prophet Muhammad as the "Perfect Man," whose life symbolizes the total receptivity to the divine that characterizes the archetypal, ideal human being. Just as the feats of a dancer or an athlete are impossible for an untrained body and seem superhuman to most of us, these people all developed a spiritual capacity that took them beyond the norm and revealed to their followers the untapped "divine" or "enlightened" potential that exists in any man or woman.

From almost the very beginning, men and women have repeatedly engaged in strenuous and committed religious activity. They evolved mythologies, rituals, and ethical disciplines that brought them intimations of holiness that seemed in some indescribable way to enhance and fulfill their humanity. They were not religious simply because their myths and doctrines were scientifically or historically sound, because they sought information about the origins of the cosmos, or merely because they wanted a better life in the hereafter. They were not bludgeoned into faith by power-hungry priests or kings: indeed, religion often helped people to oppose tyranny and oppression of this kind. The point of religion was to live intensely and richly here and now. Truly religious people are ambitious. They want lives overflowing with significance. They have always desired to integrate with their daily lives the moments of rapture and insight that came to them in dreams, in their contemplation of nature, and in their intercourse with one another and with the animal world. Instead of being crushed and embittered by the sorrow of life, they sought to retain their peace and serenity in the midst of their pain. They yearned for the courage to overcome their terror of mortality; instead of being grasping and mean-spirited, they aspired to live generously, large-heartedly, and justly, and to inhabit every single part of their humanity. Instead of being a mere workaday cup, they wanted, as Confucius suggested, to transform themselves into a beautiful ritual vessel brimful of the sanctity that they were learning to see in life. They tried to honor the ineffable mystery they sensed in each human being and create societies that protected and welcomed the stranger, the alien, the poor, and the oppressed. Of course, they often failed, sometimes abysmally. But overall they found that the disciplines of religion helped them to do all this. Those who applied themselves most assiduously showed that it was possible for mortal men and women to live on a higher, divine, or godlike plane and thus wake up to their true selves.

One day a Brahmin priest came across the Buddha sitting in contemplation under a tree and was astonished by his serenity, stillness, and self-discipline. The impression of immense strength channeled creatively into an extraordinary peace reminded him of a great tusker elephant. "Are you a god, sir?" the priest asked. "Are you an angel . . . or a spirit?" No, the Buddha replied. He explained that he had simply revealed a new potential in human nature. It was possible to live in this world of conflict and pain at peace and in harmony with one's fellow creatures. There was no point in merely believing it; you would discover its truth only if you practiced his method, systematically cutting off egotism at the root. You would then live at the peak of your capacity, activate parts of the psyche that normally lie dormant, and become a fully enlightened human being. "Remember me," the Buddha told the curious priest, "as one who is awake."[9]

# Acknowledgments

As always, I have so many people to thank. First, my agents, Felicity Bryan, Peter Ginsberg, and Andrew Nurnberg, who have given me indispensable encouragement, affection, and support for so many years, as well as my wonderful editors, Jane Garrett, Robbert Ammerlaan, Louise Dennys, and Will Sulkin. I know how fortunate I am to have each one of you as a beloved friend and colleague.

But I must also express my gratitude to Michele Topham, Jackie Head, and Carole Robinson in Felicity Bryan's office for their unfailing patience, kindness, and practical help, and to Leslie Levine, Jane Garrett's assistant at Knopf. Many thanks, too, to the host of people who have worked on the text and production of this book with such skill, dedication, and commitment: Louise Collazo, Wesley Gott, Ellen Feldman, Claire Bradley Ong, Gabriele Wilson, and Jörg Hensgen. Finally, my thanks to the publicists, some of whom have become old and valued friends after our years on the road together: Sheila O'Shea, Kim Thornton, Sheila Kay, Laura Hassan, and Francien Schuursma. It is a joy to work with each and every one of you.

In the autumn of 2007, I had the good fortune to give the William Belden Noble Lectures at Harvard University, which gave me the opportunity to present some of the ideas that I have developed in this book. I also aired some of these themes at the Chautauqua Institution in the summer of 2008. I want to thank all my friends at the Harvard Memorial Church (especially the Faith & Life Forum) and at Chautauqua, who have listened to me so loyally and kindly over the years and given me such encouragement.

During the last year, it has been a great delight and privilege to work with TED Conferences on the Charter for Compassion, an attempt to implement practically the thesis of this book. Thanks especially to Chris Anderson and Amy Novogratz, and to all the TED-sters who have contributed to this project with such extraordinary generosity, creativity, and awe-inspiring commitment. It has been an inspiration.

Finally, a big thank-you to Eve, Gary, Stacey, and Amy Mott and to Michelle Stevenson, who make it possible for me to do my work by looking after Poppy so devotedly during my many absences.

I could not have managed without any of you.

# Notes

## Introduction

1. Johannes Sloek, *Devotional Language,* trans. Henrick Mossin (Berlin and New York, 1996), pp. 53–96.
2. I have discussed the role of mythology more fully in *A Short History of Myth* (Edinburgh, 2005).
3. Mircea Eliade, *Patterns in Comparative Religion,* trans. Rosemary Sheed (London, 1958), pp. 453–55.
4. Joseph Campbell, *The Hero with a Thousand Faces* (Princeton, N.J., 1949).
5. Sloek, *Devotional Language,* pp. 75–76.
6. *The Book of Zhuangzi* 17.3 in Martin Palmer with Elizabeth Breuilly, trans., *The Book of Chuang Tzu* (London and New York, 1996).
7. Ibid.
8. Denys Turner, *Faith, Reason and the Existence of God* (Cambridge, U.K., 2004), pp. 108–15.
9. George Steiner, *Real Presences: Is There Anything* in *What We Say?* (London, 1989), p. 217.
10. George Steiner, *Language and Silence* (London, 1967), pp. 58–59.
11. Steiner, *Real Presences,* p. 217.
12. Steiner, *Language and Silence,* p. 59.
13. I have discussed this more fully in *The Battle for God: A History of Fundamentalism* (London and New York, 2000), and there is a more extended discussion of fundamentalism in chapter 12.

## ONE  *Homo religiosus*

1. Joseph Campbell, *Primitive Mythology: The Masks of God,* rev. ed. (New York, 1988), p. 305; Joseph Campbell with Bill Moyers, *The Power of Myth* (New York, 1988), p. 79.
2. André Leroi-Gourhan, *Treasures of Prehistoric Art* (New York, n.d.), p. 112. This rules out the suggestion that the paintings were simply a form of hunting magic.
3. Ibid., p. 118.
4. John E. Pfeiffer, *The Creative Explosion* (New York, 1982), p. viii.

5. André Leroi-Gourhan, *Les religions préhistorique: Paléolithique* (Paris, 1964), pp. 83–84; Mircea Eliade, *A History of Religious Ideas,* 3 vols., trans. Willard R. Trask (Chicago and London, 1978, 1982, 1985), 1:16.

6. Joseph Campbell, *Historical Atlas of World Mythologies,* 2 vols. (New York, 1988), I, 1: 58.

7. Ibid., I, 1: 65.

8. Leo Frobenius, *Kulturgeschichte Africas* (Zurich, 1933), pp. 131–32; Campbell, *Primitive Mythology,* p. 300.

9. Eliade, *History of Religious Ideas,* 1: 24.

10. Campbell with Moyers, *Power of Myth,* pp. 85–87.

11. Ibid., pp. 72–79; *Historical Atlas,* I, 1: 48–49; Eliade, *History of Religious Ideas,* 1: 7–8.

12. Walter Burkert, *Homo Necans: The Anthropology of Ancient Greek Sacrificial Ritual and Myth,* trans. Peter Bing (Berkeley, Los Angeles, and London, 1983), pp. 16–22.

13. Walter Burkert, *Structure and History in Greek Mythology and Ritual* (Berkeley, Los Angeles, and London, 1980), pp. 54–56; Burkert, *Homo Necans,* pp. 42–45.

14. Campbell, *Historical Atlas,* I, 2: xiii.

15. Ibid., I, 1: 93.

16. Campbell, *Primitive Mythology,* p. 66.

17. Mircea Eliade, *The Myth of the Eternal Return, or Cosmos and History,* trans. Willard R. Trask (Princeton, N.J., 1954), pp. 1–34.

18. Huston Smith, *The World's Religions,* rev. ed. (New York, 1991), p. 367.

19. Eliade, *History of Religious Ideas,* 1:17.

20. Mircea Eliade, *Birth and Rebirth: The Religious Meanings of Initiation in Human Cultures* (New York, 1958); Mircea Eliade, *Myths, Dreams and Mysteries: The Encounter Between Contemporary Faiths and Archaic Realities,* trans. Philip Mairet (London, 1960), pp. 194–226; Campbell with Moyers, *Power of Myth,* pp. 81–85.

21. Eliade, *Myths, Dreams,* p. 225.

22. Herbert Kuhn, *Auf den Spuren des Eiszeitmenschen* (Wiesbaden, 1953), pp. 88–89; Campbell, *Primitive Mythology,* pp. 307–8.

23. Abbé Henri Breuil, *Four Hundred Centuries of Cave Art* (Montignac, France, 1952), pp. 170–71.

24. Campbell, *Primitive Mythology,* p. 311.

25. Burkert, *Homo Necans,* pp. 27–34.

26. Mircea Eliade, *Patterns in Comparative Religion,* trans. Rosemary Sheed (London, 1958), pp. 331–43.

27. Alexander Marshack, "Lunar Notations on Upper Palaeolithic Remains," *Scientia* 146 (1964).

28. Eliade, *Patterns in Comparative Religion,* pp. 146–85.

29. Burkert, *Homo Necans,* pp. 78–82.

30. Eliade, *Patterns in Comparative Religion,* pp. 1–124, 216–39.

31. Mary Boyce, *Zoroastrians: Their Religious Beliefs and Practices,* 2nd ed. (London and New York, 2001), p. 2; Peter Clark, *Zoroastrians: An Introduction to an Ancient Faith* (Brighton and Portland, Ore., 1998), p. 18.

32. Boyce, *Zoroastrians,* pp. 9–11.

33. Jan Gonda, *Change and Continuity in Indian Religion* (The Hague, 1965), p. 200; Louis Renou, "Sur la notion de *brahman,*" *Journal Asiatique* 237 (1949).

34. Louis Renou, *Religions of Ancient India* (London, 1953), pp. 10, 16–18; Michael Witzel, "Vedas and Upanishads" in Gavin Flood, ed., *The Blackwell Companion to Hinduism* (Oxford, 2003), pp. 70–71.

35. J. C. Heesterman, *The Inner Conflict of Tradition: Essays in Indian Ritual, Kingship and Society* (Chicago and London, 1985), pp. 70–72, 126.

36. Zhuangzi, *The Book of Zhuangzi* 6:29–31.

37. Mark S. Smith, *The Origins of Biblical Monotheism: Israel's Polytheistic Background and the Ugaritic Texts* (New York and London, 2001), pp. 41–79.

38. Eliade, *Patterns in Comparative Religion,* pp. 367–88; Mircea Eliade, *The Sacred and the Profane: The Nature of Religion,* trans. Willard R. Trask (New York, 1959), pp. 50–54, 64; Mircea Eliade, *Images and Symbols: Studies in Religious Symbolism,* trans. Philip Mairet (Princeton, N.J., 1991), pp. 37–56.

39. Eliade, *Patterns in Comparative Religion,* pp. 38–63; Eliade, *Myths, Dreams,* pp. 172–78; Wilhelm Schmidt, *The Origin of the Idea of God* (New York, 1912), passim.

40. Eliade, *The Sacred and the Profane,* pp. 120–25.

41. Rig Veda 10.129.

42. Rig Veda 10.90.

43. Gwendolyn Leick, *Mesopotamia: The Invention of the City* (London, 2001), p. 268.

44. Thorkild Jacobsen, "The Cosmos as State," in H. and H. A. Frankfort, eds., *The Intellectual Adventure of Ancient Man: An Essay on the Speculative Thought in the Ancient Near East* (Chicago, 1946), pp. 186–97.

45. "The Babylonian Creation" 1.1 in N. K. Sanders, trans. and ed., *Poems of Heaven and Hell from Ancient Mesopotamia* (London, 1971).

46. *Enuma Elish* 6.19, in Sanders, *Poems of Heaven and Hell.*

47. E. O. James, *The Ancient Gods* (London, 1960), pp. 87–90.

48. Psalms 89:10–13; 93:1–4; Isaiah 27:1; Job 7:12; 9:8; 26:12; 38:7.

49. Eliade, *Myths, Dreams,* pp. 80–81.

50. Chandogya Upanishad (CU) 6.13; my italics. All quotations from the Upanishads are from Patrick Olivelle, trans. and ed., *Upaniṣads* (Oxford and New York, 1996).

51. CU 6.11–12.

52. CU 6.10.

53. Brhadaranyaka Upanishad (BU) 4.5.15.

54. BU 3.4.

55. BU 4.5.13–15.

56. BU 3.5.1.

57. Mircea Eliade, *Yoga, Immortality and Freedom,* trans. Willard R. Trask (New York, 1958).

58. Women participated in Upanishadic spirituality and, later, in Buddhist practice.

59. Patanjali, Yoga Sutra 2.42, in Eliade, *Yoga,* p. 52.

60. BU 1.4.1–5.

61. BU 1.4.6.

62. BU 1.4.10.

63. BU 4.3.21.

64. Samyutta Nikaya 53:31. The quotations from the Pali Canon of Buddhist scriptures are my own version of the texts cited.

65. Sutta-Nipata 43:1–44.

66. Majjima Nikaya 29.

67. *Vinaya:* Mahavagga 1.6.

68. Confucius, Analects 17.19. Unless otherwise stated, quotations from the Analects are taken from Arthur Waley, trans. and ed., *The Analects of Confucius* (New York, 1992).

69. Analects 4.15.

70. Analects 15.23.

71. Ibid.

72. Analects 12.1. Translation suggested by Benjamin I. Schwartz, *The World of Thought in Ancient China* (Cambridge, Mass., and London, 1985), p. 77.

73. Ibid.

74. Analects 9.10.

## two God

1. Genesis 2:23. All quotations from the Pentateuch—Genesis, Exodus, Leviticus, Numbers, and Deuteronomy—are taken from Everett Fox, trans., *The Five Books of Moses* (New York, 1993); all other biblical quotations are taken from *The Jerusalem Bible* (London, 1966) unless otherwise stated.

2. I have discussed this at length in *The Bible: The Biography* (London and New York, 2007).

3. Michael Fishbane, *Text and Texture: Close Readings of Selected Biblical Texts* (New York, 1979), pp. 21–22.

4. Genesis Rabbah Ecclesiastes 4:4.10.

5. Margaret Barker, *The Gate of Heaven: The History and Symbolism of the Temple in Jerusalem* (London, 1991), pp. 26–29; R. E. Clements, *God and Temple*, (Oxford, 1965), p. 64.

6. Psalms 89:9–19; 65:2; 78:69. Ben C. Ollenburger, *Zion, the City of the Great King: A Theological Symbol of the Jerusalem Cult* (Sheffield, U.K., 1987), pp. 54–58.

7. Genesis 3:8.

8. Genesis 3:24.

9. 1 Kings 6:15–38; 2 Chronicles 3:8–13.

10. Numbers 21:8–9; 2 Kings 18:14.

11. See, for example, Psalm 122.

12. Psalm 42:4.

13. Psalm 84:2, 3, 6, 10.

14. William G. Dever, *What Did the Biblical Writers Know and When Did They Know It? What Archaeology Can Tell Us About the Reality of Ancient Israel* (Grand Rapids, Mich., and Cambridge, U.K., 2001), p. 280.

15. Frank Moore Cross, *From Epic to Canon: History and Literature in Ancient Israel* (Baltimore and London, 1998), pp. 41–42.

16. George W. Mendenhall, *The Tenth Generation: The Origins of Biblical Traditions* (Baltimore and London, 1973); N. P. Lemche, *Early Israel: Anthropological and Historical Studies on the Israelite Society Before the Monarchy* (Leiden, the Netherlands, 1985).

17. R. E. Clements, *Abraham and David* (London, 1967); Fishbane, *Text and Texture,* pp. 64, 124–25; Peter Machinist, "Distinctiveness in Ancient Israel," in

Mordechai Cogan and Israel Ephal, eds., *Studies in Assyrian History and Ancient Near Eastern Historiography* (Jerusalem, 1991), p. 434.

18. Exodus 14:21–22.
19. Frank Moore Cross, *Canaanite Myth and Hebrew Epic: Essays in the History of the Religion of Israel* (Cambridge, Mass., and London, 1973), pp. 103–24.
20. Exodus 15:1.
21. Exodus 15:14–15. "Rams" was probably a technical term for "chieftains" in Canaan, as it was in Ugarit.
22. Joshua 3:1–5:15; Cross, *From Epic to Canon,* p. 44; Cross, *Canaanite Myth,* pp. 103–5, 133–38.
23. Joshua 5:1.
24. Joshua 4:10–12.
25. Deuteronomy 32:8–9.
26. Mark S. Smith, *The Early History of God: Yahweh and the Other Deities in Ancient Israel* (New York and London, 1990), pp. 44–49.
27. Genesis 28:10–19.
28. Genesis 28:10–11.
29. Genesis 28:12–13.
30. Genesis 28:16–17.
31. Genesis 18:1–22.
32. Genesis 22:1–10.
33. Martin Buber, *On the Bible: Eighteen Studies,* ed. Nahum Glatzer (New York, 1982), p. 42.
34. I have described this in detail in *A History of God: The 4,000-Year Quest of Judaism, Christianity and Islam* (New York, 1993), pp. 27–66, and in *The Great Transformation: The Beginning of Our Religious Traditions* (New York, 2006), pp. 86–101, 157–83, 211–20.
35. Psalm 135:15–18; see also Psalm 115:4–8; Jeremiah 10.
36. 2 Kings 22:8.
37. Deuteronomy 7:5.
38. 2 Kings 23:4–20.
39. Deuteronomy 12:20–24; 16:18–20; 17:8–13; Bernard M. Levinson, *Deuteronomy and the Hermeneutics of Legal Innovation* (Oxford and New York, 1998), pp. 50, 114–37.
40. Deuteronomy 17:18–20; Levinson, *Deuteronomy,* pp. 138–43.
41. Deuteronomy 11:21, 12:5.
42. Clements, *God and Temple,* pp. 89–95; Barker, *Gate of Heaven,* pp. 7–8; S. David Sperling, *The Original Torah: The Political Intent of the Bible's Writers* (New York and London, 1986), pp. 146–47.
43. 1 Kings 8:27.
44. 2 Kings 23:29.
45. Exodus 3:14.
46. Exodus 24:10–11.
47. Exodus 33:22–23.
48. Exodus 19:18; 24:15–17.
49. Psalm 137:7–9.
50. Elias J. Bickerman, *The Jews in the Greek Age* (Cambridge, Mass., and London, 1988), pp. 47–48.
51. Ezekiel 1:1–2:15.
52. Leviticus 17–26.

53. Exodus 25–31; 35–38; 40.
54. Exodus 29:46.
55. Cross, *Canaanite Myth,* pp. 298–300; Clements, *God and Temple,* pp. 114–21.
56. Cross, *Canaanite Myth,* 321.
57. Andrew Mein, *Ezekiel and the Ethics of Exile* (Oxford and New York, 2001), p. 137.
58. Leviticus 19:2.
59. Leviticus 26:12.
60. Leviticus 19:34. Jerusalem Bible translation.
61. Mary Douglas, *In the Wilderness: The Doctrine of Defilement in the Book of Numbers* (Oxford and New York, 2001), pp. 25–26.
62. Leviticus 1:1–3; Mary Douglas, *Leviticus as Literature* (Oxford and New York, 1999), pp. 68–69.
63. Douglas, *Leviticus as Literature,* pp. 150–73.
64. Leviticus 11:31–39, 43–44.
65. Numbers 11:31–33.
66. Genesis 1:2.
67. Genesis 1:14–18.
68. Genesis 1:21–22.
69. Genesis 1:3, 11, 14.
70. Mark S. Smith, *The Origins of Biblical Monotheism: Israel's Polytheistic Background and the Ugaritic Texts* (New York and London, 2001), pp. 161–71.
71. Genesis 1:31.
72. Exodus 25–31, 35–40.
73. Exodus 39:32, 43; 40:33; 40:2, 17; 31:3, 13.
74. Isaiah 40:1.
75. Isiaah 43:11, 12.
76. Isaiah 11:15–16.
77. Isaiah 46:1; see also Isaiah 45:21.
78. Isaiah 42:13.
79. Isaiah 41:17–24.
80. Isaiah 41:12, 16; 51:23.
81. Isaiah 42:1–4; 49:1–6; 50:4–9; 52:13–53:12.
82. Isaiah 42:2–3.
83. Isaiah 50:5–6, 9.
84. Isaiah 52:13–53:5.
85. Isaiah 49:6.
86. Ezra 7:6, translated by Michael Fishbane, in *The Garments of Torah: Essays in Biblical Hermeneutics* (Bloomington and Indianapolis, 1989), p. 66.
87. It is notoriously difficult to date this period. See Gosta W. Ahlstrom, *The History of Ancient Palestine* (Minneapolis, 1993), pp. 880–83; Elias J. Bickerman, *The Jews in the Greek Age* (Cambridge, Mass., 1988), pp. 29–32.
88. Nehemiah 8:7–8. The Levites were second-ranking priests, serving those who were the direct descendants of Aaron, Moses's brother.
89. Ezra 10.
90. Fishbane, *Garments of Torah*, pp. 64–65; Gerald L. Bruns, "Midrash and Allegory; the Beginnings of Scriptural Interpretation," in Robert Alter and Frank Kermode, eds., *The Literary Guide to the Bible* (London, 1987), pp. 626–27.
91. Wilfred Cantwell Smith, *What Is Scripture? A Comparative Approach* (London, 1993), p. 290.

THREE Reason

1. Jonathan Barnes, ed. and trans., *Early Greek Philosophy* (London and New York, 1987), pp. 55–80; Anthony Gottlieb, *The Dream of Reason: A History of Philosophy from the Greeks to the Renaissance* (London, 2000), pp. 4–20; Walter Burkert, *Greek Religion,* trans. John Raffan (Cambridge, Mass., 1985), pp. 305–11; Richard Tarnas, *The Passion of the Western Mind: Understanding the Ideas That Have Shaped Our World View* (New York and London, 1991), pp. 19–25; Oswyn Murray, *Early Greece,* 2nd ed. (London, 1993), pp. 247–51; Huston Smith, "The Western Way: An Essay on Reason and the Given," in *Essays on World Religion* (New York, 1992), pp. 179–85.

2. Jean-Pierre Vernant, *Myth and Society in Ancient Greece,* 3rd ed., trans. Janet Lloyd (New York, 1996), pp. 102–4, 113; Burkert, *Greek Religion,* pp. 219–25.

3. Burkert, *Greek Religion,* pp. 114, 152: S. L. Schein, *The Mortal Hero: An Introduction to Homer's* Iliad (Berkeley, Los Angeles, and London, 1984), pp. 57–58.

4. George Steiner, introduction to *Is Science Nearing Its Limits? Conference Convened by George Steiner* (Manchester, U.K., 2008), p. xvi.

5. Barnes, *Early Greek Philosophy,* pp. 129–43; Tarnas, *Passion of the Western Mind,* pp. 20–21; Charles Freeman, *The Greek Achievement: The Foundation of the Western World* (New York and London, 1999), pp. 154–55; Gottlieb, *Dream of Reason,* pp. 51–64; Vernant, *Myth and Society,* pp. 98–99; Burkert, *Greek Religion,* pp. 310–11.

6. Barnes, *Early Greek Philosophy,* pp. 242–89; Tarnas, *Passion of the Western Mind,* pp. 21–22; Freeman, *Greek Achievement,* pp. 105–6.

7. Barnes, *Early Greek Philosophy,* pp. 81–89; Gottlieb, *Dream of Reason,* pp. 23–40; Burkert, *Greek Religion,* pp. 200–304.

8. Gottlieb, *Dream of Reason,* pp. 123–25, 138–40; Burkert, *Greek Religion,* pp. 134–35, 200.

9. Walter Burket, *Ancient Mystery Cults* (Cambridge, Mass., and London, 1986), pp. 7–9.

10. Robert Parker, *Athenian Religion: A History* (Oxford and New York, 1996), pp. 97–100; Burkert, *Ancient Mystery Cults*, pp. 7–95; Burkert, *Homo Necans: The Anthropology of Greek Sacrificial Ritual and Myth,* trans. Peter Bing (Berkeley, Los Angeles, and London, 1983), pp. 248–97.

11. Burkert, *Ancient Mystery Cults,* p. 78.

12. Demetrius, *On Style* 101, ibid., p. 79.

13. Aristotle, fragment 15, ibid., p. 89.

14. Dio of Prusa, *Oration* 12.33, ibid., pp. 89–90.

15. Plutarch, fragment 168, ibid., pp. 91–92.

16. Ibid., p. 90.

17. Cited ibid., p. 114.

18. Xenophanes B.14, B.12, B.15 in Barnes, *Early Greek Philosophy,* p. 95.

19. Xenophanes B.23, B.26, B.25, ibid., pp. 95, 97.

20. Protagoras, fragment 4, in Tarnas, *Passion of the Western Mind,* p. 28.

21. Aeschylus, *Agamemnon* 177–84 in *Aeschylus: The Oresteia,* trans. Robert Fagles (Harmondsworth, U.K., 1976).

22. Euripides, *Trojan Women* 884–88 in John Davie, trans. and ed., *Euripides: Electra and Other Plays* (London and New York, 1998).

23. Euripides, fragment 1018, in Burkert, *Greek Religion,* p. 319.

24. Plato, *Phaedrus* 274c–275b. All quotations from *Phaedrus* are from "Phaedrus," trans. Alexander Nehamas and Paul Woodruff, in John M. Cooper, ed., *Plato: The Complete Works* (Indianapolis, 1997).

25. Plato, *Phaedrus* 275d–e.

26. Plato, *Phaedrus* 276e–277a.

27. Plato, *Apology* 21d. All quotations from the *Apology* are taken from "Apology," trans. G. M. A. Grube, in Cooper, *Plato*.

28. Plato, *Phaedo* 96a. All quotations from *Phaedo* are taken from "Phaedo," trans. G. M. A. Grube, in Cooper, *Plato*.

29. Plato, *Phaedo* 98b–d.

30. Plato, *Phaedo* 98e–99a.

31. Pierre Hadot, *Philosophy as a Way of Life: Spiritual Exercises from Socrates to Foucault,* intro. and ed. Arnold I. Davidson, trans. Michael Chase (Oxford, 1995).

32. Xenophon, *Memorabilia* 4.4.10, cited in Hadot, *Philosophy,* p. 23.

33. P. Friedlander, *Plato—an Introduction,* 2 vols., trans. H. Meyenhoff (Princeton, N.J., 1969), 1:53.

34. Plato, *Symposium* 175b. All quotations from the *Symposium* are taken from "Symposium," trans. Alexander Nehemas and Paul Woodruff, in Cooper, *Plato*.

35. Plato, *Symposium* 220c.

36. Plato, "Laches" 187e–188a in "Laches," trans. Rosamund Kent Sprague, in Cooper, *Plato*.

37. Plato, *Apology* 38a.

38. Plato, *Apology* 30e–31c, 29d, 31b, 36c.

39. Hadot, *Philosophy,* pp. 152–70.

40. Ibid., pp. 91–93.

41. Plato, *Meno* 75c–d in "Meno," trans. G. M. A. Grube, in Cooper, *Plato;* my italics.

42. Plato, *Theatetus* 149a.

43. Plato, *Symposium* 211a.

44. Plato, *Symposium* 211b.

45. Plato, *Symposium* 212a.

46. Plato, *Symposium* 212a–b.

47. Plato, *Symposium* 216a.

48. Plato, *Symposium* 216e–217a.

49. Hadot, *Philosophy,* pp. 56–59.

50. Plato, *Apology* 36c.

51. Huston Smith, "Western Philosophy as a Great Religion," in *Essays on World Religion,* pp. 215–16; Josef Pieper, *Leisure, the Basis of Culture* (London, 1952), p. 77.

52. Hadot, *Philosophy,* pp. 94–96; Tarnas, *Passion of the Western Mind,* pp. 4–54; Bernard Williams, "Plato: The Invention of Philosophy," in Frederic Raphael and Ray Monk, eds., *The Great Philosophers* (London, 2000), pp. 41–75; Gottlieb, *Dream of Reason,* pp. 169–219; Burkert, *Greek Religion,* pp. 321–23.

53. Plato, *Phaedo* 67e.

54. Plato, *The Republic* 486a. Quotations from *The Republic* are taken from "The Republic," trans. G. M. A. Grube and C. D. C. Reeve, in Cooper, *Plato*.

55. Plato, *The Republic* 485d–486e.

56. Plato, *The Republic,* 571b–d.
57. Mark A. McIntosh, *Mystical Theology, The Integrity of Spirituality and Theology* (Oxford, 1998), p. 70.
58. Mircea Eliade, *The Myth of the Eternal Return, or Cosmos and History,* trans. Willard R. Trask (Princeton, N.J., 1954), pp. 34–35.
59. Plato, *Phaedrus* 250b.
60. Plato, Seventh Letter 344, in Walter Hamilton, trans., *Plato: Phaedrus and Letters VII and VIII* (London, 1973).
61. Plato, Seventh Letter 341.
62. Plato, *The Republic,* 504d–509d.
63. Plato, *The Laws* 716bc in "The Laws," trans. Trevor J. Saunders, in Cooper, *Plato;* my italics.
64. Burkert, *Greek Religion,* pp. 333–34.
65. Plato, *The Laws* 907d, 909d.
66. Plato, *Timaeus* 28c in "Timaeus,"trans. Donald J. Zeyl, in Cooper, *Plato.*
67. Plato, *Timaeus* 90a.
68. Hadot, *Philosophy,* pp. 29, 68.
69. Aristotle, *Nichomachean Ethics* 1178a. Unless otherwise stated, all quotations from Aristotle's works are taken from Richard McKeon, ed. and trans., *The Basic Works of Aristotle* (New York, 2001); italics in original.
70. Aristotle, *Nichomachean Ethics* 1177b.
71. Aristotle, *On the Parts of Animals* 645a.
72. Burkert, *Greek Religion,* p. 331.
73. Aristotle, *Metaphysics* 1072, 20–30; italics in original.
74. Hadot, *Philosophy,* pp. 60–65.
75. Freeman, *Greek Achievement,* pp. 362–65.
76. Gottlieb, *Dream of Reason,* pp. 283–345; Tarnas, *Passion of the Western Mind,* pp. 73–85; Hadot, *Philosophy,* pp. 57–60, 80–89, 103–4.
77. Epicurus, letter to Pythoclus 85 in A. A. Long and D. N. Sedely, *The Hellenistic Philosophers: Translations of the Principal Sources with Philosophical Commentary,* 2 vols., (Cambridge, U.K., 1987), 1:91–92.
78. Epicurus, *Letter to Menoecius* 125, ibid., 1:149–50.
79. Hadot, *Philosophy,* p. 266.
80. Proverbs 8:30–31.
81. Ben Sirah 24:3–6.
82. *The Wisdom of Solomon* 7:25–26.
83. Philo, *The Special Laws* 1.43.

FOUR Faith

1. Douglas Harman Akenson, *Surpassing Wonder: The Invention of the Bible and the Talmuds* (New York, San Diego, and London, 1998), pp. 19–209.
2. Ibid., pp. 319–25.
3. B. Shabbat 31a in A. Cohen, ed., *Everyman's Talmud* (New York, 1975), p. 65. Some authorities attribute this story to another rabbi.
4. Aboth de Rabbi Nathan I. N, 11a in C. G. Montefiore and H. Loewe, eds., *A Rabbinic Anthology* (New York, 1976), pp. 430–31.
5. Sifra on Leviticus 19:11 in Samuel Belkin, *In His Image: The Jewish Philosophy of Man as Expressed in Rabbinic Tradition* (London, 1960), p. 241.

6. Genesis 5:1 in Montefiore and Loewe, *A Rabbinic Anthology,* p. xl.

7. Mekhilta on Exodus 20.13 in Belkin, *In His Image,* p. 50.

8. B. Sanhedrin 4:5.

9. Baba Metziah 58b.

10. Arakim 15b.

11. M. Avoth 6:1; Michael Fishbane, *The Garments of Torah: Essays in Biblical Hermeneutics* (Bloomington and Indianapolis, 1989), p. 77.

12. M. Pirke Avoth 3:3 in Montefiore and Loewe, *A Rabbinic Anthology,* p. 23.

13. J. Hagigah 2.1.

14. Midrash Rabbah 1.10.2 in Gerald Bruns, "Midrash and Allegory: The Beginnings of Scriptural Interpretation," in Robert Alter and Frank Kermode, eds., *The Literary Guide to the Bible* (London, 1987), p. 627.

15. Matthew 5:39–48; 26:53; Luke 22:34.

16. 1 Corinthians 15:3–8.

17. Acts 4:32–5; Matthew 5:3–12; Luke 6:20–23; Matthew 5:38–48; Luke 6:27–38; Romans 12:9–13, 14; 1 Corinthians 6:7; Akenson, *Surpassing Wonder,* p. 102; Paula Fredricksen, *Jesus of Nazareth, King of the Jews: A Jewish Life and the Emergence of Christianity* (London, 2000), p. 243.

18. Matthew 5:17–19; Luke 16:17; 23:56; Galatians 2:11–12.

19. Matthew 7:12; Luke 6:31; see Romans 13:10.

20. Acts 2:1–13.

21. Acts 8:1, 18; 9:2; 11:19.

22. Isaiah 2:2–3; Zephaniah 3:9; Tobit 14:6; Zechariah 8:23.

23. Romans 8:9; Galatians 4:16; Fredricksen, *Jesus,* pp. 133–35.

24. 1 Corinthians 1:22.

25. Mark 13:14; Daniel 9:27.

26. Mark 11:15–19; Isaiah 56:7; Jeremiah 7:11.

27. Matthew 18:20.

28. I have discussed this more fully in *The Bible: A Biography* (London, 2007), pp. 55–78.

29. Luke is traditionally held to be a gentile, but there is no hard evidence for this, and his gospel gives a more positive account of Judaism than any of the others.

30. Luke 24:13–35; Julia Galambush, *The Reluctant Parting: How the New Testament's Jewish Writers Created a Christian Book* (San Francisco, 2005), pp. 67–68; Gabriel Josipovici, "The Epistle to the Hebrews and the Catholic Epistles," in Alter and Kermode, *The Literary Guide to the Bible,* pp. 506–7.

31. Philippians 2:6–11.

32. Philippians 2:2–4.

33. Exodus 4:22; Hosea 11:1; see Romans 8:14–17; Galatians 4:4–7.

34. Matthew 7:11.

35. Mark 6:3.

36. Mark 6:4; see Luke 24:19.

37. Romans 1:4.

38. Mark 1:11; Luke 3:22; see Psalm 2:7.

39. Matthew 17:5.

40. See, for example, Luke 8:25; Matthew 8:10; 13:58; 15:28.

41. Mark 9:24–25.

42. This has been explored exhaustively by Wilfred Cantwell Smith in *Belief and History* (Charlottesville, Va., 1977) and *Faith and Belief* (Princeton, N.J., 1979), and I rely greatly on his thesis in these pages.

43. Mark 11:22–23.
44. *Oxford English Dictionary,* 1888; Smith, *Belief in History,* p. 110.
45. Smith, *Belief in History,* pp. 41–44.
46. *All's Well That Ends Well,* act 2, scene 3, line 59.
47. E. P. Sanders, *The Historical Figure of Jesus* (London, 1993), pp. 133–68; Fredricksen, *Jesus,* pp. 110–17; John Dominic Crossan, *The Birth of Christianity: Discovering What Happened in the Years Immediately After the Execution of Jesus* (San Francisco, 1998), pp. 302–4.
48. Geza Vermes, *Jesus the Jew: A Historian's Reading of the Gospels* (London, 1973), pp. 69–78.
49. Matthew 17:20.
50. Mark 1.44; 8:26; 7:36.
51. Matthew 8:17; Isaiah 53:4.
52. Luke 7:11–17; see 1 Kings 17:9, 17–24.
53. Mark 6:52.
54. Matthew 14:33.
55. Matthew 14:27–31; 16:21–33; 26:46.
56. Matthew 12:28; Luke 10:17.
57. Deuteronomy 30:12.
58. Baba Metziah 59b in Montefiore and Loewe, *A Rabbinic Anthology,* pp. 340–41.
59. Fishbane, *Garments of Torah,* pp. 64–65.
60. B. Menahoth 29b.
61. Midrash Rabbah on Numbers 19:6, in Bruns, "Midrash and Allegory," p. 632.
62. Eliyahu Zatta 2.
63. Bruns, "Midrash and Allegory," p. 629.
64. Fishbane, *Garments of Torah,* p. 37.
65. Ibid., pp. 22–32.
66. Jacob Neusner, *Medium and Message in Judaism* (Atlanta, 1989), p. 3; Jacob Neusner, "The Mishnah in Philosophical Context and Out of Canonical Bounds," *Journal of Biblical Literature* 11 (Summer 1993); Akenson, *Surpassing Wonder,* pp. 305–20.
67. Louis Jacobs, *The Talmudic Argument: A Study in Talmudic Reasoning and Methodology* (Cambridge, U.K., 1983), pp. 20–23, 203–13.
68. B. Baba Batara 12a.
69. Jaroslav Pelikan, *Whose Bible Is It? A History of the Scriptures Through the Ages* (New York, 2005), pp. 67–68.
70. Akenson, *Surpassing Wonder,* p. 379.
71. B. Qedoshim 49b; Smith, *What Is Scripture? A Comparative Approach* (London, 1993), pp. 116–17.
72. John 1:1.
73. Origen, *On First Principles* 4.2.9, in G. W. Butterworth, trans., *Origen: On First Principles* (Gloucester, Mass., 1973).
74. Origen, *On First Principles* 4.2.7.
75. Origen, *On First Principles* 4.1.6.
76. Origen, *On First Principles* preface, 8.
77. Mark A. McIntosh, *Mystical Theology: The Integrity of Spirituality and Theology* (Oxford, 1998), pp. 42–43.
78. Origen, commentary on John 6:1, in R. R. Reno, "Origen," in Justin S. Holcomb, ed., *Christian Theologies of Scripture: A Comparative Introduction* (New York and London, 2006), p. 28.

79. Smith, *What Is Scripture?*, p. 19.

80. F. L. Cross, ed. and trans., *St. Cyril of Jerusalem's Lectures on the Christian Sacraments: The Procatechesis and the Five Mystagogical Cathecheses* (London, 1951).

81. John Meyendorff, "Eastern Liturgical Theology," in Bernard McGinn and John Meyendorff, eds., *Christian Spirituality: Origins to the Twelfth Century* (London, 1986), pp. 353–56.

82. Mystagogical Cathechesis 3:1. Cross translation.

83. Theodore, *Ad Baptizandos,* Homily 13:14 in Wilfred Cantwell Smith, *Faith and Belief* (Princeton, N.J., 1979), p. 259.

84. Smith, *Faith and Belief,* pp. 37–47.

85. *The Message of the Qur'an,* trans. Muhammad Asad (Gibraltar, 1980), 3:64–68; 10:36; 41:23.

86. Qur'an 92:18; 9:103; 63:9; 102:1.

87. Qur'an 90:13–20.

88. Toshiko Izutsu, *Ethico-Religious Concepts in the Qur'an* (Montreal and Kingston, Ont., 2002), pp. 127–57.

89. Qur'an 29:61–63; 2:89; 27:14.

90. Qur'an 7:75–76; 39:59; 31:17–18; 23:4547; 38:71–75.

91. Qur'an 15:94–96; 21:36; 18:106; 40:4–5; 68:56; 22:8–9.

92. Izutsu, *Ethico-Religious Concepts,* pp. 28–45.

93. Ibid., 68–69; Qur'an 14:47; 39:37; 15:79; 30:47; 44:16.

94. Qur'an 25:63.

95. Qur'an 2:89; 16:33; 27:14; 2:34; 2:146. W. Montgomery Watt, *Muhammad at Mecca* (Oxford, 1953), p. 68.

96. Qur'an 3:84.

97. Qur'an 12:11; 5:69.

98. Qur'an 5:48.

99. Qur'an 24:35.

100. Qur'an 29:46.

101. Qur'an, 22:36–40; 2:190.

102. I have discussed this at length in my biography *Muhammad: A Prophet for Our Time* (London and New York, 2006), pp. 163–80.

FIVE  Silence

1. Clement, *Exhortation to the Greeks* 4.63.6; Jaroslav Pelikan, *The Christian Tradition: A History of the Development of Doctrine,* 5 vols. (Chicago and London, 1971–89), 1:36.

2. Irenaeus, *Against Heresies* 30.9.

3. John 1.14.

4. John 1.3.

5. John 1.1.

6. Proverbs 8:22.

7. Robert C. Gregg and Dennis E. Groh, *Early Arianism—a View of Salvation* (London, 1981), pp. 20–28.

8. G. L. Prestige, *God in Patristic Thought* (London, 1952), pp. 146–56, 197–223; Pelikan, *The Christian Tradition,* 1:194–210; Gregg and Groh, *Early Arianism*; Rowan Williams, *Arius: Heresy and Tradition* (London, 1987); Andrew

Louth, *The Origins of Christian Mysticism: From Plato to Denys* (Oxford, 1981), pp. 76–77.

9. David Christie Murray, *A History of Heresy* (Oxford and New York, 1976), p. 46.

10. John Meyendorff, "Eastern Liturgical Theology," in Bernard McGinn and John Meyendorff, eds., *Christian Spirituality: Origins to the Twelfth Century* (London, 1986), p. 354.

11. Pelikan, *The Christian Tradition,* 1:200.

12. Arius, *Epistle to Alexander* 2; Pelikan, *The Christian Tradition,* 1:194.

13. Athanasius, *On the Decrees of the Synod of Nicaea* 8.1; Pelikan, *The Christian Tradition,* 1:195.

14. Athanasius, *Against the Arians* 2.23–24.

15. Ralph Norman, "Rediscovery of Mysticism," in Gareth Jones, ed., *The Blackwell Companion to Modern Theology* (Oxford, 2004), pp. 456–58.

16. Athanasius, *Against the Arians* 1.18 in W. G. Rusch, ed., *The Trinitarian Controversy* (Philadelphia, 1980), p. 78.

17. Athanasius, *Against the Arians* 1.28, ibid., p. 84.

18. Athanasius, *On the Incarnation* 54; Louth, *Origins of Christian Mysticism,* p. 78.

19. Pelikan, *The Christian Tradition,* 1:201–4.

20. The so-called Nicene Creed was not written at Nicaea but at the Council of Constantinople in 381.

21. Maximus, *Ambigua* 42 in Andrew Louth, trans., *Maximus the Confessor* (London, 1996).

22. Maximus, *Ambigua* 5.

23. Pierre Hadot, *Philosophy as a Way of Life: Spiritual Exercises from Socrates to Foucault,* intro. and ed. Arnold I. Davidson, trans. Michael Chase (Oxford, 1995), pp. 129–32.

24. Kallistos Ware, "Ways of Prayer and Contemplation: Eastern," in McGinn and Meyendorff, *Christian Spirituality,* pp. 395–401.

25. Evagrius, *On Prayer* 67, 71 in G. E. H. Palmer, P. Sherrard, and K. Ware, eds. and trans., *The Philokalia* (London, 1979).

26. Evagrius, *On Prayer* 120.

27. A. J. Moore, *Fifty Spiritual Homilies of St Macarius the Egyptian* (London, 1921), pp. 116, 122.

28. Louis Bouyer, "Mysticism: An Essay on the History of the Word," in Richard Woods, ed., *Understanding Mysticism* (New York, 1980), pp. 42–44.

29. Sarah Coakley, ed., *Rethinking Gregory of Nyssa* (Oxford, 2003); Louth, *Origins of Christian Mysticism,* pp. 80–95.

30. Gregory, *Commentary on the Song of Songs* 12.1037, trans. C. McCambley (Brookline, Mass., 1987).

31. Gregory, *Commentary on the Song of Songs* 11.1000–1001.

32. Gregory, *The Life of Moses* 2.24, trans. A. J. Malherbe and E. Ferguson (New York, 1978).

33. Gregory, *The Life of Moses* 2.165.

34. John 1.1; Basil, *On the Holy Spirit,* ed. and trans. C. F. H. Johnston (Oxford, 1892), pp. 8–9.

35. Basil, Epistle 234.1.

36. Paul, 2 Corinthians 3:18.

37. Norman, "Rediscovery of Mysticism," p. 258.

38. Prestige, *God in Patristic Thought,* pp. 76–300; Pelikan, *The Christian*

*Tradition,* 1:52–67, 172–226; Thomas Hopko, "The Trinity in the Cappadocians," in McGinn and Meyendorff, *Christian Spirituality,* pp. 261–73; Lars Thurberg, "The Human Person and the Image of God: Eastern," ibid., pp. 292–308; Raimundo Panikkar, *The Trinity and the Religious Experience of Man* (London and New York, 1973); John Meyendorff, *Byzantine Theology: Historical Trends and Doctrinal Themes* (New York and London, 1975), pp. 131–80.

39. Gregory of Nazianzus, Oratio 29:6–20.

40. Basil, Epistle 38.4.

41. Basil, *On the Holy Spirit* 28.66; Andrew Louth, *Discerning the Mystery: An Essay on the Nature of Theology* (Oxford, 1983), pp. 85–90.

42. Louth, *Discerning the Mystery,* p. 46.

43. Gregory of Nazianzus, Oratio 40.41; Vladimir Lossky, *The Mystical Theology of the Eastern Church* (London, 1957), pp. 45–46.

44. Leonid Ouspensky, "Icon and Art," in McGinn and Meyendorff, *Christian Spirituality,* pp. 382–90.

45. Rowan Williams, "The Deflections of Desire: Negative Theology in Trinitarian Disclosure," in Oliver Davies and Denys Turner, eds., *Silence and the Word: Negative Theology and Incarnation* (Cambridge, U.K., 2002), pp. 128–30.

46. Panikkar, *Trinity,* pp. 46–67.

47. Peter Brown, *Augustine of Hippo: A Biography* (London, 1967); Louth, *Origins of Christian Mysticism,* pp. 139–56; Prestige, *God in Patristic Thought,* pp. 235–37; Mary T. Clark, "The Trinity in Latin Christianity," in McGinn and Meyendorff, *Christian Spirituality,* pp. 282–85; Denys Turner, *The Darkness of God: Negativity in Christian Mysticism* (Cambridge, 1995), pp. 50–101.

48. Augustine, *The Confessions* 8.12.29. All quotations from *The Confessions* are taken from Philip Burton, trans. and ed., *Augustine: The Confessions,* intro. by Robin Lane Fox (London, 2001).

49. Augustine, *Confessions* 10.27.38.

50. Augustine, *Confessions* 10.25.36.

51. Augustine, *Confessions* 10.6.9; John 18:25; Psalms 100.2; 99.3.

52. Augustine, *Confessions* 10.7.11.

53. Augustine, *Confessions* 10.6.8.

54. Ibid.

55. Augustine, *Confessions* 10.17.26.

56. Denys Turner, *Faith, Reason and the Existence of God* (Cambridge, U.K., 2004), pp. 81–83.

57. Augustine, *Confessions,* 7.17.23.

58. Augustine, *Ennarationes in Psalmis* 134.6; Turner, *Faith, Reason,* p. 83.

59. Augustine, *The City of God* 22.24.2; Augustine, *On Contemplation* 1.5; Turner, *Faith, Reason,* pp. 82, 83.

60. Augustine, *On the Trinity* 10.11.18 in Edmund Hill, OP, trans., *Augustine: The Trinity* (New York, 1994).

61. McIntosh, *Mystical Theology,* p. 70.

62. Augustine, *Confessions* 13.15.18.

63. Psalm 103:2.

64. Augustine, *The Literal Sense of Genesis* 1.18, 19, 21.

65. Augustine, *Confessions* 12.25.35.

66. D. W. Robertson, trans., *Augustine: On Christian Doctrine* (Indianapolis, 1958), p. 30.

67. Acts 17:34.

68. Denys Turner, "Apophaticism, Idolatry and the Claims of Reason," in Davies and Turner, *Silence and the Word,* pp. 16–21; Turner, *Darkness of God,* pp. 12–49, 252–72; McIntosh, *Mystical Theology,* pp. 46–56; Andrew Louth, *Denys the Areopagite* (Wilton, Conn., 1989); Paul Rorem, "The Uplifting Spirituality of Pseudo-Dionysius," in McGinn and Meyndorff, *Christian Spirituality,* pp. 132–49; Paul Rorem, *Biblical and Liturgical Symbols Within the Pseudo-Dionysian Synthesis* (Toronto, 1984); Norman, "Rediscovery of Mysticism," pp. 454–55, 459.

69. Denys, *The Divine Names* (hereafter *DN*) 712A–B. Quotations from Denys's writings are taken from Colm Luibheid and Paul Rorem, trans., *Pseudo-Dionysus: The Complete Works* (Mahwah, N.J., and London, 1987).

70. *DN* 596A.

71. Denys, *The Celestial Hierarchies* 141A–B.

72. Denys, Epistle 9, 1104D–1105B.

73. Denys, *Mystical Theology* (hereafter *MT*), 1033B.

74. *MT* 1048A.

75. *DN* 872A; my italics.

76. *MT* 1048B.

77. *MT* 1048A.

78. *DN* 817D.

79. *DN* 981B.

80. *MT* 1000c–1001A.

81. Rorem, *Biblical and Liturgical Symbols;* Turner, *Darkness of God,* pp. 258–59, 272; McIntosh, *Mystical Theology,* pp. 45, 54–56; Louth, *Denys,* pp. 24, 29–31, 101–9.

82. *MT* 1033C; my italics.

83. Meyendorff, "Eastern Liturgical Theology," pp. 358–59.

84. *MT* 1000C.

85. *DN* 864A.

six  Faith and Reason

1. P. A. Sigal, "Et les marcheurs de Dieu prirent leurs armes," *L'Histoire* 47 (1982); Ronald C. Finucane, *Pilgrims, Popular Beliefs in Medieval Europe* (London, 1977).

2. R. W. Southern, ed. and trans., *Vita Sancti Anselmi by Eadmer* (Oxford, 1962); Benedicta Ward, ed. and trans., *The Prayers and Meditations of St. Anselm with the Proslogion,* intro. by R. W. Southern (London and New York, 1973); Ward, "Anselm of Canterbury and His Influence" in Jill Raitt, ed., *Christian Spirituality: High Middle Ages and Reformation* (New York, 1988; London, 1989), pp. 197–203; Jaroslav Pelikan, *The Christian Tradition: A History of the Development of Doctrine,* 5 vols. (Chicago and London, 1971–89), 3:106–44, 257–63; John Macquarrie, *In Search of Deity: An Essay in Dialectical Theism* (London, 1984), pp. 201–2.

3. Anselm, Epistle 136 in Pelikan, *Christian Tradition,* 3:258.

4. Anselm, *Proslogion* 1.143–45 in Ward, trans., *Meditations and Prayers.*

5. Anselm, *Monologion* 32, 68 in F. S. Schmitt, ed., *Sancti Anselmi Cantuariensis archiepiscopi opera omnia,* 6 vols. (Edinburgh, 1938–61). My translation.

6. Anselm, *Proslogion* 1.150–51. Ward translation.

7. Anselm, *Proslogion* 1.153–57. My translation. See Wilfred Cantwell Smith, *Belief in History* (Charlottesville, Va., 1985), pp. 312–13.

8. Anselm, *Proslogion* 2.159. Ward translation.

9. Anselm, *Proslogion* 2.161. My translation. See Macquarrie, *In Search of Deity,* p. 201, who argues that the idea of "perfection" is included in *maius* as well as "greatness."

10. Anselm, *Proslogion* 3.197–98. Ward translation; my italics.

11. Psalm 14:1.

12. Anselm, *Proslogion* 2.180–83. Ward translation.

13. Anselm, *Proslogion* 2.180–86.

14. See Macquarrie, *In Search of Deity,* pp. 201–2.

15. Jean Leclerq, "Ways of Prayer and Contemplation: West," in Bernard McGinn and John Meyendorff, eds., *Christian Spirituality: Origins to the Twelfth Century* (London, 1986), pp. 417–25.

16. Anselm, *Prayers and Meditations,* preface. Ward translation.

17. Ibid.

18. Anselm, *Proslogion,* preface. Ward translation.

19. Ibid.

20. Southern, *Vita Sancti Anselmi,* p. 20.

21. Ibid.

22. I have discussed the philosophical movement in Islam and Judaism and explored its implications in greater detail in *A History of God: The 4000-Year Quest of Judaism, Christianity, and Islam* (New York, 1993), pp. 170–208.

23. Quoted in S. H. Nasr, "Theology and Spirituality," in *Islamic Spirituality: Manifestations,* ed. S. H. Nasr (London, 1991), p. 411.

24. From the *Rasa'il,* a tenth-century Ismaili text, quoted in Majid Fakhry, *A History of Islamic Philosophy* (New York and London, 1970), p. 187.

25. W. Montgomery Watt, *Muslim Intellectual: The Struggle and Achievement of al-Ghazzali* (Edinburgh, 1963), pp. 133–40.

26. Maimonides, *The Guide to the Perplexed,* trans. M. Friedlander (London, 1936), p. 87.

27. Moshe Idel, "PaRDeS: Some Reflections on Kabbalistic Hermaneutics," in John Collins and Michael Fishbane, eds., *Death, Ecstasy, and Other Worldly Journeys* (Albany, N.Y., 1995), pp. 249–57.

28. Brian Davies, *The Thought of Thomas Aquinas* (Oxford, 1992); Denys Turner, *Faith, Reason and the Existence of God* (Cambridge, U.K., 2004); Denys Turner, "Apophaticism, Idolatry and the Claims of Reason," in Oliver Davies and Denys Turner, eds., *Silence and the Word, Negative Theology and Incarnation* (Cambridge, U.K., 2002), pp. 23–34; Herbert McCabe, *God Matters* (London, 1987); Herbert McCabe, "Aquinas on the Trinity," in Davies and Turner, *Silence and the Word,* pp. 76–92; Antony Kenny, *The Five Ways* (London, 1969); Etienne Gilson, *L'Esprit de la philosophie medieval* (Paris, 1944); Pelikan, *The Christian Tradition,* 3:268–307; Ralph Norman, "Rediscovery of Mysticism," in Gareth Jones, ed., *The Blackwell Companion to Modern Theology* (Oxford, 2004), pp. 463–64.

29. Thomas, *Summa contra gentiles* 1.5.3. in *Thomas Aquinas: Selected Writings,* trans. R. McInery (Harmondsworth, U.K., 1998).

30. Ephesians 1.21; Thomas, *Commentary on St. Paul's Epistle to the Ephesians,* trans. M. L. Lamb (Albany, 1966), pp. 78–79.

31. Thomas, *Summa theologiae* (hereafter *ST*) 1a. Unless otherwise stated, all quotations from *ST* are taken from Timothy McDermott, trans. and ed., *St*

*Thomas Aquinas, Summa Theologiae: A Concise Translation* (London, 1989), p. 11.

32. Ephesians 1:20.
33. *ST* Ia.2, pp. 11–12; my italics.
34. *ST* Ia q.3 in McCabe, "Aquinas on the Trinity," p. 77; McCabe's italics.
35. *ST* Ia.2–11, pp. 12–15.
36. J. J. C. Smart and J. J. Haldane, *Atheism and Theism* (Oxford, 2003), pp. 126–37.
37. Herbert McCabe, appendix 3 to vol. 3 of the Blackfriars edition of the *Summa Theologiae;* Davies, *Thought of Thomas Aquinas*, p. 41.
38. *ST* Ia q.3.1–5, pp. 14–15.
39. Turner, *Faith, Reason*, p. 226.
40. Ibid., p. 121.
41. *ST* 2.2.4.5 as translated in Wilfred Cantwell Smith, *Faith and Belief* (Princeton, N.J., 1979), p. 87.
42. *"Credere [est] actus intellectus assentientis vero ex imperio voluntate"* (*ST* 2.2.4.5), translated ibid., p. 280.
43. Smith, *Faith and Belief*, pp. 87–89, 294–95.
44. *ST* 2.2.14.1; 2.2.1.2.
45. *ST* 8.46.2.
46. Pelikan, *The Christian Tradition*, 3:286, 305–6; Denys Turner, *The Darkness of God: Negativity in Christian Mysticism* (Cambridge, U.K., 1995), pp. 103–34; Turner, *Faith, Reason*, pp. 27–28, 52–62.
47. Bonaventure, *The Journey of the Mind to God* (hereafter *JMG*) 6.2. Quotations from Bonaventure's works are taken from Philotheus Boehner and M. Frances Laughlin, eds. and trans., *The Works of Saint Bonaventure*, 2 vols. (New York, 1958).
48. *JMG* 3.1.
49. *JMG* 5.3.
50. *JMG* 5.4.
51. Ibid.
52. *JMG* 6.3.
53. Ibid.
54. *JMG* 6.7.
55. *JMG* 6.5.
56. *JMG* 6.7.
57. John 13:1.
58. John 14:8.
59. *JMG* 7.6.
60. Richard Cross, *Duns Scotus* (Oxford, 1999); William A. Frank and Allan B. Walter, *Duns Scotus, Metaphysician* (West LaFayette, Ind., 1995); Turner, *Faith, Reason*, pp. 85–88, 125–49.
61. *ST* 1.13.10.
62. Scotus, *Ordinatio* 1 d.3, 35 in Turner, *Faith, Reason*, p. 143.
63. Scotus, *Ordinatio* 1 d.3 q.1, ibid., p. 131.
64. Eric Alliez, *Capital Times: Tales from the Concept of Time*, trans. George Van De Abbeele (Minneapolis, 1996), p. 226.
65. Scotus, *Quodlibet* q.5 a.7.
66. Scotus, *Ordinatio* 1 d.3 q.1.1–2; Cross, *Duns Scotus*, p. 39.
67. Thomas was not named in the 1277 Condemnations and those directed against him were withdrawn in 1325.

68. Edward Grant, "Science and Theology in the Middle Ages," in David C. Lindberg and Ronald L. Numbers, eds., *God and Nature: Historical Essays on the Encounter Between Christianity and Science* (Berkeley, Los Angeles, and London, 1986).

69. Amos Funkenstein, *Theology and the Scientific Imagination: From the Middle Ages to the Seventeenth Century* (Princeton, N.J., 1986), pp. 10–11, 121–22.

70. Ibid., pp. 55–58.

71. Ibid., pp. 307–12.

72. Grant, "Science and Theology," p. 61.

73. Edward Grant, *Much Ado About Nothing: Theories of Space and Vacuum from the Middle Ages* (Cambridge, U.K., 1981), pp. 260–64.

74. Edward Grant, "The Condemnations of 1277: God's Absolute Power and Physical Thought in the Late Middle Ages," *Viator* 10 (1979).

75. Grant, "Science and Theology," pp. 57–59.

76. Funkenstein, *Theology and the Scientific Imagination,* p. 11.

77. Turner, *Faith, Reason,* pp. 76–78.

78. Turner, *Darkness of God,* pp. 214–15. The great exception was Nicholas of Cusa.

79. Hans Urs von Balthasar, "Theology and Holiness," *Communio* 14 (Winter 1987); Mark A. McIntosh, *Mystical Theology: The Integrity of Spirituality and Theology* (Oxford, 1998), pp. 63–69; Colin Morris, *The Discovery of the Individual, 1050–1200* (New York, 1972), pp. 70–77, 139–52.

80. Clifford Wolters, trans. and ed., *Richard Rolle: The Fire of Love* (London, 1972), p. 45.

81. Ibid.

82. Ibid., p. 46.

83. Ibid., p. 61.

84. Rowan Williams, *The Wound of Knowledge: Christian Spirituality from the New Testament to St. John of the Cross* (Cambridge, Mass., 1991), pp. 140–42.

85. McIntosh, *Mystical Theology,* p. 74.

86. Turner, *Darkness of God,* pp. 137–85; Oliver Davies, *Meister Eckhart: Mystical Theologian* (London, 1991); Bernard McGinn, Frank Tobin, and Elvira Borgstadt, eds., *Meister Eckhart, Teacher and Preacher* (New York, 1986); J. C. Clark, *Meister Eckhart: An Introduction to the Study of His Works with an Anthology of His Sermons* (New York, 1957).

87. Eckhart, Sermon 2 in Edmund Colledge and Bernard McGinn, trans., *Meister Eckhart: The Essential Sermons, Commentaries, Treatises and Defense* (New York, 1981), p. 180.

88. Quoted Oliver Davies, *God Within* (London, 1988), p. 51.

89. Turner, *Darkness of God,* pp. 171–72.

90. Eckhart, *On Detachment,* in Colledge and McGinn, trans., *Essential Sermons,* p. 286.

91. Eckhart, Sermon 5b, ibid., p. 183.

92. Eckhart, Sermon 52, ibid., p. 201.

93. Eckhart, *Renovamini Spiritum,* ibid., p. 208.

94. Julian, *Revelations of Divine Love* 58, trans. Clifford Wolters (London and Harmondsworth, U.K., 1966), p. 166.

95. Turner, *Darkness of God,* pp. 186–210.

96. *Cloud* 6 in Clifton Wolters, trans. and ed., *The Cloud of Unknowing and Other Works* (Harmondsworth, U.K., and New York, 1961), p. 68.

97. *Cloud* 3, pp. 61–62.

98. *Cloud* 6, p. 67.
99. Ibid.
100. *Cloud* 7, pp. 68–69.
101. *Cloud* 6, p. 68.
102. *Cloud* 45, pp. 113–14.
103. Ibid.
104. *Cloud* 52, p. 122.
105. *Cloud* 68, p. 142.
106. Ibid.
107. Ibid.
108. *Cloud* 68, pp. 142–43.
109. *Cloud* 68, p. 143.
110. Ibid.
111. *Cloud* 3, p. 61.
112. Denys the Carthusian, *De contemplatione* 3.3; Turner, *Darkness of God*, p. 218.

SEVEN  Science and Religion

1. Friedrich Heer, *The Medieval World, 1100–1350,* trans. Janet Sondheimer (London, 1962), p. 318.
2. Paul Johnson, *A History of the Jews* (London, 1987), p. 229.
3. Yirmanyahu Yovel, *The Marrano of Reason,* vol. 1 of *Spinoza and Other Heretics* (Princeton, N.J., 1989), pp. 17–18.
4. Ibid., pp. 19–24.
5. Ibid., pp. 75–76.
6. Gershom Scholem, *Major Trends in Jewish Mysticism* (London, 1955), pp. 246–49.
7. Ibid., 245–800; Gershom Scholem, *The Messianic Idea in Judaism and Other Essays on Jewish Spirituality* (New York, 1971), pp. 43–48.
8. Gershom Scholem, *Sabbatai Sevi: The Mystical Messiah* (London and Princeton, N.J., 1973), pp. 37–42.
9. Ibid., pp. 23–25.
10. R. J. Werblowsky, "The Safed Revival and Its Aftermath," in Arthur Green, ed., *Jewish Spirituality,* 2 vols. (London, 1986, 1989), 2:15–19, 21–24; Lawrence Fine, "The Contemplative Practice of Yehudin in Lurianic Kabbalah," ibid., 2:73–78, 89–90; Louis Jacobs, "The Uplifting of the Sparks in Later Jewish Mysticism," ibid., 2:108–11; Gershom Scholem, *On the Kabbalah and Its Symbolism* (New York, 1965), p. 150.
11. Werblowsky, "The Safed Revival," in Green, *Jewish Spirituality,* 2:17; Jacob Katz, "Halakah and Kabbalah as Competing Disciplines of Study," ibid., 2:52–53.
12. Marshall G. S. Hodgson, *The Venture of Islam: Conscience and History in a World Civilization,* 3 vols. (Chicago and London, 1974), 2:334–60.
13. Robin Briggs, "Embattled Faiths: Religion and Natural Philosophy," in Euan Cameron, ed., *Early Modern Europe* (Oxford, 1999), pp. 197–205.
14. Richard Tarnas, *The Passion of the Western Mind: Understanding the Ideas That Have Shaped Our World View* (New York and London, 1991), p. 230.
15. Ibid., pp. 240–42.
16. Valla, *Encomion Sancti Thomae Aquinatis,* in James D. Tracy, "*Ad Fontes*: The Humanist Understanding of Scripture," in Jill Raitt, ed., *Christian Spir-*

*ituality: High Middle Ages and Renaissance* (London and New York, 1988), p. 244.

17. Petrarch to his brother Gherado, 2 December 1348, in David Thompson, ed., *Petrarch, a Humanist Among Princes: An Anthology of Petrarch's Letters and Translations from His Works* (New York, 1971), p. 90.

18. Stephen Toulmin, *Cosmopolis: The Hidden Agenda of Modernity* (New York, 1990), pp. 25–32.

19. Andrew Louth, *Discerning the Mystery: An Essay on the Nature of Theology* (Oxford, 1983), p. 54.

20. Ibid.

21. Tracy, *"Ad Fontes,"* p. 249.

22. Alister E. McGrath, *The Intellectual Origins of the European Reformation* (Oxford and New York, 1987), p. 200; Alister E. McGrath, *Reformation Thought: An Introduction* (Oxford and New York, 1988), p. 20.

23. Tarnas, *Passion of the Western Mind,* pp. 239–40; McGrath, *Intellectual Origins,* p. 197.

24. John Bossy, *Christianity in the West, 1400 to 1700* (Oxford and New York, 1985), pp. 91–93.

25. McGrath, *Reformation Thought,* p. 73.

26. Richard Marius, *Martin Luther: The Christian Between God and Death* (Cambridge, Mass., and London, 1999), pp. 73–74, 214–15, 486–87.

27. McGrath, *Intellectual Origins,* pp. 27, 199.

28. Habakkuk 2:4; Romans 1:17.

29. McGrath, *Reformation Thought,* p. 74.

30. Bossy, *Christianity in the West,* p. 94.

31. McGrath, *Reformation Thought,* pp. 73–74.

32. Ibid., p. 87.

33. Alastair McGrath, *A Life of John Calvin: A Study in the Shaping of Western Culture* (Oxford, 1990), p. 90.

34. Luther, Sermon 25:7, in Jaroslav Pelikan, *The Christian Tradition: A History of the Development of Doctrine,* 5 vols. (Chicago and London, 1971–89), 4:163.

35. Luther, Heidelberg Disputation 19–21, ibid., 4:155.

36. Ibid., 4:154.

37. Luther, Sermon 15, ibid., 4:166.

38. Tarnas, *Passion of the Western Mind,* pp. 240–42.

39. Bossy, *Christianity in the West,* p. 97.

40. Euan Cameron, "The Power of the Word: Renaissance and Reformation," in Cameron, *Early Modern Europe,* pp. 91–95.

41. James Turner, *Without God, Without Creed: The Origins of Unbelief in America* (Baltimore, 1985), pp. 10–11, 19–20.

42. Tarnas, *Passion of the Western Mind,* p. 242.

43. Cameron, "Power of the Word," pp. 88–89.

44. John Bossy, "The Counter-Reformation and the People of Catholic Europe," *Past and Present* (May 1970).

45. A. N. Galpern, *The Religions of the People in Sixteenth-Century Champagne* (Cambridge, Mass., 1976), p. 157; Benedict Philip, "The Catholic Response to Protestantism: Church Activity and Popular Piety in Rouen, 1560–1600," in James Obelkevich, ed., *Religion and the People, 800–1700* (Chapel Hill, N.C., 1979), p. 175.

46. Cameron, "Power of the Word," p. 78.

47. Ibid., pp. 78–80; Robert S. Westman, "The Copernicans and the Churches," in David C. Lindberg and Ronald L. Numbers, eds., *God and Nature: Historical Essays on the Encounter Between Christianity and Science* (Berkeley, Los Angeles, and London, 1986), pp. 76–80; Tarnas, *Passion of the Western Mind,* pp. 248–253; Thomas Kuhn, *The Copernican Revolution: Planetary Astronomy in the Development of Western Thought* (Cambridge, Mass., 1957).

48. Psalms 93:1; 103:4; Ecclesiastes 1:4.

49. Edward Rosen, trans. and ed., *Nicholas Copernicus: On the Revolutions* (Warsaw and Cracow, 1978), p. xvi.

50. Westman, "The Copernicans," p. 82.

51. John Calvin, Commentary on Genesis 1.16 in *The Commentaries of John Calvin on the Old Testament,* 30 vols. (Calvin Translation Society, 1643–48), 1:86.

52. Calvin, Commentary on Genesis 1:6, ibid. 1:79–80.

53. Frances Yates, *Giordano Bruno and the Hermetic Tradition* (Chicago, 1964).

54. J. L. Heibron, *The Sun in the Church: Cathedrals as Solar Observatories* (Cambridge, Mass., 1999), p. 10.

55. Michael J. Buckley, "The New Science and the Ancient Faith: Three Settlements at the Dawn of Modernity," in *Denying and Disclosing God: The Ambiguous Progress of Modern Atheism* (New Haven, Conn., and London, 2004), p. 16; Arthur Koestler, *The Sleepwalkers: A History of Man's Changing Vision of the Universe* (New York, 1963), p. 341.

56. Tarnas, *Passion of the Western Mind,* p. 256; Koestler, *Sleepwalkers,* pp. 258, 313–16, 394–98.

57. Tarnas, *Passion of the Western Mind,* pp. 262–63.

58. Johannes Kepler, *Mysterium Cosmographicum: The Secret of the Universe* (hereafter *MC*), trans. A. M. Duncan, intro. and commentary by E. J. Aiton, preface by I. Bernard Cohen (New York, 1981), p. 97.

59. *MC,* p. 92.

60. Kepler, *Harmonies of the World* 4:1.

61. Kepler to Hewart von Hohenburg, 9/10 April 1599, in Carole Baumgardt, *Johannes Kepler: Life and Letters* (New York, 1951), p. 50.

62. *MC,* p. 63; see Buckley "The New Science," p. 13; Westman, "The Copernicans," pp. 96–97.

63. Kepler to Michael Mästlin, 3 October 1595, in Koestler, *Sleepwalkers,* pp. 261–62.

64. *MC,* p. 149.

65. Dedication to Emperor Rudolph II, in Buckley, "The New Science," p. 15.

66. John of the Cross, "The Ascent of Mount Carmel," book I, chap. 13, no. 11, in *The Collected Works of John of the Cross,* trans. Kieran Kavanagh and Otilio Rodriguez (Washington, D.C., 1991), p. 150.

67. William R. Shea, "Galileo and the Church," in Lindberg and Numbers, *God and Nature,* p. 117.

68. Ibid., pp. 276–77; Tarnas, *Passion of the Western Mind,* pp. 263–64; Buckley, "The New Science," pp. 3–5.

69. Galileo, *Il Saggiatore,* para. 48, in Edwin Arthur Burtt, *The Metaphysical Foundations of Modern Physical Science* (London, 1949).

70. Westman, "The Copernicans," p. 98.

71. Buckley, "The New Science," pp. 8–9.

72. Galileo, "Letter to the Grand Duchess Christina," in Maurice A. Finnocchiano, ed. and trans., *The Galileo Affair: A Documentary History* (Berkeley, Calif., 1989), p. 96.

73. Ibid., pp. 92–93.

74. Ibid., pp. 90–91.

75. Ibid., p. 104.

76. Shea, "Galileo and the Church," p. 115.

77. Ibid., pp. 124–29; Westman, "The Copernicans," pp. 100–101.

78. Galileo, *Le Opere di Galileo Galilei,* 20 vols., ed. Antonio Favaro (Florence, 1899–1909), 5:138–39.

79. Bellarmine to Foscarini, 12 April 1615, ibid., 12:171–72; Shea, "Galileo and the Church," pp. 120–21.

80. Galileo, *Opere,* 5:668–70; Shea, "Galileo and the Church," p. 122.

81. Ernan McMullin, "Galileo on Science and Scripture," in Peter Machamer, ed., *The Cambridge Companion to Galileo* (Cambridge, U.K., 1998), p. 285; Buckley, "The New Science," pp. 9–10.

82. McMullin, "Galileo on Science and Scripture," p. 317.

83. Shea, "Galileo and the Church," p. 127.

84. Ibid., pp. 128–30.

85. Galileo, *Opere,* 1:489; Shea, "Galileo and the Church," pp. 130–31.

86. Yovel, *Marrano of Reason,* pp. 54–57.

87. Ibid., p. 53.

88. Isaac Orobio de Castro, prologue, *Epistola invecta contra Prado,* ibid., pp. 51–52.

89. Yovel, *Marrano of Reason,* pp. 42–51.

90. Ibid., pp. 57–73.

## EIGHT  Scientific Religion

1. John Donne, *An Anatomie of the World,* "The First Anniversary," lines 213–14, in Sir Herbert Grierson, ed., *Donne: Poetical Works* (Oxford, 1933).

2. Ibid., lines 212, 251–60.

3. Stephen Toulmin, *Cosmopolis: The Hidden Agenda of Modernity* (New York, 1990), pp. 47–55.

4. Michael J. Buckley, *At the Origins of Modern Atheism* (New Haven, Conn., and London, 1987), pp. 40–56; Michael J. Buckley, "A Dialectical Pattern in the Emergence of Atheism," in *Denying and Disclosing God: The Ambiguous Progress of Modern Atheism* (New Haven, Conn., and London, 2004), pp. 30–32.

5. *De providentia numinis et animi immortalitate* 1.2.16–19, translated into English as *Rawleigh His Ghost, Or, A Feigned Apparition of Syr Walter Rawleigh, to a friend of his, for the translating into English, the Booke of Leonard Lessius (that most learned man) entitled De providentia numinis, et animi immortalitate: written against Atheists, Polititians of these days* (hereafter *RG*), trans. "A. B." (1631), in vol. 349 of *English Recusant Literature, 1558–1640,* ed. D. M. Rogers (London, 1977), pp. 325–28.

6. Donne, "The First Anniversary," line 213.

7. *RG,* pp. 328–29.

8. P. J. S. Whitmore, *The Order of Minims in Seventeenth-Century France* (The

Hague, 1967), pp. 71–72; Ira O. Wade, *The Intellectual Origins of the French Enlightenment* (Princeton, N.J., 1971), p. 165.

9. Buckley, *Origins of Modern Atheism,* pp. 56–66; Buckley, "A Dialectical Pattern," pp. 32–33; William B. Ashworth Jr., "Catholicism and Early Modern Science," in David C. Lindberg and Ronald L. Numbers, eds., *God and Nature: Historical Essays on the Encounter Between Christianity and Science* (Berkeley, Los Angeles, and London, 1986), pp. 138–39.

10. Robert Lenoble, *Mersenne ou la naissance du mechanisme* (Paris, 1971), pp. 380–82; Whitmore, *The Order of Minims,* pp. 144–47.

11. René Descartes, *Discourse on the Method* 2.18. All quotations from *Discourse on the Method* and *Meditations on First Philosophy* are taken from Elizabeth J. Haldane and G. R. T. Ross, trans., ed., and with an introduction by Enrique Chávez-Arvizo, *Descartes: Key Philosophical Writings* (Ware, U.K., 1997).

12. Buckley, *Origins of Modern Atheism,* p. 73.

13. Descartes, *Discourse on Method,* 4.32.

14. Buckley, *Origins of Modern Atheism,* pp. 85–87.

15. Descartes, *Meditations* 2.28.

16. Descartes, *Discourse on Method* 3.34.

17. Descartes, *Meditations* 5.67.

18. Ibid.

19. Descartes, *Discourse on Method* 3.37.

20. Ashworth, "Catholicism and Early Modern Science," p. 139; Jacques Roger, "The Mechanistic Conception of Life," in Lindberg and Numbers, *God and Nature,* pp. 281–82.

21. Descartes, *Meditations* 6.80.

22. Richard Tarnas, *The Passion of the Western Mind: Understanding the Ideas That Have Shaped Our World View* (New York and London, 1991), pp. 26–68.

23. Descartes, introduction to *Les Méteors,* in Paul J. Olscamp, ed. and trans., *Discourse on Method, Optics, Geometry, and Metereology* (Indianapolis, 1965), p. 263.

24. Descartes, dedication to *Meditations* 1.

25. Buckley, "A Dialectical Pattern," p. 33.

26. Amos Funkenstein, *Theology and the Scientific Imagination: From the Middle Ages to the Seventeenth Century* (Princeton, N.J., 1986), p. 73.

27. Toulmin, *Cosmopolis,* pp. 98–104.

28. John Locke, *An Essay Concerning Human Understanding,* ed. Peter Nidditch (Oxford, 1975), p. 314; Locke's italics.

29. A. W. S. Baird, "Pascal's Idea of Nature," *Isis* 61 (1970); Ashworth, "Catholicism and Early Modern Science," pp. 142–44.

30. Pascal, *Pensées,* trans. A. J. Krailsheimer (Harmondsworth, U.K., 1966), p. 88.

31. Ibid., p. 309.

32. Ibid., pp. 169–70.

33. Alasdair MacIntyre, "The Fate of Theism," in A. MacIntyre and Paul Ricoeur, *The Religious Significance of Atheism* (New York, 1969), p. 12.

34. Pascal, *Pensées,* p. 38.

35. Yirmanyahu Yovel, *Spinoza and Other Heretics,* 2 vols. (Princeton, N.J., 1989); J. Guttmann, *Philosophies of Judaism: The History of Jewish Philosophy from Biblical Times to Franz Rosenzweig* (London and New York, 1964), pp.

265–85; R. M. Silverman, *Baruch Spinoza: Outcast Jew, Universal Sage* (Northwood, U.K., 1995).

36. Christopher Hill, *The World Turned Upside Down* (New York, 1972), pp. 112, 114, 176, 318–19; Norman Cohn, *The Pursuit of the Millennium: Revolutionary Millennarians and Mystical Anarchists of the Middle Ages* (London, 1957), pp. 303–18.

37. David J. Lovejoy, *Religious Enthusiasm in the New World: Heresy to Revolution* (Cambridge, Mass., and London, 1985), p. 69.

38. Ibid., p. 112.

39. Hill, *The World Turned Upside Down,* p. 86; Michael Barkun, *Disaster and the Millennium* (New Haven, Conn., and London, 1974), pp. 82–86.

40. Margaret C. Jacob, "Christianity and the Newtonian Worldview" in Linberg and Numbers, *God and Nature,* pp. 239–43.

41. Isaac Newton, to Robert Hooke, 5 February 1675, in *The Correspondence of Isaac Newton,* 7 vols., vols. 1–3, ed. by H. W. Turnbull; vol. 4, ed. J. F. Scott; vols. 5–7 ed. A. R. Hill and L. Tilling (Cambridge, U.K., 1959–1977), 7:254–55.

42. Isaac Newton, preface, *Philosophia Naturalis Principia Mathematica.* All quotations from the *Principia* are taken from *Sir Isaac Newton's Mathematical Principles of Natural Philosophy and His System of the World,* trans. Andrew Motte, revised by Florian Cajori (Berkeley and Los Angeles, 1962),p. xvii; henceforth referred to as *Principia.*

43. *Principia,* pp. xvii–xviii.

44. Ibid., p. 543.

45. Ibid., p. 544.

46. Ibid., p. 546.

47. Isaac Newton, *Opticks,* book 3, query 28, in *Opticks, or a Treatise of the Reflections, Refractions, Inflections and Colours of Light,* foreword by Albert Einstein, introduction by Sir Edmund Whittaker and L. Tilling (New York, 1952), p. 369.

48. Newton to Richard Bentley, 10 December 1691, in *Correspondence,* 3:233.

49. Ibid., 3:234, 236.

50. Newton to Richard Bentley, 17 January 1692, in *Correspondence,* 3:240.

51. Newton to Richard Bentley, 11 February 1692, in *Correspondence,* 3:244.

52. Buckley, *Origins of Modern Atheism,* pp. 13–37.

53. Newton, *Principia,* p. 546.

54. Ibid., p. 545.

55. Ibid., Newton's italics; A. R. and Marie Boas Hall (Cambridge, U.K., 1962), pp. 138–39; Gary B. Deason, "Reformation Theology and the Mechanistic Conception of Nature," in Lindberg and Numbers, *God and Nature,* pp. 184–85.

56. Samuel Clarke to Gottfried Wilhelm Leibniz, in H. G. Alexander, ed., *The Leibniz-Clarke Correspondence* (Manchester, U.K., 1956), p. 22; Deason, "Reformation Theology," p. 185.

57. Newton to Richard Bentley, 25 February 1693, in *Correspondence,* 3:253–54; Newton's italics.

58. Isaac Newton, "A Short Scheme of the True Religion," in Sir David Brewster, *Memoirs of the Life, Writings and Discoveries of Sir Isaac Newton,* 2 vols. (Edinburgh, 1855), 2:347–48.

59. Richard S. Westfall, "The Rise of Science and the Decline of Orthodox

Christianity: A Study of Kepler, Descartes and Newton," in Lindberg and Numbers, *God and Nature,* pp. 230–33.

60. Isaac Newton, Yehuda MS 41, fol. 7, Jewish National and University Library, Jerusalem; Westfall, "The Rise of Science," pp. 232–33.

61. Isaac Newton, MS, William Andrews Clark Memorial Library, UCLA, Los Angeles; Westfall, "The Rise of Science," p. 231.

62. Newton, *Correspondence,* 3:108.

63. Isaac Newton, unpublished manuscript, quoted in J. E. McGuire, "Newton on Time, Place and God: An Unpublished Source," *British Journal for the History of Science* 11 (1978).

64. J. C. Davis, *Fear, Myth and History: The Ranters and Their History* (New York, 1986), pp. 114–21.

65. John Bunyan, *Grace Abounding to the Chief of Sinners* and *Pilgrim's Progress,* ed. Roger Sharrock (London, 1966), pp. 33, 38.

66. Lucien Febvre, *The Problem of Unbelief in the Sixteenth Century: The Religion of Rabelais,* trans. Beatrice Gottlieb (Cambridge, Mass., and London, 1982).

67. Walter J. Ong, SJ, *Rhetoric, Romance and Technology: Studies in the Interaction of Expression and Culture* (Ithaca, N.Y., 1971), p. 279; J. E. McGuire, "Boyle's Conception of Nature," *Journal of the History of Ideas* 33 (1972).

68. Jacob, "Christianity and the Newtonian Worldview," pp. 243–46.

69. Samuel Clarke, *A Discourse Concerning the Being and Attributes of God, the Obligations of Natural Religion, and the Truth and Certainty of Christian Revelation,* 9th ed. (London, 1738), p. 51.

70. Ibid., p. 8.

71. Ecclesiasticus 43:28.

72. Clarke, *Discourse Concerning the Being and Attributes of God,* p. 126.

73. Samuel Clarke, *A Discourse Concerning the Unchangeable Obligations of Natural Religions and the Truth and Certainty of Christian Religion,* in Richard Watson, ed., *A Collection of Theological Tracts* (London, 1785), p. 246.

NINE  Enlightenment

1. John Locke, *A Letter Concerning Toleration* (Indianapolis, 1955).

2. Cotton Mather, *The Christian Philosopher: A Collection of the Best Discoveries of Nature, with Religious Improvements,* facsimile reproduction with introduction by Josephine K. Piercy (Gainesville, Fla., 1968), p. 1; Mather's italics.

3. Ibid., pp. 2–3; Mather's italics.

4. Ibid., p. 2; Mather's italics.

5. Ibid., p. 294.

6. Robert Briggs, "Embattled Faiths: Religion and Natural Philosophy" in Euan Cameron, ed., *Early Modern Europe* (Oxford, 1999), pp. 197–205.

7. Michael J. Buckley, *At the Origins of Modern Atheism* (New Haven, Conn., and London, 1987), p. 37; James Turner, *Without God, Without Creed: The Origins of Unbelief in America* (Baltimore, 1985), pp. 37–56.

8. Amos Funkenstein, *Theology and the Scientific Imagination: From the Middle Ages to the Seventeenth Century* (Princeton, N.J., 1986), pp. 357–60.

9. Voltaire, *Philosophical Dictionary,* trans. Theodore Besterman (London, 1972), p. 357.

10. Ibid., p. 57.

11. Peter Gay, *The Enlightenment: An Interpretation,* 2 vols. (New York, 1968, 1969), 2:526.

12. Mather, *Christian Philosopher,* p. 6; Mather's italics.

13. Jonathan Edwards, *The Great Awakening,* ed. C. C. Goen (New Haven, Conn., 1972), p. 249.

14. Thomas Jefferson to John Adams, 22 August 1813, in Lester J. Cappon, ed., *The Adams-Jefferson Letters,* 2 vols. (Chapel Hill, N.C., 1959), 2:368.

15. From "Seven Sermons," quoted in Turner, *Without God,* p. 50.

16. Wilfred Cantwell Smith, *Towards a World Theology: Faith and the Comparative History of Religion* (London and Basingstoke, U.K., 1981), pp. 51–54.

17. Stephen Toulmin, *Cosmopolis: The Hidden Agenda of Modernity* (New York, 1990), pp. 119–21.

18. Margaret C. Jacob, "Christianity and the Newtonian Worldview," in David C. Lindberg and Ronald L. Numbers, eds., *God and Nature: Historical Essays on the Encounter Between Christianity and Science* (Berkeley, Los Angeles, and London, 1986), pp. 249–53.

19. Commonplace Book I of George Horne, Bishop of Norwich, Cambridge University Library MS SS 8134/b/1; Jacob, "Christianity and the Newtonian Worldview," p. 252.

20. Commonplace Book I of George Horne, fol. III; Jacob, "Christianity and the Newtonian Worldview," p. 252; Christopher Wilde, "Hutchinsonianism, Natural Philosophy and Religious Controversy in Eighteenth-Century Britain," *History of Science* 18 (1980).

21. Jaroslav Pelikan, *The Christian Tradition: A History of the Development of Doctrine,* vol. 5: *Christian Doctrine and Modern Culture (Since 1700)* (Chicago and London, 1989), p. 125.

22. Ibid., p. 131.

23. Ibid.

24. Quoted by Frederick Dreyer, "Faith and Experience in the Thought of John Wesley," *American Historical Review* 88 (1983): 13–14.

25. Pelikan, *Christian Tradition,* 5:118.

26. Albert Outler, "Pietism and Christianity," in Louis Dupré and Don E. Saliers, *Christian Spirituality: Post-Reformation and Modern* (London, 1989).

27. Buckley, *Origins of Modern Atheism,* pp. 274–75.

28. Toulmin, *Cosmopolis,* pp. 121–24, 126–29.

29. Andrew Louth, *Discerning the Mystery: An Essay on the Nature of Theology* (Oxford, 1983), pp. 18–29; Funkenstein, *Theology and the Scientific Imagination,* pp. 202–12, 280–88, 328–32.

30. Giambattista Vico, *Scienza nuova,* in T. G. Bergin and M. H. Frisch, eds. and trans., *The New Science of Giambattista Vico* (New York, 1968), p. 331.

31. Ibid., pp. 141–42.

32. Isaiah Berlin, *Against the Current* (London, 1980), p. 109.

33. Vico, *Scienza nuova,* p. 122.

34. Jean-Jacques Rousseau, *Second Discourse,* in Roger D. Masters and Judith R. Masters, trans., *The First and Second Discourses* (New York, 1964), pp. 95, 132–33.

35. Joshua Mitchell, *Not by Reason Alone: Religion, History and Identity in Early Modern Political Thought* (Chicago, 1993), p. 124.

36. Jean-Jacques Rousseau, *Emile,* trans. Allan Bloom (New York, 1979), p. 444.

37. Jon Butler, *Awash in a Sea of Faith: Christianity and the American People* (Cambridge, Mass., and London, 1990), pp. 218–26.

38. Ruth H. Bloch, *Visionary Republic: Millennial Themes in American Thought, 1756–1800* (Cambridge, U.K., 1985), pp. 81–88.

39. For example, Timothy Dwight, *A Valedictory Address to the Young Gentlemen Who Commenced the Bachelor of Arts, July 27, 1776* (New Haven, Conn., 1776).

40. David S. Lovejoy, *Religious Enthusiasm in the New World: Heresy to Revolution* (Cambridge, Mass., and London, 1985), p. 226.

41. Thomas Paine, *Common Sense and the Crisis* (New York, 1975), p. 59.

42. Roger Hahn, "Laplace and the Mechanistic Universe," in Lindberg and Numbers, *God and Nature,* pp. 261–62.

43. Julien Offray de La Mettrie, *Man, a Machine,* trans. Gertrude Carmen Bussey (La Salle, Ill., 1943), p. 122.

44. Ibid., pp. 123–25.

45. Buckley, *Origins of Modern Atheism,* pp. 216–22.

46. Denis Diderot, *Letter on the Blind,* in Margaret Jourdain, trans., *Diderot's Early Philosophical Works* (Chicago, 1916), p. 111.

47. Ibid., pp. 111–12.

48. Ibid., p. 110.

49. Denis Diderot to Voltaire, 11 June 1749, in Buckley, *Origins of Modern Atheism,* p. 225.

50. Paul Heinrich Dietrich, Baron d'Holbach, *The System of Nature: or, Laws of the Moral and Physical World,* with notes by Diderot, trans. H. D. Robinson (New York, 1835), p. 232.

51. Ibid., p. 12.

52. Ibid., p. 181.

53. Ibid., p. 192.

54. Ibid., pp. 226–27.

55. Nicolas-Sylvestre Bergier, *Examen de materialisme, ou réfutation du systéme de la nature* (Paris, 1771); translations cited in Buckley, *Origins of Modern Atheism,* p. 253.

56. Tarnas, *Passion of the Western Mind,* pp. 33–34; Hahn, "Laplace and the Mechanistic Universe," pp. 264–68.

57. Hahn, "Laplace and the Mechanistic Universe," p. 265.

58. Ibid., p. 268.

59. Albert C. Outler, "Pietism and Enlightenment: Alternatives to Tradition," in Dupré and Saliers, *Christian Spirituality,* p. 245.

60. Hahn, "Laplace and the Mechanistic Universe," pp. 267–73.

61. Ibid., p. 257; Buckley, *Origins of Modern Atheism,* p. 325.

62. Jacob, "Christianity and the Newtonian Worldview," p. 253; David V. Erdman, *Blake: Prophet Against Empire* (New York, 1969), pp. 224, 367, 484.

63. William Blake, "Introduction," *Songs of Experience,* in *William Blake: A Selection of Poems and Letters,* ed. with an intro. by J. Brownowski (Harmondsworth, U.K., 1958).

64. Blake, "The Tyger," lines 4–5.

65. Blake, *Jerusalem* 33, lines 1–24.

66. Blake, *Jerusalem* 96, lines 23–28.

67. Percy Bysshe Shelley, "Hymn to Intellectual Beauty," lines 1–4, in *The Complete Poetical Works of Percy Bysshe Shelley,* ed. Thomas Hutchinson (Oxford, 1921).

68. William Wordsworth, "Lines Composed a Few Miles Above Tintern

Abbey, on Revisiting the Banks of the Wye During a Tour. July 13, 1798," lines 37–49.

69. Wordsworth, "Expostulation and Reply"; "The Tables Turned."

70. Wordsworth, *The Prelude* 1.586–88.

71. Wordsworth, "Tintern Abbey," lines 37–49.

72. Wordsworth, *The Prelude* 2, lines 258–59.

73. John Keats to George and Georgiana Keats, 21 December 1817. Quotations from Keats's letters are taken from H. E. Rollins, ed., *The Letters of John Keats*, 2 vols. (Cambridge, Mass., 1958); author's italics.

74. Keats to George and Georgiana Keats, 19 March 1819.

75. Keats to Richard Woodhouse, 27 October 1818.

76. Ibid.

77. Keats to J. H. Reynolds, 3 February 1818.

78. Keats to Benjamin Bailey, 22 November 1817.

79. Michael J. Buckley, "God as the Anti-Human," in *Denying and Disclosing God: The Ambiguous Progress of Modern Atheism* (New Haven, Conn., and London, 2004), pp. 79–83; Buckley, *At the Origins of Modern Atheism*, pp. 330–32; John MacQuarrie, *Thinking About God* (London, 1975), pp. 157–65.

80. Friedrich Schleiermacher, *On Religion: Speeches to Its Cultured Despisers*, trans. John Oman (New York, 1958), p. 12.

81. Ibid., p. 87.

82. Schleiermacher, *The Christian Faith*, trans. H. R. Mackintosh and J. S. Stewart (Edinburgh, 1928), p. 12.

83. Ibid., p. 16.

84. Georg Wilhelm Friedrich Hegel, *The Phenomenology of Mind* (London, 1931), p. 86.

## TEN Atheism

1. James Turner, *Without God, Without Creed: The Origins of Unbelief in America* (Baltimore, 1985), pp. 73–97.

2. Nathan O. Hatch, *The Democratization of American Christianity* (New Haven, Conn., and London, 1989), pp. 138–39.

3. Ibid., pp. 9, 68–157.

4. Ibid., p. 71.

5. Lyman Beecher, *Lectures on Scepticism* (Cincinnati, 1835), p. 132.

6. Jon Butler, *Awash in a Sea of Faith: Christianity and the American People* (Cambridge, Mass., and London, 1990), p. 216.

7. Ibid., p. 219.

8. Lyman Beecher, *Autobiography* (1864), 2 vols., ed. Barbara M. Cross (Cambridge, Mass., 1961), 2:146.

9. Turner, *Without God*, pp. 100–101.

10. James McCosh, *The Method of the Divine Government; Physical and Moral*, 4th ed. (New York, 1855), p. 17.

11. Daniel Walker Howe, "Religion and Politics in the Antebellum North," in Mark A. Noll, ed., *Religion and American Politics: From the Colonial Period to the 1980s* (Oxford and New York, 1990), pp. 132–33; George M. Marsden, Afterword to ibid., pp. 382–83; Turner, *Without God*, pp. 78–79.

12. Turner, *Without God*, pp. 86–96.

13. Ibid., p. 125; Howe, "Religion and Politics in the Antebellum North," pp. 125–28.

14. Butler, *Awash in a Sea of Faith,* p. 270.

15. Alister McGrath, *The Twilight of Atheism: The Rise and Fall of Disbelief in the Modern World* (London and New York, 2005), pp. 52–55.

16. Patrick Masterson, *Atheism and Alienation: A Study of the Philosophic Sources of Contemporary Atheism* (Dublin, 1871), 76–93; Michael J. Buckley, "God as the Anti-human," in *Denying and Disclosing God: The Ambiguous Progress of Modern Atheism* (New Haven, Conn., and London, 2001), pp. 86–89; Richard Tarnas, *The Passion of the Western Mind: Understanding the Ideas That Have Shaped Our World View* (London and New York, 1991), pp. 329–32; McGrath, *Twilight of Atheism,* pp. 60–66; Gary Hyman, "Atheism in Modern History," in Michael Martin, ed., *The Cambridge Companion to Atheism* (Cambridge, U.K., 2007) pp. 36–37.

17. Masterson, *Atheism and Alienation,* pp. 62–76; Buckley, "God as Anti-human," pp. 83–89, 97–98; Buckley, "The Radical Finitude of Religious Ideas: Atheism and Contemplation," in *Denying and Disclosing God,* pp. 100–105; Michael J. Buckley, *At the Origins of Modern Atheism* (New Haven, Conn., and London, 1985), pp. 332–33; McGrath, *Twilight of Atheism,* pp. 51–59.

18. Ludwig Feuerbach, *The Essence of Christianity,* trans. Marion Evans (New York, 1957), p. 284.

19. Ibid., p. 5.

20. Ibid., p. 33.

21. Ibid., p. 283; Feuerbach's italics.

22. Karl Marx, "Theses on Feuerbach," in Karl Marx and Friedrich Engels, *On Religion,* intro. Reinhold Niebuhr (New York, 1964), p. 72; Marx's italics.

23. Karl Marx, "Contribution to the Critique of Hegel's Philosophy of Right, 1843–44," in Jaroslav Pelikan, ed., *Modern Religious Thought* (Boston, 1990), p. 80; Marx's italics.

24. Ibid.

25. Ibid., p. 81; Marx's italics.

26. Martin J. S. Rudwick, "The Shape and Meaning of Earth History," in David C. Lindberg and Ronald L. Numbers, eds., *God and Nature: Historical Essays on the Encounter between Christianity and Science* (New York, 1986), pp. 313–14; James R. Moore, "Geologists and Interpreters of Genesis in the Nineteenth Century," ibid., pp. 322–30.

27. Martin J. S. Rudwick, "Charles Lyell Speaks in the Lecture Theatre," *British Journal of the History of Science* 9 (1976).

28. Charles Lyell, review of *Memoir on the Geology of Central France,* by G. P. Scopes, *Quarterly Review,* 30 October 1827.

29. Turner, *Without God,* pp. 185–86, 193–95.

30. Quoted in Patricia James, *Population Malthus: His Life and Times* (London, 1979), p. 446.

31. Rudwick, "Shape and Meaning," pp. 314–15.

32. Louis Agassiz, *Essay on Classification* (1859), ed. Edward Lurie (Cambridge, Mass., 1962), p. 12.

33. Alfred Tennyson, *In Memoriam* lv, line 20, in *Tennyson: Poems and Plays,* ed., Sir Thomas Herbert Warren (Oxford, 1954).

34. Ibid., liv, lines 5–8.

35. Ibid., lvi, line 25.

36. Ibid., liv, lines 13–20.

37. Horace Bushnell, *God in Christ* (Hartford, Conn., 1849), pp. 40–42, 74.

38. Ibid., p. 55.

39. Ibid., p. 72.

40. Stephen Jay Gould, *The Flamingo's Smile* (New York, 1985), p. 397; Daniel C. Dennett, "Atheism and Evolution," in Martin, *Companion to Atheism*, pp. 135–39.

41. A. Hunter Dupree, "Christianity and the Scientific Community in the Age of Darwin," in Lindberg and Numbers, *God and Nature*, pp. 356–62.

42. Charles Darwin, 9 May 1879, in Owen Chadwick, *The Victorian Church*, 2 vols. (London, 1966), 2:20.

43. Turner, *Without God*, p. 186.

44. Charles Hodge, *Systematic Theology*, 2 vols. (Princeton, N.J., 1973), 1:16; 2:15–16.

45. Charles Hodge, *What Is Darwinism?* (Princeton, N.J., 1874), p. 142.

46. Ibid., p. 60.

47. Moore, "Geologists and Interpreters of Genesis," pp. 329–34.

48. Ibid., p. 341.

49. Ibid., pp. 333–34.

50. Ward, *Robert Elsmere* (Lincoln, Neb., 1969), p. 414.

51. Moore, "Geologists and Interpreters of Genesis," p. 341.

52. James R. Moore, *The Post-Darwinian Controversies: A Study of the Protestant Struggle to Come to Terms with Darwin in Great Britain and America* (Cambridge, U.K., 1979), 95; Frank M. Turner, "The Victorian Conflict Between Science and Religion: A Professional Dimension," *Isis* 69 (1978).

53. Moore, "Geologists and Interpreters of Genesis," pp. 342–43.

54. Archibald Hodge and B. B. Warfield, "Inspiration," *Princeton Review* 2, 11 April 1881.

55. *New York Times*, 5 April 1894.

56. *New York Times*, 18 April 1899.

57. *Union Seminary Magazine* 19 (1907–8).

58. Buckley, *Origins of Modern Atheism*, p. 10; Owen Chadwick, *The Secularization of the European Mind in the Nineteenth Century* (Cambridge, U.K., 1975), pp. 90–91.

59. Hypatia Bradlaugh Bonner, *Charles Bradlaugh: A Record of His Life and Work by His Daughter* (London, 1908), p. 337.

60. Adrian Desmond, *Huxley: The Devil's Disciple* (London, 1994), p. 373.

61. Thomas H. Huxley, *Science and Christian Tradition: Essays* (New York, 1898), pp. 245–46.

62. Quoted in Peter Gay, *A Godless Jew: Freud, Atheism and the Making of Psychoanalysis* (New Haven, Conn., and London, 1975), pp. 6–7.

63. Ibid., p. 240.

64. Robert G. Ingersoll, "Individuality" (1873), in *The Works of Robert G. Ingersoll*, 3 vols. (New York, 1909), 1:192.

65. Charles Eliot Norton to Godwin Smith, 14 June 1997, in Sara Norton and M. A. DeWolfe, eds., *Letters of Charles Eliot Norton with Biographical Comment*, 2 vols. (Boston, 1913), 2:248.

66. Joel Moody, "Science of Evil," excerpted in *The Iconoclast* 2, no. 16 (1871); Turner, *Without God*, p. 218.

67. Ingersoll, "The Great Infidels" (1881), in *Works,* 3:309.
68. John William Draper, *History of the Conflict Between Religion and Science* (New York, 1874), p. 367.
69. Andrew Dixon White, *A History of the Warfare of Science with Theology in Christendom,* 2 vols. (New York, 1896), 1:8; White's italics.
70. Ibid., 1:325.
71. J. R. Lucas, "Wilberforce and Huxley: A Legendary Encounter," *The Historical Journal* 22 (1979).
72. Turner, *Without God,* pp. 219–20.
73. J. S. Mill, "Theism," in *Three Essays on Religion* (London, 1975), p. 204.
74. Ingersoll, "The Gods" (1872), in *Works,* 1:22.
75. Chadwick, *Secularization of the European Mind,* p. 168.
76. Ibid., pp. 168–80.
77. Ibid., p. 179.
78. Arnold, "Dover Beach," lines 25, 14, 32–37, in *Arnold: Poetical Works,* ed. C. B. Tinker and H. F. Lowry (Oxford, 1945).
79. Hyman, "Atheism in Modern History," pp. 37–38; John D. Caputo, "Atheism, A/theology, and the Postmodern Condition," in Martin, *Companion to Atheism,* pp. 270–71; Buckley, *Origins of Modern Atheism,* pp. 28–30; Buckley, "God as the Anti-human," pp. 89–94; Tarnas, *Passion of the Western Mind,* pp. 317, 367–71; McGrath, *Twilight of Atheism,* pp. 149–51.
80. Friedrich Nietzsche, *The Gay Science,* trans. Walter Kaufman (New York, 1974), p. 181.
81. Ibid., p. 279.
82. Ibid., p. 181.
83. Gay, *Godless Jew,* passim; Tarnas, *Passion of the Western Mind,* pp. 328–29; Buckley, "God as the Anti-human," pp. 92–93; "The Radical Finitude," pp. 105–7; McGrath, *Twilight of Atheism,* pp. 67–77.
84. Gay, *Godless Jew,* pp. 37–50.
85. Sigmund Freud, *The Future of an Illusion,* trans. and ed. James Strachey (New York, 1961), p. 53.
86. Sigmund Freud, *Civilization and Its Discontents,* trans. and ed. James Strachey (New York, 1961), p. 21.
87. McGrath, *Twilight of Atheism,* p. 75.
88. Ingersoll, "The Gods," 1:58.
89. Ibid., pp. 57–58.
90. Speech of L. T. Brown, M.D., quoted in Turner, *Without God,* p. 237.
91. Mill, "Theism," pp. 256–57.
92. I. F. Clarke, *Voices Prophesying War: Future Wars, 1763–3749.* 2nd ed. (Oxford and New York, 1992), pp. 37–88.
93. Thomas Hardy, "The Darkling Thrush," lines 25–32, in John Wain, ed., *Selected Shorter Poems of Thomas Hardy* (London, 1966).

ELEVEN  Unknowing

1. Richard Tarnas, *The Passion of the Western Mind: Understanding the Ideas That Have Shaped Our World View* (London, 1991) p. 356.
2. Ronald W. Clark, *Einstein: The Life and Times* (New York, 1971), p. 343.

3. Arthur F. Smethurst, *Modern Science and Christian Beliefs* (New York, 1955), p. 81.

4. An unnamed theologian quoted in Philipp Frank, *Einstein, His Life and Times* (New York, 1947), p. 264.

5. Robert Jastrow, *God and the Astronomers* (New York, 1978).

6. William G. Pollard, *Chance and Providence: God's Action Is a World Governed by Scientific Law* (London, 1959), pp. 69, 72.

7. Quoted in Werner Heisenberg, *Physics and Beyond: Encounters and Conversations* (New York, 1971), pp. 82–83.

8. Quoted in Huston Smith, *Beyond the Post-Modern Mind,* rev. ed. (Wheaton, Ill., 1989), p. 8.

9. Alister McGrath, *The Twilight of Atheism: The Rise and Fall of Disbelief in the Modern World* (London, 2004), pp. 96–97.

10. Bryan Magee, *Confessions of a Philosopher: A Journey Through Western Philosophy* (London, 1997), p. 561.

11. Karl R. Popper, *Unended Quest: An Intellectual Autobiography* (London, 1992), p. 145; Mark Vernon, *After Atheism: Science, Religion and the Meaning of Life* (Basingstoke, U.K., 2007), p. 160.

12. Albert Einstein, "Strange Is Our Situation Here on Earth," in Jaroslav Pelikan, ed., *Modern Religious Thought* (Boston, 1990), p. 225.

13. Ludwig Wittgenstein, *Tractatus logico-philosophicus,* trans. C. K. Ogden (London, 1962), p. 189.

14. A. J. Ayer, *The Central Questions of Philosophy* (London, 1973), passim.

15. A. J Ayer, *Language, Truth and Logic* (Harmondsworth, U.K., 1974), pp. 152–53.

16. Wilfred Cantwell Smith, *Belief and History* (Charlottesville, Va., 1977), pp. 20–32.

17. Acts of the Apostles 2:1–6.

18. Harvey Cox, *Fire from Heaven: The Rise of Pentecostal Spirituality and the Reshaping of Religion in the Twenty-first Century* (New York, 1995), pp. 48–74.

19. Romans 8:26.

20. Cox, *Fire from Heaven,* pp. 57, 69–71.

21. Denys Turner, *The Darkness of God: Negativity in Christian Mysticism* (Cambridge, U.K., 1995), pp. 260–62.

22. A. C. Dixon, *The King's Business* 40 (1922).

23. Robert C. Fuller, *Naming the Antichrist: The History of an American Obsession* (Oxford and New York, 1995), pp. 115–17; Paul Boyer, *When Time Shall Be No More: Prophecy Belief in Modern American Culture* (Cambridge, Mass., and London, 1992); George M. Marsden, *Fundamentalism and American Culture: The Shaping of Twentieth-Century Evangelicalism, 1870–1925* (Oxford and New York, 1980), pp. 141–44, 150, 157, 207–10.

24. Marsden, *Fundamentalism and American Culture,* pp. 90–92.

25. Ferenc Morton Szasz, *The Divided Mind of Protestant America, 1880–1930* (University, Ala., 1982), p. 85.

26. See my book *The Battle for God: A History of Fundamentalism* (London and New York, 2000).

27. Marsden, *Fundamentalism and American Culture,* pp. 147–48.

28. Szasz, *Divided Mind,* p. 86.

29. Marsden, *Fundamentalism and American Culture,* pp. 147–48.

30. Dixon, *The King's Business* 19 (1918).

31. *The Watchtower Examiner,* July 1920; Fuller, *Naming the Antichrist,* p. 120.

32. Nancy T. Ammerman, "North American Protestant Fundamentalism," in Martin E. Marty and R. Scott Appleby, eds., *Fundamentalisms Observed* (Chicago and London, 1991), p. 26; Marsden, *Fundamentalism and American Culture,* pp. 169–83; Ronald E. Numbers, *The Creationists: The Evolution of Scientific Creationism* (Berkeley, Los Angeles, and London, 1992), pp. 41–44; Szasz, *Divided Mind,* pp. 107–8.

33. Marsden, *Fundamentalism and American Culture,* pp. 184–89; Szasz, *Divided Mind,* pp. 117–35; Numbers, *Creationists,* pp. 98–103; Laurence R. Moore, *Religious Outsiders and the Making of Americans* (Oxford and New York, 1986), pp. 160–63.

34. Marsden, *Fundamentalism and American Culture,* pp. 187–88.

35. Ibid.

36. Moore, *Religious Outsiders,* pp. 161–63.

37. Tarnas, *Passion of the Western Mind,* pp. 211–19; Zygmunt Bauman, *Modernity and the Holocaust* (Ithaca, N.Y., 1989); George Steiner, *In Bluebeard's Castle: Some Notes Towards the Redefinition of Culture* (New Haven, Conn., 1971), pp. 36–48; Richard L. Rubenstein, *After Auschwitz: Radical Theology and Contemporary Judaism* (New York, 1966).

38. Bauman, *Modernity and the Holocaust,* pp. 77–92.

39. Rubenstein, *After Auschwitz,* pp. 12–42.

40. Steiner, *In Bluebeard's Castle,* pp. 36–42.

41. Ibid., p. 46.

42. Ibid., pp. 47–48.

43. Elie Wiesel, *Night,* trans. Stella Rodway (Harmondsworth, U.K., 1981), p. 45.

44. Ibid., pp. 76–77.

45. Rubenstein, *After Auschwitz,* passim.

46. Ludwig Wittgenstein, *Lectures and Conversations on Aesthetics, Psychology and Religious Belief,* ed. Cecil Barrett (Oxford, 1966), p. 56.

47. Ibid., p. 53.

48. Maurice Drury, "Conversations with Wittgenstein," in Rush E. Rhees, ed., *Ludwig Wittgenstein: Personal Recollections* (Totowa, N.J., 1981), p. 117.

49. Ibid., p. 123.

50. Ibid., p. 101.

51. Ibid.

52. Ibid., p. 129.

53. Ray Monk, *Ludwig Wittgenstein: The Duty of Genius* (London, 1990), p. 410.

54. Martin Heidegger, "Only a God Can Save Us," *Der Spiegel* 23 (1976).

55. Rudolf Bultmann, "New Testament and Mythology," in Hans Werner Bartsch, ed., *Kerygma and Myth,* 2 vols. (London, 1964), 2:36.

56. Ibid., 2:11.

57. Rudolf Bultmann, *Essays: Philosophical and Theological* (London, 1955), p. 239.

58. Rudolf Bultmann, *Jesus and the Word* (London, 1958), p. 103.

59. Paul Tillich, *Theology and Culture* (Oxford and New York, 1964), p. 129.

60. Paul Tillich, *A History of Christian Thought* (New York, 1969), p. 264.

61. Paul Tillich, *Systematic Theology,* 2 vols. (Chicago, 1951), 1:205.

62. D. Mackenzie Brown, *Ultimate Concern: Tillich in Dialogue* (London, 1965), p. 88.

63. Paul Tillich, *The Courage to Be* (Glasgow, 1952), p. 183; Tillich's italics.

64. Karl Rahner, "What Is a Dogmatic Statement?" in *Theological Investigations V* (New York, 1966), pp. 18–19.

65. Michael Polyani, *Knowing and Being* (London, 1969), p. 144.

66. Ibid., p. 148.

67. Andrew Louth, *Discerning the Mystery: An Essay on the Nature of Theology* (Oxford, 1983), pp. 64–65.

68. Ibid., pp. 67–68.

69. Gabriel Marcel, *Being and Having* (London, 1965), p. 101.

70. Ibid., p. 127; author's italics.

71. Ibid., p. 128.

72. Albert Camus, *The Myth of Sisyphus,* trans. Justin O'Brien (London, 2005), p. 119.

## TWELVE Death of God?

1. Callum G. Brown, *The Death of Christian Britain: Understanding Secularisation, 1800–2000* (London, 2001).

2. Stephen Toulmin, *Cosmopolis: The Hidden Agenda of Modernity* (New York, 1990), pp. 172–81; Keith Jenkins, ed., *The Postmodern History Reader* (London, 1997), pp. 3–5.

3. Michael J. Buckley, *At the Origins of Modern Atheism* (New Haven, Conn., and London, 1987), p. 28; Karl Rahner, interview with Gwendoline Jancyk, 12 June 1981.

4. Michael Hardt and Antonio Negri, *Empire* (Cambridge, Mass., 2000), p. 46.

5. Paul Van Buren, *The Secular Meaning of the Gospel* (London, 1963), p. 138.

6. I have discussed fundamentalism in Judaism, Christianity, and Islam more fully than is possible in these pages in *The Battle for God: A History of Fundamentalism* (London and New York, 2000).

7. Afghani was alienated from Western modernity by his experience of British colonialism in India.

8. Azar Tabari, "The Role of the Clergy in Modern Iranian Politics," in Nikki R. Keddie, ed., *Religion and Politics in Iran: Shiism from Quietism to Revolution* (New Haven, Conn., and London, 1983), pp. 58–59.

9. Richard Mitchell, *The Society of Muslim Brothers* (London, 1969), pp. 152–61.

10. Yvonne Hadad, "Sayid Qutb: Ideologue of Islamic Revival," in John Esposito, ed., *Voices of Resurgent Islam* (New York and Oxford, 1993), p. 70.

11. Charles J. Adams, "Mawdudi and the Islamic State," ibid., pp. 99–133.

12. Qur'an 2.256. The Arabic is very strong: *"La ikra fi'l-din."*

13. Sayyid Qutb, *Milestones* (Delhi, 1988), p. 90.

14. Khomeini, *Islam and Revolution,* trans. Hamid Algar (Berkeley, Calif., 1981), p. 28.

15. Interview with Scott McConnell, "The Logic of Suicide Terrorism," *The American Conservative,* 18 July 2005; John L. Esposito and Dalia Mogahed, *Who Speaks for Islam? What a Billion Muslims Really Think* (New York, 2007), p. 77.

16. Qur'an 5:32.

17. Esposito and Mogahed, *Who Speaks for Islam?,* p. 80.

18. Ibid., pp. 86–87.

19. Ibid., p. 97.

20. Jacques Monod, *Chance and Necessity: An Essay on the Natural Philosophy of Modern Biology,* trans. Austryn Wainhouse (New York, 1972), pp. 160–80.

21. Richard Dawkins, *The God Delusion* (London, 2006), p. 188.

22. Sam Harris, *The End of Faith: Religion, Terror, and the Future of Reason* (New York, 2004); Sam Harris, *Letter to a Christian Nation* (New York, 2007); Christopher Hitchens, *God Is Not Great: How Religion Poisons Everything* (New York, 2007).

23. Stephen Jay Gould, *Rocks of Ages: Science and Religion in the Fullness of Life* (London, 2001), p. 6.

24. Ibid., p. 7.

25. Ibid., pp. 58–59.

26. John F. Haught, *God and the New Atheism: A Critical Response to Dawkins, Harris, and Hitchens* (Louisville and London, 2008); Alister McGrath, *Dawkins' God: Genes, Memes, and the Meaning of Life* (Malden, Mass., 2005); John Cornwell, *Darwin's Angel: An Angelic Response to "The God Delusion"* (London, 2007).

27. Harris, *End of Faith,* p. 35.

28. Hitchens, *God Is Not Great,* p. 120.

29. Dawkins, *God Delusion,* pp. 237–67.

30. Daniel Dennett, "Atheism and Evolution," in Michael Martin, ed., *The Cambridge Companion to Atheism* (Cambridge, U.K., 2007), p. 137.

31. Dawkins, *God Delusion,* p. 31; Dawkins's italics.

32. Ibid.

33. Ibid., pp. 31–73; Haught, *New Atheism,* pp. 41–44.

34. Harris, *End of Faith,* pp. 58–73.

35. Ibid., p. 73.

36. Ibid., p. 45.

37. Dawkins, *God Delusion,* p. 306.

38. Harris, *End of Faith,* pp. 14–15.

39. Harris, *Letter to a Christian Nation,* p. 85; Harris's italics.

40. Dawkins, *God Delusion,* p. 1.

41. Haught, *New Atheism,* p. 63.

42. Dawkins, *God Delusion,* p. 221.

43. Alister McGrath, *The Twilight of Atheism: The Rise and Fall of Disbelief in the Modern World* (London and New York, 2005), p. 93.

44. Esposito and Mogahed, *Who Speaks for Islam?,* pp. 86–91.

45. Paul Davies, *The Mind of God: Science and the Search for Ultimate Meaning* (London, 1992), p. 176.

46. Roger Penrose, *The Emperor's New Mind: Concerning Computers, Mind, and the Laws of Physics* (Oxford, 1989), p. 421.

47. Haught, *New Atheism,* pp. 44–49.

48. Robert Bellah, *Beyond Belief: Essays on Religion in a Post-traditionalist World* (New York, 1970), p. 254.

49. George Steiner, ed., *Is Science Nearing Its Limits? Conference Convened by George Steiner* (Manchester, U.K., 2008), p. xxii.

50. Ibid., pp. xxii–xxiii.

51. Mark Vernon, *After Atheism: Science, Religion and the Meaning of Life* (Basingstoke, U.K., 2007), pp. 49–51.

52. Ibid., pp. 45–47.

53. Paul Davies in an interview with Bel Mooney, ed., *Devout Sceptics* (London, 2003), p. 57.
54. Paul Davies, *God and the New Physics* (New York, 1983), p. ix.
55. Jacques Derrida, *On Grammatology,* corrected ed., trans. Gayatri Spivak (Baltimore, 1992), p. 323.
56. Gianni Vattimo, "Towards a Non-Religious Christianity," in John D. Caputo and Gianni Vattimo, *After the Death of God,* ed. Jeffrey W. Robbins (New York, 2007), p. 43.
57. Ibid.
58. Gianni Vattimo, *After Christianity,* trans. Luca D'Isanto (New York, 2002), p. 17.
59. Gianni Vattimo, *The Transparent Society,* trans. David Webb (Baltimore, 1992), pp. 2–9.
60. Vattimo, "Towards a Non-Religious Christianity," p. 45. Vattimo refers to the Latin hymn *"Ubi caritas et amor, Deus ibi est."*
61. John D. Caputo, "Atheism, A/theology and the Postmodern Condition," in Michael Martin, ed., *The Cambridge Companion to Atheism* (Cambridge, U.K., 2007), p. 277.
62. John D. Caputo, *On Religion* (London, 2001), p. 60.
63. Ibid., p. 61.
64. Ibid., p. 63.
65. John D. Caputo, "Spectral Hermeneutics: On the Weakness of God and the Theology of the Event," in Caputo and Vattimo, *After the Death of God,* pp. 57–59.
66. John D. Caputo, "The Power of the Powerless," in Caputo and Vattimo, *After the Death of God,* pp. 115–16.
67. Caputo, *On Religion,* p. 115.
68. Caputo, "Spectral Hermeneutics," p. 47.
69. Caputo, "Power of the Powerless," p. 147.
70. Caputo, "Atheism, A/theology," p. 283.

## Epilogue

1. Julian Baggini, *Atheism: A Very Short Introduction* (Oxford, 2003), p. 106.
2. J. J. C. Smart and J. J. Haldane, *Atheism and Theism* (Oxford, 1996).
3. Peter Berger, *A Rumour of Angels* (London, 1970), p. 58; see John Macquarrie, *Thinking About God* (London, 1975), p. 54.
4. *Shorter Oxford English Dictionary* (Oxford, 1968).
5. Charles Webster, "Puritanism, Separatism and Science" in David C. Lindberg and Ronald L. Numbers, eds., *God and Nature: Historical Essays on the Encounter Between Christianity and Science* (Berkeley, Los Angeles, and London, 1986), pp. 192–217.
6. William B. Ashworth, Jr., "Catholicism and Early Modern Science," ibid., pp. 154–60.
7. Denys Turner, *Faith, Reason and the Existence of God* (Cambridge, U.K., 2004), pp. 114–15.
8. Xunzi, "The Book of Master Xan" 21:34–39, in Burton Watson, ed. and trans., *Xunzi: Basic Writings* (New York, 2003).
9. Anguttara Nikaya 4.36; my translation.

# Glossary

**agnosticism** (Latin derivation from *agnosco*: "I do not know"). The principled refusal to suspend belief in a doctrine, teaching, or idea that is incapable of proof.

*ahimsa* (Sanskrit). "Harmlessness"; nonviolence.

**allegory** (Greek *allegoria*). A discourse that describes one thing under the guise of another.

**anagogical** (Greek derivation). The mystical or eschatological meaning of a biblical text.

*apokalypsis* (Greek). "Apocalypse"; literally an "unveiling" or "revelation"; an eternal truth hitherto hidden that has suddenly become clear; often used to refer to a revelation about the last days or the End-time.

**apologia** (Latin). A rational explanation.

*apophatic* (Greek derivation). "Speechless"; wordless; silent.

*arche* (Greek). The "beginning"; the original substance of the universe.

**archetype** (Greek derivation). The "original pattern" or paradigm. A term connected with the perennial philosophy, which sees every earthly object or experience as a replica, a pale shadow of a more powerful, richer reality in the heavenly world. In ancient religion, the return to the archetypal reality was regarded as the fulfillment of a person or object. One thus attained a fuller, more complete existence.

*ataraxia* (Greek). Freedom from pain.

**atheism.** Today this means the outright denial of God's existence; until the nineteenth century, however, it was usually a term of abuse applied to others, and people generally did not call *themselves* atheists. Before this time, it commonly referred to a "false belief." It was used to describe a way of life, an idea, or a form of religion that people disapproved of.

*atman* (Sanskrit). The immortal or eternal "self" sought by yogins and the sages of the Upanishads that was believed to be identical with the Brahman.

**atomism** (Greek derivation). A scientific theory developed by the Greek physicist Democritus (c. 466–370 BCE), who believed that the raw material of the universe consisted of innumerable tiny, indivisible *atomos* (particles) that swirled eternally in empty space. Periodically the atoms would collide and stick together, forming the objects of our world. Eventually these objects would disintegrate, and the atoms that composed them returned to mill around in space until they formed their next combination. This theory was revived by European philosophers during the scientific revolution of the seventeenth century.

*atopos* (Greek). Unclassifiable; untypical; outside the norm; extraordinary.

**avatar** (Sanskrit: *avatara*). "Descent"; "manifestation"; the earthly appearance of one of the gods; an incarnation of the divine.

*ayah* (Arabic); plural *ayat*. "Sign, symbol, parable." The Qur'an distinguishes between the absolute reality of God and the "signs" or "manifestations" of God that we see in the world. Muslims are commanded to contemplate the marvelous "signs" of God's benevolence and generosity in the natural world. The Qur'an is also a "symbol" of the divine, and every single one of its verses is called an *ayah,* a reminder that we can only speak of God in signs and symbols. The great images of the Qur'an, such as the Creation, Last Judgment, or Paradise, are also *ayat,* "symbols" that make an inexpressible reality known to us.

**Bavli.** See *Talmud.*

**Being.** The fundamental energy that supports, animates, and sustains everything that exists; to be carefully distinguished from *a being,* which is a finite, particular, and limited manifestation of Being itself.

**belief.** Originally the Middle English verb *bileven* meant "to love; to prize; to hold dear"; and the noun *bileve* meant "loyalty; trust; commitment; engagement." It was related to the German *liebe* ("beloved") and the Latin *libido* ("desire.") In the English versions of the Bible, the translators used these words to render the Greek *pistis; pisteuo;* and the Latin *fides; credo.* Thus "belief" became the equivalent of "faith." But "belief" began to change its meaning during the late seventeenth century. It started to be used of an intellectual assent to a particular proposition, teaching, opinion, or doctrine. It was used in this modern sense first by philosophers and scientists, and the new usage did not become common in religious contexts until the nineteenth century.

**Brahman** (Sanskrit). "The All"; the whole of reality; the essence of existence; the foundation of everything that exists; being itself. The power that holds the cosmos together and enables it to grow and develop. The supreme reality of Vedic religion.

**Brahmodya** (Sanskrit). A ritual competition. The contestants each tried to find a verbal formula that expressed the mysterious and ineffable reality of the Brahman. The contest always ended in silence when contestants were reduced to wordless awe. In the silence they felt the presence of the Brahman.

**bricolage.** A term in modern design that refers to the process of creating something new out of old materials that happen to lie at hand. Applied analogically to the transmission of tradition, it refers to the premodern habit of taking ancient texts and giving them an entirely fresh interpretation to suit the needs of the time and the requirements of a particular group of students. When written material was scarce, this was a recognized method of moving a tradition forward. It was used not only by religious teachers but also by Hellenistic philosophers.

**Buddha** (Sanskrit). An enlightened or "awakened" person.

*buddhi* (Sanskrit). The "intellect"; the highest category of the human mind; the only part of the human person that was capable of reflecting the ultimate reality. Not dissimilar to the Latin *intellectus.*

*Christos* (Greek). Christ; a Greek translation of the Hebrew *messhiach.*

*coincidentia oppositorum* (Latin). The "coincidence of opposites"; the ecstatic experience of a unity that exists beyond the apparent contradictions of earthly life.

**compassion** (Greek and Latin derivation). The ability to "feel with" another, "experience with" another; empathy; sympathy. It does *not* mean "pity." Compassion is regarded as the highest of the virtues in all the major religious traditions; it is the test of genuine religious experience and practice and one of the chief means of encountering the sacred. All the traditions also insist that you cannot confine your benevolence to your own group but must have "concern for everybody"; honor the stranger; love even your enemies.

**cosmology** (Greek derivation). Literally "discourse/speech about the cosmos"; a creation story; *cosmogony* refers to the birth of the cosmos.

**credo** (Latin); *credere*. Today this is usually translated as "I believe" and "to believe," respectively. But this is a relatively recent development (see *belief*). *Credo* derives from *cor do*: "I give my heart." It originally meant "trust; commitment; engagement; involvement." When Saint Jerome translated the Bible into Latin during the fourth century, he used *credo* as the equivalent of *pisteuo*.

**Dao** (Chinese). The Way; the correct course or path. The object of much Chinese ritual was to ensure that human affairs were aligned with the Way of Heaven—or as we might say, were in tune with Being. In the tradition known as Daoism, it would become the ultimate, indescribable, and impersonal reality; the source from which all appearance derives, unproduced producer of all that exists that guarantees the stability and order of the world.

***demiourgos*** (Greek). "Craftsman." The creator god in Plato's *Timaeus,* which shaped the raw materials of the universe into an ordered cosmos modeled on the eternal forms.

***deva*** (Sanskrit); plural *devas*. "The shining ones"; the gods of the Vedic Aryans. Like all gods in the ancient world, they were not omnipotent or omniscient; they were animated by the same Spirit as all other creatures—men, women, animals, plants, rocks, trees, or stars—and were bound by the sacred order of the universe like everything and everybody else. They were a higher form of being because they were immortal, just as animals have a greater share of being than plants. But they were not supernatural in our sense, because they were simply members of the cosmos.

**dialectic** (Greek derivation). The art of critical examination into the truth of an opinion or statement; sometimes applied to a process of thought whereby contradictions are seen to merge in a higher truth that transcends them.

***din*** (Arabic). "Religion"; "way of life."

***dogma*** (Greek). The Greek fathers of the church distinguished this "teaching" from *kerygma,* the public, readily explicable and overt message of the gospel. *Dogma* could not be expressed verbally but could be suggested and intuited in the symbolic gestures of the liturgy and in silent, apophatic contemplation. *Dogma* was only comprehensible after years of immersion in the ritual and liturgy; it represented the tacit tradition of the Church that was not fixed or static but changed as the worshipping community deepened its understanding of revealed truth.

***dunamis*** (Greek). The "powers" of God, a term used by Greeks to denote God's activity in the world that was quite distinct from the indescribable and unknowable essence (*ousia*) of God.

***ekstasis*** (Greek). Ecstasy; literally "stepping out"; going beyond the self; transcending normal experience.

***ellu*** (Akkadian). Holiness, literally "cleanliness; brilliance; luminosity"; related to the Hebrew *elohim*. The gods were not the source of this holiness but merely participated in it to a high degree; they were known as the "holy ones."

**Elohim** (Hebrew). The term denoting the God of the Bible; usually translated

"God," but more accurately, it refers to everything that the gods could mean for human beings.

**En Sof** (Hebrew). "Without end"; the inaccessible and unknowable essence of the Godhead in Kabbalah.

*energeiai* (Greek). "Energies"; the term used to distinguish God's "activities" or "manifestations" in the world, which enable us to glimpse something of the otherwise inaccessible divine. Like *dunamis,* it is used to distinguish the human perception of God from the ineffable, unknown reality itself. The Greek fathers saw the Logos and the Holy Spirit as the *energeiai* that had, as it were, translated the divine into terms that human beings could to an extent grasp and comprehend.

*Enuma Elish.* The Babylonian epic recounting the creation of the world chanted annually in the temple of Esagila during the New Year festival.

**eschatology.** Derived from the Greek *eschaton,* "the end." The study of the last days.

**exegesis** (Greek derivation). "To guide; lead out"; the art of interpreting and explaining the text of scripture.

*ex nihilo* (Latin). "Out of nothing"; the phrase used to distinguish the new doctrine of creation that emerged in the Christian world during the fourth century and stated that God had created the world out of absolute nothingness. This cosmology had been unknown in the ancient world. Hitherto the gods had been regarded as created beings; they could only assist a creation process that was already under way and, as it were, work on the raw materials of the universe and finish it off.

**faith.** Trust; loyalty; the English translation of the Latin *fides* ("loyalty"; "fealty") and the Greek *pistis.* It did not originally mean acceptance of orthodox theology. See *belief.*

*falsafah* (Arabic). "Philosophy"; the attempt by Muslim scientists, known as the *faylasufs* ("philosophers"), to interpret Islam according to Greek philosophical rationalism.

**Golah** (Hebrew). The community of the exiles who returned from Babylon to Judaea.

**gospel** (derived from the Anglo-Saxon *god spel*). "Good news"; the proclamation (Greek: *evangelion*) of the early church.

**goyim** (Hebrew). The "foreign nations"; non-Jews; when translated into Latin, this became *gentes,* hence the English "gentiles."

*halakah* (Hebrew). A rabbinical legal ruling.

*hasid* (Hebrew); plural *hasidim.* A devout Jew; a holy man.

*hesychia* (Greek); adj. *hesychast.* "Inner tranquillity; interior silence"; a contemplative, apophatic spirituality that stripped the mind of theological ideas and tried to rise above words, concepts, and sensations.

**High God.** A supreme deity, worshipped in remote antiquity and still remembered in indigenous communities today, who was thought to have created the world single-handedly; he was so elevated that he had no cult and gradually faded from the minds and hearts of his worshippers. He was usually superseded by more immediate and dynamic deities.

*hilm* (Arabic). Forbearance; mercy; patience; tranquillity.

**Holy Spirit.** Translation of the Hebrew *ruach* ("spirit"); term used by the rabbis, often interchangeably with Shekhinah, to refer to God's presence on earth; distinct from God itself, the essence of the Godhead that exceeded human understanding or experience. The early Jewish Christians used the term to describe the immanent divine force within them that filled them with an empowering energy and enabled them to understand the deeper meaning of Jesus's mission.

*hypostasis* (Greek); plural *hypostases*. Used in a secular context to express the exterior expression of a person's inner nature; an object or person viewed from the outside; the Greeks used the term to describe the external, earthly manifestations of the unknown God as Logos and Holy Spirit.

**hypothesis** (Greek derivation). A proposition put forward as the basis for discussion; a supposition or conjecture that accounts for known facts and serves as a starting point for further investigation that may or may not be proved.

**idolatry.** The worship or veneration of a human or humanly constructed reality instead of the transcendent God.

*ilam* (Akkadian). "Divinity," which, in Mesopotamia, referred to a radiant power that lay beyond the gods and transcended any particular deity; a fundamental reality that could not be tied to a distinct form. The gods were not the source of *ilam,* but like all other creatures, they participated in this holiness.

*iman* (Arabic). Translated as "faith," but this does not mean "belief" in the modern sense. The *mu'min* ("faithful," often misleadingly translated "believers") are those who live up to the Muslim ideal, pray regularly, give alms, help the poor, perform the works of justice, and free their slaves.

**incarnation** (Latin derivation). The embodiment of the divine in a human bodily form; see *avatar.*

*intellectus* (Latin). "Intellect," the most refined region of our reasoning powers, where reason, pushed as far as it can go, subverts itself and experiences the divine. Not dissimilar to *buddhi.*

**Islam** (Arabic). An existential "surrender" of one's entire being to God.

*jahiliyyah* (Arabic). Traditionally translated as "time of ignorance" and used in Muslim sources to refer to the pre-Islamic period in Arabia. In English translations of the Qur'an, the noun *jahl* and the adjective *jahili* are often rendered as "unbelief" or "unbelieving." This is not accurate. In the early sources, the primary meaning is violent and explosive; irascible; arrogant; chauvinist.

*jihad* (Arabic). Struggle; endeavor; effort.

**Kabbalah** (Hebrew). "Inherited tradition"; the mystical tradition of Judaism.

*kaddosh* (Hebrew). Holy; literally "separate; other."

*kafir* (Arabic); plural *kafirun.* Traditionally translated as "unbeliever"; but more accurately it refers to somebody who ungratefully, churlishly, and aggressively rejects God; refuses to translate his belief in God's creation of the world into benevolent and generous action; hoards wealth to build up a private fortune; and does not care for the poor and deprived. *Kufr* is not "unbelief" but "ingratitude" and "insolence."

*kenosis* (Greek). "Emptying"; the emptying of the self; the dismantling of egotism.

*kerygma* (Greek). The public teaching of the Church, that, unlike *dogma,* can be expressed clearly and rationally and understood by people who do not participate in the rituals and ethical practices of Christianity.

*lectio divina* (Latin). "Sacred study"; the monastic practice of reading scripture slowly and meditatively, identifying with the action, and experiencing moments of *ekstasis.*

*logos* (Greek). "Dialogue speech"; reasoned, logical, and scientific thought. Ancient Greek philosophers used the term to denote the pragmatic, accurate mode of thought that was distinct from *mythos.* In Stoicism, *Logos* referred to the underlying rational, ruling processes of nature that were also called "God" or "Spirit." Christians identified the Logos with the Word and Wisdom of God that brought everything into being and had given human beings intimations of the divine throughout history. In the prologue to his gospel, Saint John claimed that the Logos ("Word") had taken flesh in the person of Jesus. As Christian theology developed, the Logos would become one of the *hypostases, prosopoi, dunamis,* and *energeiai* of the otherwise unknown and unknowable God.

**messiah.** From the Hebrew *messhiach* ("anointed one"); originally the term referred to the king of Israel, who was anointed during the coronation ceremony and achieved a special, cultic intimacy with God. He became a "son of God" and had a particular divine task. Priests and prophets were also given this title to denote their special mandate and closeness to Yahweh. By the time of Jesus, some Jews were looking forward to a future redeemer, possibly a king in the line of King David, who would usher in the Kingdom of God, an era of peace and justice.

**midrash** (Hebrew). Jewish exegesis; derived from the verb *darash* ("to study, investigate, go in search of"). Jewish interpretation always retained the sense of a quest for something fresh, expectant inquiry; the investigation of something that was not immediately self-evident.

*miqra* (Hebrew). "Call to action;" the early rabbis' name for the scripture.

**Mishnah** (Hebrew). Literally "learning by repetition"; a Jewish scripture composed between 135 and 200 CE that consisted of a collection of oral traditions and rabbinical legal rulings.

**monotheism.** The form of religion that has only a single god as its chief symbol of the divine.

**Muslim** (Arabic). A man or woman who has made the surrender of *islam.*

*musterion* (Greek). "Mystery"; derived from the verb *muein* ("to close the eyes or the mouth"), it refers to an obscure reality, hidden from ordinary sight, that exists beyond the reach of language. It was also linked to the related word *myein* ("to initiate") and *myesis* ("initiation"), hence the Mystery Cults that developed in the Greek world during the sixth century BCE, notably at Eleusis, secret rites that gave participants an overwhelming experience of the sacred. The term *musterion* was later applied by Greek Christians to describe the initiations of baptism and the Eucharist. Exegesis, the quest for the hidden meaning of scripture, was also a *musterion,* a transformative, initiatory process. Therefore *musterion* was not something that one was obliged to think and "believe" (in the modern sense) but was something that one did. This was particularly evident in the *dogma* of the Trinity, which was not simply a doctrinal formulation but also a meditative exercise.

*mystes* (Greek); plural, *mystai.* An "initiate"; somebody who takes part in a Mystery (*musterion*).

*mythos* (Greek); plural *mythoi.* Myth; a story that was not meant to be historical or factual but expressed the meaning of an event or narrative and encapsulated its timeless, eternal dimension. A myth can be described as an occurrence that in some sense happened once but also happens all the time. Myth can also be seen as an early form of psychology, describing the labyrinthine and obscure world of the psyche. Derived from the verb *muein* ("to close the eyes or the mouth"), it is related to "mystery" and "mysticism" and has connotations of darkness and silence. It refers to experiences and convictions that cannot be easily put into words, that elude the clarity of *logos* and are different from the discourse and thought habits of practical, everyday reality.

**Nirvana** (Sanskrit). "Extinction"; "blowing out"; the extinction of the self in Buddhism that brings enlightenment and liberation from pain and suffering; a sacred haven of peace discovered in the depths of the self; an indefinable reality, because it corresponds to no concept and is incomprehensible to those still enmeshed in the toils of selfishness and egotism.

*nous* (Greek). "Mind."

*ontos* (Greek). "Being"; "nature." Hence the *ontological proof* of Saint Anselm, which argues from an examination of the workings of human nature and the nature of the divine.

**orthodox; orthodoxy** (Greek derivation). "Right teaching."

*otiosus* (Latin). "Useless"; "superfluous."

*ousia* (Greek). Essence; nature; that which makes a thing what it is; a person or object seen from within; when applied to what we call God, the term denotes that divine essence, nature, or substance that will always elude human understanding or experience.

**Pentateuch** (Greek derivation). The first five books of the Bible, also called the Torah: Genesis, Exodus, Leviticus, Numbers, and Deuteronomy.

*persona* (Latin); plural *personae*. "Mask"; "face"; the translation of the Greek *prosopon;* the mask worn by an actor to enable the audience to recognize his character and make his voice audible (the "sound" [*sonus*] was amplified as it went "through" [*per*] it). Hence in English, the *hypostases* of the Trinity have been called the three divine "persons."

*pesher* (Hebrew). "Deciphering"; a form of exegesis used by the Qumran sect and by the early Christians, who saw the whole of scripture as a code, referring to their own community in the last days.

*philosophia* (Greek). "The love of wisdom" (*sophia*).

*phusikoi* (Greek). The "naturalists" of Miletus and Elea, who developed a purely physical and material vision of the cosmos and laid the foundations of Western science.

*pistis* (Greek); verbal form *pisteuo*. Trust; loyalty; commitment; often translated as "faith."

**polis** (Greek). The Greek city-state.

*prosopon* (Greek); plural *prosopoi*. "Face"; "mask"; also used of a facial expression that reveals one's inner thoughts or a role that one has decided to play in either life or the theater. Often used by the Greek fathers as an alternative to *hypostasis.*

**Purusha** (Sanskrit). "Person"; the term was first applied to the primordial human "Person" who voluntarily allowed the gods to sacrifice him in order to bring the world into being.

*ren* (Chinese). Originally "human being." Confucius gave the word new significance, but refused to describe it because it transcended any of the intellectual categories of his time. It was a transcendent value, the highest good. *Ren* would always be associated with the concept of humanity and has been translated as "human-heartedness." Later Confucians specifically associated *ren* with compassion and benevolence.

**revelation** (Latin derivation). "Unveiling"; the Latin translation of *apokalypsis;* it was not regarded as a set of unalterable truths, doctrines, or propositions, but as an ongoing process that depended on human ingenuity and innovation.

**Rig Veda** (Sanskrit). "Knowledge in Verse"; the most sacred part of the Vedic scriptures of the Aryans, consisting of over a thousand inspired hymns.

*rishi* (Sanskrit). "Seer"; the term applied to the inspired poets of the Rig Veda; also a visionary, mystic, or sage.

*secundum imaginationem* (Latin). "According to the imagination"; an idea presented hypothetically.

*sefer torah* (Hebrew). The "Scroll of the Law," discovered by the seventh-century reformers in the time of Josiah, which purported to be the document written by Moses on Mount Sinai.

*shalom* (Hebrew). Often translated as "peace," but more accurately "wholeness; completion."

**Shekhinah** (Hebrew). From the Hebrew verb *shakan* ("to pitch one's tent"); the rabbinic term for God's presence on earth, distinguishing a Jew's experience of God from the ineffable reality itself. Originally the Shekhinah, the Divine Presence had been enshrined in the Holy of Holies in the Jerusalem temple; after the temple's destruction in 70 CE, the rabbis taught Jews to experience the Shekhinah when two or three sat together and studied the Torah. Jewish Christians experienced the Shekhinah in the person of Jesus when they studied scripture together and in the Eucharist.

**Sky God.** See *High God.*

**symbol** (Greek derivation). A material object, person, icon, or idea that stands for something immaterial. The Greek *symbalon* indicates something that is "thrown together." Human beings have never experienced the unknowable reality that we call God directly but always in an earthly object, such as a human person, a scripture, a law code, a mountain, a temple, an idea, or a doctrine. The creeds of the Church were originally called "symbols." In the premodern world, the earthly symbol and the reality to which it pointed were experienced as inseparable. They had indeed been "thrown together" and fused, like gin and tonic in a cocktail. In the sixteenth century, however, as the scientific quest for accuracy and univocity took hold, people started to see the symbol as distinct from the transcendent reality to which it pointed. Thus the Protestant reformers claimed that the Eucharist was *only* a symbol. The gods and *devas* were "symbols" of the transcendent reality of Being. The idea of God was also a symbol, directing our attention to a transcendent reality beyond itself.

**Talmud** (Hebrew). "Teaching; study"; the term refers to two scriptures, the Jerusalem Talmud, completed in the early fifth century CE, and the Bavli, the Babylonian Talmud, completed in the sixth century CE. Both took the form of a *gemara* ("commentary") on the Mishnah.

*theoria* (Greek). "Contemplation"; in the modern West, a "theory" is a mental construct; a hypothesis.

**Torah** (Hebrew). "Teaching"; often translated as "law"; in the Bible, the word *torah* included God's perceived guidance in the world and the words he used to formulate it. Thus the Torah often refers to the Pentateuch, the first five books of the Bible, which contains stories about God's guidance and care. Later Torah was linked with God's Wisdom and the Word that brought the world into being and became synonymous with the highest knowledge and with transcendent goodness.

**transcendence** (Latin derivation); adj. *transcendent*. That which "climbs beyond" known reality and cannot be categorized.

*ummah* (Arabic). The Muslim community.

**univocal** (Latin derivation). "With one sense"; a proposition that has only one meaning; a word that is unambiguous.

**Upanishads** (Sanskrit). "To sit down near to"; esoteric scriptures revered as the culmination of Vedic religion. Thirteen of the classical Upanishads were composed between the seventh and second centuries BCE.

**Veda** (Sanskrit); adj. *Vedic*. "Knowledge"; the term used to denote the huge corpus of sacred literature of the Aryan Indians.

**Wisdom** (translation of the Hebrew *Hokhmah*). A personified figure in the book of Proverbs who represents God's divine plan that governs the universe; the blueprint of creation; identified later with the Torah, the highest wisdom, and the divine Word that brought the world into being. A method of describing God's activity in the world that human beings can experience as opposed to the inaccessible reality itself.

**Word.** See *wisdom; logos.*

**yoga** (Sanskrit). "Yoking"; the yoking of the powers of the mind to achieve enlightenment. The meditative discipline designed to eliminate the egotism that holds us back from Nirvana and enlightenment.

**zannah** (Arabic). Guesswork; surmise; used in the Qur'an to denote pointless and divisive theological speculation.

**ziggurat** (Akkadian). Temple towers built by the Sumerians in a form found in other parts of the world; huge stone ladders that men and women could climb to meet their gods.

# Selected Bibliography

Abelson, J. *The Immanence of God in Rabbinical Literature.* London, 1912.

Akenson, Donald Harman. *Surpassing Wonder: The Invention of the Bible and the Talmuds.* New York, San Diego, and London, 1998.

Alter, Robert, and Frank Kermode, eds. *The Literary Guide to the Bible.* London, 1987.

Altizer, Thomas J. *The Gospel of Christian Atheism.* Philadelphia, 1966.

———, with William Hamilton. *Radical Theology and the Death of God.* New York and London, 1966.

Anonymous. *The Cloud of Unknowing.* Trans. Clifton Wolters. Harmondsworth, U.K., 1980.

Anselm of Laon. *The Prayers and Meditations of Saint Anselm, with the Proslogion.* Trans. and introduction by Sister Benedicta Ward, SLG. Foreword by R. W. Southern. London, 1973.

Aristotle. *The Basic Works of Aristotle.* Ed. Richard McKeon. New York, 2001.

Atran, Scott. *In Gods We Trust: The Evolutionary Landscape of Religion.* New York and Oxford, 2002.

Augustine. *The Confessions.* Trans. and ed. Philip Burton. Introduction by Robin Lane Fox. London, 2007.

———. *On Christian Doctrine.* Trans. and ed. D. W. Robertson. Indianapolis, 1958.

———. *The Trinity.* Ed. and trans. Edmund Hill, OP. New York, 1994.

Ayer, A. J. *The Central Questions of Philosophy.* London, 1973.

———. *Language, Truth and Logic.* Harmondsworth, U.K., 1974.

Baggini, Julian. *Atheism: A Very Short Introduction.* Oxford, 2003.

Balthasar, Hans Urs von. *The Glory of the Lord: A Theological Aesthetics.* Vol. 4: *The Realm of Metaphysics in the Middle Ages.* Trans. Oliver Davies, Andrew Louth, Brian McNeill CRV, John Saward, and Rowan Williams. Edinburgh, 1991.

Barbour, Ian. *Religion in an Age of Science.* San Francisco, 1990.

Barker, Margaret. *The Gate of Heaven: The History and Symbolism of the Temple in Jerusalem.* London, 1991.

Barnes, Jonathan, trans. and ed. *Early Greek Philosophy* London, 1987.

Basil of Caesarea. *On the Holy Spirit.* Ed. C. F. H. Johnston. Oxford, 1982.

Bauman, Zymunt. *Modernity and the Holocaust.* Ithaca, N.Y., 1989.

Belkin, Samuel. *In His Image: The Jewish Philosophy of Man as Expressed in Rabbinic Tradition*. London, 1961.

Bellah, Robert. *Beyond Belief: Essays on Religion in a Post-traditionalist World*. New York, 1970.

Bloch, Ruth H. *Visionary Republic: Millennial Themes in American Thought, 1756–1800*. Cambridge, U.K., 1985.

Bonaventure (John of Fidanza). *The Works of St Bonaventure*. 2 vols. Ed. and trans. Philotheus Boehner OFM and Sister Mary Frances Laughlin SMIC. New York, 1990.

Bossy, John. *Christianity in the West, 1400 to 1700*. Oxford and New York, 1985.

Boyer, Paul. *Religion Explained: The Human Instincts That Fashion Gods, Spirits and Ancestors*. London, 2001.

Breuil, Abbe Henri. *Four Hundred Centuries of Cave Art*. Montignac, France, 1952.

Brewster, Sir David. *Memoirs of the Life, Writings and Discoveries of Sir Isaac Newton*. 2 vols. Edinburgh, 1885.

Brown, Callum G. *The Death of Christian Britain: Understanding Secularization, 1800–2000*. London, 2001.

Brown, D. Mackenzie, ed. *Ultimate Concern: Tillich in Dialogue*. London, 1965.

Buckley, Michael J. *At the Origins of Modern Atheism*. New Haven, Conn., and London, 1987.

———. *Denying and Disclosing God: The Ambiguous Progress of Modern Atheism*. New Haven, Conn., and London, 2001.

Bultmann, Rudolf. *Essays: Philosophical and Theological*. London, 1955.

———. *Jesus and the Word*. London, 1958.

———. *Jesus Christ and Mythology*. New York, 1958.

———. *The Gospel of John*. Oxford, 1971.

———. *The Theology of the New Testament*. 2 vols. London, 1952, 1955.

Burkert, Walter. *Ancient Mystery Cults*. Cambridge, Mass., and London, 1986.

———. *Greek Religion*. Trans. John Raffan. Cambridge, Mass., 1985.

———. *Homo Necans: The Anthropology of Ancient Greek Sacrificial Rites and Myth*. Trans. Peter Bing. Berkeley, Los Angeles, and London, 1983.

———. *Structure and History in Greek Mythology and Ritual*. Berkeley, Los Angeles, and London, 1979.

Bushnell, Horace. *God in Christ*. Hartford, Conn., 1849.

Butler, Jon. *Awash in a Sea of Faith: Christianizing the American People*. Cambridge, Mass., and London, 1990.

Cameron, Euan, ed. *Early Modern Europe*. Oxford, 1999.

Campbell, Joseph. *The Hero with a Thousand Faces*. Princeton, N.J., 1949.

———. *Historical Atlas of World Mythologies*. 2 vols. New York, 1988.

———. *Primitive Theology: The Masks of God*. Rev. ed. New York, 1969.

———, with Bill Moyers. *The Power of Myth*. New York, 1988.

Caputo, John. *On Religion*. London, 2001.

———. *The Prayers and Tears of Jacques Derrida: Religion Without Religion*. Bloomington, Ind., 1997.

———. *The Weakness of God: A Theology of the Event*. Bloomington, Ind., 2006.

———, with Gianni Vattimo. *After the Death of God*. Ed. Jeffrey W. Robbins. New York, 2007.

Cassirer, Ernst. *The Philosophy of Enlightenment*. Princeton, N.J., 1951.

Certeau, Michel de. *The Mystic Fable*. Vol. 1: *The Sixteenth and Seventeenth Centuries*. Trans. Michael B. Smith. Chicago, 1992.

Chadwick, Owen. *The Secularization of the European Mind in the Nineteenth Century.* Cambridge, U.K., 1975.

———. *The Victorian Church.* 2 vols. London, 1966.

Clark, J. C., trans. and ed. *Meister Eckhart: An Introduction to the Study of His Works with an Anthology of His Sermons.* New York, 1957.

Clarke, Samuel. *A Discourse Concerning the Being and Attributes of God, the Obligations of Natural Religion, and the Truth and Certainty of the Christian Revelation.* 9th ed. London, 1738.

———. *A Discourse Concerning the Unchangeable Obligations of Natural Religion and the Truth and Certainty of the Christian Religion.* In Richard Watson, ed., *A Collection of Theological Tracts.* London, 1785.

Clements, R. E. *God and Temple.* Oxford, 1965.

———, ed. *The World of Ancient Israel: Sociological, Anthropological and Political Perspectives.* Cambridge, U.K., 1989.

Coakley, Sarah, ed. *Rethinking Gregory of Nyssa.* Oxford, 2003.

Cohen, A., ed. *Everyman's Talmud.* New York, 1975.

Cohn, Norman. *The Pursuit of the Millennium: Revolutionary Millenarians and Mystical Anarchists of the Middle Ages.* London, 1957.

Collins, James. *God in Modern Philosophy.* Chicago, 1959.

Confucius. *The Analects of Confucius.* Trans. Arthur Waley. New York, 1992.

Copernicus, Nicolaus. *Nicholas Copernicus: On the Revolutions.* Trans. Edward Rosen. Warsaw and Cracow, 1978.

Cornwell, John. *Darwin's Angel: An Angelic Response to "The God Delusion."* London, 2007.

Cox, Harvey. *Fire from Heaven: The Rise of Pentecostal Spirituality and the Reshaping of Religion in the Twenty-first Century.* New York, 1995.

———. *The Secular City: Secularization and Urbanization in Theological Perspective.* New York, 1966.

Cross, Frank Moore. *Canaanite Myth and Hebrew Epic: Essays in the History of the Religion of Israel.* Cambridge, Mass., and London, 1973.

———. *From Epic to Canon: History and Literature in Ancient Israel.* Baltimore and London, 1998.

Cross, Richard. *Duns Scotus.* Oxford, 1999.

Cupitt, Don. *Is Nothing Sacred?* New York, 2002.

———. *Taking Leave of God.* London, 1980.

Darwin, Charles. *The Descent of Man, and Selection in Relation to Sex.* Princeton, N.J., 1981.

———. *On the Origin of Species by Means of Natural Selection.* Oxford, 1986.

Darwin, Francis. *The Life and Letters of Charles Darwin.* 2 vols. New York, 1911.

Davies, Brian. *The Thought of Thomas Aquinas.* Oxford, 1992.

Davies, Oliver. *God Within.* London, 1988.

———. *Meister Eckhart: Mystical Theologian.* London, 1991.

———, and Denys Turner, eds. *Silence and the Word: Negative Theology and Incarnation.* Cambridge, U.K., 2002.

Davies, Paul. *God and the New Physics.* London, 1984.

———. *The Mind of God: Science and the Search for Ultimate Meaning.* London, 1992.

Dawkins, Richard. *The Blind Watchmaker.* London, 1986.

———. *The God Delusion.* London and New York, 2006.

———. *River Out of Eden.* London, 2001.

Deleuze, Gilles. *The Logic of Sense*. Trans. Mark Lester. New York, 1990.

———, and Félix Guattari. *What Is Philosophy?* Trans. Hugh Tomlinson and G. Burchill. London, 1994.

De Lubac, Henri, SJ. *The Drama of Atheist Humanism*. London, 1949.

Dennett, Daniel. *Breaking the Spell: Religion as a Natural Phenomenon*. New York, 2006.

Denys the Areopagite. *Pseudo-Dionysius: The Complete Works*. Trans. Colm Luibheid and Paul Rorem. Mahwah, N.J., and London, 1987.

Derrida, Jacques. *Of Grammatology*. Corrected ed. Trans. Gayatri Spivak. Baltimore, 1992.

———. *Points . . . Interviews, 1974–94*. Ed. Elisabeth Weber. Trans. Peggy Kamuf. Stanford, Calif., 1995.

Descartes, René. *Discourse on Method, Optics, Geometry, and Meteorology*. Trans. Paul J. Olscamp. Indianapolis, 1965.

———. *Key Philosophical Writings*. Trans. Elizabeth S. Haldane and G. R. T. Ross. Ed. and intro. by Enrique Chávez-Arvizo. Ware, U.K., 1997.

Dever, William G. *What Did the Biblical Writers Know and When Did They Know It? What Archaeology Can Tell Us About the Reality of Ancient Israel*. Grand Rapids, Mich., and Cambridge, U.K., 2001.

Dewey, John. *Experience and Nature*. La Salle, Ill., 1971.

Diderot, Denis. *Diderot's Early Philosophical Works*. Trans. and ed. Margaret Jourdain. Chicago, 1916.

———. *Diderot: Interpreter of Nature: Selected Writings*. Ed. J. Kemp. New York, 1963.

Dillenberger, John. *Protestant Thought and Natural Science*. Nashville, Tenn., 1960.

Drake, Stillman, ed. *Discoveries and Opinions of Galileo*. Garden City, N.Y., 1957.

Draper, John William. *History of the Conflict Between Religion and Science*. New York, 1894.

Dupré, Louis, and Don E. Saliers. *Christian Spirituality: Post-Reformation and Modern*. London and New York, 1989.

Dyson, Freeman. *Disturbing the Universe*. New York, 1979.

Eckhart, Meister. *Meister Eckhart: The Essential Sermons, Commentaries, Treatises and Defense*. Trans. and ed. Edmund Colledge and Bernard McGinn. New York, 1981.

———. *Meister Eckhart: Teacher and Preacher*. Ed. and trans. Bernard McGinn, Frank Tobin, and Elvira Borgstadt. New York, 1986.

Edwards, Jonathan. *The Great Awakening*. Ed. C. C. Goen. New Haven, Conn., 1972.

Eliade, Mircea. *Birth and Rebirth: The Religious Meanings of Initiation in Human Culture*. Trans. Willard R. Trask. New York, 1958.

———. *A History of Religious Ideas*. 3 vols. Trans. Willard R. Trask. London and New York, 1985.

———. *Images and Symbols: Studies in Religious Symbolism*. Trans. Philip Mairet. Princeton, N.J., 1991.

———. *The Myth of the Eternal Return, or Cosmos and History*. Trans. Willard R. Trask. Princeton, N.J., 1954.

———. *Myths, Dreams and Mysteries: The Encounter between Contemporary Faiths and Archaic Realities*. Trans. Philip Mairet. London, 1960.

———. *Patterns in Comparative Religion*. Trans. Rosemary Sheed. London, 1958.

———. *The Sacred and the Profane*. Trans. Willard R. Trask. New York, 1959.

———. *Yoga, Immortality and Freedom*. Trans. Willard R. Trask. London, 1958.

Esposito, John L., ed. *Voices of Resurgent Islam*. New York and Oxford, 1983.

————, and Dalia Mogahed. *Who Speaks for Islam? What a Billion Muslims Really Think, Based on the Gallup World Poll*. New York, 2007.

Fakhry, Majid. *A History of Islamic Philosophy*. New York and London, 1970.

Fantoli, Annibule. *Galileo: For Copernicanism and the Church*. Trans. George Coyne. Vatican City, 1996.

Febvre, Lucien. *The Problem of Unbelief in the Sixteenth Century: The Religion of Rabelais*. Trans. Beatrice Gottlieb. Cambridge, Mass., and London, 1982.

Feuerbach, Ludwig. *The Essence of Christianity*. Trans. George Eliot. New York, 1957.

Findlay, J. N. *The Philosophy of Hegel: An Introduction and Re-examination*. New York, 1966.

Fingarette, Herbert. *Confucius: The Secular as Sacred*. New York, 1972.

Finkelstein, Israel, and Neil Asher Silberman. *The Bible Unearthed: Archaeology's New Vision of Ancient Israel and the Origin of Its Sacred Texts*. New York and London, 2001.

Finnocchiano, Maurice A., ed. and trans. *The Galileo Affair: A Documentary History*. Berkeley, Calif., 1989.

Fishbane, Michael. *The Exegetical Imagination: On Jewish Thought and Theology*. Cambridge, Mass., and London, 1998.

————. *The Garments of Torah: Essays in Biblical Hermeneutics*. Bloomington and Indianapolis, 1989.

————. *Text and Texture: Close Readings of Selected Biblical Texts*. New York, 1979.

Frank, William A., and Allan B. Wolter. *Duns Scotus: Metaphysician*. West Lafayette, Ind., 1995.

Fredricksen, Paula. *Jesus of Nazareth, King of the Jews: A Jewish Life and the Emergence of Christianity*. London, 2000.

Freeman, Charles. *The Greek Achievement: The Foundation of the Western World*. New York and London, 1999.

Frei, Hans. *The Eclipse of Biblical Narrative*. New Haven, Conn., and London, 1974.

Freud, Sigmund. *Civilization and Its Discontents*. Trans. and ed. James Strachey. New York, 1961.

————. *The Future of an Illusion*. Trans. and ed. James Strachey. New York, 1961.

————. *Moses and Monotheism*. London, 1990.

————. *New Introductory Lectures on Psychoanalysis*. Newly trans. and ed. James Strachey. New York, 1965.

————. *Totem and Taboo*. London, 1990.

Friedman, Richard Eliot. *Who Wrote the Bible?* New York, 1987.

Fuller, Steve. *Kuhn vs Popper: The Struggle for the Soul of Science*. London, 2003.

Funkenstein, Amos. *Theology and the Scientific Imagination: From the Middle Ages to the Seventeenth Century*. Princeton, N.J., 1986.

Gadamer, Hans-Georg. *Truth and Method*. London, 1975.

Galambush, Julia. *The Reluctant Parting: How the New Testament's Jewish Writers Created a Christian Book*. San Francisco, 2005.

Galilei, Galileo. *Dialogues Concerning Two Sciences*. Trans. Henry Crew and Alfonso de Salvio. New York, 1914.

Gay, Peter. *The Enlightenment: An Interpretation*. 2 vols. Vol. 1: *The Rise of Modern Paganism*. New York, 1968; vol. 2: *The Science of Freedom*. New York, 1969.

————. *A Godless Jew: Freud, Atheism and the Making of Psychoanalysis*. New Haven, Conn., and London, 1987.

Gilson, Etienne. *L'Esprit de la philosophie medievale*. Paris, 1944.

————. *The Unity of Philosophical Experience*. New York, 1937.

————, and Thomas Langan. *Modern Philosophy: Descartes to Kant*. New York, 1963.

Gottlieb, Anthony. *The Dream of Reason: A History of Philosophy from the Greeks to the Renaissance*. London, 2000.

Gould, Stephen Jay. *The Flamingo's Smile*. New York, 1985.

————. *Rocks of Ages: Science and Religion in the Fullness of Life*. London, 2001.

Grant, Edward, ed. *A Source Book in Medieval Science*. Cambridge, Mass., 1974.

————. "The Condemnations of 1277: God's Absolute Power and Physical Thought in the Late Middle Ages." *Viator* 10 (1979).

————. *Much Ado About Nothing: Theories of Space and Vacuum from the Middle Ages*. Cambridge, U.K., 1981.

Green, Arthur, ed. *Jewish Spirituality*. 2 vols. London, 1986, 1989.

Gregory of Nyssa. *The Catechetical Oration of St. Gregory of Nyssa*. Trans. J. H. Strawley. London, 1903.

————. *Commentary on the Song of Songs*. Trans. Casimer McCambley. Brookline, Mass., 1987.

————. *The Life of Moses*. Trans. A. J. Malherbe and E. Ferguson. New York, 1978.

————. *Select Writings and Letters of Gregory, Bishop of Nyssa*. Trans. H. A. Wilson, New York, 1893.

Griffith, Ralph T. H., trans. *The Rig Veda*. New York, 1992.

Guthrie, W. K. C. *The Greek Philosophers*. London, 1967.

Guttmann, Julius. *Philosophies of Judaism: The History of Jewish Philosophy from Biblical Times to Franz Rosenzweig*. Trans. David W. Silverman. New York, 1964.

Habermas, Jürgen. *Knowledge and Human Interests*. Trans. Jeremy J. Shapiro. 2nd ed. London, 1978.

Hadot, Pierre. *Philosophy as a Way of Life: Spiritual Exercises from Socrates to Foucault*. Trans. Michael Chase. Intro. and ed. Arnold I. Davidson. Oxford, 1995.

Harris, Sam. *The End of Faith: Religion, Terror, and the Future of Reason*. New York, 2004.

————. *Letter to a Christian Nation*. New York, 2007.

Hatch, Nathan O. *The Democratization of American Culture*. New Haven, Conn., and London, 1989.

Haught, John F. *God and the New Atheism: A Critical Response to Dawkins, Harris, and Hitchens*. Louisville, Ky., and London, 2008.

Hegel, Georg Wilhelm Friedrich. *Essays on the History of Philosophy*. Trans. E. S. Haldanne and Frances H. Simson. Atlantic Highlands, N.J., 1983.

————. *The Phenomenology of Mind*. Trans. J. B. Baillie. London, 1931.

Heidegger, Martin. *Being and Time*. Trans. John Macquarrie and Edward Robinson. New York, 1962.

————. *Identity and Difference*. Trans. Joan Stambaugh. New York, 1969.

————. *The Principle of Reason*. Trans. Reginald Lilly. Bloomington, Ind., 1991.

Heisenberg, Werner. *Physics and Beyond: Encounters and Conversations*. New York, 1971.

Hick, John. *The Existence of God*. London, 1964.

Hill, Christopher. *The World Turned Upside Down*. New York, 1972.

Hitchens, Christopher. *God Is Not Great: How Religion Poisons Everything*. New York, 2007.

Hodgson, Marshall G. S. *The Venture of Islam: Conscience and History in a World Civilization.* 3 vols. Chicago and London, 1974.

Holbach, Paul Heinrich Dietrich, Baron d'. *The System of Nature: or, Laws of the Moral and Physical World, with notes by Diderot.* Trans. H. D. Robinson. New York, 1835.

Holcomb, Justin E., ed., *Christian Theologies of Scripture: A Comparative Introduction.* New York and London, 2006.

Hudson, Donald. *Wittgenstein and Religious Belief.* London, 1975.

Hume, David. *Principal Writings on Religion Including Dialogues Concerning Natural Religion and The Natural History of Religion.* Oxford, 1993.

Huxley, Thomas H. *Science and Christian Tradition: Essays.* New York, 1898.

Ingersoll, Robert G. *The Works of Robert G. Ingersoll.* 3 vols. New York, 1909.

Izutsu, Toshiko. *Ethico-Religious Concepts in the Qur'an.* Montreal and Kingston, Ont., 2002.

Jaspers, Karl. *The Great Philosophers: The Foundations.* Ed. Hannah Arendt. Trans. Ralph Mannheim. London, 1962.

———. *The Origin and Goal of History.* Trans. Michael Bullock. London, 1953.

Jones, Gareth. *The Blackwell Companion to Modern Theology.* Oxford, 2004.

Julian of Norwich. *Revelations of Divine Love.* Trans. Clifton Wolters. London, 1966.

Kant, Immanuel. *Critique of Practical Reason.* Trans. Lewis White Beck. Chicago, 1949.

———. *Critique of Pure Reason.* Trans. Norman Kemp Smith. London, 1963.

———. *Religion Within the Limits of Reason Alone.* Trans. Theodore M. Greene and Hoyt H. Hudson. New York, 1960.

Katz, Steven, ed. *Mysticism and Philosophical Analysis.* Oxford, 1992.

Kearns, Edward John. *Ideas in Seventeenth-Century France: The Most Important Thinkers and the Climate of Ideas in Which They Worked.* Manchester, U.K., and New York, 1979.

Keddie, Nikki R. *Religion and Politics in Iran: From Quietism to Revolution.* New Haven, Conn., and London, 1983.

Kenny, Antony. *The Five Ways.* London, 1969.

Kepler, Johannes. *Mysterium cosmographicum: The Secret of the Universe.* Trans. A. M. Duncan. Intro. and commentary by E. J. Aiton. Preface by I. Bernard Cohen. New York, 1981.

Kerr, Fergus. *After Aquinas: Versions of Thomism.* Oxford, 2002.

Khomeini, Sayeed Ruhollah. *Islam and Revolution.* Trans. and ed. Hamid Algar. Berkeley, Calif., 1981.

Koestler, Arthur. *The Sleepwalkers: A History of Man's Changing Vision of the Universe.* Intro. by Herbert Butterfield. New York, 1963.

Kors, Alan Charles. *Atheism in France, 1650–1729: The Orthodox Sources of Disbelief.* Princeton, N.J., 1990.

———. *D'Holbach's Coterie: An Enlightenment in Paris.* Princeton, N.J., 1976.

Koyre, Alexandre. *From the Classical World to the Infinite Universe.* Baltimore, 1957.

———. *Metaphysics and Measurement.* Cambridge, Mass., 1968.

Kuhn, Thomas. *The Copernican Revolution: Planetary Astronomy in the Development of Western Thought.* Cambridge, Mass., 1957.

———. *The Structure of Scientific Revolutions.* Chicago and London, 1963.

La Mettrie, Julien Offray de. *Man a Machine.* Ed. and trans. Gertrude Carman Bussey. La Salle, Ill., 1943.

Langford, Jerome L. *Galileo, Science and the Church*. Rev. ed. Ann Arbor, Mich. 1971.

Laplace, Pierre-Simon de. *Exposition du système du monde*. Paris, 1865.

Leaman, Oliver. *An Introduction to Medieval Islamic Philosophy*. Cambridge, U.K., 1985.

Leclercq, Jean. *Love of Learning and the Desire for God: A Study of Monastic Culture*. Trans. Catherine Misrahi. New York, 1974.

Leroi-Gourhan, André. *Les Religions de la préhistoire: Paléolithique*. Paris, 1964.

———. *Treasures of Prehistoric Art*. New York, n.d.

Levinas, Emmanuel. *On Escape*. Trans. Beltina Bergo. Stanford, Calif., 2004.

———. *Otherwise Than Being, or Beyond Essence*. Trans. Alphonso Lingis. Pittsburgh, 1998.

Lindberg, David C., and Ronald L. Numbers, eds. *God and Nature: Historical Essays on the Encounter Between Christianity and Science*. Berkeley, Los Angeles, and London, 1986.

Locke, John. *An Essay Concerning Human Understanding*. Oxford, 1975.

Lossky, Vladimir. *In the Image and Likeness of God*. London, 1975.

———. *The Mystical Theology of the Eastern Church*. London, 1957.

Louth, Andrew. *Denys the Areopagite*. Wilton, Conn., 1989.

———. *Discerning the Mystery: An Essay on the Nature of Theology*. Oxford, 1983.

———. *Maximus the Confessor*. London, 1996.

———. *The Origins of Christian Mysticism: From Plato to Denys*. Oxford, 1981.

Lovejoy, David. *Religious Enthusiasm in the New World: From Heresy to Revolution*. Cambridge, Mass., and London, 1985.

Lucas, J. R. "Wilberforce and Huxley: A Legendary Encounter." *The Historical Journal* 22 (1979).

Lyotard, Jean-François. *The Postmodern Condition*. Trans. Geoff Bennington and Brian Massami. Minneapolis, 1984.

MacHamer, Peter, ed. *The Cambridge Companion to Galileo*. Cambridge, U.K., 1998.

MacIntyre, Alasdair, and Paul Ricoeur. *On the Religious Significance of Atheism*. New York, 1969.

Mackie, J. L. *The Miracle of Theism: Arguments For and Against the Existence of God*. Oxford, 1982.

MacQuarrie, John. *In Search of Deity: An Essay in Dialectical Theism*. London, 1984.

———. *Thinking About God*. London, 1975.

Marcel, Gabriel. *Being and Having*. London, 1965.

Marion, Jean-Luc. *God Without Being*. Trans. Thomas A. Carlson. Chicago, 1991.

Marsden, George M. *Fundamentalism and American Culture: The Shaping of Twentieth-Century Evangelicalism, 1870–1925*. Oxford and New York, 1980.

Martin, Michael, ed. *Atheism: A Philosophical Justification*. Philadelphia, 1991.

———. ed. *The Cambridge Companion to Atheism*. Cambridge, U.K., 2007.

Marty, Martin E., and R. Scott Appleby, eds. *Accounting for Fundamentalisms*. Chicago and London, 1994.

———. *Fundamentalisms and Society*. Chicago and London, 1993.

———. *Fundamentalisms and the State*. Chicago and London, 1993.

———. *Fundamentalisms Comprehended*. Chicago and London, 1995.

———. *Fundamentalisms Observed*. Chicago and London, 1991.

Marx, Karl. *Early Writings*. Trans. Rodney Livingstone and Gregor Benton. London, 1975.

————, and Friedrich Engels. *On Religion*. Intro. by Reinhold Niebuhr. New York, 1964.

Masterson, Patrick. *Atheism and Alienation: A Study in the Philosophic Sources of Contemporary Atheism*. Dublin, 1971.

Mather, Cotton. *The Christian Philosopher: A Collection of the Best Discoveries of Nature, with Religious Improvements*. Facsimile reproduction. Intro. by Josephine K. Piercy. Gainesville, Fla., 1968.

Maximus the Confessor. *Maximus Confessor: Selected Writings*. Trans. George C. Berthold. New York, 1985.

McCabe, Herbert, OP. *God Matters*. London, 1987.

————. *God Still Matters*. London and New York, 1992.

McGinn, Bernard, and John Meyendorff. *Christian Spirituality: Origins to Twelfth Century*. London, 1985.

McGrath, Alister. *Dawkins' God: Genes, Memes, and the Meaning of Life*. Malden, Mass., 2005.

————. *The Intellectual Origins of the European Reformation*. Oxford and New York, 1987.

————. *A Life of John Calvin: A Study in the Shaping of Western Culture*. Oxford, 1990.

————. *Reformation Thought*. Oxford and New York, 1988.

————. *The Twilight of Atheism: The Rise and Fall of Disbelief in the Modern World*. London and New York, 2005.

McIntosh, Mark A. *Mystical Theology: The Integrity of Spirituality and Theology*. Oxford, 1998.

McLeod, Hugh. *The Decline of Christendom in Western Europe, 1750–2000*. Cambridge, U.K., 2003.

Meslier, Jean. *Oeuvres complètes de Jean Meslier*. Ed. Deprun Desne and Albert Seboul. Paris, 1970.

Meyendorff, John. *Byzantine Theology: Historical Trends and Doctrinal Themes*. New York and London, 1975.

Mill, John Stuart. *Three Essays on Religion*. London, 1974.

Monod, Jacques. *Chance and Necessity: An Essay on the Natural Philosophy of Modern Biology*. Trans. Austryn Wainhouse. New York, 1972.

Montefiore, C. G., and H. Loewe, eds. *A Rabbinic Anthology*. New York, 1974.

Moore, James R. *The Post-Darwinian Controversies: A Study of the Protestant Struggle to Come to Terms with Darwin in Great Britain and America*. Cambridge, U.K., 1979.

Moore, R. Lawrence. *Religious Outsiders and the Making of Americans*. Oxford and New York, 1986.

Nasr, Seyyed Hossein. *Ideals and Realities in Islam*. London, 1971.

————. *Islamic Spirituality: Foundation*. London and New York, 1987.

————. *Islamic Spirituality: Manifestations*. London and New York, 1991.

Newton, Isaac. *The Correspondence of Isaac Newton*. 7 vols. Vols. 1–3, ed. H. W. Turnbull. Vol. 4, ed. J. F. Scott. Vols. 5–7, ed. A. R. Hall and L. Tilling. Cambridge, U.K., 1959–77.

————. *Opticks, or a Treatise on the Reflections, Refractions, Inflections and Colours of Light*. Foreword by Albert Einstein. Intro. by Sir Edmund Whittaker and L. Tilling. New York, 1952.

————. *Sir Isaac Newton's Mathematical Principles of Natural Philosophy and His System of the World*. Trans. Andrew Motte (1729). Revised by Florian Cajori. Berkeley and Los Angeles, 1962.

————. *Unpublished Scientific Papers of Isaac Newton*. Ed. and trans. A. R. and Marie Boas Hall. Cambridge, U.K., 1962.

Nicholson, Ernest. *The Pentateuch in the Twentieth Century: The Legacy of Julius Wellhausen*. Oxford, 1998.

Nietzsche, Friedrich. *The Birth of Tragedy*. Trans. Shaun Whiteside. Ed. Michael Turner. London, 1993.

————. *The Gay Science*. Trans. Walter Kaufman. New York, 1974.

————. *Thus Spoke Zarathustra*. Trans. R. J. Hollingdale. London, 1961.

————. *Twilight of the Idols and The Antichrist*. Trans. R. J. Hollingdale. London, 1968.

Noll, Mark A., ed. *Religion and American Politics: From the Colonial Period to the 1980s*. Oxford and New York, 1990.

Norton, Charles Eliot. *Letters of Charles Eliot Norton with Biographical Comment*. 2 vols. Ed. Sara Norton and M. A. DeWolfe. Boston, 1913.

Numbers, Ronald E. *The Creationists: The Evolution of Scientific Creationism*. Berkeley, Los Angeles, and London, 1992.

Olivelle, Patrick, ed. and trans. *Upaniṣads*. Oxford and New York, 1992.

Ong, Walter J., SJ. *Rhetoric, Romance, and Technology: Studies in the Interaction of Expression and Culture*. Ithaca, N.Y., 1971.

Origen. *Origen: On First Principles*. Ed. and trans. G. W. Butterworth. Gloucester, Mass., 1973.

Otto, Rudolf. *The Idea of the Holy: An Inquiry into the Non-rational Factor in the Idea of the Divine and Its Relation to the Rational*. Trans. John W. Harvey. Oxford, 1923.

Paley, William. *Natural Theology, or Evidences of the Existence and Attributes of the Deity*. Oxford, 1802.

Pascal, Blaise. *Pensées*. Trans. and ed. A. J. Krailsheimer. Harmondsworth, U.K., 1966.

Panikkar, Raimundo. *The Trinity and the Religious Experience of Man*. London and New York, 1973.

Pelikan, Jaroslav. *The Christian Tradition*. 5 vols. Chicago and London, 1971–89.

————, ed. *Modern Religious Thought*. Boston, 1990.

Plato. *Plato: The Complete Works*. Ed. John M. Cooper. Indianapolis, 1997.

————. *Plato: Phaedrus and Letters VII and VIII*. Ed. William Hamilton. London, 1973.

Polyani, Michael. *Knowing and Being*. London, 1969.

Popper, Karl. *The Logic of Scientific Discovery*. London, 1959.

————. *Unended Quest*. London, 1992.

Prestige, G. L. *God in Patristic Thought*. London, 1952.

Qutb, Sayyid. *Milestones*. Delhi, 1981.

Rahner, Karl. *Foundations of Christian Faith: An Introduction to the Idea of Christianity*. Trans. William V. Dych. New York, 1982.

————. *Theological Investigations III*. Trans. Karl-H. Kruger and Boniface Kruger. London, 1966.

————. *Theological Investigations IV*. Trans. Kevin Smith. London, 1966.

————. *Theological Investigations V*. Trans. Karl-H. Kruger. London, 1966.

Raitt, Jill, with Bernard McGinn and John Meyendorff, eds. *Christian Spirituality: High Middle Ages and Reformation*. London, 1988.

Rhees, Rush, ed. *Ludwig Wittgenstein: Personal Recollections*. Totowa, N.J., 1981.

Robinson, John. *Honest to God*. London, 1963.

Rolle, Richard. *The Fire of Love*. Trans. Clifton Wolters. London, 1972.

Rorem, Paul. *Biblical and Liturgical Symbols Within the Pseudo-Dionysian Synthesis.* Toronto, 1984.

Rousseau, Jean-Jacques. *Emile.* Trans., Allan Bloom. New York, 1979.

———. *The First and Second Discourses.* Trans. Roger T. Masters and Judith R. Masters. New York, 1964.

———. *The Social Contract.* Trans. Maurice Cranston. New York, 1984.

Rubenstein, Richard L. *After Auschwitz: Radical Theology and Contemporary Judaism.* New York, 1966.

Rusch, W. G., ed. *The Trinitarian Controversy.* Philadelphia, 1980.

Sanders, E. P. *The Historical Figure of Jesus.* London, 1993.

Schleiermacher, Friedrich. *The Christian Faith.* Trans. H. R. Mackintosh and J. S. Stewart. Edinburgh, 1928.

———. *On Religion: Speeches to Its Cultured Despisers.* Trans. John Oman. New York, 1958.

Scholem, Gershom. *Major Trends in Jewish Mysticism.* New York, 1954.

———. *The Messianic Idea in Judaism and Other Essays in Jewish Spirituality.* New York, 1971.

———. *On the Kabbalah and Its Symbolism.* Trans. Ralph Manheim. New York, 1965.

———. *Sabbetai Sevi: The Mystical Messiah.* London and Princeton, N.J., 1973.

Scotus, Duns. *Philosophical Writings.* Ed. and trans. Allan Wolter. Edinburgh, 1962.

Sherrard, Philip, and Kallistos Ware, eds. and trans. *The Philokalia.* London, 1979.

Silverman, R. M. *Baruch Spinoza: Outcast Jew, Universal Sage.* Northwood, U.K., 1995.

Sloek, Johannes. *Devotional Language.* Trans. Henry Mossin. Berlin and New York, 1996.

Smalley, Beryl. *The Study of the Bible in the Middle Ages.* Oxford, 1941.

Smart, J. J. C., and J. J. Haldane. *Atheism and Theism.* Oxford, 1996.

Smith, Mark S. *The Early History of God: Yahweh and the Other Deities in Ancient Israel.* New York and London, 1990.

———. *The Origins of Biblical Monotheism: Israel's Polytheistic Background and the Ugaritic Texts.* New York and London, 2001.

Smith, William Cantwell. *Belief and History.* Charlottesville, Va., 1985.

———. *Faith and Belief.* Princeton, N.J., 1987.

———. *The Meaning and End of Religion: A New Approach to the Religious Traditions of Mankind.* New York, 1962.

———. *Towards a World Theology: Faith and the Comparative History of Religion.* London, 1981.

———. *What Is Scripture? A Comparative Approach.* London, 1993.

Southern, R. W., ed. and trans. *Vita sancti Anselmi by Eadmer.* London, 1962.

Steiner, George. *In Bluebeard's Castle: Some Notes Towards the Redefinition of Culture.* New Haven, Conn., 1971.

———, ed. *Is Science Nearing Its Limits? Conference Convened by George Steiner.* Manchester, U.K., 2008.

———. *Language and Silence.* London, 1967.

———. *Real Presences: Is There Anything in What We Say?* London, 1989.

Szasz, Ferenc Morton. *The Divided Mind of Protestant America, 1880–1930.* University, Ala., 1982.

Tarnas, Richard. *The Passion of the Western Mind: Understanding the Ideas That Have Shaped Our World View.* London and New York, 1991.

Taylor, Mark C. *Erring: A Postmodern A/Theology.* Chicago, 1984.

Temple, Richard. *Icons and the Mystical Origins of Christianity.* London, 1990.

Thomas Aquinas. *Commentary on St. Paul's Epistle to the Ephesians.* Ed. and trans. M. L. Lamb. Albany, 1966.

———. *St Thomas Aquinas, Summa Theologiae: A Concise Translation.* Trans. and ed. Timothy Mc Dermott. London, 1989.

———. *Thomas Aquinas: Selected Writings.* Trans. R. McInery. Harmondsworth, U.K., 1998.

Tillich, Paul. *The Courage to Be.* Glasgow, 1962.

———. *A History of Christian Thought.* New York, 1969.

———. *The Religious Situation.* Trans. H. Richard Niebuhr. New York and London, 1956.

———. *Systematic Theology.* 2 vols. Chicago, 1951, 1957.

———. *Theology of Culture.* London, 1959.

Tindal, Matthew. *Christianity as Old as the Creation, or The Gospel a Republication of the Religion of Nature.* London, 1730.

Toland, John. *Christianity Not Mysterious.* London, 1696.

Toulmin, Stephen. *Cosmopolis: The Hidden Agenda of Modernity.* New York, 1990.

Turner, Denys. *The Darkness of God: Negativity in Christian Mysticism.* Cambridge, U.K., 1995.

———. *Faith, Reason and the Existence of God.* Cambridge, U.K., 2004.

Turner, Frank M. "The Victorian Conflict Between Science and Religion: A Professional Dimension." *Isis* 69 (1978).

Turner, James. *Without God, Without Creed: The Origins of Unbelief in America.* Baltimore, 1985.

Van Buren, Paul. *The Secular Meaning of the Gospel.* London, 1963.

Vattimo, Gianni. *After Christianity.* Trans. Luca D'Isanto. New York, 1999.

———. *Belief.* Trans. Luca D'Isanto and David Webb. New York, 1999.

———. *Nihilism and Emancipation.* Ed. Santiago Zabala. New York, 2004.

———. *The Transparent Society.* Trans. David Webb. Baltimore, 1992.

Vermes, Geza. *Jesus the Jew: A Historian's Reading of the Gospels.* London, 1973.

Vernant, Jean-Pierre. *Myth and Society in Ancient Greece.* 3rd ed. Trans. Janet Lloyd. New York, 1996.

Vernon, Mark. *After Atheism: Science, Religion and the Meaning of Life.* Basingstoke, U.K., 2007.

Voltaire. *Philosophical Dictionary.* Ed. and trans. Theodore Besterman. London, 1972.

Ward, Lester. *Dynamic Sociology.* New York, 1883.

Watt, W. Montgomery. *Muhammad at Mecca.* Oxford, 1953.

———. *Muhammad at Medina.* Oxford, 1956.

———. *Muhammad's Mecca: History and the Qur'an.* Edinburgh, 1988.

———. *Muslim Intellectual: The Struggle and Achievement of Al-Ghazzali.* Edinburgh, 1963.

Weinberg, Steven. *Dreams of a Final Theory: The Search for the Fundamental Laws of Nature.* London, 1993.

White, Andrew Dixon. *History of the Warfare of Science with Theology in Christendom.* 2 vols. New York, 1936.

Wittgenstein, Ludwig. *Lectures and Conversations on Aesthetics, Psychology and Religious Belief.* Ed. Cyril Barrett. Oxford, 1966.

———. *Tractatus logico-philosophicus.* Trans. C. K. Ogden. London, 1962.

Yovel, Yirmanyahu. *Spinoza and Other Heretics.* 2 vols. Princeton, N.J., 1989.

# Index

## Permissions Acknowledgments

Grateful acknowledgment is made to the following for permission to reprint previously published material:

Franciscan Institute Publications: Excerpts from *The Journey of Mind to God* by St. Bonaventure from *The Works of Saint Bonaventure,* translated by Philotheus Boehner and M. Francis Laughlin. Reprinted by permission of Franciscan Institute Publications, The Franciscan Institute, St. Bonaventure University, St. Bonaventure, New York 14778.

Hackett Publishing Company: Excerpts from "Apology" and "Phaedo," translated by G. M. A. Grube, and "Phaedrus" and "Symposium," translated by Alexander Nehamas and Paul Woodruff, from *Plato: The Complete Works,* edited by John M. Cooper. Reprinted by permission of Hackett Publishing Company.

## THE GREAT TRANSFORMATION
*The Beginning of Our Religious Traditions*

In the ninth century BCE, events in four regions of the civilized world led to the rise of religious traditions that have endured to the present day—the development of Confucianism and Daoism in China, Hinduism and Buddhism in India, monotheism in Israel, and philosophical rationalism in Greece. Armstrong, one of our most prominent religious scholars, examines how these traditions began in response to the violence of their time. Studying figures as diverse as the Buddha and Socrates, Confucius and Jeremiah, Armstrong reveals how these long-standing philosophies can help address our contemporary problems.

Religion/History

### ALSO AVAILABLE
*Holy War*
*The Spiral Staircase*

**ANCHOR BOOKS**
Available wherever books are sold.
www.anchorbooks.com